Italian Yearbook
of Human Rights 2019

PETER LANG

Bruxelles · Bern · Berlin · New York · Oxford · Wien

Research and Editorial Board
Paolo De Stefani (editor-in-chief),
Pietro de Perini (co-editor-in-chief),
Andrea Cofelice, Paola Degani,
Ino Kehrer, Marco Mascia

Advisory Editorial Board
Léonce Bekemans, University of Padova
Bojko Bucar, University of Ljubljana
Gabor Halmai, European University Institute, Florence
Jean-Paul Lehners, Université du Luxembourg
Gianni Magazzeni, Office of the UN High Commissioner
for Human Rights
Marco Mascia, University of Padova
Stelios Perrakis, Panteion University, Athens
Ugo Villani, LUISS University, Rome
Peter G. Xuereb, University of Malta

Translator from the Italian version
Rosemary Claire Burnham

The Yearbook is edited by the
University of Padova
Human Rights Centre "Antonio Papisca"
via Martiri della Libertà 2
35137 Padova
tel. +39 049.8271817
centro.dirittiumani@unipd.it
http://www.italianhumanrightsyearbook.eu

Italian Yearbook
of Human Rights 2019

Italian Yearbook of Human Rights
Vol. 10

UNIVERSITÀ
DEGLI STUDI
DI PADOVA

HUMAN RIGHTS CENTRE
"ANTONIO PAPISCA"

United Nations
Educational, Scientific and
Cultural Organization*

UNESCO Chair "Human Rights,
Democracy and Peace",
University of Padova

* The authors are responsible for the choice and presentation of information contained in this publication as well as for the opinions expressed therein, which are not necessarily those of UNESCO and do not commit the Organization

First Italian edition: *Annuario italiano dei diritti umani 2019*, Padova, Padova University Press, 2019.

No part of this book may be reproduced in any form, by print, photocopy, microfilm or any other means, without prior written permission from the publisher. All rights reserved.

© P.I.E. PETER LANG s.a.
Éditions scientifiques internationales
Brussels, 2020
1 avenue Maurice, B-1050 Bruxelles, Belgique
brussels@peterlang.com; www.peterlang.com

ISSN 2294-8848
ISBN 978-2-8076-1445-1
ePDF 978-2-8076-1458-1
ePub 978-2-8076-1459-8
Mobi 978-2-8076-1460-4
DOI 10.3726/b16725
D/2020/5678/11

Bibliographic information published by "Die Deutsche Nationalbibliothek"

"Die Deutsche Nationalbibliothek" lists this publication in the "Deutsche Nationalbibliografie"; detailed bibliographic data is available in the Internet at http://dnb.d-nb.de.

Contents

List of Acronyms 13
Italy and Human Rights in 2018: Does Omission Follow Inaction? 17
Italian Agenda of Human Rights 2019 23
Structure of the Yearbook 2019 31

In-depth Analysis. The Italian System to Protect Trafficked Persons and the National Action Plan against Trafficking 2016–2018. 33

    I. Legal Framework 34
    II. The Italian Anti-trafficking System 35
    III. The National Action Plan against trafficking 2016–2018 ... 38
    IV. The Single Public Calls for Funding 41
    V. Human Trafficking in Italy 44
    VI. Monitoring Projects and the Role of the National Hotline against Trafficking 45
    VII. Governance of the Anti-Trafficking System 46
    VIII. Update and Assessment of the National Action Plan against Trafficking. The Problem with Prostitution 48

PART I The Reception of International Human Rights Law in Italy 53

International Human Rights Law 55

    I. Legal Instruments of the United Nations 55
    II. Legal Instruments on Disarmament and Non-proliferation 56
    III. Legal Instruments of the Council of Europe 56
    IV. European Union Law 56

Italian Law 63

  I. Constitution of the Italian Republic 63
  II. National Legislation 64
  III. Municipal, Provincial and Regional Statutes 67
  IV. Regional Laws 68

PART II The Human Rights Infrastructure in Italy 75

National Bodies with Jurisdiction over Human Rights 77

  I. Parliamentary Bodies 78
  II. Prime Minister's Office (Presidency) 104
  III. Ministry of Foreign Affairs and International Cooperation 108
  IV. Ministry of Labour and Social Policies 111
  V. Ministry of Justice 115
  VI. Judicial Authorities 115
  VII. Independent Authorities 116
  VIII. Non-Governmental Organisations 124
  IX. Teaching and Research on Human Rights in Italian Universities 127

Sub-national Human Rights Structures 143

  I. Peace Human Rights Offices in Municipalities, Provinces and Regions 143
  II. Ombudspersons in the Italian Regions and Provinces 144
  III. National Coordinating Body of Ombudspersons 145
  IV. Network of Ombudspersons for Children and Adolescents 147
  V. National Coordinating Body of Local Authorities for Peace and Human Rights 148
  VI. Archives and Other Regional Projects for the Promotion of a Culture of Peace and Human Rights 150

Region of Veneto 153

  I. Department for International Relations, Communications and SISTAR 155
  II. Committee for Human Rights and the Culture of Peace 155

III.	Committee for Development Cooperation	156
IV.	Regional Table on Human Rights and Sustainable Development Cooperation	157
V.	Venice for Peace Research Foundation	157
VI.	Human Rights Authority	158
VII.	Regional Commission for Equal Opportunities between Men and Women	161
VIII.	Regional Observatory on Immigration	162
IX.	Regional Archive «Pace Diritti Umani - Peace Human Rights»	163

PART III Italy in Dialogue with International Human Rights Institutions 165

The United Nations System 167

I.	General Assembly	167
II.	Human Rights Council	177
III.	High Commissioner for Human Rights (OHCHR)	201
IV.	High Commissioner for Refugees (UNHCR)	203
V.	Human Rights Treaty Bodies	204
VI.	Specialised United Nations Agencies, Programmes and Funds	212

Council of Europe 223

I.	Parliamentary Assembly	224
II.	Committee of Ministers	226
III.	European Court of Human Rights	230
IV.	Committee for the Prevention of Torture	231
V.	European Committee of Social Rights	237
VI.	Commissioner for Human Rights	243
VII.	European Commission against Racism and Intolerance	245
VIII.	Advisory Committee on the Framework Convention for the Protection of National Minorities	247
IX.	European Commission for Democracy through Law	248
X.	Group of experts on Action against Trafficking in Human Beings	248

XI.	Group of States against Corruption	256
XII.	Group of Experts on action against Violence against Women and Domestic Violence	259
XIII.	Lanzarote Committee	260

European Union 263

I.	European Parliament	263
II.	European Commission	264
III.	Council of the European Union	265
IV.	Court of Justice of the European Union	265
V.	European External Action Service	266
VI.	Special Representative for Human Rights	266
VII.	Fundamental Rights Agency (FRA)	266
VIII.	European Ombudsman	269
IX.	European Data Protection Supervisor	269

Organization for Security and Cooperation in Europe (OSCE) 271

I.	Office for Democratic Institutions and Human Rights (ODIHR)	273
II.	High Commissioner on National Minorities	277
III.	Representative on Freedom of the Media	278
IV.	Special Representative and Coordinator for Combating Trafficking in Human Beings	279

Humanitarian and Criminal Law 281

| I. | Adaptation to International Humanitarian and Criminal Law | 281 |
| II. | Italian Contribution to "Peacekeeping" and to Other International Missions | 282 |

Part IV National and International Case-Law 287

Human Rights in Italian Case-Law 289

| I. | Aspects of the Relationship between the Italian Justice System and European Case-Law | 293 |

II.	Dignity of the Person, Right to Identity	296
III.	Political Rights and Freedom of Association; Citizenship; Freedom of the Press	303
IV.	Asylum and International Protection	305
V.	Discrimination – General Issues	308
VI.	Rights of Persons with Disabilities	312
VII.	Social Rights	316
VIII.	Immigration	319
IX.	Right to Private and Family Life. Right to Property	325
X.	Children's Rights	330
XI.	Due Process and the Pinto Act	339
XII.	Criminal Issues	342

Italy in the Case-law of the European Court of Human Rights 353

I.	Ban on Torture, Inhuman and Degrading Treatment, Right to Liberty, Right to Life	353
II.	Fair Trial, Right to Private Property	356
III.	Retroactive Laws with Effects on Ongoing Procedures Concerning Property	363
IV.	Nulla poena sine lege: confiscation of land and buildings	364
V.	Private and Family Life	366

Italy in the Case-law of the Court of Justice of the European Union 371

I.	Limitation to the Possibility of Appeal Decisions Regarding International Protection	371
II.	Gender Discrimination among Theatre Workers	372
III.	Administrative and Penal Sanctions: Ban on ne bis in idem	373

Index 375
Table of Cases 385
Research and Editorial Committee 393

List of Acronyms

C.l.:	Constitutional Law (legge costituzionale)
CAT:	Convention against Torture and Other Cruel, Inhuman or Degrading Treatment or Punishment
CDFUE:	Charter of Fundamental Rights of the European Union
CEDAW:	Convention on the Elimination of All Forms of Discrimination against Women
CIDU:	Inter-Ministerial Committee for Human Rights *(Comitato interministeriale dei diritti umani)*
CJEU:	Court of Justice of the European Union
CM:	Committee of Ministers of the Council of Europe
CoE:	Council of Europe
CPED:	International Convention for the Protection of All Persons from Enforced Disappearance
CPR:	Repatriation Centre *(Centro di permanenza per i rimpatri)*
CPT:	European Committee for the Prevention of Torture and Inhuman or Degrading Treatment or Punishment
CRC:	Convention on the Rights of the Child
CRPD:	Convention on the Rights of Persons with Disabilities
D.p.c.m.:	Decree of the President of the Council of Ministers (decreto del Presidente del Congilio dei Ministri)
DPO:	Department for Equal Opportunities of the Presidency of the Council of Ministers
D.p.r.:	Decree of the President of the Republic (decreto del Presidente della Repubblica)
ECHR:	European Convention for the Protection of Human Rights and Fundamental Freedoms
ECOSOC:	United Nations Economic and Social Council
ECRI:	European Commission against Racism and Intolerance
ECtHR:	European Court of Human Rights

ESC-R:	European Social Charter (revised)
FAO:	Food and Agriculture Organisation of the United Nations
FRA:	Fundamental Rights Agency of the European Union
FRONTEX:	European Border and Coast Guard Agency
GRECO:	Group of States against Corruption (Council of Europe)
GRETA:	Group of Experts on Action against Trafficking in Human Beings (Council of Europe)
ICC:	International Criminal Court
ICCPR:	International Covenant on Civil and Political Rights
ICERD:	International Convention on the Elimination of all forms of Racial Discrimination
ICESCR:	International Covenant on Economic, Social and Cultural Rights
ICRMW:	International Convention on the Protection of the Rights of all Migrant Workers and their Families
ILO:	International Labour Organisation
IOM:	International Organisation for Migration
L.:	Law
L.d.:	Law Decree (decreto-legge)
Lgs.D.:	Legislative Decree (decreto legislativo)
NATO:	North Atlantic Treaty Organisation
ODIHR:	Office for Democratic Institutions and Human Rights (OSCE)
OHCHR:	Office of the High Commissioner of the United Nations for Human Rights
OPCAT:	Optional Protocol to the Convention against Torture
OSCE:	Organisation for Security and Cooperation in Europe
P.l.:	Provincial Law
PACE:	Parliamentary Assembly of the Council of Europe
R.l.:	Regional Law
TAR:	Administrative Regional Court (Tribunale Amministrativo Regionale)
TFUE:	Treaty on the Functioning of the European Union
TUE:	Treaty on European Union

UNAR:	Office for the Promotion of Equal Treatment and the Fight against Racial Discrimination (*Ufficio per la promozione della parità di trattamento e la rimozione delle discriminazioni fondate sulla razza e sull'origine etnica*)
UNDP:	United Nations Development Programme
UNEP:	United Nations Environmental Programme
UNESCO:	United Nations Educational, Scientific and Cultural Organisation
UNGA:	United Nations General Assembly
UNHCR:	United Nations High Commission for Refugees
UNICEF:	United Nations Children's Fund
UPR:	Unitersal Periodic Review
WHO:	World Health Organisation

Italy and Human Rights in 2018: Does Omission Follow Inaction?

The introduction of the previous *Italian Yearbook of Human Rights*, 2018 edition, focused on Italy's urgent need to change pace and shake off the long-standing immobility that was undermining the country's ability to make policies to promote and protect fundamental rights; a call to fight some of the dangerous signs of regression that were emerging around the general health state of human rights in Italy and around the world with a renewed sense of leadership.

In this context, the election of Italy to the UN Human Rights Council for 2019–2021 (on 12 October 2018) seemed to be a good omen. To have Italy's voice heard for the third time among the 47 members of the main political body for promoting and protecting human rights on an international level could and should have driven the country into activism. It gives Italy more responsibility and visibility to implement an international political human rights agenda, providing the government with the opportunity to steer the international conversation to issues that interest Italy, with positive impacts on a national and sub-national level.

One year on, the Research and Editorial Committee of the *Yearbook* cannot fail to notice the lack of positive developments in this direction. As stated by Prime Minister Conte in his opening speech of the 63rd General Assembly of the United Nations, on 26 September 2018, the "respect for the inviolable rights of man is one of the pillars on which the Italian Republic is founded, our beacon, especially today, when we are called upon to address the immense challenges of the grave and prolonged crises in the EuroMediterranean area, including migratory flows" remains unchanged. However, if we look at the practical application of these principles, it is difficult to see the much-anticipated change of pace, both in international relations and internal matters.

The awaited contribution of the country in the Human Rights Council has, so far, been limited; out of 40 resolutions adopted during the 40th ordinary session (March 2019 – the first session in which Italy participated as a renewed member of the Council), Italy sponsored just one single resolution (A/HRC/40/L.7, on the situation on human rights in Syria). Every year for the three years prior, from outside the Council, Italy sponsored five resolutions in the first ordinary session of the year. On an informal level, the Permanent Representative of Italy co-promoted one single event out of the 93 that were organised during the session (on promoting alternative treatment for children with disabilities). Of course, the change of the head of the Permanent Representative of Italy in Geneva had some effect on this, although this effect is minimal. Yet still, Italy's election to the Human Rights Council created some expections, in light of the important commitments made by the Government in Italy's letter of candidacy (see *Yearbook 2018*, p. 15–19).

It cannot be denied that, just in the matter the Prime Minister evoked in the aforementioned passage, that is migrations, which is a sensitive issue for a country such as Italy, the attitudes of the national institutions have been anything but coherent. Moreover, while during the speech to the General Assembly, Italy announced its official participation to the intergovernmental conference of Marrakech, aimed at adopting the Global Compact for safe, orderly and regular migration, a few weeks later the Government decided not to participate, joining the 33 States that backed out (conversely to the 161 other countries, plus the EU). Out of the European countries, other than Italy, Austria, Bulgaria, Czech Republic, Estonia, Hungary, Iceland, Poland, Switzerland and Ukraine were also absent from the Conference.

In this year, therefore, Italy has not been the shining light of activism or spirit of iniative concerning the reflection and development of human rights in multi-lateral institutions. At the same time, in 2018 and the first months of 2019, the dialogue and in some cases, the discussion between national authorities and the institutions created at a European and international level to monitor human rights was intense and at times rough.

The arguements taking place between some Governmental and Parliamentary representatives and United Nations bodies (the newly elected High Commissioner for Human Rights, Michelle Bachelet, and various *special rapporteurs*) and the Council of Europe (Commissioner for Human Rights, Special Rapporteur for the Freedom of the Media) broke through into national news. A rising number of recommendations and urgent requests for information were addressed to the Italian authorities outside the usual monitoring cycles, relating to a series of developments at national level concerning critical human rights issues, namely: the aggressive management of policies against irregular migration, with particular consideration for asylum seekers, with the consequent climate of hostility towards them and those who protect them (international and Italian NGOs and human rights defenders); the potential obstacles to advancing the rights of women and protection against domestic and gender-based violence, as shown in those law bills tabled by representatives of the majority parties; hate speech directed towards minorities (especially Roma and Sinti communities) were common place in public speeches; the rise in episodes of racial and xenophobic violence reported in the news and followed up by the police force (for more details on the requests for information and advanced recommendations from the Special Rapporteurs of the UN, see Part III, The United Nations System, VI); the restriction of civil society space and the criminalisation of solidarity.

In front of all these international requests, the reaction of the Italian authorities was incoherently articulated: rather accurate and punctual answers provided by competent technical authorities; and ostensibly unavailable to review the choices that had given rise to requests and recommendations in the public and media discourse.

From an international political perspective, it is essential to look at the behaviour of the Italian authorities last year and at the start of 2019, which marks an unprecedented break with the role that the country has traditionally filled within the international community. Italy has always been considered a responsible actor, committed to the promotion of peace and human rights within a stable and recognisable allied group. The ongoing confrontation with some authoritative requests that protect the fundamental standards for the respect of human dignity - rules that Italy itself contributed to defining and disseminating and to which it is bound – shows a worrying regressive movement regarding fundamental rights and even of fundamental humanitarian guarantees, as it seems on a domestic level.

The "stagnation" of Italy on matters related to human rights, which has been observed for many years by the Research and Editorial Committee of this publication, but also by civil society organisations and numerous national and international experts, has finally translated into action, although in this moment, action which is contrary to that which we anticipated: not the honest and transparent opening to ethical, juridical and "strategic" (medium-long term) imperatives of protecting the human rights of every person, but a "tactical" compression of those rights.

The choices of the previous Governments, unopposed by Parliament, favoured immobility on some crucial issues. An example, and the *leit motiv* of the pages of this *Yearbook*, is the continuing lack of an Independent National Institution on Human Rights in line with the Paris Principles. Immobility has, in turn, generated and legitimised a form of restriction of human rights "by omission": the voices defending fundamental rights and the most disadvantaged groups are silenced, marginaliszed or denigrated and delegitimised, through calls of "conflicts of interest", crimes of corruption or anti-national plots. In this way, in Italy – as well as, it is worth noting, in many other countries of the world – the public debate on fundamental rights is being degraded and is losing its value. The civil society voices (NGOs, human rights defenders, representatives of schools and the cultural sector, local administrators and academic circles, religious groups, voluntary associations etc.) who, over the years, have sustained the cause of universal and equal human rights for everyone, find themselves facing a political and social climate that is sometimes openly hostile, without the suitable instruments to effectively combat it.

There were many "pro-human rights" initiatives in the period under review. Considering just those that made the most impact in the media, those initiatives included the ongoing "humanitarian corridors" project of the Waldensian Evangelical Church and the Community of Sant'Egidio, and the initiatives organised by "*In Difesa di*" network to establish "shelter cities" for human rights defenders (see Part II, Sub-national Human Rights Structures, I). It is worth remembering also, in these regards, that a number of local administrations expressed perplexity when faced with the "security decree" of 2018 (l.d. 113/2018), due to the negative impact that the application of this bill could have on the life conditions of migrants and asylum seekers, and also on the peaceful coexistence within local communities.

Also, on an institutional level, a number of practices have developed against the trend. It is worth mentioning the ability to respond and recover demonstrated by the National Ombudsperson for the Rights of Persons in Prison or Deprived of Liberty, or the support shown by the Prime Minister and the Minister of Foreign Affairs and International Cooperation to relevant and strategic projects aimed at teaching human rights and international solidarity to future generations, via the continuing experimentation of the "Civil Peace Corps" and financing projects for implementation of the Third Italian Action Plan on "Women, Peace, Security".

The territory on which these initiatives are developing seems to be visibly less receptive, and their impact on the public opinion looks limited. If we consider that these non-governmental actors have often contributed to keeping the country straight on the path of human rights through a continuous commitment on the front line even in times of immobility or political neglect, the situation can only arouse concern.

The new version of the *Italian Agenda of Human Rights*, a guidance tool aimed at promoting the sustainability and development of the Italian human rights system, presents this situation from another perspective. On one hand, it was not possible for the Research and Editorial Committee – observing the period between 2018 and the first months of 2019 – to eliminate any point or sub-point of the previous Agenda (an indicator of the characterizing stagnation the Italian situation, already highlighted also in Agenda 2018 compared to the previous year). On the other hand, the 2019 Agenda further expands with some new points aimed at providing ideas and suggestions to decision-makers and civil society representatives to reverse or slow down the current regressive tendencies.

With this complex domestic and international situation, Italy will be subjected to its third Universal Periodic Review (UPR) before the Human Rights Council. The UPR will constitute a new benchmark in which to measure whether in the view of the international community human rights in our country are healthy or not. The Human Rights Council will also have the Government report and various reports prepared by Italian non-governmental organisations. From this new periodic examination, we expect stimuli and suggestions to arrive both for State institutions and civil society organisations who are committed to overcoming the current stalemate and to helping the country to follow the right course.

Italian Agenda of Human Rights 2019

Like every year, the Research and Editorial Committee of the *Italian Yearbook of Human Rights* at the University of Padova Human Rights Centre "Antonio Papisca" offers the updated version of the *Italian Agenda of Human Rights*, built on the basis of an analysis of the recommendations received by Italy in the international sphere and of the most critical aspects identified in the various editions of the same Yearbook.

As already mentioned in the *Introduction* of this edition of the *Yearbook*, in preparing for the new one, it was not possible to delete any points or sub-points from the 2018 version of the Agenda, as proof of the country's continuing immobility on human rights. Some points or sub-points have been slightly reformulated in consideration of some developments during the year under review in terms of regulations or public policies. Specifically, with reference to points 23, 33, 34 and 35 of the Agenda 2019 some important regulatory measures have been adopted in the social field (citizenship income, measures on pensions) and on security (legitimate defence, security decrees) that largely concern the enjoyment of human rights in Italy and can therefore impact the structure and contents of this guidance tool. However, for the moment, these consequences cannot be analysed since there is still no concrete feedback on the implementation of these developments.

Compared to the 2018 version, the new Agenda adds two points. One concerns the adoption of national action plans on human rights and reveals the need to continue updating and implementing the policy approaches on aspects to which the Italian Government had already committed in the past (point 20). The other new point concerns the need to ensure adequate working spaces for non-governmental organisations involved in search and rescue operations in the Mediterranean Sea (point 32).

Italian Agenda of Human Rights 2019

Normative Level	1) Ratify the following legal instruments at the United Nations and the Council of Europe:
	   a. International Convention on the Protection of the Rights of All Migrant Workers and Members of their Families;
	   b. Protocol XII to the European Convention on Human Rights;
	   c. Protocol XV to the European Convention on Human Rights;
	   d. Protocol XVI to the European Convention on Human Rights;
	   e. European Convention on Nationality;
	   f. Additional Protocol to the Criminal Law Convention on Corruption.

	2) Deposit the instruments of ratification for the following legal instruments for which Parliament has already adopted the relative ratification and implementation laws:
	   a. Convention on Human Rights and Biomedicine (Oviedo Convention);
	   b. Additional Protocol to the Convention on Human Rights and Biomedicine Concerning Transplantation of Organs and Tissues of Human Origin.

Normative Level	3) Promote the awareness and application of the Declaration on the Right to Peace adopted by the Human Rights Council on 1 July 2016 before the UN General Assembly.
	4) Accept Article 25 of the European Social Charter (revised), on the right of workers to protection of their claims in the event of insolvency of their employer.

	5) Withdraw the declaration that excludes the application for Italy of Chapter C of the European Convention on the Participation of Foreigners in Public Life at Local Level and, accordingly, provide for the introduction of active and passive voting rights in local elections for foreigners who have been residing in Italy for a certain number of years.
	6) Include hate motivation as an aggravating circumstance in Article 61 of the Italian criminal code.
	7) Bring the crime of torture, introduced under Article 613-*bis* of the Criminal Code, in line with Article 1 of the UN Convention Against Torture.
	8) Expressly recognise representative non-governmental organisations within Italian jurisdiction having particular competence in issues regulated by the European Social Charter (revised) the right to present collective complaints pursuant to the 1995 Protocol.
	9) Complete the adoption process of parliamentary bill No. 925 on defamation in light of the of United Nations, Council of Europe and OSCE standards.
	10) Continue efforts to reform the system for the prevention and repression of corruption in both the public and private sector, with special reference to the most recent recommendations made by GRECO on the following subjects: indictment for corruption, transparency in party financing, and preventing corruption in Members of the Chamber of Deputies and magistrates.

Infrastructural Level	11) Complete the system of independent national human rights institutions in line with the Paris principles adopted by the United Nations: a. establish the National Human Rights Commission; b. establish the National Ombudsperson.
	12) Ensure the existence of a permanent parliamentary Human Rights Commission, in one or both Chambers.
	13) Assign all Ministries an ad hoc human rights office.
	14) Assign all necessary personnel and financial resources to the independent human rights authorities working in the sector.
Implementation of International Obligations and Commitments	15) Complete the legislative process for the implementation of the Statute of the International Criminal Court as concerns substantive law.
	16) Increase the timeliness and full execution of European Court of Human Rights rulings, including paying out compensation awarded, and improve Italy's capacity to conform to the standards defined by the same Court.
Implementation of International Obligations and Commitments	17) Address as a matter of urgency the issue of the excessive duration of legal proceedings, including those initiated to seek remedy for their excessive duration.
Adoption of policies	18) Hold an annual debate on human rights in Parliament.
	19) Adopt the following national action plans, providing them with suitable tools for monitoring and assessment: a. National Action Plan on the human rights situation within detention structures; b. National Programme on education for democratic citizenship and education and training on human rights.

	20) Update the following national action plans upon expiry: a. National Strategy for Preventing and Combating Discrimination on grounds of gender identity or sexual orientation (last reference period: 2013–2015); b. National action plan against racism, xenophobia and intolerance (last reference period: 2013–2015); c. National Action Plan against Trafficking in and Serious Exploitation of Human Beings (2016–2018).
	21) Implement and provide information on the impact of the following national action plans: a. National Strategy for the inclusion of Roma, Sinti and Travellers – 2012–2020; b. National Action Plan on Business and Human Rights (2016–2021); c. National Action Plan on "Women, Peace and Security" (2016–2019); d. Fourth National Action Plan for the protection of the rights and of the development of children and adolescents (2016–2017); e. National Strategic Plan on male violence against women (2017–2020); f. Second two-year Action Programme for the promotion of the rights and the integration of persons with disabilities (2018–2020); g. National Plan for the Prevention and Fight against Abuse and Sexual Exploitation of Children (2015–2017).
	22) Formally extend the remit of UNAR to include all forms of discrimination, including those based on language, religion, nation of origin, disabilities, sexual orientation and gender identity.

	23) Ensure sufficient public social spending in the various categories (illness, disability, family support, unemployment, social housing and combating social exclusion).
	24) Continue with efforts to resolve the problem of overcrowding in prisons, making further progress on the structural measures and deflation mechanisms introduced.
Initiatives in specific areas	
Women's Rights	25) Promote actual equality between men and women in all aspects of public and private life, specifically through the adoption of policies and actions directed at: a. reducing the deficit in the number of women represented in the highest decision-making roles in political bodies, including Parliament and Regional Councils, public administration including the Diplomatic Service and in the private sector; b. reducing the salary gap between men and women; c. fostering a more balanced sharing of family duties between men and women, both in running the home and in care-giving duties; d. eliminating stereotypical attitudes on the roles and responsibilities of women and men in the family, in society and in the workplace; e. encouraging plans for the integration of foreign women f. tackling and resolving the phenomenon of resignations without a justified reason ("blank resignation letters") for pregnant women and working mothers.

Children's Rights	26) Adopt a general legislative measure which enshrines the right of children to be listened to in court, in administrative bodies, in the institutions, at school and in the family on every issue which concerns them directly and establish suitable mechanisms and procedures to this end, to ensure that the participation of children really takes place.
	27) Amend the criminal code so as to explicitly forbid and criminalise the recruitment and the deployment, by either the armed forces or armed groups, of young people under the age of 18 in the course of armed conflicts.
	28) Adopt legislation prohibiting and criminalising the sale of light and small calibre arms to Countries which deploy child soldiers.
Citizenship Rights; Rights of Migrants, Refugees and Asylum Seekers	29) Address migratory flows as a structural phenomenon, the systematic planning for which must be assigned to instruments of an ordinary nature (rather than to emergency measures linked to a purely security- oriented viewpoint) and to multi- level governance with the involvement of the relevant Ministries, Regions, local administrations and civil society.
	30) Respect the principle of non- refoulement, the right of asylum seekers to an individual examination of their case, as well as immediate access to asylum procedures and other forms of national and international protection, including where there are bilateral agreements for return or for cooperation in management of migratory flows.

	31) Implement initiatives that aim to overcome the rigid nature of the Dublin III regulations, in order to meet both the expectations of those seeking international protection and the needs of those communities in Europe who are particularly exposed to the impact of potential asylum seekers.
	32) Maintain the working spaces for non-governmental organisations involved in search and rescue operations at sea, as required by existing international standards.
Citizenship Rights; Rights of Migrants, Refugees and Asylum Seekers	33) Support the activities of the "Roundtable on the Legal Status of Roma", established on 30 January 2013 as part of the National Strategy for Inclusion of the members of these communities, with the objective of finding solutions to the situation of statelessness of large numbers of Roma and Sinti originally from the former Yugoslavia, and of their children born in Italy (the so- called "de facto stateless people").
	34) Develop a more expeditious identification system, in order to reduce as far as possible the period that migrants are detained while waiting for the identification procedures to be completed, ensuring complete respect of the rights of people detained in repatriation centres.
	35) Re-examine laws on citizenship in the light of the principle of *ius humanae dignitatis*, continuing in the direction taken by the simplification of the process for acquiring citizenship status pursuant to Article 33 of l.d. 21 June 2013, No. 69.

Structure of the Yearbook 2019

Like in its previous editions, the *Italian Yearbook of Human Rights 2019* aims at presenting a snapshot of the human rights situation in Italy, both from a legislative and "infrastructural" point of view, and from that of the practical implementation of policies and initiatives to promote and protect them. This version of the *Yearbook* looks specifically at the calendar year 2018. The level of detail and background analysis provided in the various sections allows for crosscutting and targeted readings, which can also be developed by consulting the analytical indexes.

Information presented in the first three parts of the *Yearbook* come from public documents, which are normally consultable via the official webpage for each body examined. For Part IV, the databases of the specific courts cited were used (for Italian case-law, most data were taken from the Giuffrè *"De Iure"* database).

Part I of the *Yearbook* illustrates the main developments in Italy's incorporation of international and regional standards into its domestic legislation. The overview starts from international level (United Nations) and moves on to regional level, comprising legislation drawn up by the Council of Europe and the European Union, before presenting domestic legislation that transposes international obligations into national and regional laws.

Part II illustrates the human rights infrastructure in Italy and is divided into three chapters. The first describes the structure, functions and activities of State bodies (Parliament, Government, the Judiciary, independent authorities) and also presents the activities of civil society organisations and academic institutions operating at State level. The second chapter considers the sub-national level of the Italian legal order and illustrates the variegated local and regional human rights infrastructure and the relative coordinating bodies. The third chapter is devoted to the "peace human rights" infrastructure and to initiatives developed in this area by the Region of Veneto. The specific focus on this Region is explained by the pioneering commitment shown by Veneto, dating back to its 1998 r.l. 18, in promoting a culture of human rights, peace and international solidarity.

Part III deals with Italy's position with reference to the international and regional bodies and mechanisms for monitoring the implementation of human rights. It includes the assessments and recommendations that these bodies have addressed to Italy following specific missions to the State and periodic monitoring activities. The role of Italy within these organisations and the contribution of its diplomatic representatives for the promotion of human rights at regional and global level are considered. This Part is subdivided into five chapters. The first focuses on the United Nations system, analysing in particular the activities of the General Assembly, the Human Rights Council, the Treaty Bodies and the specialised Agencies. The second chapter is devoted to the Council of Europe, while the third to the European Union. These two chapters complement the information presented in Part I (concerning legislation) and in Part IV (concerning case-law), relative to Council of Europe and EU activities in 2016. The fourth chapter deals with the Organisation for Security and Cooperation in Europe (OSCE) and its bodies for the promotion of the human dimension of security. The fifth and final chapter is on international humanitarian and criminal law. In this area, in addition to providing updates on Italy's level of conformity, there is a list of all international peace missions to which Italian troops contributed in 2018.

Finally, Part IV presents a selection of domestic and international case-law concerning Italy over the year in question. In the three chapters, the cases are subdivided according to the subject to which the judgment refers. The chapters respectively deal with the internal case-law (mainly of the Constitutional Court, the Court of Cassation and the State Council), the case-law of the European Court of Human Rights and the case-law of the Court of Justice of the European Union, the latter with reference to the cases directly concerning Italy. A targeted reading of the case-law is also possible by using the index of case-law cited at the end of the book.

The section of the Introduction devoted to examining in-depth some specific human rights subjects in Italy concerns, for this edition, the Italian system for the protection of victims of trafficking and the formulation and implementation of the 2016–2018 national anti-trafficking plan. The in-depth analysis is edited by Professor Paola Degani.

In-depth Analysis. The Italian System to Protect Trafficked Persons and the National Action Plan against Trafficking 2016–2018.

Trafficking in human beings is certainly not a a recent phenomenon, and still constitutes a widespread problem and a grave violation of human rights. The fight against human trafficking is one of the priorities of the Sustainable Development Goals (SDG) which the whole international community must turn its attention to Goal 5 cites trafficking directly: in the framework for measures promoting gender equality, Goal 5.2 identifies that it is necessary to eliminate all forms of violence against all women and girls in public and private spheres, including trafficking and sexual and other types of exploitation, while Goal 16.2. adds a specific reference to children: end abuse, exploitation, trafficking and all forms of violence and torture against children.

In the last few years, Europe has taken centre stage as the setting for this phenomenon, which itself has taken on different and increasingly complex forms, changing in many respects: the victims' profile, above all their nationality, arrival method, forms of recruitment and exploitation, and the sectors in which the victims are employed.

Human trafficking for the purpose of sexual exploitation is the most well-known form of trafficking, although it is not necessarily the most serious or violent; this form has also changed over the years in the route profile, the structure of the criminal organisations and the types of duress exercised over the victim. Moreover, other trafficking contexts have overlapped with trafficking for the purpose of sexual exploitation; in particular, human trafficking to Italy and Europe also takes place with the purpose of labour exploitation in the agricultural or services sector, or even in some manufacturing sectors (in particular the textile industry). At times, victims are exploited in criminal activities, begging, organ harvesting or for illegal international adoption (all of which are areas that are still relatively unexplored).

Italy is a destination and transit country on the specialised trafficking routes used by criminal organisation. The country is strongly affected by these dynamics, not only because of its geographical position, but also by virtue of a strong demand for low-cost labour from various sectors of the economy. More generally, Italy is involved due to the existence of small parts of the territory under the control of organised crime, where illicit activities are not always effectively countered and where local mafias negotiate criminal partnerships with criminal groups of different ethnicities aiding and abetting illegal immigration and trafficking in human beings.

I. Legal Framework

The international community is committed to the fight against human trafficking and has adopted in the last few decades many provisions aimed at both tackling the crime and providing protection to the victims. The turning point was when the United Nations adopted the United Nations Convention against Transnational Organized Crime, more specifically its Additional Protocol to Prevent, Suppress and Punish Trafficking in Persons Especially Women and Children, in 2000. The Convention and Protocol introduce a new definition of *trafficking in persons*, setting out its limits compared to *smuggling of migrants*. Trafficking and smuggling are two distinctly different concepts, even if they seem the same when talking about the concrete facts of a case.

On a regional level, the legal source of reference is the Council of Europe Convention on Action against Trafficking in Human Beings, approved in Warsaw on 16 May 2005. The main value of the Council of Europe treaty lies in the adoption of a human rights perspective, following the fundamental principle that protecting and promoting the rights of victims of trafficking must be ensured without any discrimination. In the EU law framework, the most recent document on the subject is Directive 2011/36/EU, introducing important provisions aimed at combating human trafficking, preventing the crime and protecting the victim. On this last point, the Directive establishes specific measures for rapid identification, assistance and support, which must be guaranteed, with the victim's informed consent, from when the authorities have "reasonable motives" to suppose that the person is a victim of trafficking, and for an appropriate time period with respect to the duration of the undergoing criminal proceedings.

II. The Italian Anti-trafficking System

Italy has an efficient protection system for victims of human trafficking, at the forefront both in terms of current legislation and as as regards the effective interventions by public and private social bodies tasked to implement protection and assistance programmes for victims of slavery, human trafficking or other serious forms of exploitation. The anti-trafficking system was put in place earlier than the aforementioned international standards were adopted. Legislative decree 286/1998, Consolidated law on provisions concerning immigration regulations, contained provisions (Article 18) which were subsequently used as a model for other European systems. Even now, Article 18 is an important instrument to protect victims of human trafficking or in general of serious exploitation. The norm, in conjunction with Article 27 of the implementing regulation (Presidential Decree 394/99), establishes the issue of a special residence permit for foreign citizens who are victims of violence or severe explotation and who are endangered as a consequence of statements made in the course of court proceedings against their exploiters or as a consequence of to their decision to escape exploitation. The person's situation of exploitation and danger must be verified in a criminal proceeding for any offence set out by the law, as in Article 3 of l. 75/1958 (facilitating or exploiting prostitution) and crimes pursuant to Article 380 of the Criminal Procedure Code, or those for which compulsory arrest is envisaged, including, in particular, crimes referred to in Articles 600 (enslaving or holding in slavery), 601 (human trafficking) and 602 (purchase or sale of slaves) of the Criminal Code. Furthermore, situations of serious exploitation may also emerge during interventions to protect victims. The residence permit provided for in Article 18 of legislative decree 286/1998 can be issued both following the victim reporting the crime and in cases where the victim cannot or does not want to contact the Judicial Authority. In this sense, there is a "double track" system in place.

This provision establishes the victim's access to a "social assistance and integration programme", laying the basis for a protection and assistance system for victims of serious exploitation and human trafficking. Therefore, Italy has had programmes aiming at emergence, assistance and social integration of the victims since the 1990s (as defined nowadays by Article 18(3-*bis*) as amended by legislative decree 24/2014 of transposition of European Directive 2011/36). These are services aimed at ensuring necessary assistance and protection measures to those who have experienced trafficking or serious exploitation. These programmes are entrusted to public sector or private social bodies and are financed by the Department for Equal Opportunities of the Presidency of the Council of Ministers (DPO). Since 2000, over 22,000 people have been directly assisted by the system.

The programs supported by the DPO are articulated in interventions such as: street units, aimed at directly contacting people who prostitute themselves on the street; help and information desks; reception services in sheltered homes with secret addresses; support for social and labour inclusion, which encompasses initiatives aimed at acquiring a residence permit for work or study reasons replacing the the social protection permit. Furthermore, the National Hotline against Trafficking (800.290.290) provides detailed information 24 hours a day about services for victims of trafficking and, upon request, directs them to the most appropriate social-assistance services for each specific case (information, psychological advice, legal counselling, social and health support, etc.). This toll-free number is managed by the Municipality of Venice on the mandate of the DPO. As part of this referral activity, the National Hotline receives important data on the trafficking in general and on the profile of the people accessing the anti-trafficking system. Legislative decree 24/2014 identified the the DPO as the responsible body for coordinating, monitoring and assessing the outcomes of the prevention, combat and social protection policies, giving it a central role in national policies. It must also draw up a plan of the financial needs for assistance and social integration of victims.

The most relevant new elements that were introduced by the 2014 decree are:

- adopting the first National Action Plan against Trafficking, across all levels of governance, though especially at the level of Regions and local authorities, which, implement the system of interventions in support of victims of trafficking and/or other serious forms of exploitation, especially through agencies of the private social sector;
- unifying the two existing types of projects (based respectively on Article 13, l. 228/2003 – Measures against human trafficking, and Article 18, lgs.d. 2896/1998) in a single program of emergence, assistance and social integration, with the main aim of active integration of the victim by the end of the programme. Unifying

these has brought clear advantages in terms of activity management and overcoming traditional planning of territorial services;
- obligatory training for all social and other workers involved;
- a system of compensation and relief for the victims.

In recent years, the Italian protection system of victims of human trafficking has been based on a composite structure fundamentally based on three pillars of action, connected to corresponding operational dispositives.

The first of these dispositives is Article 18 of lgs.d. 286/1998, which authorises the issuing of residence permits "for reasons of social protection". Victims of human trafficking can obtain a residence permit following a judicial process (when they decide to cooperate with judicial and police authorities during the investigation and criminal proceedings against traffickers) or via a social route (when a situation of violence or severe exploitation has been verified, regardless of the victim's willingness to testify in court). As seen above, the second type of protective measure is based on Article 13 of law 228/2003. The law provides for an assistance programme for victims of the crimes within Articles 600 and 601 of the Criminal Code to guarantee the first forms of protection and reception for a short period of time (three months, which is then extendable for another three) necessary to identify situations of violence.

Article 12 of l. 228/2003 established a fund for anti-trafficking measures, again managed by the Presidency of the Council of Ministers. The fund finances assistance, social integration programmes and various other activities implementing Article 18 of lgs.d. 286/1998.

Today these programmes appear to be operationally unified within the so-called "single programme of emergence, assistance and social integration", defined by the Decree of the President of the Council of Ministers (d.p.c.m.) relating to the Single Programme of emergence, assistance and social integration, of 16 May 2016. The goal of the single programme is to provide reception and protection facilities to the person in the preliminary phase of verifying the condition of victim of trafficking and, subsequently, to provide them with the tools necessary to become fully autonomous. There are active projects carrying out the single programme all across Italy.

The legal framework also includes law 29 October 2016, No. 199, which lays down the "provisions on the fight against the phenomena of undeclared work, the exploitation of labour and the pay realignment in the agricultural sector", which rewrites the crime of illegal hiring. The law introduces a specific aggravating circumstance in the case of child victims, and extends the fund for victims of trafficking to benefit the victims of the illegal hiring. It becomes an important tool to fight against labour exploitation, reinforced by the law 14 September 2011, No. 148 which introduced the crime of illicit intermediation and exploitation of labour (Article 603-*bis* of the Criminal Code), and of lgs.d. 23 October 2018, No. 119 which set up a working group on tackling illegal hiring ("*caporalato*") at the Ministry of Labour and Social Policies.

On protecting children's rights, it is necessary to mention law 7 April 2017, No. 47 (the so-called Zampa Law) containing "provisions regarding the protection measures for unaccompanied foreign minors", which, in Article 17, provides for a specific assistance programme for child victims of trafficking and introduces important measures on age assessment.

III. The National Action Plan against Trafficking 2016–2018

In 2016, the Council of Ministers adopted the first "National Action Plan against trafficking and the serious exploitation of human beings" (NAP) (http://www.pariopportunita.gov.it/wp-content/uploads/2017/12/Piano-nazionale-di-azione-contro-la-tratta-e-il-grave-sfruttamento-2016-2018.pdf), implementing Article 9, lgs.d. 24/2014. The Plan aimed to "define multi-year intervention strategies to prevent and fight against trafficking and the serious exploitation of human beings, as well as actions aimed at raising awareness, social prevention, and the emergence and social integration of the victims". The practical goal is to define a coordinated and systematic national intervention policy, involving the various competent administrations at national and regional level, with a collaborative approach aimed at optimising financial resources.

The NAP explicitly recognises the complexity of the human trafficking phenomenon and the need to act simultaneously on multiple fronts, taking into account its multiple aspects. A multi-level and multi-agency approach to governance is therefore needed to tackle this issue.

The services system offered in Italy is funded via various channels, including those deriving from the application of Article 13 of l. 11 August 2003, No. 228, Article 18 of l. 25 July 1998, No. 286, and d.p.c.m. 16 May 2016, reflects the welfare protection system outlined by the national anti-trafficking legal frame. Social services are delivered in 4 phases:

– Phase 1: Contact, emergence and protection of the person;
– Phase 2: First assistance to prepare for social inclusion processes;
– Phase 3: Professional training and labour insertion;
– Phase 4: Social inclusion and beginning autonomous living.

Initiatives to combat trafficking in human beings for the purpose of serious exploitation move substantially on two channels, which follow the Italian "double track" system. The first concerns the combat and repression of the crime of exploitation of human being, which is entrusted to all law enforcement agencies. The second concerns preventing trafficking and protecting victims, and is within the competency of the public social services, accredited private social bodies via the appropriate section (section II) of the register of the associations which carry out activities on behalf of immigrants, established by Article 52(1) of the Presidential Decree 334/2004 (Regulation to implement the consolidated law on immigration).

In addition to thoroughly considering all institutional subjects involved in multi-level governance, the NAP also identifies some strategic stakeholders:

– voluntary organisations, committed to helping people in conditions of social marginalisation and severe hardship;
– the third sector, with NGOs, cooperatives, associations or other institutions that manage contact services, referral, protection, training and social integration for anyone in difficulty, which, over the years, have developed professional skills with regard to integrating immigrants, asylum seekers and refugees;
– migrant and immigrant and/or refugee associations that mainly work towards intercultural mediation and in favour of second-generation migrants in reception services, in teaching Italian and other native languages and in supporting administrative procedures (renewal of residence permits, acquisition of Italian citizenship, etc.);

- international organisations that work at all levels on protecting victims of trafficking;
- trade union organisations and their service networks, which play an active role in workplace protection;
- universities and the academic world in general, carrying out research and in-depth studies on the trafficking in human beings and its developments.

The NAP therefore aims to transfer the legal norms and the existing institutional apparatus at international and European level to the national level, making it more functional. Directive 2011/36/EU (and lgs.d. 24/2014 implementing the directive) remains as the main legal references, establishing minimum rules concerning the definition of crimes and sanctions in the area of human trafficking and common provisions for all EU Member States. It aims both at strengthening crime prevention and repression and at protecting victims, whilst referring to the national intervention system.

The action strategy of the NAP was based on the "EU Strategy towards the eradication of trafficking in human beings 2012-2016", adapted to Italian law via Commincation COM(2012) 286 of 19 June 2012.

The Plan is therefore structured according to the five priorities identified by the EU Strategy:

- identifying, protecting and assisting victims of trafficking;
- stepping up the prevention of trafficking in human beings;
- increased prosecution of traffickers;
- enhanced coordination and cooperation among key actors and policy coherence;
- increased knowledge of and effective response to emerging concerns related to all forms of trafficking in human beings.

Considering the four key purposes (*prevention, prosecution, protection, partnership*) identified by European documents, the NAP foresees action on four strategic goals:

- coordination (strengthen the national integrated anti-trafficking system);
- prevention;
- assistance, protection and recovering victims of trafficking;
- investigation and combating trafficking.

IV. The Single Public Calls for Funding

The NAP is particularly significant for operators within the anti-trafficking system, given that in 2016, the plan made it possible to draft the working programme and related implementation and financing procedures, incorporated in the d.p.c.m. of 16 May 2016. It set out the "Single Programme of emergence, assistance and social integration in favour of foreigners and citizens who are victims of crimes under Articles 600 and 601 of the Criminal Code, or of crimes set out in paragraph 1 of Article 18, lgs.d. 286/1998". It is evident that the integration between the two areas (protection of asylum seekers and the fight against trafficking for serious exploitation) are closely linked. It is the recognition that there is a cross-over between the worlds of migrants, which is still not acknowledged within the legislation, which still tends to group them all together. In particular, it is the recognition that the current reality of "mixed" migratory flows does not allow to easily distinguish asylum seekers from victims of trafficking, irregular migrants who access the traffic mechanisms from those who are or become victims of serious exploitation, or who fear persecution in their country. This is the complicated and ever-changing reality envisaged in the NAP and in the related "single public calls for proposals".

In the first few months of 2019, there were two "single public calls for proposals", issued by the Government for the distribution of loans for the planned initiatives: the call for tenders for 2016/2017 and the one for 2017/2018.

The projects envisaged by the single public call for proposals are carried out by public bodies or private companies that work in favour of immigrants as previously mentioned, and have the following series of activities as their goal:

– first contact with persons at risk of exploitation, aimed at protecting their health and the emergence of potential victims of trafficking and/or serious exploitation, with particular attention to applicants or holders of international protection;
– proactive multi-agency actions to identify the state of victim, also in the Territorial Commissions for the recognition of international protection;
– immediate protection and first assistance, including: prompt reception, health care and legal protection, in accordance with the provisions of Article 13 of the l. 228/2003;

- assistence in obtaining the residence permit pursuant to Article 18 of lgs.d. 286/98;
- training activity (linguistic and/or computer literacy, job orientation, professional training) and social-work placement;
- integration of the protection system for victims of trafficking with the system to protect applicants/holders of international/humanitarian protection, including integrated protection paths between the two systems.

The currently active projects reported on the official National Observatory website (managed by the National Hotline against Trafficking) are the following (we report: proposing authority; name of the project; territorial competence):

- On the Road Association; "ASIMMETRIE – Multi-regional integrated system actions: Mid-Adriatic against human trafficking and exploitation and for the social-work inclusion of the victims"; Macerata, Fermo, Ascoli Piceno, Abruzzo and Molise Provinces;
- Pisa Health Society; "SATIS – Tuscan Anti-trafficking System and Social Interventions"; Tuscany;
- Emilia-Romagna Region; "Beyond the road– 2016/2017"; Emilia-Romagna;
- *La Strada* Assocation; "Dawn"; Trentino-Alto Adige;
- Dedalus Coop.; "Outside trafficking– Actions for the emergence, assistance and social integration of victims of trafficking and serious exploitation"; Campania;
- *Lule* Association; "WE WEAR WINGS – from emergence to integration"; Bergamo, Cremona, Lecco, Lodi, Mantua, Pavia;
- Lazio Region; "Lazio anti-trafficking network"; Lazio;
- Friuli-Venezia Giulia Region; "FVG online against trafficking"; Friuli-Venezia Giulia;
- Fight against marginalisation cooperative; "DRIFTING AND APPROACHING. Areas of freedom and rights for victims of trafficking and serious exploitation"; Monza-Brianza, Varese, Sondrio, Como;
- Congregation of the Daughters of Charity; "Elen Joy"; Sardinia;
- Umbria Region; "Away from risk Marginalisation and Exclusion – Free together to promote emergence"; Umbria;

- Proxima Social Cooperative; "LIGHTHOUSES"; Ragusa, Siracusa, Caltanissetta, Enna Provinces;
- Penelope Association; "Clouds"; Messina and Catania Provinces;
- Calabria Region; "IN.C.I.P.I.T. – INitiative of Calabria for the Identification, Protection and social Inclusion of the victims of Trafficking"; Calabria;
- CESTRIM; "People, not slaves"; Basilicata;
- Municipality of Venice; "N.A.Ve. – Veneto Anti-Trafficking Network"; Veneto;
- Free Woman Association; "Opportunity"; Ancona and Pesaro-Urbino Provinces;
- Apulia Region; "Puglia does not Traffic – together for the victims"; Apulia.

The NAP, in its operational dynamics, highlights a system of services, divided into five areas:

- proactive actions aimed at at-risk populations (e.g. through contact units);
- proactive multi-agency actions for emergence, identification, reporting and referral of potential victims of trafficking and serious exploitation;
- social protection: protecting rights and compensation;
- reception and residency;
- training and work access.

The range of services provided for victims of trafficking within the NAP is accordingly made up of five steps, two of which relate to the area of emergence, i.e. to proactive contact initiatives aimed at at-risk populations and proactive multi-agency actions of emergence, identification, reporting and referral of potential victims; two relating to the field of assistance; the last towards social inclusion.

According to the government proposal, the system of the single public calls for tenders, in the two-year period 2016–2018, should facilitate multi-agency and multidisciplinary coordination, in particular through the national referral mechanism: a set of recommendations and practical measures that guides all the actors involved in the anti-trafficking action. This institutional working model should make it possible to intervene on all forms of trafficking and on the various target victims, as well as facilitating the professionalisation process of everyone involved. Among the main innovations introduced by the NAP is the mandatory training for everyone working within the anti-trafficking field. In this context, the document provides for a series of measures, among which:

- the multidisciplinary training of all the subjects that potentially come into contact with victims of trafficking: law enforcement officers, border police, reception centre operators, magistrates, legal operators;
- setting outguidelines aimed at correctly identifying potential victims of trafficking in various contexts, including during the procedure for recognising international protection;
- the abovementioned introduction of a National Referral Mechanism, which Italy does not yet have, aimed at creating a system of cooperation through which state actors are able to fulfill their obligations to protect and promote human rights of victims of trafficking, in coordination with civil society;
- updating the reception measures, in order to respond to the constantly changed characteristics of the victims;
- the implementation of specific protection measures for trafficked children.

V. Human Trafficking in Italy

As has been repeatedly emphasised, human trafficking is an extremely complex and constantly evolving problem. It is therefore necessary to develop adequate monitoring tools that can provide an up-to-date and in-depth insight, to support the creation of policies and contribute to planning targeted response initiatives. In recent years, due to the characteristics of the migration phenomenon, the problem caused by people potentially exposed or at risk of trafficking (or even already victimised) requesting international protection has significantly involved the operators within the anti-trafficking system. This constituted a significant amount of the most important reference target of their work. The anti-trafficking interventions involving international protection applicants have almost always been carried out following an alert from within the "asylum system", or from humanitarian workers and border police forces. The network of asylum system operators was faced with the phenomenon of mixed flows and found themselves systematically managing situations at risk of serious exploitation. This need for a specialised response brought about a partial adaptation of what was drawn up within the NAP. The problem emerged specifically in regards to Nigerian girls in Italy, who, in recent years, have arrived in truly unprecedented number (up to 11,000 arrivals in 2016; more than 5,000 in 2015 and in 2017). They have often endured negative experiences (both in their country of origin and in transit countries, especially Libya) and face greater problems (in Italy or elsewhere in Europe) that are tragic from a perspective of human rights violations.

In the face of this scenario, it is evident that projects at a territorial level in the years between 2016 and 2018 planned their work on the basis of their "geographical exposure" to arrivals by sea, and in particular to their proximity to places of arrival of Nigerian women.

However, this does not diminish the crucial importance of the proactive intiatives that allow the emergence of the problem of trafficking. Emergence activities can be carried out by various social actors independently or on a multi-agency basis, involving police forces or those performing inspection roles; for example, in the workplace. In fact, for many operators, most of their time was spent responding to requests for help and extraction from a situation of risk of serious exploitation and/or trafficking from asylum seekers, in the accompanying these people to the Territorial Commissions and preparing reports often requested by the Commissions themselves to support and supplement the application for international protection. The same operators have also often reported the need to strengthen protection of asylum seekers from the risk of serious labour exploitation upon arrival in Italy, including in the northern regions of the country. This highlights, once again, the pervasive and multifaceted nature of trafficking.

VI. Monitoring Projects and the Role of the National Hotline against Trafficking

Data collected by the National Hotline against Trafficking allow us to appreciate the multi-faceted nature of this phenomenon, and the initiatives that individual parties and the anti-trafficking system as a whole must put in place. In particular, we notice that, as shown in the graphic, still a majority of trafficked persons are victims of sexual exploitation: around 60 %, on approximately 1,000 persons taken in charge annually by the system in the years 2015–2019), while the percentage of persons experiencing labour explotation is relatively low.

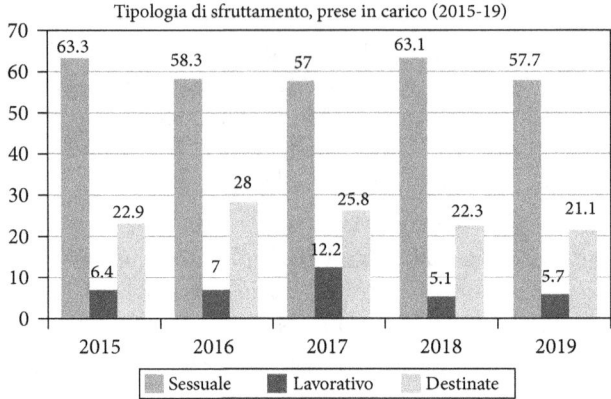

Percentage of persons taken in charge by the Italian antitrafficking system distributed along the two main types of exploitation they experienced in Italy (sexual, labour). The category of "Destinate" (intended) identifies persons exploited or at risk of exploitation before their arrival in Italy. In each year the number of persons in charge of the antitrafficking system have been about 1,000. Source: Data provided by the National Hotline against Trafficking

As regards the comphensive number of persons being treated, in 2018 the new cases amounted to around 1,000, and the total numberd of persons in charge of the system was of around 2,000.

The operators believe that there is a need to encourage the emergence activities in other contexts and to strengthen collaboration between agencies, in a historical moment in which the human rights of migrants are being openly discussed and challenged. Guidelines and political decisions that have recently been adopted at local and national level do not facilitate the construction of cooperative networks between the actors involved, nor do they improve performance.

VII. Governance of the Anti-trafficking System

Over the years, the multi-agency network strategy has been applied in different ways depending on the territory and has been characterised by varying development, alternating moments of growth and regression or stagnation. For example, collaboration between Anti-Trafficking Services and Police Forces in the field of the emergence and identification of victims of trafficking in street prostitution seem to be less efficient today; this however used to be the area where multi-agency action historically began and that, until to 2014–2015, was the main area of collaboration.

In this regard, it should be noted that the same NAP envisaged national governance based at the DPO of the Presidency of the Council, with a single Control Room, making up a to define activities and finance interventions. The NAP, however, does not seem to attribute a coordinator to manage strategies of fighting trafficking within the country.

The National Control Room, according to the NAP, can go ahead via proposals and in-depth analyses by the third sector subjects and trade unions in order to facilitate the exchange of best practise within the territory, to support continuous and effective dialogue and to interact with the scientific and academic community.

The NAP, however, does not outline an equally clear governance at the territorial level. The size of the territories is actually very important, given the plural and "geographically distinctive" nature of trafficking, as well as being crucial to rationalise interventions.

Another objective of the DPO is to createa a centralised, computerised database, capable of performing processing in real time. This is crucial for identifying early signs of evolution and change of the trafficking phenomenon. In recent years, creating and implementing this database, that was developed by the National Hotline against Trafficking (the result, in turn, of a "system action") has contributed to improving the response of the services, facilitating a culture of monitoring and therefore of evaluation. In this context, the National Hotline has also promoted numerous exchanges of best practice initiatives for the winners of the single public calls for proposals.

Although the National Hotline against Trafficking was initially conceived as a instrument with functions concerning emergence, reporting and referral to territorial projects for victims, it has increasingly taken on a "system" profile, providing both support for projects, facilitating the referral process, networking and transfer of victims from one structure to another. It does so both by responding directly to the needs of the DPO, in relation to data collection on trafficking and on the interventions, and of the territorial projects. The National Hotline is able to provide support and connection services between the managing bodies of the projects and between these and the central coordination at the DPO. More specifically, the new data collection system called SIRIT (Computerised System for Collecting Information on Trafficking), updated by the owners/coordinators of the projects for assistance and social protection for victims of trafficking and exploitation (co-financed by the DPO pursuant to Article 18 of lgs.d. 286/1998 and to Article 13, l. 228/2003 and now funded by the single public call for proposals) has made it possible to rationalise the referral system and get a lot of information on the victims and their pasts, thus providing very important elements for combating criminal organisations and protecting victims. The National Hotline has also acted as a catalyst for the "demand" coming from the implementing bodies towards political institutions, in the absence of a real central coordinating body for interventions.

In practice, in recent years the National Hotline, in addition to carrying out its own tasks, has taken on the coordination of the 21 territorial projects organised and managed on a predominantly regional basis, making the collected data available to the operators and facilitating the use of data for planning interventions.

VIII. Update and Assessment of the National Action Plan against Trafficking. The Problem with Prostitution

The NAP, a programming and policy tool, and its monitoring, which is necessary to effectively assess the achieved progress and verify the impact of the policies adopted, are among the measures Italy is obliged to activate with respect to its international commitments.

The monitoring and evaluation process conditions the functioning of a system. Human trafficking is notoriously constantly evolving; defining the policies for the intervention system reflects the current decision-making process.

The NAP acknowledges that monitoring and evaluation make it possible to measure the impact of anti-trafficking measures on the human rights of victims. It is therefore necessary to take into consideration the opinion of the victims themselves about the quality and value of the assistance received. However, experience shows that this measurement is not immediately feasible, as it would require the people passing through the system to be traceable, which is not guaranteed. Beyond any contingency, the fact remains that working with migrant marginality requires a non-judgmental and inclusive point of view.

This consideration directly involves the issue of prostitution. In this regard, a clash emerges between this non-judgmental and inclusive approach and certain positions expressed by bodies of civil society and also present at a political level, which favour legislative reforms that prohibit street prostitution (or at least push to move it into a closed environment). More often, it appears evident that street prostitution is treated as a matter of urban degradation and public order, rather than a problem of serious exploitation and a violation of the dignity and rights of vulnerable people.

In November 2018, the fourth mapping of street daytime and nighttime prostitution was organised, in order to observe the phenomenon and its variations and to collect up-to-date information, and facilitate a comparison among territories and a debate operators. The mapping was carried out with the substantial contribution of the National Hotline against Trafficking. The Contact and Street Units operating on the national territory were therefore asked to try to "count" any persons who were prostituting themselves on the street, monitoring at different moments the same places, including areas not normally covered by local police or social services. 68 % of the Italian Provincial capitals and Metropolitan Cities' territories was covered (as regards metropolitan cities, only Bari at night was not mapped); five Regions (Veneto, Emilia-Romagna, Trentino Alto Adige, Friuli Venezia-Giulia and Umbria) resulted completely mapped.

While it is evident that no definitive conclusions can be drawn, the four mappings conducted in 2017 and 2018 provide useful indications for the daily work of operators, especially if analysed over time. They also allow a more precise classification of the characteristics of street prostitution, which have witnessed many important changes, as often mentioned. In particular, some developments may alarm operators, since the reduction in the number of Nigerian women seems to match an increase in the number of young Albanian women involved in prostitution, who are often victims of serious violence.

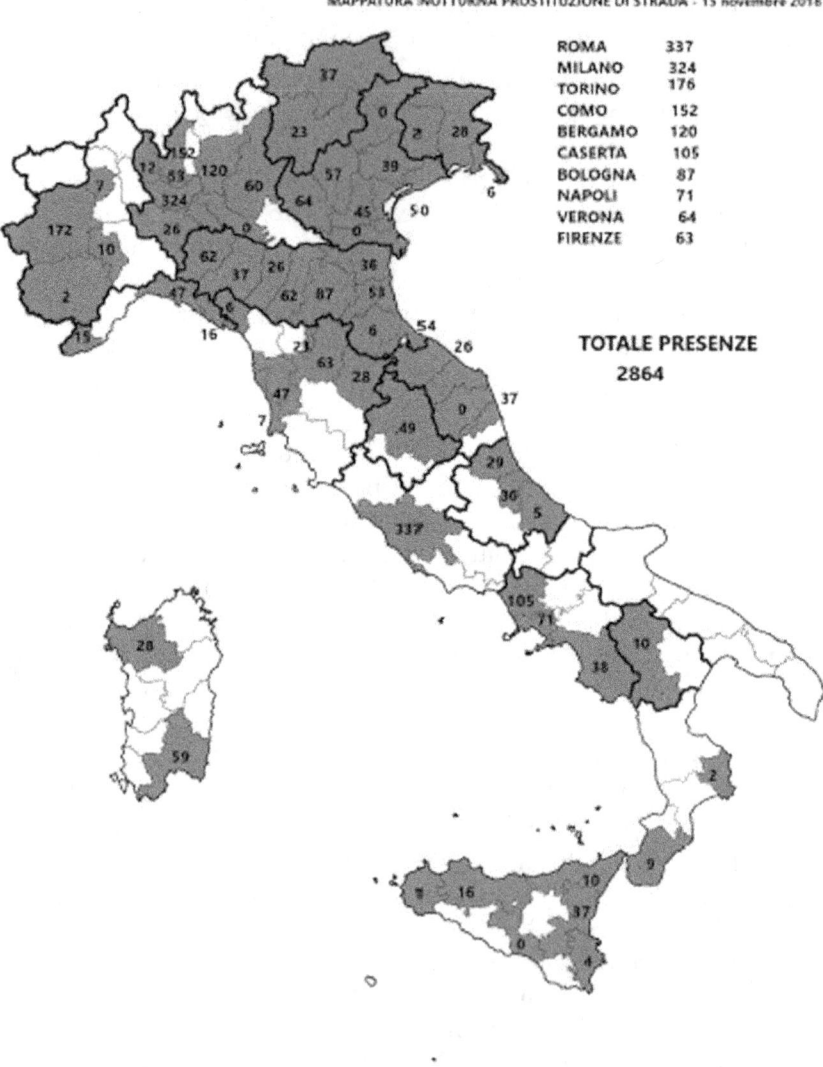

Street prostitution in Italy. Total number of outdoor prostitutes in Italian cities at November 15, 2018, during nighttime. Total number of recorded presences: 2,864. Source: Data provided by the National Hotline against Trafficking

Update and Assessment of the National Action Plan against Trafficking

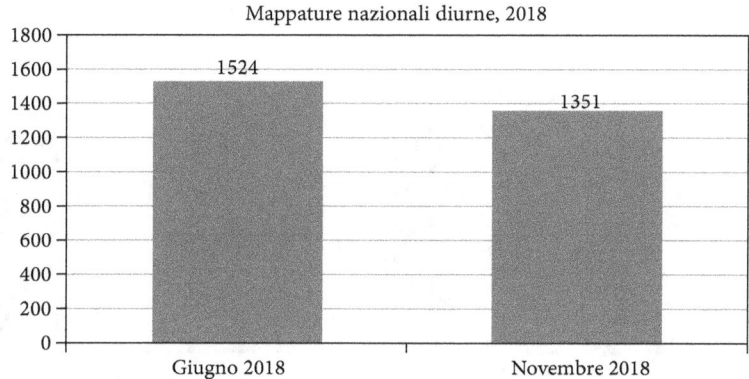

Street prostitution in Italy. Total number of street prostitutes during daytime, June and November 2018. Source: Data provided by the National Hotline against Trafficking

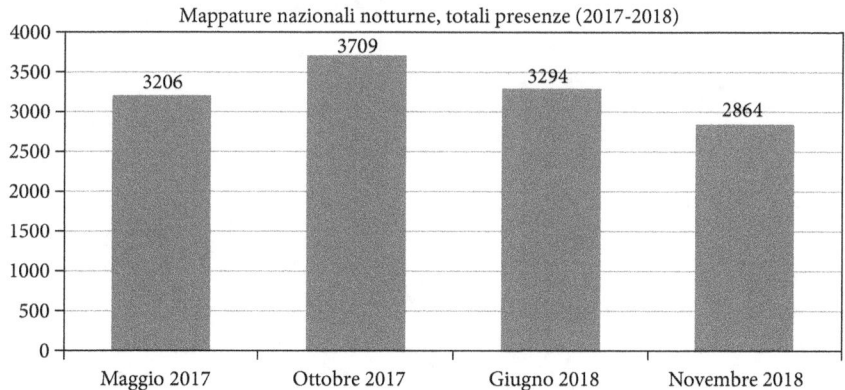

Street prostitution in Italy. Total number of street prostitutes during nighttime, 2017 and 2018. Source: Data provided by the National Hotline against Trafficking

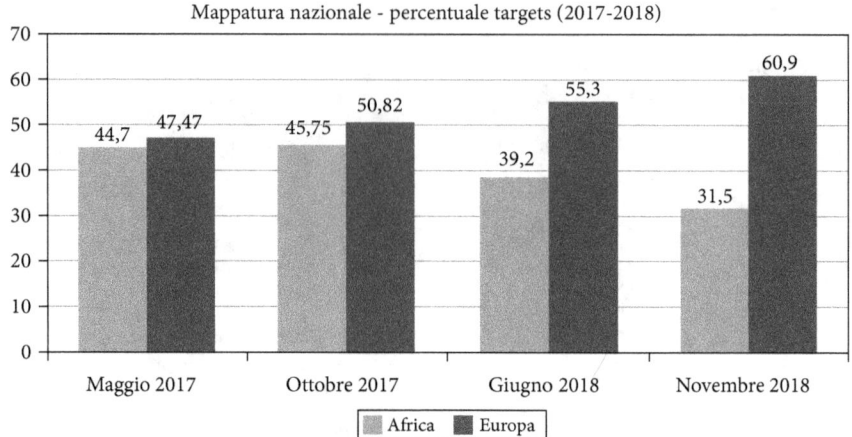

Street prostitution in Italy. Geographical origin of prostitutes (Africa and Europe) in May 2017, October 2017, June 2018, November 2018. Source: Data provided by the National Hotline against Trafficking

PART I

The Reception of International Human Rights Law in Italy

International Human Rights Law

The first Part of the *Yearbook* is divided into two chapters. The first is devoted to updates concerning the major international human rights instruments that Italy has ratified, as well as to the identification of both those international instruments signed but not ratified by the Country and those adopted in 2018 that have not been subjected to any initiative of acceptance yet.

This summary is particularly relevant in view of the implementation of the Agenda 2030 for Sustainable Development, which is deeply rooted in the numerous international instruments that constitute international human rights law (according to the Danish Institute for Human Rights, more than 90 % of the targets of the Sustainable Development Goals are connected to international human rights and workers' rights standards). From this perspective, Italy's lack of ratification of the International Convention on the Protection of the Rights of All Migrant Workers and Members of Their Families – the only core human rights treaty that Italy has not signed and ratified – has consequences on the country's commitment to carrying out a series of Agenda 2030 targets, with particular reference to Goal 3 (Good Health and Well-being), 4 (Quality Education), 8 (Decent Work and Economic Growth), 10 (Reduced Inequalities) and 16 (Peace, Justice and Strong Institution).

The framework of Italy's international obligations takes into consideration the universal conventions adopted within the system of the United Nations, the conventions of the Council of Europe, and also the European Union treaties and secondary law. Accordingly, the information provided is preliminary to the presentation of the national normative apparatus – the Constitution, national and regional laws – which is the subject of the following chapter.

I. Legal Instruments of the United Nations

During 2018, Italy did not file new instruments of ratification.

II. Legal Instruments on Disarmament and Non-proliferation

During 2018, Italy did not file new instruments of ratification.

III. Legal Instruments of the Council of Europe

On 20 February 2018, Italy signed the Protocol amending the Additional Protocol to the Convention on the Transfer of Sentenced Persons (adopted by the Council of Europe on 22 November 2017).

IV. European Union Law

A. Treaties

As envisaged by the Treaty of Lisbon, since 1 December 2009, the EU legal framework has consisted of two fundamental instruments: the Treaty on the European Union (TEU) and the Treaty on the Functioning of the European Union (TFEU). Article 6 TEU attributes the status of primary law to the Charter of Fundamental Rights of the EU, and also refers specifically to the rights guaranteed by the European Convention for the Protection of Human Rights and Fundamental Freedoms (ECHR) and those deriving from the constitutional traditions common to the Member States, which are part of EU law as general principles.

Furthermore, in the Preamble of the TEU, explicit reference is made to the 1989 Community Charter of Fundamental Social Rights of Workers and the 1961 European Social Charter of the Council of Europe (revised in 1996). Both these instruments are also mentioned in the TFEU in the context of Title X on Social Policy (Article 151).

B. EU Law in 2018

During 2017, the European Parliament and the Council of the EU adopted directives, regulations and decisions with particular relevance for human rights. For its part, the European Commission presented significant communications and legislative proposals.

In 2018, the following directives were adopted: combating money laundering by means of criminal law, enabling more efficient and swifter cross-border cooperation between competent authorities (2018/1673 of 23 October 2018); establishing the European Electronic Communications Code that fundamentally aims to proliferate directives 2002/19/EC1, 2002/20/EC2, 2002/21/EC3 and 2002/22/EC4, which have been subject to substantial amendment (2018/1972 11 December 2018); on the coordination of certain provisions laid down by law, regulation or administrative action in Member States concerning the provision of audiovisual media services (Audiovisual Media Services Directive) in view of changing market realities, amending Directive 2010/13/EU, extending its application from audiovisual media services to include social media services (2018/1808 of 14 November 2018); on the prevention of the use of the financial system for the purposes of money laundering or terrorist financing, and amending Directives 2009/138/EC and 2013/36/EU, extending their scope so as to include providers engaged in exchange services between virtual currencies and fiat currencies as well as custodian wallet providers (2018/843 of 30 May 2018); on the promotion of the use of energy from renewable sources that recasts directive 2009/28/EC and establishes a framework and common targets for promoting energy from renewable sources (2018/2001 of 11 December 2018); on a proportionality test before adoption of new regulation of professions to avoid disproportionate restrictions by national regulations on access to freedom to choose an occupation, as well as the freedom to conduct a business (2018/958 of 28 June 2018); amending Directive 96/71/EC concerning the posting of workers in the framework of the provision of services (2018/957 of 28 June 2018).

Various regulations in the field of human rights were adopted in 2018: Regulation 2018/1725 of 23 October 2018 on the protection of natural persons with regard to the processing of personal data by the Union institutions, bodies, offices and agencies and on the free movement of such data, and repealing Regulation (EC) No. 45/2001 and Decision No. 1247/2002/EC; Regulation 2018/1805 of 14 November 2018 on the mutual recognition of freezing orders and confiscation orders; Regulation 2018/1139 of 4 July 2018 on common rules in the field of civil aviation and establishing a European Union Aviation Safety Agency, and amending Regulations (EC) No. 2111/2005, (EC) No. 1008/2008, (EU) No. 996/2010, (EU) No. 376/2014 and Directives 2014/30/EU and 2014/53/EU of the European Parliament and of the Council, and repealing Regulations (EC) No. 552/2004 and (EC) No. 216/2008 of the European Parliament and of the Council and Council Regulation (EEC) No. 3922/91; Regulation 2018/302 of 28 February 2018 on addressing unjustified geo-blocking and other forms of discrimination based on customers' nationality, place of residence or place of establishment within the internal market and amending Regulations (EC) No. 2006/2004 and (EU) 2017/2394 and the Directive 2009/22/CE; Regulation 2018/1860 of 28 November 2018 on the use of the Schengen Information System for the return of illegally staying third-country nationals; Regulation 2018/1475 of 2 October 2018 laying down the legal framework of the European Solidarity Corps and amending Regulation (EU) No. 1288/2013, Regulation (EU) No. 1293/2013 and Decision No. 1313/2013/EU.

Furthermore, some decisions were adopted that are particularly relevant: Commission Decision 2018/262 of 14 February 2018 registering the proposed citizens' initiative entitled 'We are a welcoming Europe, let us help!' related to the signing, on behalf of the European Union, of the Council of Europe Convention on preventing and combating violence against women and domestic violence regarding asylum and non-refoulement; Council Decision 2018/1925 of 18 September 2018 on the position to be taken on behalf of the European Union position within the Association Council set up by the Euro-Mediterranean Agreement establishing an association between the European Community and its Member States, of the one part, and the Republic of Tunisia, of the other part, with regard to the adoption of the EU-Tunisia strategic priorities for the period 2018–2020, established with Council Decision 1/2018 of 9 November 2018; Council Decision 2018/1789 of 19 November 2018 in support of combating the illicit trade in and proliferation of small arms and light weapons in the Member States of the League of Arab States within the framework of the EU strategy against illicit firearms, SALW and their ammunition entitled 'Securing Arms, Protecting Citizens'; Commission Decision 2018/1962 of 11 December 2018 laying down internal rules concerning the processing of personal data by the European Anti-Fraud Office (OLAF) in relation to the provision of information to data subjects and the restriction of certain of their rights in accordance with Article 25 of Regulation (EU) 2018/1725 of the European Parliament and of the Council; European Parliament decision C 463/21 of 7 February 2018 on the revision of the Framework Agreement on relations between the European Parliament and the European Commission (2017/2233(ACI)) which provides for the selection of lead candidates ('Spitzenkandidaten') openly, inclusively and transparently and their candidates for President of the Commission (a system put in place for the first time during the 2014 European Parliamentary elections) and the amendment of Code of Conduct for the Members of the Commission so that the latter can stand for election to the European Parliament without first requesting a leave of absence.

Concerning Communications adopted by the Commission during 2018: Report on the evaluation of the EU Framework for National Roma Integration Strategies up to 2020 (COM/2018/785 of 4 December 2018); a more efficient decision-making for EU Common Foreign and Security Policy to have a more incisive role at a world level (COM/2018/647 of 12 September 2018); adapting the common visa policy to new challenges (COM/2018/251 of 14 March 2018); education in Emergencies and Protracted Crises (COM/2018/304 of 18 May 2018); strengthening whistleblower protection at EU level (COM/2018/214 of 23 April 2018); on the Seventeenth Progress Report towards an effective and genuine Security Union (COM/2018/845 of 11 December 2018); on the Progress report on the Implementation of the European Agenda on Migration, (COM/2018/301 of 16 May 2018); on the 2018 EU Justice Scoreboard for an independant, effective and quality national justice systems (COM/2018/364 of 28 May 2018); on monitoring the implementation of the European Pillar of Social Rights, which is part of the broader debate about the future of Europe, which was launched by the Commission's White Paper of 1 March 2017 (COM/2018/130 of 13 March 2018); on the role of youth, education and culture policies given that at the November 2017 Gothenburg Summit, EU Leaders chose education and culture for the Leaders' Agenda debate, informed by a Commission contribution on "Strengthening European Identity through Education and Culture" (COM/2018/268 of 22 May 2018); on the possible European Approach to tackle online disinformation in order to create a more transparent, trustworthy and accountable online ecosystem with regards to the freedom of expression (COM/2018/236 of 26 April 2018); on the European Approach to artificial intelligence (AI) aiming to build the EU's technological and industrial strengths and to adopt AI in all economic sectors and aiming to ensure an appropriate ethical and legal framework in line with fundamental rights, aboveall with regard to data protection (COM/2018/237 of 25 April 2018).

From the adoption of l. 24 December 2012, No. 234, the adaptation of the Italian legal system in line with the European system is achieved through two legislative instruments: the European Law and the Law of European delegation. While the former contains regulations for the direct implementation of EU law aimed at remedying cases of incorrect transposition of EU legislation, the latter contains the delegation provisions required for the transposition of directives and other Union acts.

On 25 October 2017, the Parliament adopted the 2016–2017 law of European delegation. With particular reference to the protection of fundamental rights, the provision confers the Government delegation to implement regulation 2016/679 of 27 April 2016 concerning the protection of natural persons with regard to the processing of personal data, while adopting principles and criteria for the implementation of directive 2016/681 of 27 April 2016 on the use of passenger name record (PNR) data for the purposes of prevention, detection, investigation and prosecution of terrorist offences and serious crimes.

On 11 May 2019, law No. 37 was published in the Official Gazzette, which contains provisions for the fulfilment of Italy's obligations deriving from the European Union (European Law 2018). As such, Italy must deal with 6 infringement procedures, 4 EU-Pilot cases (situations that can precede an infringement) and in one EU-Pilot case, the Government was delegated to adopt a legislative decree. It also resolves two cases of illegal State aid; two expired directives were implemented and national legislation was brought in line with five European Regulations. European Law 2018 also implements the Agreement between the European Union and the Republic of Iceland and the Kingdom of Norway (done at Vienna on 28 June 2006) on the surrender procedure between the Member States of the European Union and Iceland and Norway, to be applied within the limits of the principles of human rights and fundamental freedoms laid out in the Constitution. The infringement produres resolved by the cited law concerning human rights are as follows: Infringement 2018/2175 concerning professional qualifications and specifically the definition of "legally established"; Infringement 2018/0354 regarding the failure to notify on time the implementation of Directive (EU) 2017/1564, on certain permitted uses of certain works and other subject matter protected by copyright and related rights for the benefit of persons who are blind, visually impaired or otherwise print-disabled which is directly implemented in European Law 2018; Infringement 2018/2021 concerning the primary liability and ultimate responsibility for spent fuel and radioactive waste. As regards the EU-Pilot cases, the following cases are reported: 2079/11/EMPL concerning provisions for native language assistants; 8718/16/ENVI concerning the incorrect implementation of Directive 2012/19/EU with regard to disposal of electric and electronic equipment; 9180/17/ENVI concerning the disposal of garden and agricultural waste, referring particularly to the need for materials used for agriculture, forestry or energy production to not cause harm to human health and the environment

Alongside the aforementioned Directive 2017/1564, that expired on 11 October 2018, Directive 2017/1572 was also implemented, expired on 31 March 2018, concerning the principles and guidelines regarding good manufacturing practice for human pharmaceuticals.

Regarding the adaptation of the national legislation to European regulations, the following are relevant: Regulation 2018/302 on addressing unjustified geo-blocking and other forms of discrimination based on customers' nationality, place of residence or place of establishment within the internal market; Regulation 1031/2010 on the timing, administration and other aspects of auctioning of greenhouse gas emission allowances; Regulations No. 745/2017 and 746/2017 concerning medical provisions and in vitro diagnostic medical devices.

As regards to certain infringement procedures that were opened in previous years, in 2018, the Commission appealed to the EU Court of Justice pursuant to Article 258 TFEU for the following cases: Infringement No. 2014/0386 concerning the violation of Directive 2012/39/EU of 26 November 2012 amending Directive 2006/17/EC concerning certain technical requirements for the testing of human tissues and cells; Infringement No. 2014/2147 for excess levels of fine particulate matter (PM 10) in the air, which is a grave risk for human health; Infringement No. 2016/2027 for the failure to notify the national programme for the implementation of a spent fuel and radioactive waste management policy, in accordance with Council Directive 2011/70/Euratom.

In 2018, the following infringement procedures were closed: No. 2014/2171 on the situation of unaccompanied minors seeking asylum, No. 2015/2165 for non-compliance with the requirements of Articles 28 and 30 of Directive 2008/98/EC on Waste Management Plans; No. 2017/0127 regarding Directive 2015/720 of 29 April 2015 amending Directive 94/62/EC as regards reducing the consumption of lightweight plastic carrier bags; No. 2018/0028 concerning the lack of application of the Commission Implementing Directive (EU) 2017/1279 of 14 July 2017, amending annexes I to V of Council Directive 2000/29/EC on protective measures against the introduction into the Community of organisms harmful to plants or plant products and against their spread within the Community; No. 2018/0080 on Commission Directive (EU) 2016/1214 of 25 July 2016, amending Directive 2005/62/EC regarding quality system standards and specifications for blood establishments; No. 2017/0129 for the non-communication of national transposition measures of Directive (EU) 2015/2203 regarding marketing standards for certain dairy products- caseins and caseinates intended for human consumption.

The Commission sent a letter of formal notice concerning Article 258 of the TFEU: on 19 July 2018 for Infringement No. 2017/2181 for breaching its obligations under the Urban Waste Water Treatment Directive; 8 November 2018 for Infringement No. 2018/2249 calling on Italy and Spain over the insufficient protection of waters against pollution caused by nitrates from agricultural sources in accordance with Council Directive 91/676/EC; 24 September 2018 for Infringement No. 2018/0264 establishing a fourth list of indicative occupational exposure limit values pursuant to Council Directive 2017/164 of 31 January 2017.

On 17 May 2018, regarding Infringement No. 2009/2034, the Commission sent a letter of formal notice concerning Article 260 of the TFEU calling on Italy to fully comply with the ruling of the Court of Justice of the EU of 10 April 2014 in case C-85/13, for failing to fulfil its obligations under Article 258 TFEU and Council Directive 91/271 amended by Regulation No. 1137/2008 on the collection, treatment and discharge of urban waste water and the treatment and discharge of waste water from certain industrial sectors, particularly areas which are protected.

On 25 January 2018, the Commission sent a reasoned opinion based on Article 258 of the TFEU concerning Infringement No. 2013/2022 in which the Commission calls on Italy to comply with the key provisions of Directive 2002/49/EC of 25 June 2002 relating to the assessment and management of environmental noise which establishes activities for Member States to avoid and reduce environmental noise where they can be harmful to human health.

Italian Law

I. Constitution of the Italian Republic

"The Republic recognises and guarantees the inviolable rights of the persons, both as an individual and in the social group where the human personality is expressed. The Republic expects that the fundamental duties of political, economic and social solidarity be fulfilled" (Article 2).

"All citizens have equal social dignity and are equal before the law, without distinction of sex, race, language, religion, political opinion, personal and social conditions.

It is the duty of the Republic to remove those obstacles of an economic or social nature which constrain the freedom and equality of citizens, thereby impeding the full development of the human person and the effective participation of all workers in the political, economic and social organisation of the Country" (Article 3).

"The Italian legal system conforms to the generally recognised principles of international law. The legal status of foreigners is regulated by law in conformity with international provisions and treaties. A foreigner who, in his home Country, is denied the actual exercise of the democratic freedoms guaranteed by the Italian Constitution shall be entitled to the right of asylum under the conditions established by law. A foreigner may not be extradited for a political offence" (Article 10).

"The Italian legal system conforms to the generally recognised principles of international law. The legal status of foreigners is regulated by law in conformity with international provisions and treaties. A foreigner who, in his home Country, is denied the actual exercise of the democratic freedoms guaranteed by the Italian Constitution shall be entitled to the right of asylum under the conditions established by law. A foreigner may not be extradited for a political offence" (Article 10).

The whole of Fundamental Principles and Part I of the Constitution (Articles 1–54) is devoted to the fundamental rights and duties of citizens, which are grouped into four areas: civil relations, ethical and social relations, economic relations and political relations.

II. National Legislation

During 2018, the Parliament and the Government adopted legislative acts (laws, decree-laws, legislative decrees) that are directly and indirectly related to the protection and protection of internationally recognised human rights. Below the legislative acts are listed on the basis of the following typologies:

a) general legislative acts;

b) legislative acts concerning specific subjects;

c) legislative acts concerning the protection of particular groups

a) General legislative acts

L. 16 November 2018, No. 130 (Converting into law, with amendments, l.d. 28 September 2018, No. 109, containing urgent provisions for the City of Genova, the safety of the national infrastructure and transport network, seismic events of 2016 and 2017, work and other emergencies).

L. 1 December 2018, No. 132 (Converting into law, with amendments, l.d. 4 October 2018, No. 113 containing urgent provisions for international protection and imigration, public security, measures supporting the funtions of the Ministry for Internal Affairs and the organisation and operation of the national agency for administration and the disposal of goods confiscated from organised crime. Delegation to the Government regarding the reorganisation of the roles and careers of Police and Armed Forces personnel).

b) Legislative acts concerning specific subjects

Crime, criminal procedure

Lgs.d. 1 March 2018, No. 21 ((Provisions for implementing the principle of delegation for preserving the Criminal Code pursuant to Article 1, comma 85, letter q), of l. 23 June 2017, No. 103).

L. 7 August 2018, No. 100 (Establishing a Parliamentary enquiry commission on the illegal activities connected to waste cycle and related environmental offences).

L. 7 August 2018, No. 99 (Establishing a Parliamentary enquiry commission on the mafia and criminal associations, both Italian and foreign).

Lgs.d. 10 August 2018, No. 104 (Directive (EU) 2017/853 of the European Parliament and of the Council of 17 May 2017 amending Council Directive 91/477/EEC on control of the acquisition and possession of weapons).

Lgs.d. 22 December 2018, No. 151 (Regulation for implementing directive 2009/52/EC providing for minimum standards on sanctions and measures against employers of illegally residing third-country nationals).

Penitentiary law

Lgs.d. 2 October 2018, No. 123 (Reforming the penitentiary law, in implementing the delegate pursuant to Article 1, paragraphs 82, 83 and 85, letters a), d), i), l), m), o), r), t) and u), of l. 23 June 2017, No. 103).

Lgs.d. 2 October 2018, No. 124 (Reforming the penitentiary law concerning the prison life and penitentiary work, in implementation of the delegate of which Article 1, commas 82, 83 and 85, letters g), h) and r), of l. 23 June 2017, No. 103).

Civil service

Lgs.d. 13 April 2018, No. 43 (Integrative and corrective provisions to lgs.d. 6 March 2017, No. 40, concerning: «Institution aand regulation of Universal Civil Service, pursuant to Article 8 of l. 6 June 2016, No. 106»).

Third sector

Lgs.d. 3 August 2018, No. 105 (Integrative and corrective provisions to lgs.d. 3 July 2017, No. 117, concerning: «Third Sector Code, pursuant to Article 1, comma 2, letter b), of l. 6 June 2016, No. 106. »).

Personal data and cyber security

D.p.r. 15 January 2018, No. 15 (Regulation pursuant to Article 57 of lgs.d. 30 June 2003, No. 196, concerning identifying the way to implement the principles of the Code on the protection of personal data and treatment of data, for use by the police, offices and in police reports.

Lgs.d. 18 May 2018, No. 51 (Implementing directive (EU) 2016/680 of the European Parliament and the Council of 27 April 2016, on the protection of natural persons with regard to the processing of personal data by competent authorities for the purposes of the prevention, investigation, detection or prosecution of criminal offences or the execution of criminal penalties, and on the free movement of such data, and repealing Council Framework Decision 2008/977/JHA).

Lgs.d. 21 May 2018, No. 53 (Implementing directive (EU) 2016/681 of the European Parliament and the Council of 27 April 2016 on the use of passenger name record (PNR) data for the prevention, detection, investigation and prosecution of terrorist offences and serious crime and on the obligation of carriers to communicate passenger data 2004/82/EC of the Council of 29 April 2004).

Lgs.d. 18 May 2018, No. 65 (Implementing directive (EU) 2016/1148 of the European Parliament and of the Council of 6 July 2016 concerning measures for a high common level of security of network and information systems across the Union).

Lgs.d. 11 May 2018, No. 63 (Implementing directive (EU) 2016/943 of the European Parliament and of the Council of 8 June 2016 on the protection of undisclosed know-how and business information (trade secrets) against their unlawful acquisition, use and disclosure).

Lgs.d. 10 August 2018, No. 101 Provisions for adapting the national legislation to implement Regulation (EU) 2016/679 of the European Parliament and of the Council of 27 April 2016 on the protection of natural persons with regard to the processing of personal data and on the free movement of such data, and repealing Directive 95/46/EC (General Data Protection Regulation).

Education, culture

Lgs.d. 11 May 2018, No. 71 (Implementing directive (EU) 2016/801 of the European Parliament and of the Council of 11 May 2016 on the conditions of entry and residence of third-country nationals for the purposes of research, studies, training, voluntary service, pupil exchange schemes or educational projects and au pairing).

Lgs.d. 24 May 2018, No. 92 (Regulations concerning the guidelines for school leavers from vocational study programmes, pursuant to Article 3, paragraph 3, of legislative decree 13 April 2017, No. 61, on the revision of vocational courses in compliance with Article 117 of the Constitution, as well as liaisoning with vocational education and training, in accordance with Article 1, paragraphs 180 and 181, lettera d), of law 13 July 2015, No. 107).

Health

Lgs.d. 22 January 2018, No. 33 (Regulation on measures and the requirements of plant protection products for safe use by non-professional users).

L. 11 January 2018, No. 3 (Delegation to the Government in the field of clinical trials of medicines and provisions for the reorganization of the health professions and management of the Ministry of Health).

Lgs.d. 19 March 2018, No. 19 Implementing Commission directive (EU) 2016/1214 of 25 July 2016 amending Directive 2005/62/EC as regards quality system standards and specifications for blood establishments).

Lgs.d. 30 May 2018, No. 81 (Implementing directive (EU) 2016/2284 of the European Parliament and of the Council of 14 December 2016 on the reduction of national emissions of certain atmospheric pollutants, amending Directive 2003/35/EC and repealing Directive 2001/81/EC).

Work

Lgs.d. 18 May 2018, No. 72 (Protection of work within the seized and confiscated companies in implementation of Article 34 of l. 17 October 2017, No. 161).

L.d. 12 July 2018, No. 87 (Urgent provisions for dignity of workers and businesses, converted with amendments to l. 9 August 2018).

c) Legislative acts concerning the protection of particular groups

Minors

L. 1 October 2018, No. 117 (Introducing of the obligation to install provisions to prevent the abandonment of children in closed vehicles).

Lgs.d. 2 October 2018, No. 121 (Framework for the execution of sentences of juvenile offenders, in implementation of the delegate pursuant to Article 1, commas 82, 83 and 85, lettera p), of l. 23 June 2017, No. 103).

Linguistic Minorities

D. p. r. 3 December 2018, No. 150 (Regulation to amend and integrate the decree of the President of the Republic 27 February 2002, No. 65, concerning the institution and operation of the Joint institutional committee for issues of the Slovenian minority, pursuant to Article 3 of l. 23 February 2001, No. 38).

L.d. 1 March 2018, No. 24 (Regulation for the implementation of the special Statute for Trentino-Alto Adige / Südtirol containing amendments to the lgs.d. 16 December 1993, No. 592, concerning schools located in localities of the province of Trent in which Ladino, Mocheno and Cimbro are spoken).

Victims and witnesses of disaster/crime

L.11 January 2018, No. 4 (Amending the Civil Code, Criminal Code, Criminal Procedure Code and other provisions regarding orphans of domestic crimes).

L. 11 January 2018, No. 6 (Provisions for the protection of witnesses).

III. Municipal, Provincial and Regional Statutes

Starting from 1991, following the adoption of l. June 8, 1990, No. 142 (Arrangement of local autonomies), the so-called "peace human rights" norm, originally contained in Article 1 of the Veneto Regional Law of 30 March 1988, No. 18 (now updated by L. 55/1999) on "Regional interventions for the promotion of a culture of peace", has been included in the statutes of numerous Italian Municipalities, Provinces and Regions.

The standard text indicates:

"The Municipality ... (the Province ... the Region ...), in accordance with constitutional principles and international norms that recognise the innate rights of human persons, sanction the rejection of war as a means of resolving international disputes and promote cooperation between the peoples, peacefully recognises a fundamental right of the person and of the peoples.

For this reason, the Municipality ... (the Province ... the Region ...) promotes the culture of peace and human rights through cultural initiatives and research, education, cooperation and information that tend to transform the City into a land of peace.

The Municipality ... (the Province ... the Region ...) will take direct initiatives and will favour those of cultural and scholastic institutions, associations, voluntary groups and international cooperation".

There are also numerous statutes of local and regional authorities that contain a specific reference to international human rights norms and principles, in particular the UN Charter, the Universal Declaration of Human Rights, the International Covenant on Civil and Political Rights, the International Covenant on Social and Cultural Economic Rights, the International Convention on the Rights of the Child, the Charter of Fundamental Rights of the EU (see *Yearbook 2011*, p. 55–58)

In 2018, no changes were made to the regional statutes with reference to the "peace human rights" norm. There are 14 Italian Regions that contain this standard within its statutory law in its standard formulation or in alternative formulations (Apulia, Basilicata, Calabria, Campania, Emilia-Romagna, Lazio, Liguria, Lombardy, Marche, Molise, Piedmont, Tuscany, Umbria and Veneto).

IV. Regional Laws

This section lists the laws on human rights, equal opportunities, development cooperation, fair trade, minorities, migration, Ombudspersons and the protection of children's rights, workers' rights, the rights of persons with disabilities, solidarity, social advancement, family assistance, and citizenship and legality education adopted by the Councils of the Italian Regions and Autonomous Provinces in 2018. The laws are divided according to topics and listed, for each authority, in chronological order.

Peace, human rights, development cooperation, fair trade

R.l. Basilicata 30 November 2018, No. 48 (Guidelines and interventions for the development of fair trade in Basilicata).

R.l. Piedmont 20 December 2018, No. 21 (Piedmont Region – Arsenal of Peace).

R.l. Veneto 21 June 2018, No. 21 (Regional interventions for promoting human rights and sustainable development cooperation).

R.l. Veneto 25 October 2018, No. 35 (Veneto, Land of Peace).

Equal opportunities, gender

R.l. Friuli-Venezia Giulia 21 March 2018, No. 11 (New amendments to r.l. 21 May 1990, No. 23 (Establishing a regional committee for equal opporunities between men and women)).

R.l. Molise 17 December 2018, No. 10 (Amending and integrating r.l. 10 October 2013, No. 15 (Measures for preventing and combating gender-based violence)).

R.l. Sardinia 2 August 2018, No. 33 (Establishing a "freedom" wage to support women who are victims of violence).

P.l. Trent 12 March 2018, No. 4 (Amending provincal electoral law 2003 regarding gender equality and promoting access to elections for men and women).

R.l. Veneto 21 June 2018, No. 22 (Amending r.l. 23 April 2013, No. 5 (Interventions to prevent and combat violence against women)).

Ombudspersons, children's Ombudspersons

R.l. Abruzzo 2 August 2018, No. 24 (Establishing an Ombudsperson for Children and Adolescents).

R.l. Calabria 29 January 2018, No. 1 (Establishing a regional Ombudsperson for the rights of persons detained or deprived of their liberty).

R.l. Campania 11 April 2018, No. 16 (Attributing the role of health Ombudsperson to the Civic Defender in accordance with law 8 March 2017, No. 24 (Provision regarding the safety of treatments and of assisted persons, including the professional responsibility of health workers)).

R.l. Friuli-Venezia Giulia 30 October 2018, No. 23 (Amending and integrating r.l. 16 May 2014, No. 9 concerning "Institution of Guarantor for the Rights of Persons and of the Regional Ombudsperson).

R.l. Lombardy 6 December 2018, No. 22 (Institution of Regional Ombudsperson for the protection of victims of crime).

R.l. Marche 12 December 2018, No. 48 (Amending r.l. 28 July 2008, No. 23 (Monitoring authority for the respect of children's rights and human rights – Regional Ombudsperson)).

R.l. Umbria 12 October 2018, No. 7 (Futher modifying and integrating r.l. 27 November 2007, No. 30 (New framework on Regional Ombudsperson. Abrogating r.l. 30 November 1995, No. 45)).

Persons with disabilities

R.l. Apulia 3 October 2018, No. 49 (Interventions supporting disadvantaged individuals with the capacity to work).

R.l. Apulia 3 October 2019, No. 48 (Regulation supporting accessibility to the state-owned bathing areas for persons with disabilities).

R.l. Campania 2 August 2018, No. 27 (Provisions for social inclusion, removal of communication barriers, recognition and promotion of Italian sign language and Italian touch language).

R.l. Marche 28 June 2018, No. 21 (Regional interventions to promote an independent life for persons with disabilities).

R.l. Marche 6 August 2018, No. 34 (Provisions to promote access for persons with disabilities to the state-owned areas intended for bathing).

R.l. Sardinia 12 June 2018, No. 18 (Contributions for transport for persons with disabilities. Amending r.l. No. 1 of 2018).

R.l. Sardinia 14 May 2018, No. 15 (Regulations concerning specific learning disabilities).

P.l. Trent 13 June 2018, No. 8 (Amending p.l. on the handicap 2003, p.l. on the social policies 2007, p.l. 24 July 2012, No. 15 (Protecting non self-sufficient persons and their families of the p.l. 3 August 2010, No. 19, and p.l. 29 August 1983, No. 29, concerning health), p.l. on the protection of health 2010 and of p.l. transposing the European directives concenring public contracts 2016).

R.l. Veneto 23 February 2018, No. 11 (Provisions for social inclusion, removal of communication barriers and recognition and promotion of Italian Sign Language and Italian Tactile Sign Language.).

Immigration

R.l. Apulia 5 October 2018, No. 51 (Amending r.l. 4 December 2009, No. 32 (Standards for the reception, civil coexistence and integration of immigrants in Apulia)).

Minority rights

R.l. Trentino-Alto Adige 24 May 2018, No. 3 (Standards for protecting and promoting the minority languages Cimbric, Mòchena and Ladin of the Autonomous Region Trentino-Alto Adige/ South Tirol).

Workers' rights

R.l. Abruzzo 24 August 2018, No. 35 (Measures supporting businesses and employment in the regional territory and combating against manufacturing relocation).

R.l. Apulia 29 June 2018, No. 29 (Standards for regional policy of services for active work policies and combating illegal work and employment).

R.l. Apulia 3 October 2018, No. 49 – see above: *People with disabilities*

R.l. Marche 31 July 2018, No. 30 (Amending r.l. 22 April 2014, No. 7 (Standards for prevention and protection measures for high fall risks to display in building during maintenance work in safety conditions)).

R.l. Sardinia 12 June 2018, No. 19 (Measures in favour of former SAREMAR workers).

R.l. Sardinia 24 July 2018, No. 25 (Measures in favour of former workers of the Ottana industrial complex).

R.l. Tuscany 29 June 2018, No. 32 (Provisions for special recruitment aiming to resolve the issue of precarious work. Amending R.l. 1/2009 regarding hiring capacity and temporary work situations for employees).

R.l. Umbria 14 February 2018, No. 1 (Integrated system for the job market, life-long learning and promoting employment. Institution of the Regional Agency for Active Labour Policies).

R.l. Veneto 25 October 2018, No. 36 (Amending r.l. 13 March 2009, No. 3 (Provisions for employment and the job market) and subsequent amendments).

Solidarity, social promotion, assistance to families

R.l. Aosta Valley 17 December 2018, No. 10 (Measures to prevent and combat pathological gambling. Amending r.l. 15 June 2015, No. 14 (Provisions concerning the preventing, combating and treatment of pathological gambling addiction. Amending r.l. 29 March 2010, No. 11 (Regional policies and initiatives for promoting safety and legality))).

R.l. Basilicata 4 December 2018, No. 50 (Right to education and support to permanent and active life-long learning).

P.l. Bolzano 13 March 2018, No. 21 (Promoting initiatives against food and non-alimentary waste).

P.l. Bolzano 22 June 2018, No. 81 (Social Agriculture).

R.l. Calabria 16 May 2018, No. 12 (Regulations concerning the protection, promotion and enhancement of active aging).

R.l. Calabria 3 August 2018, No. 27 (Promoting recovery and redistribution activities of excess food to combat poverty and social unrest).

R.l. Campania 12 February 2019, No. 2 (Regulations promoting active aging and amending r.l. 3 August 2013, No. 9 (Establishing the Psychology Service in the Campania Region)).

R.l. Campania 30 October 2018, No. 31 (Amending r.l. 12 February 2018, No. 2 (Regulations promoting active aging and amending r.l. 3 August 2013, No. 9 (Establishing the Psychology Service in the Campania Region)).)).

R.l. Emilia-Romagna 8 June 2018, No. 7 (Amending and intergrating r.l. 19 December 2016, No. 24 (Measures combating poverty and wage support)).

R.l. Emilia-Romagna 25 June 2018, No. 8 (Further amending r.l. 4 July 2013, No. 5 (Regulations combating, preventing and reducing the risk of pathological gambling addiction and its related problems and illnesses)).

R.l. Friuli-Venezia Giulia 23 February 2018, No. 7 (Growing up in Friuli-Venezia Giulia: harmonising regional politics with the well-being of children and adolescents).

R.l. Lazio 18 December 2018, No. 12 (Provisions concerning the prevention and reduction of seismic risk. Further provisions for the simplification and acceleration of reconstruction operations in the areas hit by seismic activity in 2016 onwards).

R.l. Lombardy 6 December 2018, No. 18 (Initiatives for minors attending nursery and micro-nursery).

R.l. Marche 12 March 2018, No. 3 (Establishing Voluntary Civil Service for the elderly).

R.l. Marche 17 May 2018, No. 16 (Amending r.l. 24 March 2015, No. 11 (Provisions for establishing the Regional Earth Bank to promote jobs in the agricultural sector)).

R.l. Marche 5 June 2018, No. 17 (Amending r.l. 12 March 2018, No. 3 (Establishing Voluntary Civil Service for the elderly).

R.l. Sardinia 6 July 2018, No. 24 (Interventions for promoting and enhancing the support administrator for the protection of vulnerable individuals).

R.l. Tuscany 23 January 2018, No. 4 (Preventing and combating pathological gambling addiction. Amending r.l. 57/2013).

R.l. Tuscany 17 April 2018, No. 16 (Extraordinary solidarity contribution for the wife of Idy Diene).

R.l. Tuscany 30 May 2018, No. 27 (Preventing compulsive gambling. Amending r.l. 57/2013).

R.l. Tuscany 31 October 2018, No. 58 (Regulations for social cooperation in Tuscany).

R.l. Tuscany 28 December 2018, No. 76 (Revising the assistance for victims of terrorism and organised crime. Amending R.l. 55/2006).

P.l. Trent 8 March 2018, No. 3 (Amending p.l. on volunteering 1992).

P.l. Trent 11 July 2018, No. 13 (Integrating p.l. on education 2006: actions and operations for preventing drug addiction).

R.l. Umbria 22 October 2018, No. 8 (Regulations on reconstructing areas hit by the seismic activity of 24 August 2016, 26 and 30 October 2016 onwards. Amending integrations to regional laws).

R.l. Veneto 4 October 2018, No. 32 (Amending and integrating r.l. 3 November 2006, No. 23 (Regulations for promoting and developing social cooperation)).

Education for citizenship and legality, fight against bullying

R.l. Aosta Valley 17 December 2018, No. 10 – see above *Solidarity, social promotion, assistance to families*

R.l. Apulia 3 October 2018, No. 50 (Provisions for preventing and fighting bullying and cyberbullying).

R.l. Apulia 8 November 2018, No. 52 (Prorogation of the end of Article 7, paragraph 3, of r.l. 13 December 2013, No. 43 (Fight against the spread of pathologic gambling addition).

R.l. Apulia 20 December 2018, No. 58 (Amending r.l. 3 October 2018, No. 50 (Provisions for preventing and fighting bullying and cyberbullying)).

R.l. Basilicata 30 November 2018, No. 45 (Regional interventions for preventing and fighting crime, promoting a culture of legality and for an intergrated security system in the region).

R.l. Calabria 26 April 2018, No. 9 (Regional interventions for preventing and fighting the 'ndrangheta mafia group and for promoting legality, responsible economics and transparency)).

R.l. Calabria 28 December 2018, No. 51 (Amending r.l. 26 April 2018, No. 9 (Regional interventions for preventing and fighting the 'ndrangheta mafia group and for promoting legality, responsible economics and transparency)).

R.l. Marche 6 August 2018, No. 32 (Guidelines for regional educational interventionsto prevent and fight bullying, cyberbullying, sexting and cyberpaedophilia).

R.l. Molise 10 December 2018, No. 9 (Establishing a temporary Special Advisory Commission to study organised crime in Molise).

R.l. Piedmont 5 February 2018, No. 2 (Provisions for preventing and fighting bullying and cyberbullying).

R.l. Umbria 9 May 2018, No. 4 (Guidelines for regional interventions for preventing and fighting bullying and cyberbullying – amending regional laws).

R.l. Veneto 26 January 2018, No. 1 (Amending r.l. 28 December 2012, No. 48 (Measures for coordinated implementation of regional policies to prevent organised and mafia crime and corruption, and to promote a culture of legality and responsible citizenship)).

PART II

The Human Rights Infrastructure in Italy

National Bodies with Jurisdiction over Human Rights

International human rights law requires States to set up structures that are adequately specialised in promoting and protecting fundamental rights. In this regard, a distinction shall be made between strictly governmental bodies independent structures directly emanating from civil society. The latter in particular, through channels different from those classically used by governmental powers, aim to participate in policy-making and to promote and develop a human rights culture, as well as to prevent violations.

In this Part, the composition, mandate and activities of the following institutions will be illustrated:

- *Parliamentary bodies*: The Special Commission for the Promotion and Protection of Human Rights of the Italian Senate; the Permanent Committee on Human Rights instituted within the Foreign Affairs Commission (III) of the Italian Chamber of Deputies; the Parliamentary Commission for Children and Adolescents.
- *Governmental bodies*: Bodies established within the Prime Minister's Office: Department for Equal Opportunities; Commission for International Adoptions; National Committee on Bioethics. Bodies established within the Ministry of Foreign Affairs: Inter-Ministerial Committee for Human Rights; National Commission for UNESCO. Bodies established within the Ministry of Labour and Social Policy: National Observatory for Children and Adolescents; National Observatory Monitoring the Condition of Persons with Disabilities; and other departments and bureaus of the Ministry of Justice which work specifically on human rights matters.
- *The Constitutional Court*
- *Judicial authorities*: The Court of Cassation, acting as the supreme judge of legitimacy.
- *Independent authorities*: The Communications Regulatory Authority; the Data Protection Authority; the Committee Guaranteeing the Implementation of the Law on Strikes Affecting Essential Public Services; the National Ombudsperson for Children and Adolescents; National Ombudsperson for the Rights of Persons in Prison or Deprived of Liberty.

Italy's national human rights infrastructure is completed by academic institutions promoting not only research, but also education and training in human rights issues, and by several non-governmental organisations, some of which function through networking.

I. Parliamentary Bodies

A. *Senate of the Republic: Special Commission for the Protection and Promotion of Human Rights*

The Senate's Special Commission for the Protection and Promotion of Human Rights was first set up during the 14th legislature (motion 20, 1 August 2001) and is the fruit of long-term experience by the Committee against Death Penalty (1996–2001). Since the Commission is not permanent, it must be instituted formally at the beginning of each legislature and the Senate did so during the 15th legislature (motion 20, 12 July 2006), the 16th legislature (motion 13, 26 June 2008) and the 17th legislature (motion 7, 26 March 2013). In the latter motion, the Senate decided to commence the proceedings for the establishment of a permanent human rights commission.

The Commission has the task of studying, observing and taking initiatives on issues concerning the protection and promotion of internationally recognised human rights. To this end, it can establish relations with institutions of other countries and with international bodies; carry out missions in or outside Italy, in particular with foreign Parliaments, even – if necessary – in order to establish agreements fostering human rights or to facilitate other forms of collaboration; it can carry out informational procedures and formulate proposals and Assembly reports; and provide its advisory opinions on proposed legislation as well as on matters deferred to other Commissions.

The Commission is made up of 25 members, present in proportion to the size of the parliamentary groups to which they belong. Among these members, the Commission elects the bureau, made up of the Chair, two Vice Chairs and two Secretaries.

Since July 2018, the Commission has been made up as follows: *Chair*: Stefania Pucciarelli; *Vicechair*: Alberto Airola, Paola Binetti; *Segretaries*: Elena Botto, Monica Cirinnà; *Members*: Emma Bonino, Marzia Casolati, Stefania Gabriella Anastasia Craxi, William De Vecchis, Daniela Donno, Valeria Fedeli, Gabriella Giammanco, Barbara Guidolin, Vanna Iori, Alessandra Maiorino, Gaspare Antonio Marinello, Barbara Masini, Assuntela Messina, Michela Montevecchi, Cesare Pianasso, Isabella Rauti, Mariarosaria Rossi, Loredana Russo, Julia Unterberger, Orietta Vanin.

In 2018, for the survey on the levels and mechanisms in force in Italy and internationally for the protection of human rights, the Commission held two hearings:

- 11 December: Andrea Iacomini, spokesperson for UNICEF Italy, and Marta Fiasco, advocacy UNICEF, on child marriage.
- 18 December: Filomena Albano, National Ombudsperson for Children and Adolescents.

B. Chamber of Deputies: Permanent Committee on Human Rights

The international protection of human rights is one of the focal points of the activities performed by the Commission for Foreign and European Union Affairs (Third Commission) of the Chamber of Deputies. As from the 10th legislature (1987–1992), the Commission set up within it the Permanent Committee on Human Rights, which, especially through hearings, ensures that Parliament is kept continually informed and up-to-date with regard to the status of international human rights. The Committee also has the task of following the course of individual human rights measures, performing preliminary tasks pertinent to the activities of the Commission. The Committee for the current legislature (18th) was set up on 5 December 2018.

In 2018, the Committee was composed as follows: *Chair*: Iolanda Di Stasio; *Vice Chair*: Maurizio Lupi; *Segretary*: Ivan Scalfarotto; *Members*: Michaela Biancofiore, Simone Billi, Laura Boldrini, Mario Alejandro Borghese, Pino Cabras, Emilio Carelli, Maria Rosaria Carfagna, Edmondo Cirielli, Andrea Colletti, Vito Comencini, Sabrina De Carlo, Andrea De Maria, Chiara Ehm Yana, Mirella Emiliozzi, Piero Fassino, Paolo Formentini, Lia Quartapelle Procopio, Valentino Valentini.

In 2018, The Commission for Foreign Affairs conducted a fact-finding investigation into Italy's commitment within the International Community to the promotion and defence of human rights and the fight against discrimination. It held the following hearings:

- 4 October: Urmila Bhoola, Special Rapporteur on Contemporary forms of slavery of the UN Human Rights Council;
- 23 October: Ignace Youssif III Younan, Patriarch of Antiochia (Syrian);

- 25 October: Sam Rainsy and Saumura Tioulong, respectively ex-chair and representative of the *Cambodia National Rescue Party*;
- 15 November: Alessandro Monteduro, director of the Aid to the Church in Need Italy Foundation;
- 18 December: Manlio Di Stefano, Undersecretary of Foreign Affairs and International Cooperation;
- 19 December: Emanuela Del Re, Viceminister of Foreign Affairs and International Cooperation, and Stavros Lambrinidis, Special Rapporteur for Human Rights of the European Union.

C. Bicameral Bodies: Parliamentary Commission for Children and Adolescents

The Parliamentary Commission for Children and Adolescents was set up by l. 23 December 1997, No. 451, although its name and responsibilities were modified by l. 3 August 2009, No. 112.

> Essentially, the Commission is entrusted with a supervisory and policymaking role related to the enforcement of international obligations and domestic law on children's rights. It may also present to the two Houses of Parliament observations and proposals concerning the effects and limitations of current legislation, and the possible need to amend it to ensure compliance with international law concerning the rights of the child.
>
> The Commission is composed of 20 Senators and 20 Representatives appointed, respectively, by the Chair of the Italian Senate and the Chair of the Italian Chamber of Deputies, proportionately to the total number of members in the various parliamentary groups. In 2018, the Commission was composed as follows: *Chair*: Licia Ronzulli; *Vice Chairs*: Caterina Bini, Simone Pillon; *Segretaries*: Grazia D'angelo, Veronica Giannone; *Members from the Chamber of Deputies*: Maria Teresa Bellucci, Rossana Boldi, Fabiola Bologna, Vittoria Casa, Laura Cavandoli, Rosa Maria Di Giorgi, Ketty Fogliani, Claudia Gobbato, Carmela Grippa, Anna Macina, Patrizia Marrocco, Ubaldo Pagano, Patrizia Prestipino, Michela Rostan, Paolo Siani, Maria Spena, Gilda Sportiello, Giuseppina Versace, Leda Volpi; *Members from the Senate*: Luisa Angrisani, Stefano Bertacco, Paola Binetti, Paola Boldrini, Lello Ciampolillo, Barbara Floridia, Francesco Maria Giro, Lucio Malan, Raffaela Fiormaria Marin, Susy Matrisciano, Raffaele Mautone, Edoardo Patriarca, Maria Saponara, Liliana Segre, Pierpaolo Sileri, Julia Unterberger.

In 2018, the Commission did not conduct any fact-finding surveys or hearings.

D. Parliamentary Acts Concerning Human Rights

Presented below is a brief overview of the main human rights legislation produced by the Italian Parliament in 2018, subdivided into bills and guidelines and watchdog initiatives (motions, interpellations, questions for an oral or written answer, resolutions and agenda proposals). The proposer or first signer, the code (the letter 'C' indicating that the initiative was presented in the Chamber of Deputies and the letter 'S' that it was presented in the Senate), the title, the date of presentation and the most recent update are listed for each initiative.

Bills

Starting from this *Yearbook*, the bills presented in Parliament are organised into 11 categories refering to the main legal instruments adopted by the United Nations in the field of human rights, disarmament and international humanitarian and criminal law (see Part I, the Reception of International Human Rights Law in Italy, I and II; Part III, The United Nations System, V and Humanitarian and Criminal Law, II), and also to the Sustainable Development Goals (SDGs), adopted by the United Nations in 2015. To codify the bills, 50 descriptors were used within the classification system for parliamentary documents, TESEO (*TEsauro SEnato per l'Organizzazione dei documenti parlamentari*).

Category	International reference instrument	Descriptor (TESEO)	SDGs
1) Racism	International Convention on the Elimination of All Forms of Racial Discrimination	Racism	10 – Reduced Inequalities
2) Civil and political rights	International Convenant on Civil and Political Rights	Civil and political rights Freedom of Correspondence Right to housing Freedom of press Religious freedoms Protection of Privacy	16 – Peace, Justice and Strong Institutions

Category	International reference instrument	Descriptor (TESEO)	SDGs
		(personal or sensitive data, privacy, personal computer systems) Freedom of Association Freedom of Thought Freedom of Assembly Freedom of the Individual	
3) Economic, social and cultural rights (including bioethics and environmental rights)	International Covenant on Economic, Social and Cultural Rights	Social Security Protection of workers Freedom of teaching Protection of health Human Life	1 – No Poverty 3 – Good Health and Well-being 4 – Quality Education 6 – Clean Water and Sanitation
			8 – Decent Work and Economic Growth 13 – Climate Action 15 – Life on Land 17 – Partnerships for the Goals
4) Women's Rights	Elimination of All Forms of Discrimination against Women	Women Equality (discrimination, equality balance) Gender relations Equality between the sexes (equal opportunities)	5 – Gender Equality
		Sexual Offences (sexual harrassment, abuse within the family, sexual violence) Violence and Threats (domestic and family violence)	

Category	International reference instrument	Descriptor (TESEO)	SDGs
5) Torture, Prison Conditions, Rights of Detained Persons	Convention against Torture	Prison Systems Inmates (mothers in prison) Work of inmates Mistreatment and torture (torture, mutilation) abuse	16 – Peace, Justice and Strong Institutions
6) Children's Rights	Convention on the Rights of the Child	Minors Sexual Crimes (sexual harrassment, abuse within the family, sexual violence, corruption of minors, exploitation and sexual abuse, paedophilia)	16 – Peace, Justice and Strong Institutions
7) Migrants, Refugees, Asylum Seekers, Minorities	The International Convention on the Protection of the Rights of All Migrant Workers and Members of Their Families	Foreign nationals' rights Migrant workers Immigration Religious and ethnic minorities Citizenship	10 – Reduced Inequalities
8) Persons with Disabilities	Convention on the Rights of Persons with Disabilities	People with disabilities	10 – Reduced Inequalities
9) Enforced Disappearances	The International Convention for the Protection of All Persons from Enforced Disappearance	Political or racial persecution	16 – Peace, Justice and Strong Institutions

Category	International reference instrument	Descriptor (TESEO)	SDGs
10) National institutions and ratification of international instruments	A/RES/48/134 (Paris Principles)	Rights and duties of the person Non-traditional fundamental rights Traditional human rights Rights of man Crimes against fundamental rights	16 – Peace, Justice and Strong Institutions
		Non-governmental organizations (NGOs) Right to self-determination of peoples Treaty ratification	
11) Disarmament, international humanitarian law and criminal law	See Part I, *The Reception Of International Human Rights Law in Italy*, II and Part III, *Humanitarian and Criminal Law*	Disarmament International crimes War (cyber warfare) War crimes, crimes against humanity, genocide Peace Prisoners of war War zones, military operation zones International tribunals	16 – Peace, Justice and Strong Institutions

In 2018, a total of 232 initiatives were presented in parliament concerning human rights. More than half of these fit into the following categories: economic, social and cultural rights (66), women's rights (37) and children's rights (29). Around a third are then distributed quite evenly in three other categories: civil and political rights (26), national institutions and ratification of international instruments (24), and rights of persons with disabilities (23). The remaining categories make up just over 10 % of the law proposals presented: rights of migrants, refugees, asylum seekers and minorities (11), torture and prison conditions (8), racism (4), enforced disappearnances (2), disarmament, international humanitarian law and criminal law (2).

95 % of the initiatives are presented though parliamentary process. There were, however, eight initiatives presented via government initiatives, in particular concerning:

- *Economic, social and cultural rights*: Converting into law del l.d. 12 July 2018, No. 87, concering urgent provisions for workers' dignity and for businesses (C.924 and S.741);
- *Women's rights*: provisions concerning protection of domestic violence and gender-based violence victims (C.1455);
- *Ratification of the following international instruments*: Convention of the Coucil of Europe against the Trafficking of Human Organs (C.1122); Protocol No. 15 and 16 to the Convention for the Safeguarding of the Rights of Man and Fundamental Freedoms (C.1124); Additional Protocol of Nagoya - Kuala Lumpur, regarding responsibility and compensation, to the Protocol of Cartagen on Biosecurity (C.1123 and S.926); ILO Convention No. 155, on the Health and Safety of Workers, and No. 187 on the promotional framework for health and safety at work (S.986).

There were three proposals made through public initiative (which had still not been examined by December 2018), concerning:

- *Economic, social and cultural rights*: "Zero waste law: for a truely sustainable society" (bill C.3) and "Charter of universal labour rights. New statute for all female and male workers" (bill C.11);
- *Migrants' rights*: "New standard for promoting regular residency and social and labour inclusion for non-EU citizens" (C.13).

Only two of the 232 (therefore less than 1 %) bills concerning human rights were definitively approved by parliament (update: April 2019). In both cases they are Government initiative bills: "Converting into law, with amendments, decree law 12 July 2018, No. 87, concerning urgent provisions for the dignity of workers and businesses" (bill S.741, now l. 9 August 2018, No. 96) and "Ratification and execution of Nagoya – Kuala Lumpur Supplementary Protocol on Liability and Redress to the Cartagena Protocol on Biosafety, done in Nagoya on 15 October 2010" (bill S.926, now l. 16 January 2019, No. 7).

Two other projects were approved by a branch of Parliament: the text "Amending the procedural criminal code: provisions for protecting the victims of domestic and gender-based violence" (Government initiative bill C.1455, approved by the Chamber on 3 April 2019) and the bill "Measures to prevent and fight mistreatment and abusive behaviour, including psychological abuse, of children in nurseries and infant schools and for persons accomdated in social health and assistance structures for older people and persons with disabilities, delegating staff training programmes to the Government" (bill C.1066, the only parliamentary initiative to be approved by the Chamber on 23 October 2018).

The complete list of bills concerning human rights that were presented in parliament in 2018 (updated December 2018) can be found online: www.annuarioitalianodirittiumani.it, in the section «Allegati».

Racism

Even though the UNAR has reported an increase in hate speech and intolerance online and in the media, (see Part II, National Bodies with Jurisdiction over Human Rights, II, A), only around 2 % of the bills presented in parliament in 2018 concerned the subject:

S.362 - *Sen. Liliana Segre (Mixed) and others*
Institution of a parliamentary watchdog and guidelines committee on racism, intolerance, hate speech and violence
14 May 2018: Presented to the Senate
26 June 2018: Assigned (examination not yet begun)

S.634 - *Sen. Paola Boldrini (PD) and others*
Amendments to the Criminal Code and other provisions regarding the fight against hate speech and discrimination
11 July 2018: Presented to the Senate
1 August 2018: Assigned (examination not yet begun)

C.1082 - *Hon. Lia Quartapelle Procopio (PD)*
Amendments to Article 604-b of the Criminal Code and to l. 13 October 1975, No. 654, and other provisions regarding apology for crimes against humanity, hate crimes and discrimination
6 August 2018: Presented to the Chamber of Deputies
To be assigned

C.1420 - *Hon. Ivan Scalfarotto (PD)*
Institution of a watchdog and guideline parliamentary committee on racism, intolerance, hate speech and violence
6 December 2018: Presentated to the Chamber of Deputies
To be assigned

Civil and Political Rights

Of the 26 bills concerning civil and political rights, the promotion of which is outlined in the targets of Goal 16 (Promote peaceful and inclusive societies for sustainable development, provide access to justice for all and build effective, accountable and inclusive institutions at all levels), almost half (12) concern the fight against mistreatment and abuse in kindergartens, infant schools and social assistance structures for minors, the elderly and persons with disabilities, using videosurveillance; four concern the fight against discrimination due to sexual orientation or gender identity; four concern the protection of privacy and personal data; three concern the freedom of religion and prevention of all types of fundamentalism and radicalism; two concern the right to vote and one concerns access to justice.

The following are particularly worthy of note:

C.220 - *Hon. Deborah Bergamini (FI) and others*

Institution of a parliamentary enquiry commission into the use of big data, on violations of the protection of personal data, on data manipulation on online platforms and on technological support and e-services for social networks

23 March 2018: Presented to the Chamber of Deputies

5 February 2019: Assigned (examination not yet begun)

C.1013 - *Hon. Manfred Schullian (Mixed, Linguistic Minorities)*

Amending Article 134 of the Constitution concerning direct recourse to the Constitutional Court for the protection of fundamental rights

26 July 2018: Presented to the Chamber of Deputies

31 October 2018: Assigned (examination not yet begun)

C.1056 - *Hon. Emanuele Fiano (PD) and others*

Institution of a parliamentary enquiry commission into the mass intentional spreading of false information online and into the right to information and the forming of public opinion

3 August 2018: Presented to the Chamber of Deputies

19 December 2018: Assigned (examination not yet begun)

Economic, social and cultural rights (including bioethics and environmental rights)

Economic, social and cultural rights were not only the highest presented category of bills in 2018 (66) but also the category that showed greatest relevance to pursuing the SDGs. Around 80 % of the legislation proposed in this category directly refers to four main areas:

- *employment-related rights:* right to work, protection from being fired illegally, health and safety in the workplace, workers' participation in the management and output of the company, equal pay (Goal 8: Promote sustained, inclusive and sustainable economic growth, full and productive employment and decent work for all);
  - *education*, particularly referring to two educational projects launched in primary and secondary schools: "constitutional culture, civic education and European citizenship" and "active citizenship and direct democracy" (Goal 4: Ensure inclusive and equitable quality education and promote lifelong learning opportunities for all);
  - *social security*, above all in the form of funds, tax breaks, checks and pensions (Goal 1: End poverty in all its forms everywhere);
  - *health and bioethics* (Goal 3: Ensure healthy lives and promote well-being for all at all ages).

11 % of bills aimed to promote fair trade (Goal 10: Reduce Inequality within and among countries; Goal 17: Strengthen the means of implementation and revitalize the global partnership sustainable development). The remaining 10 % aimed to protect environmental rights (Goal 13: Take urgent action to combat climate change and its impacts; Goal 15: Protect, restore and promote sustainable use of terrestrial ecosystems, sustainably manage forests, combat desertification, and halt and reverse land degradation and halt biodiversity loss), the right to water (Goal 6: Ensure availability and sustainable management of water and sanitation for all) and the right to sport.

Women's rights

In line with Goal 5 (Achieve gender equality and empower all women and girls), almost half the 37 bills regarding the protection of women's rights speak about gender equality and equal opportunities for men and women. They focus on the gender pay gap and equal representation in the following fields: municipal councils, legal authorities, administration offices and checks of companies listed on regulated markets, means of comunication, professional sport. Eight bills concern the combat against violence against women, five speak about social security (intended aboveall in the form of pensions for women and mothers who work); three discuss civil rights (the reacquisition of citizenship for women who have renounced it by marrying a foreign national); two concern the promotion of gender education; and two about women's health.

The following two projects financed to institute further parliamentary enquiry commissions are particularly noteworthy:

C.508 - *Hon. Susanna Cenni (PD) and others*
Institution of a parliamentary enquiry commission on the social and economic status of women, on equal opportunities and the implementation of gender politics in Italy
13 April 2018: Presented to the Chamber of Deputies
4 July 2018: Assigned (examination not yet begun)
S.313 - *Sen. Donatella Conzatti (FI-BP) and others*
Insitution of a parliamentary commission for women's rights and gender equality
2 May 2018: Presented to the Senate
27 June 2018: Assigned (examination not yet begun)

Torture, prison conditions and the rights of detained persons

In 2018, two bills were presented amending l. 14 July 2017, No. 110 to introduce the crime of torture into Italian law.

S.93 - *Sen. Vanna Iori (PD) and others*
Amending law 26 July 1975, No. 354, concerning the relationship between inmates and their underage children
23 March 2018: Presented to the Senate
21 June 2018: Assigned (examination not yet begun)
S.77 - *Sen. Loredana De Petris (Mixed)*
Standards for including the teaching of non-violence (in theory and practice) and including non-violence within the teaching materials of initial and ongoing police force training
23 March 2018: Presented to the Senate
21 June 2018: Assigned (examination not yet begun)
C.123 - *Hon. Edmondo Cirielli (FDI) and others*
Establishing a parliamentary enquiry commission into the lack of adequate prison facilities and prison overcrowding
23 March 2018: Presented to the Chamber of Deputies
26 June 2018: Assigned (examination not yet begun)
C.494 - *Hon. Edmondo Cirielli (FDI) and others*

Abrogation of Articles 613-b and 613-c of the Criminal Code concerning torture and the instigation of a public official to commit torture, and introducing common aggravating circumstance for public officials

11 April 2018: Presented to the Chamber of Deputies

10 July 2018: Assigned (examination not yet begun)

S.382 - *Sen. Antonio Iannone (FdI) and others*

Establishing a parliamentary enquiry commission into the lack of adequate prison facilities and prison overcrowding

16 May 2018: Presented to the Senate

3 July 2018: Assigned (examination not yet begun)

S.409 - *Sen. Antonio Iannone (FdI) and others*

Abrogation of the crime of torture and the instigation of a public official to commit torture, and introducing common aggravating circumstance for public officials

21 May 2018: Presented to the Senate

3 July 2018: Assigned (examination not yet begun)

S.958 - *Sen. Angela Anna Bruna Piarulli (M5S) and others*

Provisions for the promotion of physical and sports activity in juvenile prison institutes

26 November 2018: Presented to the Senate

14 February 2019: Assigned (examination not yet begun)

C.1457 - *Hon. Lucia Annibali (PD) and others*

Amendments to Article 90-c of the Criminal Procedure Code, regarding the evasion and release from prison from the offended person and pursuant to law 26 July 1975, No. 354, in the granting of penitentiary benefits and cognitive behaviour therapy for the inmate, to protect the victim and prevent reoffending for serious crimes against the person

18 December 2018: Presented to the Chamber of Deputies

3 April 2019: Accepted

Rights of the child

Two thirds of the bills proposed regarding children's rights can be divided into four areas: combat against violence against children (including sexual exploitation, paedophilia and child-pornography; civil rights (with particular reference to abduction or detention, including foreign minors); right to a family (including children's rights in fostering and adoption); and prevention and fight against forced marriage. The remaining third can be divided as follows: social security (in the form of benefits and work permits); right to health; right of children to express an opinion and be heard; environmental rights; and the fight against bullying.

The following project financed to institute a further parliamentary enquiry commission is particularly noteworthy:

C.643 - *Hon. Federica Zanella (FI) and others*
Institution of a parliamentary enquiry commission on bullying and cyberbullying
18 May 2018: Presented to the Chamber of Deputies
16 October 2018: Assigned (examination not yet begun)

Migrants, refugees, asylum seekers, minorities
Over half of the 11 bills presented concern amendments to l. 5 February 1992, No. 91, regarding the acquisition of Italian citizenship.

C.13 *–People's initiative*
New regulations promoting the regular residency and social inclusion and labour inclusion of non-EU citizens
23 March 2018: Presented to the Chamber of Deputies
26 June 2018: Assigned (examination not yet begun)

S.70 - *Sen. Pietro Grasso (Mixed) and others*
Amending law 5 February 1992, No. 91, introducing new regulations on citizenship
23 March 2018: Presented to the Senate
21 June 2018: Assigned (examination not yet begun)

C.105 - *Hon. Laura Boldrini (Mixed) and others*
Amending law 5 February 1992, No. 91, introducing new regulations on citizenship
23 March 2018: Presented to the Chamber of Deputies
31 October 2018: currently under examination by the Commission

C.555 - *Hon. Galeazzo Bignami (FI)*
Introducing Article 42-b of the text of provisions concerning immigration guidelines and standards for the condition of foreign nationals with reference to legislative decree 25 July 1998, No. 286, with regard to establishing a National Register of Cultural Mediators
23 April 2018: Presented to the Chamber of Deputies
7 August 2018: Assigned (examination not yet begun)

S.359 - *Sen. Roberto Rampi (PD)*

Recognition of foreign nationals as an active and passive electorate in administrative elections

2 May 2018: Presentated to the Senate

26 June 2018: Assigned (examination not yet begun)

C.679 - *Hon. Massimo Bitonci (Lega)*

Amending law 15 December 1999, No. 482, laying down regulations regarding the protection of historic linguistic minorities

31 May 2018: Presented to the Chamber of Deputies

To be assigned

C.717 - *Hon. Renata Polverini (FI)*

Amending law 5 February 1992, No. 91, concerning citizenship

11 June 2018: Presented to the Chamber of Deputies

26 November 2018: Assigned (examination not yet begun)

S.520 - *Sen. Edoardo Patriarca (PD) and others*

Amending law 5 February 1992, No. 91, concerning acquiring Italian citizenship

25 June 2018: Presentated to the Senate

8 November 2018: Assigned (examination not yet begun)

C.797 - *Hon. Fausto Longo (Misto, Civica Popolare-AP-PSI-Area Civica)*

Amending law 5 February 1992, No. 91, concerning the recognition of Italian citizenship for foreign nationals with Italian origins

27 June 2018: Presented to the Chamber of Deputies

To be assigned

C.920 - *Hon. Matteo Orfini (PD)*

Amending law 5 February 1992, No. 91, and other provisions regarding citizenship

12 July 2018: Presented to the Chamber of Deputies

To be assigned

C.1152 - *Hon. Stefania Ascari (M5S)*

Amending consolidated law of provisions about the subject of imigration and the regulations on the condition of foreign nationals pursuant to legislative decree 25 July 1998, No. 286, as well as legislative decree 19 November 2007, No. 251, regarding the impediments to the issue or renewal of residency permits and recognition of refugee status

11 September 2018: Presented to the Chamber of Deputies

To be assigned

Rights of persons with disabilities

Almost a third of all 23 bills presented are concerning social security (in the form of parental leave, benefits and healthcare and homecare); 6 bills aim to promote independent life of persons with disabilities (particularly removing architectual barriers, the right to urban mobility and to a life of quality); five favour social and work insertion; three promote the right to sport; one regards the right to education (attributing resources and support for students with disabilities); and finally, a text concerning the crime of sexual violence against persons with disabilities.

Enforced disappearances

S.340 - *Sen. Stefano Bertacco (FdI) and others*
Amendments to law 30 March 2004, No. 92, concerning the extension of the right to request recognition for the relatives of those cast out and to grant a public contribution to the Society of Rijekan Studies
8 May 2018: Presentated to the Senate
26 June 2018: Assigned (examination not yet begun)
C.1049 - *On. Fabio Rampelli (FDI) and others*
Amendments to Article 3 of law 30 March 2004, No. 92, concerning the extension of the right to request recognition for the relatives of those cast out and to grant a public contribution to the Society of Rijekan Studies
1 August 2018: Presented to the Chamber of Deputies
4 April 2019: Assigned (examination not yet begun)

National human rights institution and ratification of internatioanl instruments

Eight bills deal with the creation of national human rights institutions (Goal 16: promote peaceful and inclusive societies for sustainable development, provide access to justice for all and build effective, accountable and inclusive institutions at all levels), with particular reference to the National Commission for the promotion and the protection of fundamental rights (acts C.855, the only one currently in examination by the commission, S.593, S.654, C.917, C.1323), the National Office against Racism and Discrimination (act C.1058), and the National Ombudsperson of family rights (acts S.108 and S.129).

Moreover, 16 bills promote the ratification and execution of the the following international instruments:

> ILO Convention No. 169 concerning Indigenous and Tribal Peoples in Independent Countries, Geneva 27 June 1989 (acts S.38 and C.1096);

- Protocols No. 12, 15 and 16 to the Convention for the safeguarding of human rights and fundamental freedoms (acts C.35, C.1077, C.1106, C.1107, C.1124);
- Chapter C of the Council of Europe Convention on the Participation of Foreigners in Public Life at Local Level, Strasbourg 5 February 1992 (act C.1076);
- Additional Protocol to the Council of Europe Convention concerning the criminalisation of acts of racist or xenophobic nature committed through computer systems, Strasbourg 28 January 2003 (act C.1094)
- Council of Europe Convention against Trafficking in Human Organs (acts C.1091 and C.1122);
- Supplementary Protocol Nagoya – Kuala Lumpur to the Cartagena Protocol on Biosafety (acts C. 1098, C.1123 and S.926, the latter definitely approved in 2019: l. 16 January 2019, No. 7);
- ILO Convention No. 155, concerning Occupational Safety and Health and the Working Environment, and No. 187 Promotional Framework for Occupational Safety and Health Convention (act S.986);
- ILO Convention No. 188 Work in Fishing Convention, Geneva 14 June 2007 (act S.932).

Disarmament, international humanitarian and criminal law

S.667 - *Sen. Alberto Airola (M5S) and others*
Ratification and execution of amendments to the Statue of the International Criminal Court, ratified pursuant to law 12 July 1999, No. 232, Kampala, 11 June 2010
17 July 2018: Presented to the Senate
5 March 2019: Currently under examination by the Commission

C.1288 - *Hon. Stefania Pezzopane (PD)*
Amending law 20 July 2000, No. 211, concerning the extension of "Holocaust Memorial Day" to all victims of ethnic, sexual, social and religious persecution who were deported to Nazi extermination camps
19 October 2018: Presented to the Chamber of Deputies
24 January 2019: Assigned (examination not yet begun)

Guidelines and watchdog initiatives

In addition to the aforementioned bills, in 2018, Parliament adopted a total of 59 human rights initiatives, of which there were 6 motions,

3 interpellations, 3 questions for an oral answer, 22 questions for a written answer, 12 questions submitted to Commissions, 6 Commission resolutions and 7 Assembly agenda proposals.

These instruments were used by parliament mainly to investigate, monitor and guide the actions taken by the government concerning the human rights situation in other countries: almost half the initiatives refer to Hungary, Cambodia, Saudi Arabia, Russia, Nigeria, Thailand, China, Tanzania, Turkey, Eritrea, Cameroon, Mauritania, Pakistan, Yemen and Libya. Almost a third of the non-legislative initiatives concerned rights of migrants, refugees, asylum seekers and minorities (particularly the conditions of landing and reception centres for migrants and asylum seekers, the rights of Roma, Sinti and Caminanti peoples, and the UN Global Compact for Safe, Orderly and Regular Migration) and economic, social and cultural rights (particularly bioethics and right to health and international development cooperation. The remaining other categories include: racism and hate speech (5 %), civil and political rights (aboveall private and family life, freedom of expression, protection of privacy and sensitive data: 5 %), torture, inhumane and degrading treatment and the rights of detained persons (3 %), national human rights institutions (particularly public defenders and dialogue with the UN Human Rights Council: 3 %), rights of persons with disabilities (particularly personal mobility: 2 %), children's rights (particularly right to education: 2 %) and women's rights (particularly combating all forms of violence against women: 2 %).

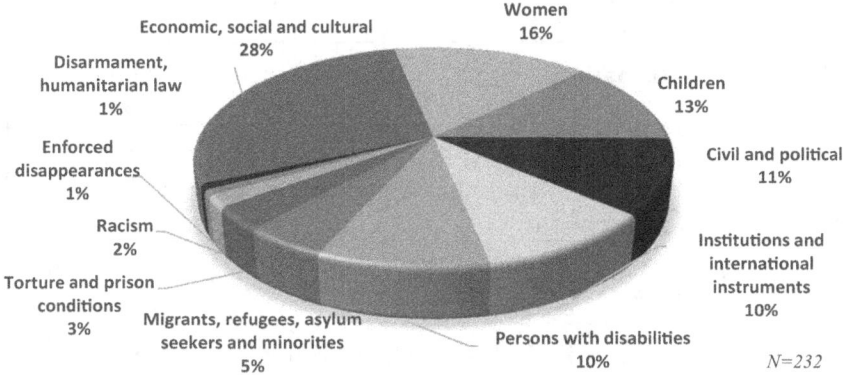

Source: Openparlamento (search criteria: "human rights", "rights of the person")

Motions

Date	Initiative	Latest update
07/05/2018	Massimo BITONCI (Lega) - C.1/00002 Bioethics: case of Alfie Evans, an English 23-month-old child with a neurodegenerative disease	07/05/2018 presentated
30/07/2018	Maria Rosaria CARFAGNA (FI) - C.1/00028 Bioethics: practise of third-party reproduction (*Gestazione per altri*)	02/08/2018 appending of new signatures
19/09/2018	Graziano DELRIO (PD) - C.1/00036 Human rights situation in Hungary	27/09/2018 not accepted
21/11/2018	Anna Maria BERNINI (FI) - S.1/00053 Violence against women	29/11/2018 accepted
11/12/2018	Andrea ORSINI (FI) - C.1/00093 Racism, xenophobia, intolerance	11/12/2018 accepted
18/12/2018	Emanuela ROSSINI (Mixed) - C.1/00096 United Nations Global Compact for Safe, Orderly and Regular Migration	19/12/2018 not accepted

Interpellations

Date	Initiative	Latest update
02/08/2018	Elvira SAVINO (FI) - C.2/00068 ACP-EU Partnership Agreement, signed in Cotonou	02/08/2018 presented
06/11/2018	Francesco SILVESTRI (M5S) - C.2/00169 Public defender	09/11/2018 concluded
27/11/2018	Stefano FASSINA (LeU) and others - C.2/00190 Human rights situation in Ecuador	25/01/2019 concluded

Questions for an oral answer

Date	Initiative	Latest update
07/08/2018	Alessandro ALFIERI (PD) - S.3/00177 Human rights situation in Cambodia	07/08/2018 assigned to a Commission
19/09/2018	Alessandro ALFIERI (PD) - S.3/00205 Dialogue between Italy and the United Nations, regarding the intention of the High Commissioner for Human Rights, Michelle Bachelet, to send investigators into the country to evaluate the high increase in violent and racist acts	19/09/2018 assigned to a Commission
27/11/2018	Daniela SBROLLINI (PD) - S.3/00418 Human rights situation in Saudi Arabia	27/11/2018 presented

Questions for a written answer

Date	Initiative	Latest update
07/05/2018	Lia QUARTAPELLE PROCOPIO (PD) - C.4/00155 Human rights situation in the Philippines	07/05/2018 presented
07/05/2018	Massimo BITONCI (Lega) - C.4/00178 Bioethics: case of Alfie Evans, an English 23-month-old child with a neurodegenerative disease	07/05/2018 presented
07/05/2018	Alessandro PAGANO (Lega) - C.4/00180 Bioethics: case of Alfie Evans, an English 23-month-old child with a neurodegenerative disease	07/05/2018 presented

Date	Initiative	Latest update
05/06/2018	Erasmo PALAZZOTTO (LeU) and others - C.4/00277 Migrants and asylum seekers: construction of a recption and first response centre in Palermo	05/06/2018 presented
26/06/2018	Riccardo MAGI (Mixed) - C.4/00529 Human rights situation in Russia	26/06/2018 presented
17/07/2018	Roberto RAMPI (PD) - S.4/00376 Migrants and asylum seekers: health assistence for migrants who land in Italian territories	17/07/2018 presented
18/07/2018	Massimo UNGARO (PD) - .4/00730 Torture and prison conditions: Italian citizens detained abroad in degrading situations, in terms of human rights, hygiene, relations with other detainees and health, right of defence	28/11/2018 concluded
30/07/2018	Gennaro MIGLIORE (PD) - C.4/00834 Rights of minorities: eviction of a settlement of Roma persons on the Via Tiberina in Rome	30/07/2018 presented
30/07/2018	Elvira SAVINO (FI) - C.4/00838 Human rights situation in Nigeria	15/10/2018 concluded
02/08/2018	Roberto RAMPI (PD) - S.4/00460 Human rights situation in Cambodia	02/08/2018 presented
11/09/2018	Ubaldo PAGANO (PD) - C.4/01033 Migrants and asylum seekers: situation in the hotspot of Taranto	28/02/2019 solicited
11/09/2018	Roberto RAMPI (PD) - S.4/00510– Human rights situation in Thailand	08/11/2018 concluded

Date	Initiative	Latest update
19/09/2018	Sara CUNIAL (M5S) - C.4/01152 Ratification of the Convention of Oviedo for the Protection of Human Rights and Dignity of the Human Being with regard to the Application of Biology and Medicine	19/09/2018 presented
25/09/2018	Luciano NOBILI (PD) - C.4/01190 RacismL violent agression towards Gerges Bolas, of Egyptian origin	25/09/2018 presented
04/10/2018	Luca PASTORINO (LeU) and others - C.4/01284 Rights of persons with disabilities: personal mobility	04/10/2018 presented
09/10/2018	Valeria FEDELI - S.4/00650 Migrants and asylum seekers: problems related to the "Porte d'Europa" competition, aimed at students from 16 and 18 to make and present visual, multimedia and literary works on the theme of migration	09/10/2018 presented
22/10/2018	Debora SERRACCHIANI (PD) - C.4/01444 Human rights situation in China	22/10/2018 presented
24/10/2018	Giorgio SILLI (FI) - C.4/01468 Bioethics: practise of third party reproduction	24/10/2018 presented
21/11/2018	Alessandro ZAN (PD) - C.4/01675 Human rights situation in Tanzania	07/02/2019 concluded
27/11/2018	Erasmo PALAZZOTTO (LeU) and others - C.4/01732 Human rights situation in Saudi Arabia	27/11/2018 presented
28/11/2018	Erasmo PALAZZOTTO (LeU) and others - C.4/01749 Human rights situation in Turkey	07/02/2019 concluded

Date	Initiative	Latest update
12/12/2018	Gaetano QUAGLIARIELLO (FI) - S.4/01012 Civil rights: right to respect for private and family life of the citizens of the Tamburi neighbourhood of Taranto	12/12/2018 presented

Questions submitted to Commissions

Date	Initiative	Latest update
04/07/2018	Gennaro MIGLIORE (PD) - C.5/00086 Migrants and asylum seekers:case of the container carrier ship Alexander Maersk, flying the Danish flag with 113 migrants aboard from Libya, aided in sea then left aboard ship for almost 4 days outside the port of Pozzallo, in the province of Ragusa, waiting to receive instructions for the Rome Lifeguard coordination centre on the where to disembark	04/07/2018 amended for assigned commission
09/07/2018	Enrico BORGHI (PD) - C.5/00098 Migrants and asylum seekers: on the ban on docking following a note from the Ministry of the Interior against the NGO ship "Astral" for public order reasons	09/07/2018 amended for assigned commission
01/08/2018	Stefania PEZZOPANE (PD) - C.5/00297 Racism: case of racial hate verified in the office of ASL of Giulianova, in Teramo province	01/08/2018 amended for assigned commission

Date	Initiative	Latest update
17/09/2018	Lia QUARTAPELLE PROCOPIO (PD) - C.5/00445 Development cooperation: on the fund for Africa, set up in law No. 232, 11 December 2016 (balance law 2017)	24/10/2018 concluded
02/10/2018	Lia QUARTAPELLE PROCOPIO (PD) - C.5/00588 Development cooperation: on resources allocated for the Italian Agency for Development Coordination	02/10/2018 amended for assigned commission
12/10/2018	Gennaro MIGLIORE (PD) - C.5/00717 Torture and rights of detained persons: case of Omar Jallow, of Gambian origins, arrested and handcuffed to the wheel of a police car	12/10/2018 amended for assigned commission
12/10/2018	Lia QUARTAPELLE PROCOPIO (PD) - C.5/00715 Human rights situation in Saudi Arabia	24/10/2018 concluded
22/10/2018	Laura BOLDRINI (LeU) and others - C.5/00786 Human rights situation in Eritrea	24/10/2018 concluded
30/10/2018	Andrea ROSSI (PD) - C.5/00855 Diritti civili (libertà di espressione): accesso impedito allo Stadio Olimpico di Roma, da parte dei funzionari della questura romana, ai tifosi della Spal che indossavano delle magliette riportanti l'effige di Federico Aldrovandi	30/10/2018 amended for assigned commission

Date	Initiative	Latest update
05/11/2018	Emanuele SCAGLIUSI (M5S) - C.5/00877 Civil rights (personal data): the way in which the Government guarentees that collecting, analysising and divulging Passenger Name Records does not violate human rights and fundamental freedoms	20/11/2018 amended for delegated ministry
12/11/2018	Yana Chiara EHM (M5S) - C.5/00929 Human rights situation in Cameroon	24/01/2019 concluded
10/12/2018	Lia QUARTAPELLE PROCOPIO (PD) - C.5/01084 Human rights situation in Mauritania	10/12/2018 amended for assigned commission

Commission resolutions

Date	Initiative	Latest update
23/10/2018	Andrea DELMASTRO DELLE VEDOVE (FdI) - C.7/00081 Human rights situation in Pakistan	23/10/2018 presented
30/10/2018	Lia QUARTAPELLE PROCOPIO (PD) - C.7/00088 Human rights situation in Yemen	03/04/2019 Rescheduled for another session
30/10/2018	Lia QUARTAPELLE PROCOPIO (PD) - C.7/00091 Human rights situation in Eritrea	29/01/2019 not accepted
07/11/2018	Andrea DELMASTRO DELLE VEDOVE (FdI) - C.7/00098 Human rights situation in Pakistan	08/11/2018 not accepted
22/11/2018	Andrea DE MARIA (PD) - C.7/00112 Human rights situation in Cambodia	12/02/2019 not accepted

Date	Initiative	Latest update
27/11/2018	Sabrina DE CARLO (M5S) - C.7/00115 Human rights situation in Yemen	03/04/2019 Rescheduled for another session

Assembly agenda proposals

Date	Initiative	Latest update
06/08/2018	Federico FORNARO (LeU) and others - C.9/01004/001 Human rights situation in Libya	06/08/2018 not accepted
06/08/2018	Stefano CECCANTI (PD) - C.9/01004/006 Human rights situation in Libya	06/08/2018 accepted
06/08/2018	Alberto PAGANI (PD) - C.9/01004/007 Human rights situation in Libya	06/08/2018 not accepted
06/08/2018	Simona SURIANO (M5S) - C.9/01004/009 Human rights situation in Libya	06/08/2018 accepted
27/11/2018	Alessia MORANI (PD) - C.9/01346/133 Migrants and asylum seekers: changes in the Italian legal system regarding rights of asylum, immigration and citizenship	28/11/2018 not accepted
27/11/2018	Giuseppe BRESCIA (M5S) - C.9/01346/145 Migrants and asylum seekers: progressive reduction of high capacity reception structures for asylum seekers	28/11/2018 accepted

Date	Initiative	Latest update
13/12/2018	Vittoria CASA (M5S) - C.9/01408/032 Children's rights: evaluate the opportunity for specific and urgent educational inteventions in the regions of Southern Italy to fight educational poverty in minors and school dropouts	13/12/2018 declared inadmissible

II. Prime Minister's Office (Presidency)

The organisation of the Prime Minister's Office is regulated by the decree of the Prime Minister of 1 October 2012. The Prime Minister's Office has a number of departments and offices (the so-called general structures), which the Prime Minister draws on for guideline and coordination functions regarding specific political and institutional fields. Of particular importance for human rights is the Department for Equal Opportunities.

A number of committees and commissions with specific tasks of economic and social relevance operate within the ambit of the Prime Minister's Office. These include the Commission for International Adoptions and the National Committee on Bioethics.

A. Department for Equal Opportunities: UNAR and Observatory for the Fight against Paedophilia and Child Pornography

The Department for Equal Opportunities, established under the auspices of the Prime Minister's Office, plans and coordinates legislative, administrative and research initiatives in all areas pertaining to equal opportunities policies. In June 2018, its management was entrusted to Undersecretary of State to the Prime Minister's Office Vincenzo Spadafora.

> The Department was instituted by d.p.c.m. 28 October 1997, No. 405, subsequently amended by various decrees (the most recent being d.p.c.m. 4 December 2012). It comprises three offices: the Office of General Affairs, International Affairs and Social Measures; the Office for Measures to Promote Equality and Equal Opportunities; and the National Anti-Racial Discrimination Office (UNAR).

UNAR was established by lgs.d. 9 July 2003, No. 215, in compliance with the European Community directive 2000/43/CE. Its mission is to guarantee observance of the principle of equal treatment of individuals, to monitor the efficacy of current instruments against discrimination and to help to stamp out forms of discrimination based on race or ethnic origin, while analysing their diversified impact on gender and their connection with other forms of racism of a cultural and religious nature.

In October the new edition of the *Statistical Dossier on Immigration* was published and edited by the IDOS/Immigration Study and Research Centre in collaboration with the UNAR. The Dossier estimates that the number of foreign citizens living regularly in Italy in 2017 was 5,333,000, 26,000 fewer than the estimate for 2016. In particular, there were 3,700,000 from States outside the EU, a figure that has remained almost the same for three years, also due to the consistent reduction of arriving by sea: 119,000 (-62,000 compared to 2016).

Immigrants residing in Italy come from almost 200 different countries from around the world. Half of these (2.6 million) are citizens of a country in Europe (of whom 1.6 million, equal to 30 %, are European Union Member States), while around 1 million come from African countries, just fewer from Asia and around 370,000 from Latin America. The biggest group from a single country are the Romanians, who constitute 23.1 % of all foreign residents, followed by the Albanians (8.6 %), Moroccans (8.1 %), Chinese (5.7 %) and Ukrainians (4.6 %). These five nationalities make up over half (50.1 %) of all foreign nationals in Italy.

With 83.1 % of all foreign residents, the Centre-North is consistently the geographical area hosting the largest number by far. The region with the highest number is Lombardy (22.9 % of the national total), followed by Lazio (13.5 %), Emilia Romagna (10.6 %, which has the highest number relative to its overall population at a national level: 12.0 %), Veneto (9.7 %) and Piedmont (8.4 %).

In 2015, the UNAR established the Media & Web Observatory, which aimed to research, monitor and analyse potentially discriminatory content coming from social network (Facebook, Twitter, YouTube and Google+) or that are published on social media (blogs with comments, fake news sites, online newspaper articles). In 2018, the Observatory flagged up 10,229 messages with offensive antisemitic content compared to 7,485 in 2017, increasing by 27.4 % in one year.

In October 2018, the Permanent Consultation Table for the Promotion of Rights and the Protection of LGBT people was established.

It is a working instrument to allow associations within the LGBT rights sector (both for promotion of rights and initiatives to fight sexual and gender- identity discrimination) and to converse and compare their work. It is a participative body that aims to share knowledge, data, best practices and carry out action proposals to promote a climate of respect for the dignity of LGBT persons and a culture of differences.

In addition to the three abovementioned, the following collegial bodies also have their secretariat within the Department for Equal Opportunities: the Inter-Ministerial Commission for support to victims of trafficking, violence and severe exploitation (as per Presidential Decree 14 May 2007, No. 102); the Committee for Prevention and Combating Female Genital Mutilation; the Committee to Evaluate the Legitimacy to Act on Behalf of People with Disabilities; the Committee for Equal Opportunities for Men and Women; the Observatory for the Fight against Paedophilia and Child Pornography.

The Observatory for the Fight against Paedophilia and Child Pornography was established in accordance with l. 3 August 1998, No. 269, as amended by l. 6 February 2006, No. 38, with the task of acquiring and monitoring data and information relating to activities carried out by all Government bodies to prevent and stamp out the sexual abuse and exploitation of minors. A further significant task of the Observatory is to prepare the National Plan for preventing and combating sexual abuse and exploitation of minors.

B. Commission for International Adoptions

Article 6 of the Hague Convention on the Protection of Minors and Cooperation in Respect of Intercountry Adoption, which was adopted on 29 May 1993 and came into force on 1 May 1995, requires State Parties to establish a central authority to ensure that adoptions of foreign children adhere to the principles established by the Convention itself. To comply with this requirement, via l. 31 December 1998, No. 476, Italy instituted the Commission for International Adoptions, which operates through the Prime Minister's Office. The Commission is Italy's central authority for the implementation of the Hague Convention.

> The Commission is comprised of a Chair, nominated by the Prime Minister (since July 2018: Giuseppe Conte, Prime Minister) and the following members:: three representatives from the Prime Minister's office; one from the Ministry of Foreign Affairs; one from the Ministry of Education; one

from the Ministry for Labour and Social Policy; one from the Ministry of the Interior; two from the Ministry of Justice; one from the Ministry of Health; one from the Ministry of Economy; four from the Unified Conference between State and Region; three from family associations; and experts.

According to the data provided by the Commission, in 2018, 1,394 minors were allowed to enter into Italy (in line with the figures from 2017). Specifically, 640 minors came from Europe, 121 from Africa, 330 from Central and South America and 303 from Asia. The country wuth the highest number of minors adopted was the Russian Federation (200), followed by Colombia (169), Hungary (135), Belarus (112) and China (84).

C. National Committee on Bioethics

The National Committee on Bioethics performs an advisory role vis-à-vis the Government, Parliament and other institutions, with a view to providing guidelines on legislative and administrative instruments designed to define the criteria to use in medical and biological practice in order to protect human rights. It also has a role in informing the public and in raising awareness with regard to ethical problems arising in connection with progress in scientific research and in technological applications in the life sciences and in healthcare.

The Committee was established by the d.p.c.m. 28 March 1990. It is made up of the following bodies: Chair (Lorenzo d'Avack, Professor in Philosophy of Law); Vice Chairs (Riccardo Di Segni, Chief Rabbi of Rome; Laura Palazzani, Professor in Philosophy of Law); Office of the President (made up of the Chair and the Vice Chairs); Assembly.

One of the tasks of the Committee is to produce studies and make recommendations that can also be used for legislative purposes. The Committee's documents offer in-depth focus and reflection on ethical and legal issues that arise as knowledge in the field of the life sciences advances. According to their nature and purpose, the documents are classified as: *opinions* (approved in the Committee's assembly on the basis of inquiries conducted by working groups); *motions* (urgent documents approved with a two-thirds majority of those present in the assembly); *responses* (documents in which the Committee makes recommendations on issues about which its opinion has been sought by other bodies or by physical persons).

The following opinions and motions were approved in 2018: "On the use of organs from anti-HCV-positive and HCV-RNA positive donors for transplantation in anti-HCV negative patients" (12 July); "On the question of AIFA's request regarding the ethicality of the use of the drug triptorelin in the treatment of adolescents with gender dysphoria (GD)" (13 July); "On the preservation of anonymity of donors" (27 September).

III. Ministry of Foreign Affairs and International Cooperation

The Ministry of Foreign Affairs has a number of directorate-generals and offices that deal specifically with human rights, disarmament and cooperation. Since August 2018, responsibility for issues dealt with in the United Nations ambit have been entrusted to Undersecretary Manlio Di Stefano.

> Particularly worthy of note is Office II – Human rights advocacy and international humanitarian law, Council of Europe, which falls within the directorate-general for Political Affairs and Security. Other offices in the same directorate are: Office I – The United Nations system and the institutional reform process, peacekeeping operations and preventive diplomacy; Office V – Disarmament, arms control and nuclear, biological and chemical non proliferation, Office of the national authority for the banning of chemical weapons; Office VI – Organisation for Security and Cooperation in Europe. The theme of human rights also relates across the board to the directorate-general for Global Affairs (Office IV – Energy, environmental protection and sustainable global development policies), the directorate-general for the European Union (Office III – European space of freedom, security and justice, the free movement of people and migratory flows towards the European Union) and the directorate-general for Development Cooperation (Office I – Development of cooperation policies within the European Union; Office II – Multilateral development cooperation; Office VI – Emergency and humanitarian aid; Office VIII – Planning and monitoring of the cooperation budget; gender issues, the rights of children and people with disabilities).

A. Inter-Ministerial Committee for Human Rights (CIDU)

The Inter-Ministerial Committee for Human Rights (CIDU) was established by decree of the Minister of Foreign Affairs on 15 February 1978, No. 519; its composition was updated by d.c.p.m. on 11 May 2007. Over 2012–2013 the CIDU was involved in a restructuring process: initially phased out as a result of the spending review, it was re-established on 5 September 2013. It maintained its functional competences because it was regarded as indispensable, both for its advice and its strategic guidance regarding the promotion and protection of human rights and in ensuring correct compliance with the obligations that Italy assumed following the signature and ratification of conventions and international agreements in this field.

> The CIDU is chaired by a functionary of the diplomatic service appointed by the Minister of Foreign Affairs: Fabrizio Petri in 2017. Committee members include representatives of the Prime Minister's Office, of various Ministries and of many different institutions (such as the Association of Italian Municipalities (ANCI); the Conference of Presidents of the Regions and Autonomous Provinces; the Union of Italian Provinces (UPI); the National Commission for UNESCO; the Italian Committee for UNICEF; the Italian Society for International Organisation (SIOI); as well as three eminent personalities in the field of human rights.
>
> The CIDU has the following tasks: to promote measures necessary for ensuring full compliance with international obligations assumed by Italy; to facilitate the implementation of international conventions in Italy; to draft the reports Italy is required to submit to the pertinent international organisations; to maintain and develop appropriate relations with civil society organisations engaged in promoting and protecting human rights.

In November 2018, the report on the activities carried out by the CIDU for the year 2017 was sent to the Chamber of Deputies The report provides Parliament with the results of collaborative activities with the bodies of the United Nations, the Council of Europe and the European Union on the submission of the periodic reports provided by the international human rights instruments of which Italy is a part; as well as visits prepared by the aforementioned organisations in order to obtain specific elements or to identify concrete situations in areas deemed to be particularly sensitive to human rights. In this regard, in 2017 the CIDU carried out the following activities.

United Nations

– Discussing the sixth periodic report on the International Covenant on Civil and Political Rights;
– Discussing the seventh periodic report on the Convention on the Elimination of All Forms of Discrimination against Women;
– Publishing V-VI Periodic Report for the Convention of the Rights of the Child, in collaboration with the National Observatory for Children and Adolescents;
– Follow-up on the discussion on the first periodic report of the Convention on the Rights of Persons with Disabilities;

- Discussing the fifth to seventh periodic report on the Convention against Torture;
- Producing the First National Report for the International Convention for the Protection of All Persons from Enforced Disappearance;
- Follow-up on the discussion on the nineteenth and twentieth periodic reports on the implementation of the International Convention on the Elimination of All Forms of Racial Discrimination;
- Implementing the Third National Action Plan on Women, Peace and Security (2016–2019);
- Following the first National Action Plan on "Business and Human Rights" (2016–2021);
- Producing the mid-term report for the second cycle of the Universal Period Review of the UN Human Rights Council;
- Visit to Italy of the Special Rapporteur on extrajudicial, summary or arbitrary executions (10–16 May 2017);
- Follow-up visit by the Subcommittee for Prevention of Torture (12 December 2017).

Council of Europe

- Visit of a delegation from the Local and Regional Authorities Congress (21–23 March 2017);
- Visit of the Special Representative of the Secretary General on migration and refugees, Amb. Tomáš Boček (31 May 2017);
- Visit to Italy of the Committee for the Prevention of Torture (7-13 June 2017).

European Union

- Visit to Italy of the Fundamental Rights Agency (FRA) (15–18 September 2017).

B. Italian National Commission for UNESCO

The Commission was established by inter-ministerial decree on 11 February 1950, at the Ministry of Foreign Affairs, two years after Italy entered the Organisation, and pursuant to Article 7 of the UNESCO Charter.

Members of the Commission include representatives from Parliament, the Prime Minister's Office, various Ministries, public and private agencies, local authorities and civil society.

The Commission's mission is to promote the implementation of UNESCO programmes in Italy; to spread the ideals of the Organisation, especially among the younger generations; to disseminate information on its principles, goals and activities, thus stimulating action by institutions, civil society and the world of culture, education and science. The Commission also advises the Government regarding its dealings with UNESCO.

In 2018, as nominated by the Ministry of Foreign Affairs, Franco Bernabè was president, while the post of Secretary General was held by Enrico Vicenti.

The National Commission receives funding for institutional activities and its functioning through chapter 2471/10 of the budget forecast of the Ministry of Foreign Affairs. In 2018, this funding was around €10,000 which covers no more than the basic functioning of the Commission, making it extremely difficult to perform its public activities.

Despite these shortages, in 2018, the National Commission carried out many activities (seminars, conferences, meetings in schools, competitions, exhibitions, workshops, shows) in various Italian cities, especially regarding the different UN International Days, including International Mother Language Day (21 February), World Poetry Day (21 March), World Book and Copyright Day (23 April) and International Jazz Day (30 April).

IV. Ministry of Labour and Social Policies

Many departments and offices within the Ministry of Labour and Social Policies deal specifically with human rights.

The following are particularly worthy of note:

- *Directorate-General for Inclusion and Social Policies.* Functions: promoting policies to combat poverty, social exclusion and severe marginalisation; promoting and monitoring policies for children and adolescents, and the protection of minors; coordination policies for the social inclusion, protection and promotion of the rights and opportunities of persons with disabilities; managing the National Fund for Social Policies, the National Fund for the Non Self-Sufficient, the National Fund for Childhood and Adolescence and other funds for financing social policies and monitoring transferred resources; study, research and investigations concerning social policies; participation in all the pertinent internationally significant activities, and managing relations with the European Union, the Council of Europe, the International Labour Organisation, the United Nations and the Organisation for Economic Cooperation and Development.

- *Directorate-general for the third sector and social groups.* Functions: promoting and supporting the activities carried out by third sector subjects, especially initiatives relating to social promotion and voluntary associations, in order to facilitate the growth of an active society welfare to support policies of social inclusion and integration; promotion, development and coordination of policies, initiatives and activities to support the spread of corporate social responsibility.
- *Directorate-general for immigration and integration policies.* Functions: programming migratory flows, and managing and monitoring entry quotas of foreign workers as well as bilateral cooperation agreements with countries of origin; coordinating policies for social and job integration of foreign immigrants and initiatives designed to prevent and combat discrimination, xenophobia and racism; developing international cooperation for activities to prevent and study social and employment emergencies, and for initiatives regarding work-related migratory flows.

In 2012, the Directorate-General for immigration and integration policies took over the functions of the Committee for Foreign Minors, which was abolished in accordance with the decree on the so-called spending review (Article 12, para. 20 of l.d. 95/2012, converted into law, with amendments, in l. 135/2012). Consequently, the Directorate-General is now responsible for monitoring the presence of foreign minors temporarily present on Italian territory, whether they be unaccompanied minors present on Italian territory or admitted minors.

As regards unaccompanied minors, the Directorate-General may adopt two kinds of measures: the first is "no repatriation", which amounts to activating the procedures for integrating the person into Italy; the second is "assisted repatriation", designed to reunite the child with his or her family in their Country of origin. As regards the first option, responsibility for managing and monitoring the measures is placed in the hands of local authorities. The most frequent choice made for unaccompanied minors in Italy is to place them in residential care facilities for children.

As regards admitted minors, the Directorate-General makes decisions, following due appraisal and according to predetermined criteria, at the request of organisations, associations or Italian families, regarding the temporary admission of children into the framework of humanitarian programmes. The Committee then makes decisions on temporary fostering and repatriation. It keeps a register of minors already admitted into the framework of humanitarian programmes and defines criteria for assessing requests for the admission of temporarily admitted minors.

By 31 December 2018, 10,787 unaccompanied foreign minors were registered with the Commission, around eight thousand fewer than on 31 December 2017. The majority of these were boys, around 92.7 % of the total. The main countries of origin were Albania (14.4 %), Egypt (8.6 %), Gambia (8.3 %), Guinea (7.4 %), Eritrea (7.1 %) and the Ivory Coast (7.1 %): together, these six represent just over half of all unaccompanied foreign minors in Italy (52.9 %). The region with the highest number of minors (about 38 % of the total) in reception centres is still Sicily, in line with a trend which has consolidated over many years, followed by: Lombardy (8.1 %), Emilia Romagna (7.3 %), Friuli Venezia Giulia (7.3 %) and Lazio (7.1 %).

A. *National Observatory for Children and Adolescents*

The Observatory performs a role of coordination among central administrations, local and regional bodies, associations, professional groups and non-governmental organisations dedicated to children's issues.

It was instituted by l. 23 December 1997, No. 451, and is currently regulated by decree of the President of the Republic (d.p.r.), 14 May 2007, No. 103, which assigns it joint chairmanship by the Ministry of Labour and Social Policies and the Undersecretary of State to the Prime Minister's Office mandated with family policies. It is made up of representatives from national and local public administrations, associations and professional orders, voluntary and third sector organisations as well as experts in the field of children's rights.

Presidential decree 103/2007 assigns the Observatory the task of preparing three documents about the condition of childhood and adolescence in Italy:

- The *National Plan of Action and of Measures to Safeguard the Rights and Development of Children and Adolescents.* Drawn up every two years, the plan contains the fundamental strategic guidelines and concrete commitments that the Government intends to pursue in order to develop a satisfactory policy for children and adolescents in Italy. The last National Plan adopted by the Observatory refers to the years 2016/2017.
- The *Report on the Condition of Children and Adolescents in Italy.* It aims to provide an updated picture of the aspects that characterise the condition of children and adolescents in Italy, and of the social services system and measures for promoting and protecting the rights of children and adolescents. In October 2017, the Observatory published the Report on the Condition of Childhood and Adolescence in Italy 2012–2015.

- The Periodic Report of the Government to the UN Committee on the Rights of the Child regarding the application of the 1989 International Convention on the Rights of the Child, pursuant to article 44 of the Convention. The latest report (combining the 5th and 6th reports) was sent by Italy in July 2017 and is awaiting discussion (see *Yearbook 2018*, p. 134–135).

In carrying out its functions, the National Observatory uses the National Centre of Documentation and Analysis for Children and Adolescents, which performs documentation, analysis, research, monitoring and training tasks.

More specifically, the National Centre of Documentation deals with:

- collecting and disseminating regional, national, European, and international norms and regulations, as well as statistical data and scientific studies;
- collecting and disseminating regional, national, European, and international norms and regulations, as well as statistical data and scientific studies;
- analysing the situation of childhood and adolescence in Italy, including the conditions of foreign minors;
- preparing an outline, based on National Observatory directives, of the biennial report on the condition of children in Italy, and of the Government report to the United Nations Committee on the Rights of the Child on the domestic implementation of the Convention on the Rights of the Child;
- formulating proposals, also at the request of local authorities, for the creation of pilot projects designed to improve children's living conditions as well as to assist mothers during the prenatal period.

B. National Observatory Monitoring the Conditions of Persons with Disabilities

The Observatory is an advisory body offering technical and scientific support in defining national policies regarding disabilities.

It was instituted by l. 3 March 2009, No. 18, at the Ministry of Labour, Health and Social Policies. It is chaired by the Ministry of Labour and includes a maximum of 40 members, who are appointed by ministerial decree and represent central administrations involved in defining and implementing disability-related policies; regional and local authorities; social security institutions; the National Statistics Institute; trade unions; and most representative associations and organisations of persons with disabilities, joined by a maximum of five experts of proven experience in the field of disabilities. Within the Observatory there is also a technical-scientific Committee, with the purpose of analysis and scientific direction in relation to the activities and tasks of the organism.

The Observatory's tasks include the following: to promote the implementation of the United Nations Convention on the Rights of Persons with Disabilities and to prepare, together with CIDU, the national report for the monitoring procedure established by that Convention; to prepare a biennial Plan of Action on disability implementing national and international laws; promotes the realisation of studies and research that can help to identify priority areas in which to direct actions and actions for the promotion of the rights of persons with disabilities.

With the Presidential Decree of the Council of Ministers of 5 December 2016, the duration of the Observatory has been extended for the three-year period 2017–2020. The new Observatory took office on 11 October 2017 and did not carry out any activities in 2018.

V. Ministry of Justice

Within the Ministry of Justice there are various departments and bureaus specifically involved with human rights. The most relevant are:

- *Office II*: (Directorate-General for litigation and human rights – Department of legal affairs): it is actively involved in examining cases pending before the European Court of Human Rights. In addition, it is responsible for drafting the reports requested by international human rights bodies, mainly by the Council of Europe and UN bodies and committees
- *Department for Juvenile Justice and Community:* the office deals with promoting and protecting the rights of unaccompanied foreign minors and of persons at risk of social exclusion.

VI. Judicial Authorities

The judiciary, that is to say the various organs of justice – ordinary, administrative and auditing – constituting judicial power, is the fundamental guarantee of rights and legality in a State that respects the principles of democracy, the division of powers and the rule of law. The Italian courts – the Constitutional Court, which delivers judgments regarding the constitutionality of laws, the Supreme Court, which is the court of last resort, the penal and civil tribunals and trial courts, and those concerned with administrative, audit and military matters – deal in a contentious manner with cases which often affect human rights in the most various ways and according to the most disparate perspectives. Access to a judge to obtain a ruling on a right that a plaintiff claims has been breached is a fundamental human right, linked to which are the many other procedural rights that distinguish the fair trial.

> The judiciary, that is to say the various organs of justice – ordinary, administrative and auditing – constituting judicial power, is the fundamental guarantee of rights and legality in a State that respects the principles of democracy, the division of powers and the rule of law. The Italian courts – the Constitutional Court, which delivers judgments regarding the constitutionality of laws, the Supreme Court, which is the court of last resort, the penal and civil tribunals and trial courts, and those concerned with administrative, audit and military matters – deal in a contentious manner with cases which often affect human rights in the most various ways and according to the most disparate perspectives. Access to a judge to obtain a ruling on a right that a plaintiff claims has been breached is a fundamental human right, linked to which are the many other procedural rights that distinguish the fair trial.

Part IV of this *Yearbook* is specifically devoted to a summary presentation of cases in the Italian courts on which rulings were delivered in 2018 (with particular reference to the judgments of the Constitutional Court and the Supreme Court), and of case-law elaborated by the European Court of Human Rights or the Court of Justice of the European Union which directly concerns Italy, either because the Italian State was the "defendant" or because the intervention of the European judge regarded pleas presented by Italian citizens or related to Italian legal norms.

V. Independent Authorities

In this section, the five independent authorities that relate more pertinently to human rights are described: the Communications Regulatory Authority (AGCOM); the Data Protection Authority; the Committee Guaranteeing the Implementation of the Law on Strikes Affecting Essential Public Services; the National Ombudsperson for Children and Adolescents; National Ombudsperson for the Rights of Persons in Prison or Deprived of Liberty.

A. Communications Regulatory Authority (AGCOM)

> AGCOM was set up by l. 31 July 1997, No. 249. It has a dual mandate: to ensure correct competition among market actors and to guarantee the fundamental freedoms of citizens in the area of communications, particularly as regards the protection of minors.

The composition of the Authority is disciplined by decree 6 December 2011, No. 201 (the so-called Save Italy decree), and its conversion into law (22 December 2011, No. 214). In 2018, the Authority was made up as follows: Chair: Angelo Marcello Cardani; members of the *Services and Products Commission*: Antonio Martusciello and Francesco Posteraro; members of the *Commission for Infrastructure and Networks*: Antonio Nicita and Mario Morcellini (from 15 March 2017). The Council consists of the Chair and all the Commissioners.

According to the annual report on work programmes and activities in 2018 (reference period: May 2017 - April 2018), the Authority focused on carrying out surveillance activities on protecting minors, freedom of information online and the use of big data and machine learning.

On 16 January 2018, the "White Paper on Media and Children 2.0" was presented to the Chamber of Deputies, updating the previous White Paper on Media and Children. In a logical and integrated way, the volume aimed to guarantee the concept of the "best interest of the child", in the understanding that while a developing digital world implies a great opportunity for growth, there are also new risks and dangers to consider.

Regarding child protection, an intervention by the Authority in the exercise of specific regulatory power was particularly significant. Moreover, lgs.d. 7 December 2017, No. 203, containing "Reform of legislative provisions concerning child protection in the cinema and audio-visual sector, pursuant to Article 33 of law 14 November 2016, No. 220", gave AGCOM the scope to regulate the classification of film and audio work for the internet and viodeogames (Article 10) within a child protection framework. On the basis on the analysis carried out, the Authority published its classification regulations (resolution No. 186/18/CONS of 11 April 2018), by submitting it for public consultation.

The systematic approach to the various problems connected to children's use of the internet and social media and the examination of the efficiency of the measures and procedures negotiated by sector continued to dominate the Authority's activities via the "National Observatory for the Fundamental Rights of Children and Adolescents Online" (established with Resolution No. 481/14/CONS). In 2017, it carried out in-depth investigation and monitoring activities of incitement to hatred, cyberbullying and hate speech, since developing a digital education is necessary to strengthen the character and critical thinking of young people.

Furthermore, the Authority has substantially increased santionary action for violation of duties regarding broadcasting programming, focusing on user protection, especially children. The sanction procedures are also based on alerts from the Postal and Communications Police and the *Guardia di Finanza* (finance division of the police). There has been a total of 114 sanction procedures initiated (in the audio-visual commercial communication sector, following a violation of the child protection regulations) and concluded, of which 94 concluded with enforcing the foreseen sanctions and 20 with archiving measures for dismissal.

Regarding the online information system and the repercussions that some typical internet issues (first and foremost misinformation and the spreading of fake news) can present concerning informative pluralism in user protection, aboveall for electoral campaigns and referenda, in November 2017, the Authority established "Technical task-force on pluralism and correct information on digital platforms (resolution No. 423/17/CONS). The first operative phase focuses on electoral campaigns for the parliamentary elections of 4 March 2018, after which the task-force approved "Guidelines for equal access to online platforms during electoral campaigns for the parliamentary campaigns of 2018". Under the task-force, five work groups were established regarding specific topics: i) methods to find and classify online misinformation; ii) defining monitoring systems of advertising economic flows, from national and international sources, aimed at financing fake contents; iii) fact-checking: organisation, techniques, tools and effects; iv) media literacy and online misinformation; v) writing and carrying out online informative campaigns on misinformation for consumers.

Finally, concerning the use of big data and machine learning, the Authority set up various initiatives, via the technical task-force on Machine to Machine activities and Internet of Things, an investigation on the development of 5G and the joint investigation with AGCM and the Privacy Authority on big data.

B. Data Protection Authority

The Data Protection Authority was instituted by l. 31 December 1996, No. 675, later substituted by lgs.d. 30 June 2003, No. 196 (Personal data protection code), with the aim to ensure protection of the fundamental rights and freedoms and respect for the dignity of persons, in the processing of personal data.

The Data Protection Authority is a collegial body made up of four members elected by Parliament, who remain in office for a seven-year non-renewable mandate. The current body is made up of Antonello Soro (Chair), Augusta Iannini (Vice Chair), Giovanna Bianchi Clerici and Licia Califano.

During 2018, the Authority issued 479 *provisions* to protect the fundamental rights of individuals with regard to the processing and circulation of personal data, with particular reference to the following issues (among others): freedom of the press; right to education, work, health and scientific research; rights of minors; handling of sensitive data; and internet and social media.

C. Commission Guaranteeing the Implementation of the Law on Strikes Affecting Essential Public Services

The Commission was instituted by l. 12 June 1990, No. 146, and subsequent amendments. It is comprised of five members designated by the Chairs of the Chamber of Deputies and the Senate among experts in matters of constitutional law, labour law and industrial relations, and appointed by decree of the President of the Republic. In 2018, the members of the Commission were: Giuseppe Santoro Passarelli (Chair), Lauralba Bellardi, Alessandro Bellavista, Domenico Carrieri, Orsola Razzolini.

Some of the main tasks of the Commission are:

- assessing the capacity of essential services to guarantee protection of both the right to strike and the enjoyment of constitutionally guaranteed human rights;
- requesting that those calling the strike delay the date of abstention from work if the Commission intends to attempt conciliation, or if it finds that the abstention violates legal and/or contractual obligations for strikes in essential public services;
- pointing out to those calling the strike any violations of norms concerning advance notice or any other requirements relative to the phase preceding collective abstention;
- notifying the appropriate authority which can order strikers back to work of situations where the strike or collective abstention could give rise to an imminent, probable risk of infringing constitutionally protected human rights;
- taking note of behaviour by administrations or enterprises which provide essential public services in clear violation of the law;

- assessing behaviour of both parties and if any non-compliance or violation of legal or contractual obligations relative to essential services emerges, inflicting penalties pursuant to Article 4 of l. 146/1990 as amended by Article 3 of l. 83/2000, ordering the employer to apply the disciplinary actions.

The annual report on the activity carried out in 2017 was presented in June 2018. According to data contained in the report, strikes in the essential public services sector remain at rather high levels. In the year in review, a slightly increasing trend was noted compared to previous year. The overall number of strikes (national, local, sectoral, refusal of overtime, etc.) called in essential public services was 2,448, compared to 2,352 in 2016. On a practical level, following the spontaneous revoking of strikes from the parties involved and aboveall thanks to inteventions from the Commission, the strike action that effectively took place went down to around half. In particular, the conflict remains strong in the following sectors: local public transport (443 strikes called), environmental hygiene (382), air transport (260), cleaning and multi-services (207), regions and local self-government (147), postal communication (137), national health service (101).

The majority of strike actions were called in full compliance with the law: the Commission only intervened with 331 preventative actions to highlight potential breaches of legislation which led to adjustments in all of the cases.

Furthermore, in 2017, there were 13 national general strikes (and other four territorial general strikes) therefore more than one per month, although almost all with insignificant levels of participation.

D. National Ombudsperson for Children and Adolescents

The National Ombudsperson for Children and Adolescents was established with l. 12 July 2011, No. 112. It is a single presiding organ, and the holder of the post is appointed by the Presidents of the Chamber of Deputies and of the Senate, who choose a figure of unquestioned morality, independence and professional competence in the field of children's rights. The term of office lasts four years. From March 2016, Filomena Albano has held the post of Ombudsperson.

The Ombudsperson has, amongst others, the following responsibilities:

- to promote the implementation of the UN Convention on the Rights of the Child, and of other pertinent international and European instruments,

and to ensure appropriate forms of collaboration with all the national and international bodies and organisations engaged in promoting and protecting children and adolescents;
- to express opinions on legislative initiatives concerning the protection of the rights of children and adolescents, and the report that the Government presents periodically to the UN Committee on the Rights of the Child;
- to inform the Government, Regions and other local or territorial bodies involved, in relation to their respective responsibilities, of all appropriate measures to ensure full promotion and protection of the rights of children and adolescents;
- to inform judicial authorities and bodies concerned of problem cases or risks of minors' rights being infringed, as well as serious cases of neglect of minors, so that they can be taken into care by the appropriate authorities;
- to enhance knowledge of the rights of children and adolescents, organising, to this end, awareness-raising activities, studies, and research.

Article 6 of l. 112 also allows anyone to address the Ombudsperson to report violation of rights or the risk thereof. Finally, Article 3 states that the Ombudsperson is to establish appropriate forms of cooperation with the regional Ombudspersons or similar figures. The National Conference for the Rights of Children and Adolescents was set up for this purpose; coordinated by the National Ombudsperson, it brings together all the other Ombudspersons, where these have been established (see this Part, Sub-national Human Rights Structures, IV).

In June 2018, the Ombudsperson presented the report to Parliament on the actions undertaken on 2017. During the year, the Ombudsperson continued to examine relevant bills, particularly following the proposals aimed at guaranteeing the protection of young people of "new legal age" who have grown up outside the family unit (by establishing a three-year fund for 2018–2020 aimed to guarantee the continuity of care paths for care leavers up to 21 years old), of minors in the criminal system, and of children born in Italy to foreign parents. The Ombudsperson also dedicated special attention to bills concerning orphans of domestic crimes (A.S. 2719), for which the parliamentary procedure was concluded in December 2017 by adopting a number of provisions aimed at reinforcing protection for children left effectively orphaned following one parent killing the other.

In 2017, the Ombudsperson held three hearings in Parliament.

Regarding the reception of asylum seekers and provisions for unaccompanied minors, the Ombudsperson spoke before a Parliamentary Enquiry Commission on the reception, identification and expulsion system. The Enquiry also heard about public resources used for reception policies and for the integration of unaccompanied minors (21 March). It also spoke before the joint commission of Constitutional Affairs and European Union policies of the Chamber of Deputies (7 November). On this occasion, the Ombudsperson outlined the framework of reception of foreign minors, highlighting various critical issues of the protection system such as the prolonged stay in first recption centres, which risks excessively delaying the integration process, and the need to concentrate competency on migrant minors within the Juvenile Court, and also for appointing guardians.

On 12 December, the Ombudsperson was heard by the Parliamentary Enquiry Commission on femicide and all forms of gender-based violence. After highlighting the lack of official data needed to provide a full overview of the situation, the Ombusperson focused on the circumstances of episodes of violence which lead to femicide, often including minors as terrified onlookers and witnesses to violence. This did not just include direct victims of violence, but all victims, and therefore the opportunity to make victims as witnesses to violence a stand-alone crime should be taken into consideration. According to the Ombudsperson, the protection and prevention measures must take place within an interdisciplinary approach, so as to involve institutions, legal practitioners, social workers, and associative entities. Furthermore, the fragmentation of the competencies for infancy, including services for adults and those for minors, takes away from the quality of the whole system. Therefore, a control room that coordinates these interventions and ensures a coherent rehabilitation and therapy course is necessary.

With regard to gender-based violence, the Ombudsperson set out the "priority of priorities" in terms of the fight against human trafficking. It is estimated that, for example, around 80 % of Nigerian girls who land in Italy arrive via trafficking routes; more and more, the girls arriving are underage, and are on average getting younger every year. The voluntary guardian is therefore an important role: for this reason, during training events organised by the Ombudsperson, there is an in-depth presentation dedicated to trafficking.

The Ombudsperson carried out numerous actions in favour of certain categories of vulnerable minors, including meetings with children and young people, by implementing the right to be heard that is set out in Article 12 of the Convention on the Rights of the Child.

E. National Ombudsperson for the Rights of Persons in Prison or Deprived of Liberty

This Ombudsperson was established by Article 7 of l.d. 23 December 2013, No. 146, converted with amendments by l. 21 February 2014, No. 10. It is collegial, and consists of the Chair and two members chosen from independent people who are competent in areas relating to the protection of human rights. Members are nominated, following a decision of the Council of Ministers, by a Presidential Decree, having heard the competent parliamentary commissions, with a five-year mandate which may not be extended.

> In 2018, the National Ombudsperson for the Rights of Persons in Prison or Deprived of Liberty was Mauro Palma; the other members were Daniela De Robert and Emilia Rossi.
>
> The Ombudsperson is tasked with ensuring that custody of persons in prison and persons subject to other types of limitations on personal freedom is carried out in accordance with the rules and principles set out in the Constitution, in international conventions on human rights, and the laws of the land. To this end, it has the faculty to visit penitentiary institutions and other structures used to host persons subject to measures restricting their personal freedom without requiring authorisation.
>
> The Ombudsperson has been identified as an independent national monitoring mechanism required under the Optional Protocol to the Convention against Torture (OPCAT), which Italy ratified in 2012.
>
> The National Ombudsperson is also tasked with coordinating the network of local ombudspersons, promoting their solidity as an institution through the recognition of sufficient guarantees of independence and autonomy vis-à-vis the local government which appointed them.

Finally, the Ombudsperson monitors procedures relating to forced repatriations pursuant to the system provided for in Article 8, para. 6, of EU Directive No. 115 of 2008.

In the period January 2018-January 2019, the Ombudsperson conducted 42 visits for a total of 100 places visited across the national territory, monitoring the rights of persons deprived of liberty in prison, health and migratory process conditions.

For the same period, with regard to monitoring activities of forced repatriation, 34 flights were monitored, mostly destined for Tunisia (13 flights) and Nigeria (11).

Furthermore, in August 2018, a delegation of the Ombudsperson visited the Diciotti ship which was docked in the Catania port, confirming the concerns of violations of national and supranational standards. For this reason, the Ombudsperson sent their findings to the Agrigento and Catania public prosecutor's offices which opened cases on the Diciotti incident.

Finally, in 2018, two opinions on legislative proposals were adopted:

- 7 August: opinion on the legislative decree laying down the Penitentiary Law Reform (delegate law No. 103 of 2017), concerning: prison health; provisions to simplify proceedings; provisions concerning life in prison;
- 15 October: opinion on law decree 4 October 2018, No. 113, urgent provisions concerning international protection and immigration, public security and measures for the functionality of the Ministry of the Interior and the functioning of the National Agency for administrating and managing goods confiscated from organised crime.

VIII. Non-Governmental Organisations

In Italy, numerous non-governmental organisations are active in promoting and protecting human rights. Some that are organised in networks at national and international levels have gained consultative status with international organisations and actively participate in their programmes.

As of 31 December 2018, 117 Italian non-governmental organisations held consultative status with the United Nations Economic and Social Council, seven of which have general status; 92 have special status and 18 have *roster* status. There are 142 non-governmental organisations with headquarters or representative offices in Italy enjoying participatory status with the Council of Europe dealing specifically with human rights.

In addition, some of the most important international non-governmental organisations have local branches in Italy. These include Amnesty International, the International Federation on Human Rights, Save the Children, Médecins sans Frontières and ActionAid.

Non-governmental organisations play an important role in monitoring the level of compliance with and protection of human rights in Italy. In 2018, the following monitoring reports, which are of particular interest, were published.

- Antigone Association: *XIV National Report on Detention Conditions – A Year in Prison.*

In 2017, the Antigone Observatory on detention conditions visited 86 of the 190 penal institutions (36 in northern Italy, 20 in the centre and 30 in the south and on the islands). There was a significant increase in the population of detainees, from 56,289 in March 2017 to 58,223 in March 2018. Not everyone is serving a sentence, however; 34 % are in custody awaiting a final sentence, slightly less than the previous year. This percentage is slightly higher in foreign nationals, at 39 %.

Crimes that people are detained for are mainly offences against property (24.9 %), followed by violent crime (17.7 %) and crimes relating to the consolidated law on narcotics (15.2 %). In foreign nationals, violent crimes were less common compared to Italian nationals, while drug offences were higher. 4.9 % of detainees are sentenced to less that one year, rising to 7.1 % considering only foreign nationals; by contrast, foreign nationals are less represented among longer sentences. Life sentences represent 4.6 % of all inmates, yet only 0.8 % of foreign national inmates.

Considering educational and training activities, only 23 % of detainees particate in educational courses at any level. The five regions with the highest numbers of school courses participants are: Lombardy (36.7 % of the total number of inmates are enrolled), Calabria (35 %), Lazio (25.7 %), Umbria (24.1 %) and Piedmont (23.1 %).

The subject of work is extremely critical. In 2017, the rate of employment of prison population of working age (15–64 years) was 31.95 %. Antigone calculate that only 2.2 % of prisoners are employed by employers other than the penitentiary administration: some are in open prison regimes and are therefore able to leave during work hours, while others work for external employers staying inside the prison. The other 17 thousand people deemed "working" by the penitentiary administration are dependent on the administration itself, and for the most part (82 %) are employed in services within the prison (cleaning, food distribution, some segretarial roles (i.e. writing complaints and documents for other detainees)). These are jobs carried out in shifts with limited expendability in the outside world of work.

Finally, regarding the number of suicides, which is the most dramatic indicator of well-being in detention, Antigone shows that, in the last ten years, the suicide rate (deaths per 10,000 people) has gone up from 8.3 in 2008 to 9.1 in 2017: in absolute figures, this means going from 46 deaths in 2008 to 52 in 2017.

- A Buon Diritto Association: *Report on the status of rights in Italy*. The Report analyses the fulfilment of fundamental rights of the person and of the protective measures in place for minorities in Italy. The Report highlights a wide range of rights and guaranties for the full enjoyment of basic human needs: personal freedom, freedom of movement, religious freedom, freedom from discrimination of any kind, freedom of persons with disability, gender identity and sexual orientation, minority rights, rights of migrants, refugees and asylum seekers, justice and guarantees, freedom of expression and information, sensitive information, confidentiality and the right to be forgotten, protection of minors, education and social mobility, women's rights, right to health, work and wage guarantees, and environmental protection.

- Italian Alliance for Sustainable Development (*Alleanza Italiana per lo Sviluppo Sostenibile* -ASviS): *Report 2018*. Other than photographing the situation in Italy, the Report analyses the evolution of the Italian regions in achieving the Sustainable Development Goals of the Agenda 2030 for the first time. According to the Report, despite the significant mobilisation of the business world, cultural and educational institutions and civil society, political delays are particularly pronounced. This puts Italy in an unsustainable state from all points of view - economic, social, environmental and institutional. Italy has shown signs of improvement in eight areas: sustainable food and agriculture, health, education, gender equality, innovation, sustainable production and consumption models, fight against climate change, and international cooperation. However, for five areas, the situation considerably worsened: poverty, economic and work conditions, inequality, and city and ecosystems conditions, while for the remaining four (water and health-hygiene structures, energy systems, sea conditions and the quality of governance, peace, justice and stable institutions) the situation seems unchanged.

- Sbilanciamoci! Campaign: ("Let's flip it!") *2019 Report- How to use public expenditure for human rights, peace and the environment*. The Report contains 101 detailed proposals by the 47 countries signed up to the Sblianciamoci! campaign, starting from a detailed analysis of the quality of public spending in Italy. It aims to save and bring in more money, cut excessive or wasteful spending and allocate the money for more correct usage. It identified seven key areas: finance; work and wages; culture and knowledge; environment and sustainable development; welfare and rights; peace, cooperation and disarmament; fair trade.

Finally, at the end of 2016, on the initiative of *Un Ponte Per…*, the network "In defence of – for human rights and those who defend them" (*In Difesa Di – per i diritti umani e chi li difende*) was established. It was made up of over thirty Italian organisations and associations that are active in the field of human rights, environmental rights, international solidarity, peace and disarmourment, workers' rights, the freedom of press and the state of rights. The aim of the network is to promote campaigns and initiatives that protect human rights defenders, raise awareness of these subjects among public opinion, and to ask Italian institutions (Government, Parliament and local institutions) to commit to developing protective instruments and mechanisms for human rights defenders.

In 2018, the network continued the establishment of "territorial nodes" (particularly in Milan and Trent) aiming to develop shelter cities for human rights defenders who need to temporarily leave their own countries (see this Part, Sub-national Human Rights Structures, I). In June, a workshop was held in Trent on shelter cities by local organisations and by the Autonomous Province of Trent, with participation of CEAR Euskadi and the Dutch Shelter Cities Program. It marked the start of a training programme that focused on the operating procedures of shelter cities and the instruments and expertise needed at a local and network level. The workshop allowed participants to discuss the implementation of a coordinated strategy on shelter cities and a possible pilot scheme which would involve all interested administrations.

IX. Teaching and Research on Human Rights in Italian Universities

In the Italian academic world, there has been an increase in research and training regarding human rights. The subject is now present in many different modules and in the curricula of many university and post-university courses, such as transdisciplinary research programmes. In the following pages, there is a mapping of the institutions and university research centres that work specifically in human rights related subjects, from three-year (Bachelor's) and two-year specialisation (Master's) degree programmes to one-year Master's programmes and PhDs that were activated or published in 2018. The courses and structured highlighted contain "human rights" in their name, or other equivalent expressions such as "rights of people", "rights of man", or "fundamental rights". This mapping shows how widespread the teaching of human rights and its various dimensions has become in the academic environment.

University Institutions and Research Centres

University	Name	Founding year
University of Padova	University Human Rights Centre	1982
University of Salento	Inter-University Centre on Bioethics and Human Rights	1992
41 European universities in partnership	European Inter-University Centre for Human Rights and Democratisation (EIUC)	2002
University of Naples	Centre for Studies on Human Rights in the era of globalisation and conflicts	2003
University of Ca' Foscari, Venice	Human Rights Research Centre (CESTUDIR)	2003
University of Salerno	Department of Individual Rights and Comparison	2011

Source: elaboration by the 2019 *Yearbook* research and editorial committee.

Bachelor's Degree Courses

Università	Denominazione	Classe di laurea
University of Padova	Political science, international relations, human rights	L-36: Political science and International Relations
Aldo Moro University of Bari	Immigration law, human rights and interculturality	L-14: Legal services

Source: elaboration by the *2019 Yearbook* research and editorial committee.

Master's Degree Courses

University	Name	Scientific Area
University of Bergamo	Human Rights and the Ethics of International Cooperation	LM-81: Cooperation development sciences
University of Bologna	International Cooperation on Human Rights and Intercultural Heritage	LM-81: Cooperation development sciences
University of Padova	Human rights and multi-level governance	LM-52: International Relations
University of Perugia	European judicial integration and human rights	LM-90: European Studies

Source: elaboration by the *2019 Yearbook* research and editorial committee.

Teachings

In 2018 a total of 111 human rights teachings were run in 41 universities. Around 61 % of these were delivered via degree courses in the field of political and social science (68 modules), while slightly over one-third related to the area of law (39 modules); 2 modules to the area of history, philosophy, pedagogy and psychology and 3 in the area of economics and statistics.

As in the years between 2010 and 2017, in 2018 the university with the greatest number of human rights teachings was Padova (18 teachings), followed by Turin (7), Milan (6), Rome Tre (6), Bari (5) and Macerata (5 teaching). Of the 111 teachings available, 34 are taught in English - 11 of which are at the University of Padova, 3 at the University of Milan, 3 at Bologna, 3 at Trent; as well as 2 at each of the following universities: Macerata, Palermo, Roma Tre, Turin; and 1 at each of the following universities: Catania, Florence, Pavia, Rome "La Sapienza", Siena and Venice.

University	Area	Degree Course	Teaching	Lecturer/Professor
Aldo Moro University of Bari	Law	5-Year Degree in Law	International Protection of Human Rights	Andrea Cannone
		MA in Designing Social Inclusion Policy	Citizenship and Human Rights	Giuseppe Campesi
	Political and social science	BA in Political Science, International Relations and European Studies	International Protection of Human Rights	Egeria Nalin
		MA in International Relations	Legal Philosophy, Human Rights and Religion in the Middle and Far East	Gianfranco Longo
	History, philosophy, pedagogy and psychology	MA in Philosophy	History of the Philosophy of Human Rights	Francesca Romana Recchia Luciani
University of Bologna	Political and social science	MA in Local and Global Development	Human Rights and Political Institutions	Francesco Raschi
		MA in International Cooperation on Human Rights and Intercultural Heritage	Political Power Beyond State Boundaries: Migration, Development and Human Rights	Annalisa Furia
			Public Law and Protection of Fundamental Rights	Caterina Drigo
			Justice, Multiculturalism and Human Rights	Gustavo Gozzi

University	Area	Degree Course	Teaching	Lecturer/Professor
University of Calabria	Political and social science	MA in Cooperation and Development	Theory of fundamental rights	Paola Stancati
University of Catania	Political and social science	MA in Global Politics and Euro-Mediterranean Relations	International Human Rights Law	Daniela Fisichella, Calogero Alfio Pettinato
University of Camerino	Economics and Statistics	BA in Social Sciences for Non-profit Organisations and International Cooperation	International Protection of Human Rights	Agostina Latino
University of Cassino and Southern Lazio	Law	5-Year Degree in Law	Fundamental Rights	Marco Plutino
University of Enna "Kore"	Law	BA in Strategic and Security Studies	General theory of human rights	Salvatore Curreri
University of Ferrara	Law	5-Year Degree in Law	Human rights and humanitarian law in armed conflicts	Francesco Salerno
University of Florence	Law	BA in Science of Law Services	Legal systems and protection of rights	Alessandra Sanna, Caterina Silvestri
			Welfare state and rights	Emilio Santoro, Maria Cristina Grisolia, Antonio Gorgoni

University	Area	Degree Course	Teaching	Lecturer/Professor
	History, philosophy, pedagogy and psychology	BA in Economic Development, International Social-Health Cooperation and Conflict Management	Human Rights and Armed Conflicts	Antonio Bultrini
University of Foggia	Law	BA in Investigative Science	Constitutional law – fundamental rights	Daniele Sebastiano Coduti
University of Genova	Law	5-Year Degree in Law	Rights to Freedom and Social Rights	Simona Rodriguez
			Tribunal Justice and fundamental rights	Michele Marcheselli
	Political and social science	MA in International studies and Cooperation	Protection of human rights	Pierangelo Celle
University of Acquila	Economics and Statistics	BA in Economics	Theory of Interpretation and Fundamental Rights	Francesca Caroccia
University of Macerata	Political and Social Science	BA in Political Science and International Relations	Philosophy of Human Rights	Natascia Mattucci
		MA in Theories, Cultures and Techniques for Social Work	Social and Citizenship-related Rights	Angela Cossiri
	Law	MA in International Politics	Human Rights and Differences	Ines Corti

University	Area	Degree Course	Teaching	Lecturer/Professor
		MA in Global Politics and International Relations	International Human Rights	Laura Salvadego
			Human rights and constitutional adjudication	Benedetta Barbisan
University of Messina	Political and social science	MA in International Relations and Development Aid	International organisations and human rights	Carmela Panella
Sacro Cuore (Sacred Heart) Catholic University Milan	Politics and social science	BA in Politics and International Relations	International protection of Human rights	Monica Spatti
	Law	5-Year Degree in Law	Human Rights	Pasquale De Sena
University of Milan	Political and social science	BA in International Studies and European Institutions	International Protection of Human Rights	Ilaria Viarengo
		BA in Administration and Management	Theory of Equality and Rights	Alessandra Facchi, Beatrice Magni
		BA in Politics	Theory and Practice of Human Rights	Nicola Riva
		BA in Social Science for Globalisation	Fundamental Rights (Jean Monnet course)	Davide Galliani
	Law	MA in Law and MA in Sustainable Development	EU law on business and human rights	Angelica Bonfanti

University	Area	Degree Course	Teaching	Lecturer/Professor
			Sociology of Human Rights and the Ombudsman	Alessandra Raffi, Marco A. Quiroz Vitale
University of Milan-Bicocca	Political and social science	MA in Sociology	Citizenship: rights, conflicts, gender	Marina Calloni
		MA in Planning and Managing Social Policy and Social Services	Cooperation and human rights protection	Gabriella Citroni
	Law	5-Year Degree in Law	International protection of human rights	Gabriella Citroni
University of Modena and Reggio Emilia	Law	5-Year Degree in Law	Theory and practice of human rights	Thomas Casadei
Università degli Studi del Molise	Political and social science	BA in Media Studies	Human rights and globalisation	Lorenzo Scillitani
Second University of Naples	Law	BA in Legal Services	Constitutional law and protection of human rights	Maria Pia Ladicicco
Federico II University of Naples	Political and social science	MA in Social Services and Policy	International Protection of Human and Social Rights	Fabio Ferraro
University of Padova	Political and social science	BA in Politics, International Relations and Human Rights	Human Rights	Elena Pariotti
			Public Policy and Human Rights	Paola Degani
			Society, Religion and Human Rights	Giuseppe Giordan
			Economic Development and Human Rights	Mario Pomini

University	Area	Degree Course	Teaching	Lecturer/Professor
			International Protection of Human Rights	Paolo De Stefani
			Human Rights and Inclusion	Laura Nota
		MA in European and Global Studies	Fundamental Rights and Citizenship	Costanza Margiotta Broglio Massucci
		MA in Human Rights and Multi-Level Governance	European Union Law and Human Rights	Paolo Piva
			Human Rights and International Justice	Costanza Margiotta Broglio Massucci
			International Law of Human Rights	Paolo De Stefani
			Women's Human Rights	Paola Degani
			Culture, Society and Human Rights	Andrea Maria Maccarini
			Economic Globalization and Human Rights	Roberto Antonietti
			Human Rights Governance	Léonce Maria Bekemans/ Pietro de Perini
			Human Rights Practice	Sara Pennicino
			Refugee Human Rights Protection	Lisa Maria Heschl

University	Area	Degree Course	Teaching	Lecturer/ Professor
			Religions and Human Rights	Giuseppe Giordan
	Law	5-Year Degree in Law	Human Rights and Public Ethics	Umberto Vincenti
University of Palermo	Law	5-Year Degree in Law	Human Rights	Clelia Bartoli
	Political and social science	BA in Cooperation and Development	Human Rights: Theory and Policies	Serena Marcenò
University of Parma	Law	5-Year Degree in Law	Constitutional Potection of Rights	Paola Torretta
	Political and social science	MA in International and European Relations	International protection of fundamental rights	Laura Pineschi
University of Pavia	Law	5-Year Degree in Law	Constitutional Justice and fundamental rights	Francesco Rigano
	Political and social science	MA in Economic Development and International Relations	Human rights and international justice	Carola Ricci
University of Perugia	Political and social science	MA in International Relations	Human Rights, Crime and International Humanitarian Law	Amina Maneggia
		Degree in Social Services	Public law institutions and Fundamental Rights	Alessandra Valstro
	Law	MA in European Judicial Intergration and Human Rights	Protection of Human Rights in the European Judicial Space	Simone Vezzani
University of Pisa	Law	5-Year Degree in Law	Multilevel protection of human rights	Elena Malfatti

University	Area	Degree Course	Teaching	Lecturer/Professor
Guido Carli Free International University of Social Studies – LUISS	Law	5-Year Degree in Law	International protection of human rights	Pietro Pustorino
Maria SS. Assunta Libera University - LUMSA	Political and social science	Degree in International and Political Science	Fundamental freedoms and rights	Marco Olivetti
		MA in International Relations	International Law and Protection of Human Rights	Roberta Greco
Roma Tre University	Political and social science	BA in Political Science for Cooperation and Development	International organisation and protection of human rights	Cristiana Carletti
		MA in International Studies	Theory of human rights	Francesco Maiolo
	Law	5-Year Degree in Law	European Constitutions and Human Rights	Mauro Palma
			Constitutional rights and freedoms	Daniele Chinni
			International Human Rights Law	Giuseppe Palmisano
			Protection of personal data and fundamental rights – legal privacy Clinic	Carlo Colapietro

University	Area	Degree Course	Teaching	Lecturer/Professor
La Sapienza University of Rome	Political and social science	MA in Development and International Cooperation Sciences	Human rights and bioethics	Luca Marini
			European Union Law and Human Rights	Alessandra Mignolli
		MA in International Relations	International Human Rights Law	Luigino Manca
Tor Vergata University of Rome	Political and social science	BA in Global Governance	Fundamental rights	Andrea Buratti
University of Salento	Political and social science	BA in International Relations and Political Science	Human rights	Attilio Pisanò
		MA in Geopolitical and International Studies	Theory and Practice of Human Rights	Attilio Pisanò
University of Salerno	Law	5-Year Degree in Law	Human Rights	Stefano Pietropaoli
			Human Rights and Biolaw	Anna Malomo
			Rights of the Person	Maria Antonietta Urcioli
University of Siena	Political and social science	MA in International Studies	International protection of human rights	Federico Lenzerini
		MA in Public and Cultural Diplomacy	Rule of law and human rights	Federico Lenzerini
University of Torino	Political and social science	MA in Sociology	Theories of human rights	Valentina Pazé

University	Area	Degree Course	Teaching	Lecturer/Professor
		MA in Area & global studies for international cooperation	Fundamental rights in Latin America	Mia Caielli
		MA in International Studies	Human rights and immigration	Alessandra Algostino
			History of human rights	Franco Motta
			Fundamental rights in Europe	Joerg Luther
		MA in Social Policy and Social Services	Citizenship, social rights, justice	Franco Prina, Valeria Ferraris
			Vulnerable People and the Protection of Rights	Maurizio Riverditi
University of Trent	Political and social science	BA in International Studies	International Relations and Human Rights	Alessia Donà
		MA in European and International Studies	Human rights and natural resources under international law	Marco Pertile
			Democratizing Security: Human Rights, Democracy and the Rule of Law in the Age of Uncertainty	Michele Nicoletti
	Law	BA in Comparative, European and International Legal Studies	Multilevel Protection of Fundamental Rights	Roberto Toniatti
University of Udine	Law	5-Year Degree in Law	Theory of Human Rights	Giovanni Turco

University	Area	Degree Course	Teaching	Lecturer/Professor
Carlo Bo University of Urbino	Political and social science	MA in Management of Policy, Social Services and Intercultural Mediation	Fundamental Rights: history, theory and practice	Giuseppe Giliberti
Ca' Foscari University of Venezia	Political and social science	MA in Comparative International Relations	European Human rights policies and instruments	Luisella Pavan, Sara de Vido
University of Verona	Political and social science	MA in Social Services in challenging environments	Social and Citizenship-related Rights.	Marco Peruzzi
			Protection of Fundamental Rights	Stefano Catalano

Source: elaboration by the 2019 Yearbook research and editorial committee based on data from the prospectuses of each university.

Doctoral programmes (academic year 2018–2019)

University	Name	Area of scientific discipline
University of Camerino, School of Advanced Studies	Doctorate in Legal and Social Sciences-Curriculum Fundamental rights in the global society	M-STO/02; M-STO/04; M-DEA/01; M-FIL/03; M-FIL/06; IUS/04; IUS/08; IUS/09; IUS/13 - IUS/21 SECS-P/01; SECS P/02; SECS-P/04; SPS/01; SPS/02; SPS/04; SPS/06; SPS/07; SPS/11; SPS/12
University of Florence	Theory and history of law – Theory and history of human rights	IUS/18, IUS/19, IUS/20

University	Name	Area of scientific discipline
University of Padova, Western Sydney University (Australia), University of Zagrab (Croatia), Nicosia University (Cyprus)	Joint Ph.D Degree in Human Rights, Society, and Multi-level Governance	IUS/13: IUS/20; IUS/21; SPS/04; SPS/08; SECS-P/01
University of Palermo	International Doctorate in Human rights: evolution, protection and limits	IUS/01, IUS/09, IUS/12, IUS/20, SPS/02, IUS/13, IUS/19, IUS/10, SPS/09, SECS-P/01, IUS/08
Amedeo Avogadro University of Eastern Piedmont	Local autonomies, public services and citizenship rights	IUS/05, IUS/08, IUS/09, IUS/10, IUS/21
Sant'Anna School of Advanced Studies of Pisa	Human Rights and Global Politics: Legal, Philosophical and Economic Challenges	SPS/01, SPS/06, IUS/13, IUS/03, IUS/14, SPS/04, SECS-P/02, SECS-P/06, SECS-P/08
La Sapienza University of Rome	International order and human rights	IUS/13, IUS/14, IUS/08, IUS/07, IUS/01
University of Salerno	Comparative Law and Rights of the Person	IUS/01, IUS/02, IUS/07, IUS/13, IUS/14, IUS/16, IUS/17
University of Macerata	Global studies: justice, rights, politics	IUS/21, M-FIL/03, SPS/01, SPS/04, SPS/09, IUS/13, SPS/03, IUS/03, SECS-P/06, SECS-P/08

Source: elaboration by the *2019 Yearbook* research and editorial committee.

Master's degree programmes - postgraduate

University	Name	Level
University of Bologna	Human rights, migration and development	I
	Constitutional justice and human rights	I
European Inter-University Centre for Human Rights and Democratisation (EIUC, 41 European partner universities)	European Master's degree in human rights and democratisation E.MA - Master europeo in diritti umani e democratizzazione	I
Sant'Anna School of Advanced Studies of Pisa	Human rights and conflict management	I
University of Siena	Global governance, inter-cultural relations and peace-process management	I
University of Bari - Aldo Moro	Peace ethics, rights and protection of the person in productive educational and economic contexts	I
La Sapienza University of Rome	"Maria Rita Saulle" International protection of human rights	II
Italian Society for International Organisation (SIOI)	International relations and international protection of human rights	-

Source: elaboration by the *2019 Yearbook* research and editorial committee.

Sub-national Human Rights Structures

I. Peace Human Rights Offices in Municipalities, Provinces and Regions

At the sub-national level, especially by virtue of the inclusion of the "peace human rights norm" in thousands of Municipal, Provincial and Regional Statutes and of the adoption of dedicated regional laws on this topic (see Part I, Italian Law, III), Italy has a number of local consultancies, offices, departments, bureaus and centres for human rights, peace, equal opportunity, development cooperation, fair trade and international solidarity. From a subsidary point of view, these structures contribute to implementing the Agenda 2030 for sustainable development, with particular reference to Goals 5 (Gender Equality), 11 (Sustainable Cities and Communities) and 16 (Peace, Justice and Strong Institutions).

In 2018, an important initiative that interested many peace human rights offices at a local level concerned establishing "shelter cities" (*città rifugio*) for human rights defenders, based on the *Shelter City Initiative* of the NGO "Justice and Peace", which has been running in the Netherlands since 2012. The initiative aims to creates temporary reception, refuge and training programmes and opportunities for human rights defenders who are at risk across the world. The initiative was promoted by the network "In Defence of: for human rights and those who defend them" (*In Difesa di: per i diritti umani e chi li difende*) (see *Yearbook 2018*, p. 79–80). In 2018, the provincial council of Trent (followed by the city council) and the city councils of Padova, Rubano, Noventa Padovana, Cadoneghe Ponte San Nicolò and Asiago in Veneto adopted the motion on "shelter cities".

> By way of an example, the motion on "shelter cities" that was adopted by the Padova city council on 10 December 2018 commits the local authorities to:
>
> – adhere to the proposal to build a Padova territorial node to establish a pilot scheme on the territory for temporary welcoming and support for human

rights defenders threatened, able to collect different territorial availability, in collaboration with the network "In Defence of – for human rights and those defends them", and other interested local Italian administrations and present and active civil society organisations;
- promote study, training and exchange opportunities between local administrations, civil society organisations and universities (also making use of the Memorandum of Understanding 5.12.2017 between the Padova City Council and the Human Rights Centre "Antonio Papisca" of the University of Padova) on the role of local administration in the protection of human rights defenders and shelter cities;
- promote awareness initiatives for human rights in schools of all levels intended as education to assuming responsibility for fulfilling roles of active and democratic citizenship;
- solicit the national Government for active protection programmes for human rights defenders, strengthening the initiative of the Italian Diplomatic Corps for the implementation of EU and OSCE guidelines, and adhere to the Temporary Relocation Platform of the European Union;
- foresee support initiatives for programmes and aid projects and protection for human rights defenders in third countries via cooperation instruments, which is key to fulfilling the Sustainable Development Goals;
- send this motion to ANCI and the Region-State Conference to encourage local authorities to commit to protecting human rights defenders and creating temporary refuge opportunities for at-risk activists and for decentralised cooperation programmes in third countries.

II. Ombudspersons in the Italian Regions and Provinces

In 2018, there were 16 incumbent Ombudspersons (or Human Rights Authorities which also fulfil the duties of an Ombudsperson), of a total of 19 Regions and Autonomous Provinces (17+2) whose respective Statues or specific regional laws included provisions for such an institution: Abruzzo, Aosta Valley, Basilicata, Emilia-Romagna, Lazio, Liguria, Lombardy, Marche (Ombudsperson), Molise, Piedmont, Sardinia, Tuscany and Veneto (Ombudsperson for Human Rights, see this Part, Region of Veneto, VI), as well as the Autonomous Provinces of Bolzano and Trent. The post is currently vacant in Umbria. No Ombudsperson has ever been appointed in Calabria and Apulia. No legislative provision has been made for the role by the Regions of Sicily and Trentino-Alto Adige (where, however, the Region has delegated full responsibility in their respective territories to the Ombudspersons of the Autonomous Provinces), while in Friuli-Venezia Giulia, the laws establishing this institution was abrogated in 2008 (r.l. 14 August 2008, No. 9). Pending the establishment of the role of National Ombudsperson, these Regional Ombudpersons, alongside the National Coordinating Body of Ombudspersons (see this Part, Sub-national Human Rights Structures, III) and other guarantee figures who work in the field of children's and detainees' rights on a territorial level (see this Part, Sub-national Human Rights Structures, IV, and Region of Veneto, VI), contribute to Italy's commitment to build effective institutions at all levels for peace, justice and human rights, as established by Goal 16 of the Agenda 2030, and in particular target 16.10 (Ensure public access to information and protect fundamental freedoms, in accordance with national legislation and international agreements).

> At European and international levels, in 2017, the European Ombudsman Institute (EOI) confirmed as members of its Executive Committee: Gabriele Morandell, Ombudsperson of the Autonomous Province of Bolzano, Antonia Fiordelisi, Ombudsperson of the Region of Basilicata, Daniela Longo, Ombudsperson of the Autonomous Province of Trent, and Vittorio Gasparrini, Office of the Ombudsperson of the Region of Tuscany. Furthermore, the Provincial Ombudspersons of the Autonomous Provinces of Bolzano and Trent and the Regional Ombudspersons of Aosta Valley, Lombardy and Tuscany are members of the International Ombudsman Institute (IOI).

III. National Coordinating Body of Ombudspersons

The National Coordinating Body of Regional and Autonomous Provinces Ombudspersons is an associative body working to harmonise and enhance the institutional role of the Ombudsperson in Italy and to guarantee every citizen, regardless of where he or she resides, protection in dealing with the public administration at all levels, whether State, regional or local.

The Coordinating Body is made up of the incumbent Ombudspersons in the Regions and the Autonomous Provinces. It operates through the office of the Ombudsperson and is collectively elected on a case-by-case basis. Its headquarters are in Rome, at the Network of the Presidents of the Legislative Assemblies of the Regions and the Autonomous Provinces, where it usually meets. The Coordinating Body also intervenes by order of the European Ombudsperson (see Part III, European Union, VIII) at the central offices of the State and of those Regions and Italian local authorities without a regional or local Ombudsperson. Furthermore, it represents the Italian Ombudsperson with the European Ombudsperson and it also links up with the other European Ombudspersons through a liaison officer. On 14 February 2017, the Coordinating Body elected the Ombudsperson of the Region of Abruzzo, Fabrizio di Carlo, as its new President. The Vice-Presidents are Daniela Longo, Ombudsperson of the Autonomous Province of Trent, and Enrico Formento Dojot, Ombudsperson of Aosta Valley.

Other than the regular meeting held in Rome to discuss questions of development and problems related to the working of civil defence in Italy, delegations of the Coordinating Body have participated in a series of activities throughout the year: the IOI Conference on Human Rights in the Digital Age on the impact of the digital world on the exercising of rights towards public administration (Tallinn, 2 February 2018), the Annual Conference of the European Network of Ombudsmen organised by the European Ombudsman Emily O'Reilly (Bruxelles, 8–9 March 2018), the *Fundamental Rights Forum* (Vienna, 25–27 September 2018), and the Congress of French-speaking *Ombudsman* "Twenty Years at the service of Ombudsman and the rule of law" (Bruxelles, 12 November).

Furthermore, on 15 March, a meeting of the Coordinating Body delegation and the President of the IOI-Europe, Rafael Ribò, was held in Milan, where the situation of Ombudspersons in Italy (bearing in mind there is still no national Ombudsperson) and the relationship between the Coordinating Body and the IOI were discussed. Concerning the latter question, the participants evaluated the possibility of bringing the Coordinating Body into the IOI board as a host, in order to represent Italy's point of view and bring a practical contribution to assessing and further deepening the issues handled by the Institute. This possibility was confermed on 8 June 2018 with the appointment of Vice Chair of the Coordinating Body and Ombudsperson of the Aosta Valley, Enrico Formento Dojot as host to the board of the IOI.

On 12 July, the Coordinating Body organised the Convention "Civic Access, Confidentiality and Guarentee Bodies", on the initiative of the Conference of the President of the Legislative Assembly of the autonomous regions and provinces". On 9 November, the Ombudspersons of the three territories of Euregio, Trentino, Alto Adige and Tirol met in Trent with the Secretary General of Euregio, Christoph von Ach, to exchange ideas and good practices and to discuss local and European legislation on access to documents and data protection.

At the time of writing this *Yearbook 2019*, the third periodic report of the National Coordinating Body on Ombudspersons has not been presented yet to the Italian Parliament.

IV. Network of Ombudspersons for Children and Adolescents

As of today, 18 Regions and the Autonomous Provinces of Trent and Bolzano have approved legislation introducing a local Ombudsperson for Children and Adolescents at a regional level. Ombudspersons have actually been nominated in 18 Regions (Apulia, Basilicata, Calabria, Campania, Emilia-Romagna, Friuli-Venezia Giulia, Lazio, Liguria, Lombardy, Marche, Molise, Piedmont, Sardinia, Sicily, Umbria, Veneto and the Autonomous Provinces of Trent and Bolzano). Some of these are exclusively tasked with ensuring rights for children and adolescents (Apulia, Basilicata, Calabria, Campania, Emilia-Romagna, Lazio, Lombardy, Molise, Sardinia, Sicily, Tuscany, Umbria and the Autonomous Province of Bolzano), whereas others have additional competence in areas such as those dealt with by Ombudspersons and/or ensuring rights for persons whose personal freedom is restricted (Friuli-Venezia Giulia, Liguria, Marche, Veneto and the Autonomous Province of Trent).

> The approval of l. 12 July 2011, No. 112 established the figure of Ombudsperson for Children and Adolescents at the national level (see this Part, National Bodies with Jurisdiction over Human Rights, VII, D) and formally defined and established the National Network for the Protection of the Rights of Children and Adolescents, made up of the Regional Ombudspersons for Children (or equivalent).
>
> The Network is tasked with creating common lines of action to protect the rights of children and adolescents for regional and national Ombudspersons, to be promoted and supported at the international level. It is also charged with identifying ways of ensuring a constant exchange of data and information on the condition of minors living in Italy. The Network has drawn up a set of internal regulations governing its functioning.

National Conference for the Protection of the Rights of Children and Adolescents is coordinated by the National Authority. During 2018, it met three times (January, June and November) to discuss common themes of interest.

V. National Coordinating Body of Local Authorities for Peace and Human Rights

Founded on 12 October 1986, the National Coordinating Body of Local Authorities for Peace and Human Rights is the largest Italian network of municipalities, provinces and regions involved in promoting peace and human rights: it is a unique experience in Europe and worldwide. The Coordinating Body is chaired by Andrea Ferrari and directed by Flavio Lotti.

In 2018, the Coordinating body opened and closed with an appeal to once again take up the compass of human rights. Throughout the year, there were hundreds of initiatives, marches, assembleys, training courses, debates, lessons, press conferences, resolutions, position statements, reflections, appeals and interventions.

The 70th anniversary of the Universal Declaration of Human Rights proved an opportunity to plan and carry out a vast Plan of Action with five goals:

1. develop an extraordinary activity scheme for education, training, information and commitment to human rights, encouraging every person and institution, school, university, local and regional authorities, media, associations, the cultural world, Government and Parliament to assume more responsibility;
2. promote the commitment, activism, creativity and behaviour of young people in the defence and realisation of human rights, also relating to developing the social and civic competences needed to tackle the challenges of the present day;
3. promote the commitment of journalists, the media world, and especially the public broadcasting service RAI in the defence and promotion of "all human rights for all";
4. promote the commitment of local and regional authorities for implementing the local political agenda of human rights, fostering the inclusion of citizens and encouraging diplomacy in cities;
5. promote the committment of Italy and the European Union in realising the political agenda of human rights.

The most important event was the Perugia-Assisi March for Peace and Fraternity, which took place on Sunday 7 October 2018. It was organised and promoted by the Coordinating Body and Table of Peace, in collaboration with the University of Padova Human Rights Centre, the National Network of Schools for Peace and many others.

Over one hundred thousand people took part in the march: young people, children, students, teachers, schools, citizens, groups, associations, local and regional authorities from all over Italy to promote human rights and reassert that "All human beings are born free and equal in dignity and rights [...]and should act towards one another in a spirit of brotherhood". The organising committee collected 990 adhesions: 172 Schools; 287 Municipalities, Provinces and Regions; and 531 Associations.

On 5 and 6 October, as a forerunner to the march was the National Meeting "Rights and Responsabilities", which saw more than 3500 young people reflecting on the national and global situation and discussing how to tackle the challenges ahead.

To mark the end of the Year of Human Rights, on 10 December 2018, over 500 initiatives were organised on the occasion of the National Mobilisation day for Human Rights, with two hundred thousand people taking part in schools, universities, local authorities, streets and squares across Italy. On the invitation of the Coordinating Body, many local authorities discussed and approved the agenda to reaffirm their commitment to human rights. Many municipalities have adhered to the "a Declaration in every pocket" campaign, giving a copy of the Universal Declaration of Human Rights, the UN Declaration on human rights defenders and the Italian Constitution to all students in the territory.

Another important event from 2018 concerning human rights commitment was the Meeting of Peace in the Trenches of the Great War. On 16 March 2018, a thousand students and teachers in Friuli-Venezia Giulia, between 8 and 20 years old, participated in a peace protest against war, violence and the indifference to the centenary of the end of the First World War. There were also accounts by witnesses to massacres of our times: wars and also work accidents and deaths, violence against women and violence against migrants.

The Meeting of Peace in the Trenches of the Great War is an integrant part of the multi-year education programme of peace and citizenship called "From the Great War to the Great Peace" carried out in Friuli-Venezia Giulia from 2014. The programme involved 590 teachers and 113 schools across the region.

VI. Archives and Other Regional Projects for the Promotion of a Culture of Peace and Human Rights

Besides the "Pace Diritti Umani - Peace Human Rights" Archive of the Region of Veneto, established by r.l. 18/1988 and managed by the University of Padova Human Rights Centre (see this Part, Region of Veneto, IV), there are other more recent archives and similar projects set up by Italian Regions and Autonomous Provinces to foster the promotion and dissemination of a culture of human rights and peace.

The "Peace and Human Rights" project in the Region of Emilia-Romagna was set up by the Regional Council in collaboration with the Department for Social Policies, Immigration, Youth Projects and International Cooperation and the Regional Governments Management Control and Statistics Systems Department. The project has been managed by the Europe Direct Centre of the Legislative Assembly of Emilia-Romagna since 2013 and follows the principles laid out in r.l. 24 June 2002, No. 12 (Regional interventions for cooperation with developing countries and countries in transition, international solidarity and the promotion of a culture of peace). It aims to support activities described in the law. The commitment of the Legislative Assembly is illustrated in the page "Pace e Diritti" ("Peace and Rights") of the Europe Direct Centre of Emilia-Romagna, which also provides citizens with a repository of documents and videos on the topic (www.assemblea.emr.it/europedirect/pace-e-rights).

The commitment of the Regional Legislative Assembly of Emilia-Romagna for the promotion and protection of human rights has continued via support and organisation of numerous activities and initiatives. In the two-year period 2017–2018, the educational course "Rights are born" (*"Diritti si nasce"*) which includes a workshop for primary and middle school students held by two operators of the Emilia-Romagna Europe Direct Centre in the classroom, and an e-learning course reserved for teachers on the theme of European citizenship and the European Union Charter of Fundamental Rights. Furthermore, the Europe Direct Centre promoted various activities in 2018, including the XV edition of the "René Cassin" graduation prize on fundamental rights and human development for professional training, the 2018 edition of the photography competition "EurHope", and the training initiatives themed for students on how the European Union institutions and politics work within the project "Crossing Europe".

The "*Forum Trentino per la pace e i diritti umani*" ("Trentino for Peace and Human Rights Forum") standing body was established in 1991 at the behest of the Provincial Council of Trent with p.l. 10 June 1991, No. 11 (Promoting and disseminating the culture of peace). Website: http://www.forumpace.it/.

> The annual theme approved during the 2018 Forum Assembly *Resistere Oggi* ("Resisting Today"). It aimed to commemorate the 100-year anniversary of the end of the First World War and 70 years from the adoption of the Universal Declaration of Human Rights, and to reflect on the global climate of violence that is damaging the human rights won over time. During this assembly, the Forum launched a public call for proposals for associations registered with them, individual or in partnership, to develop projects that foster a culture of peace starting from everyday activities that any person could participate in. Furthermore, in 2018, the Forum supported the initiative to make the city of Trent the first "city of refuge" for Italian human rights defenders (see this Part, Sub-national Human Rights Structures, I).

Region of Veneto

The Region of Veneto has been operating organically for the promotion of human rights, the culture of peace and international cooperation since 1988, the year when the first regional law on such issues was adopted in Italy (r.l. 30 March 1988, No. 18). In 1999, r.l. 18/1988 was replaced by the current r.l. 16 December 1999, No. 55, on "Regional measures for the promotion of human rights, a culture of peace, development cooperation and solidarity and then with the current R.l. 21 June 2018, No. 21 (Regional intervention for the promotion of human rights and sustainable development cooperation)".

With r.l. 24 December 2013, No. 37, the Region established the post of *Regional Ombudsperson for the Rights of the Person* which integrates the functions of the Ombudsperson, of the Ombudsperson for Children and Adolescents (both created in 1988 and working for the implementation of the aforementioned r.l. 37/2013), as well as those of promotion and protection of the rights of persons deprived of their liberty.

In the context of the Regional Government, issues concerning human rights pertain to the Councillor on Social Services, programme implementation and relations with the Regional Council, a post currently held by Manuela Lanzarin. Measures and activities concerning international relations and development cooperation are overseen directly by the Regional Governor, Luca Zaia.

Article 2 of the new R.l. 21/2018 commits the Veneto region to promoting and sustaining the following within the territory:

a) cultural, informative, awareness, research, training and education initiatives regarding human rights, fundamental freedoms and sustainable development cooperation;

b) collecting, sorting and disseminating studies, research, publications, multi-media and documents produced in regional, national and international headquarters, in relation to other databases, on the topic of promoting and human rights and sustainable development cooperation;

c) database of human rights and sustainable developement coordination organisations working in Veneto;
d) participating [...] in projects on development cooperation, in the field of the application of public development cooperation [...] including participating in the cooperation programmes of the European Union;

To this end, the new law institutes the Regional Table on human rights and sustainable development cooperation (Article 5) with advisory status on the regional programming and on consultancy concerning regional institutions. It promotes and supports the Venice Foundation for Research on Peace (Article 8) and the work of the European Commission for Democracy through Law (*Venice Commission*) of the Council of Europe (Article 7). The regional infrastructure for peace and human rights also includes the Commission for achieving equality between men and women, the Regional Observatory on Immigration, and the Peace Human Rights Archive (established by law 18/1988).

The r. l. 23 April 2013, No. 5 (Regional Intervention to prevent and combat violence against women) established a Regional Coordination Table for Preventing and Combating Violence against Women within the Regional Government. In implementing this law, the Region has financed requests received for the year 2018 from 22 anti-violence centres and 21 shelters. In close collaboration with the Coordinating Body, in September 2018, the regional council adopted a network protocol for the fight against violence against women in the Veneto region. The aims of the protocol are to build a terriorial network between institutions, local authorities, support structures for women victims of violence (r.l. 5/2013) and profit and non-profit organisations, and to promote common operative strategies for intervention and combat of violence against women, with or without underage children, in order to identify the most efficient intervention method for each party to adopt, all of whom have their own priorities, fields of competency and expertise.

By way of r.l. 28 December 1998, No. 33, the Region promotes and supports financially the European Masters degree Programme in Human Rights and Democratisation (E.MA), located in Venice. With the adoption of r.l. 22 January 2010, No. 6, the Region has recognised the social and cultural value of fair trade, proclaiming its support for the organisations which operate in this sector.

I. Department for International Relations, Communications and SISTAR

Among other things, the Department is responsible for the implementation of r.l. 55/1999. In 2017, the Director managing this structure was Diego Vecchiato.

> The Regional Section oversees a series of international activities undertaken by the Region, including: the management of international relations; the signature of memoranda of understanding with national and foreign institutions; participating in international bodies and initiatives, participating in the European Group of Territorial Cooperation "Euregio Senza Confini", programming and/or managing of the regional interventions about international solidarity, fair trade and human rights, the culture of peace, promoting equal opportunities and protectinv of linguistic minorities. The Section also hosts the Veneto Regional Committee for UNICEF.

During 2018, among the other activities of communication and promotion of human rights, the Department published a report on the use of educational vouchers allocated during the year in question. During this period, the Region allocated a total of 70,000 euros to finance 100 vouchers to create educational courses in schools in the regional territory (35 in secondary (middle) schools, 30 in secondary (high) schools and 35 in primary schools) on the following macro-themes: women's rights and gender issues, bullying and cyber-bullying, non-discrimination and social-cultural integration and children's rights. The vouchers were introduced in 2014 to create opportunities for schools and associations in the region to meet and compare ideas on human rights issues.

II. Committee for Human Rights and the Culture of Peace

Established pursuant to Article 12 of r.l. 55/1999, the Committee is tasked with drawing up the three-year programmes and annual plans regarding initiatives of the Region of Veneto on human rights and a culture of peace (Article 13). The Committee comprises representatives from local authorities, civil society, academia, the business world and social partners. With the implementation of the new r.l. 21/2018, the Committee will be replaced by the Regional Table on Human Rights and Sustainable Development Cooperation.

With d.g.r. No. 573 of 30 April 2018, the regional council adopted the Annual Implementation plan for regional interventions for promoting human rights and a culture of peace. The plan has been allocated a total fund of 100,000 euros for its activites. In fulfilment of r.l. 55/1999, this financial support allowed the "Peace Human Rights" Archieve to assign 100 vouchers to create educational courses promoting human rights in schools in Veneto (see this Part, Region of Veneto, I). However, it was not possible to establish other direct regional initiatives promoting human rights or to fund public calls for initiatives. Among the other requirements laid out by R.l. 55/1999, the Action Plan that was developed within the three-year Regional Human Rights programme 2016–2018 (see *Yearbook 2017*, p. 127–128) underlines its commitment to the regional prize "Veneto for Peace and solidarity among peoples" and adhesion to the "Venice Foundation for Research on Peace". In 2018, both initiatives did not foresee the allocation of funding. The prize was given to Irma Dall'Armellina, a ninety-three year old lady who travelled to Kenya to donate her time to help the children she had previously sponsored, as an example both of human solidarity that knows no limits – neither age nor borders – and for younger generations, as promoters and defenders of human rights in their everyday lives.

III. Committee for Development Cooperation

The Committee for Development Cooperation was established pursuant to Article 14 of r.l. 55/1999. The Committee is charged with contributing to the drafting of the three-year programmes and annual plans for decentralised development cooperation and international solidarity activities. The Committee comprises representatives from local administrations, civil society, academia, the business world and social partners.

In the framework of the regional three-year programme of 2016–2018 in the field of development cooperation (see *Yearbook 2017*, p. 128), with decision 30 April 2018, No. 526, the Regional Council adopted the new Annual Action Plan. €400,000 were allocated on the regional budget for 2017 to implement this Action Plan for decentralised cooperation interventions promoted by private organisations and bodies. In the area of fair trade, regional planning provided a budget of €90,000 for initiatives in 2018.

IV. Regional Table on Human Rights and Sustainable Development Cooperation

The Regional Table, established pursuant to Article 5 of the new R.l. 21/2018, has advisory competences on regional programming and advisory competences for regional bodies on human rights or development cooperation. These competences were implemented by the previous R.l. 55/1999, and until 2018 were realised by Committee for Human Rights and the Culture of Peace and by the Committee for Development Cooperation (see, in these Parts, 3.2 and 3.3).

With d.g.r. 10 December 2018, No. 1856, the Regional Council chose the expert members of the Table, who are as follows:

a) President of the Regional Council: Luca Zaia; b) two experts and two substitute experts (s) nominated by Veneto NGOs that are recognised by the Ministry of Foreign Affairs and International Cooperation: Leopoldo Rebellato; Daniele Brunelli; Elena Cracco (s), Andrea Danese (s); c) three experts and three substitute experts nominated by non-profit associations working in the region for at least three years whose constitution foresees human rights and sustainable development cooperation intiatives: Lucia Tonelotto; Giuseppe Piacenza; Kaoutar Badrane d) two experts and two substitute experts chosen by the Regional Council nominated by Veneto business associations: Mario Quaresimin, Alberto Bordignon; e) an expert and a substitute expert jointly nominated by the Universities of Veneto: Maria Caterina Baruffi; Stefania Tonin (s); f) the director of the University of Padova Human Rights Centre "Antonio Papisca", Marco Mascia; g) the Regional Guarantor for the rights of the person: Mirella Gallinaro; h) a representative and a substitute representative nominated by the Regional Commission for Equal Opportunities: Alessandro Giglio, Luciana Sergiacomi (s); j) two representatives and two substitutes jointly nominated by fair trade organisations subscribed to the regional list according to Article 4 of regional law 22 January 2010, No. 6: Marta Fracasso, Giorgio Scandiuzzo, Eleonora Dal Zotto (s), Stefano Toma (s); k) a representative and a substitute representative nominated by the Regional Associations of Veneto Municipalities (ANCI Veneto): Enrico Rinuncini; Michela Gottardo (s).

V. Venice for Peace Research Foundation

As was the Regional Archive, the Foundation was established by r.l. 18/1988 and reconfirmed by r.l. 55/1999. The Foundation's main goal is to carry out research, partly in collaboration with national and international institutions, on matters of security, development and peace.

In 2018, the Foundation continued to work on the *Blind Spots* project (see *Yearbook 2016*, p. 119) and "Dropping Seeds" (see *Yearbook 2018*, p. 133), published the fourth volume in the series "*Sapere l'Europa, sapere d'Europa*" ("Knowing Europe, knowing about Europe") entitled *Cultural Heritage. Scenarios 2015–2017*, edited by S. Pinton and L. Zagato, and the sixth volume in the series "*Il genocidio. Declinazioni e risposte di inizio secolo*" ("Genocide. Declinations and responses of the beginning of the century"), edited by L. Zagato and L. Candiotto.

VI. Human Rights Authority

The Human Rights Authority of the Region of Veneto was provided for by regional law 24 December 2013, No. 37 (Regional Human Rights Authority). The first and current Authority, Mirella Gallinaro, was appointed in early 2015.

The Authority brings together the functions of the Ombudsperson and of the Ombudsperson for Children and Adolescents and the activities of promoting, protecting and facilitating the fulfilment of the rights of persons subject to restrictions to their personal freedom.

Among the various initiatives carried out by the Authority, common to its three different functions, the following are of note:

- participating, as a member, in working and discussion meeting within the institutionalised coordinating bodies of the rights Ombudspersons equally competent in the area; i.e. the Network of Ombudspersons for Children and Adolescents (see this Part, 2.4), as well as the working meetings between the National Ombudsperson for the Rights of Persons in Prison or Deprived of Liberty and the equivalent territorial Ombudspersons created by Regions and Autonomous Provinces as provided for by l. 21 February 2014, No. 10 (Urgent measures concerning the protection of the fundamental rights of prisoners and the controlled reduction of the prison population);
- participating, as a member, in coordinating meetings of the Ombudspersons of the Regions and Autonomous Provinces of Trent and Bolzano (see this Part, Sub-national Human Rights Structures, II);

- participating, as a member, in coordinating meetings of regional Ombudspersons for the Rights of Persons in Prison or Deprived of Liberty, a free and spontaneous association between regional, provincial and municipal Ombudspersons with similar functions (four working meetings in 2018);
- promoting the coordinating, discussion and working meetings with Regional Ombudspersons for the Rights of Persons with Restricted or Limited Liberty, which are established in some municipalities in Veneto;
- participating, as a member, in observatories, inter-institutional round tables and committees established at a regional level;
- participating (including as a rapporteur) in meetings, seminars and round tables; these events all seek to gain an in-depth understanding of and promote debate on questions the Authority is already acting upon or on new emerging issues;
- providing information and consultancy, facilitating and mediating on public administration office procedures and activities as well as those of public service managers in the regional context, at the request of public or private entities.

In addition, in 2018, the Veneto Human Rights Authority implemented a series of initiatives that have differently affected the various areas of activities, including:

- promoting and running training courses for people suitable and prepared to take on the protection of minors, including the possible protection of unaccompanied foreign minors and applicants for international protection (in 2018, courses were held in Verona, Venice and Padova);
- coordinating the inter-institutional task-force supporting the needs of children in prison with their mothers; on 28 February, a meeting of the taskforce took place in the Venice Attenuated Custody Institute for Mothers which aimed at monitoring the operating protocol promoted by the ombudsperson in 2015 and considering possible updates for the protocol in the light of changes to the normative plan, the organisation of services and the titles of the offices involved;
- supporting and speaking at various conferences, public events, information campaigns and study days: the conference "Family Centered Care for the treatment of new-borns and children" (2 February); the theatre show "We need to go"("*Partir bisogna*") (9 February); the conference "Promoting and protecting the dignity and rights of children. Unaccompanied Foreign Minors. Law No.

47/2017" (17 March); the awareness campaign "in May I … trust" (May); the conference "Is welfare for children possible nowadays?" (31 May); the conference "Minors and Privacy. The protection of personal data of children and adolescents in the light of EU Reg. 2016/679" (22 November); the study day "Responsability. Everyone has their own." (10 May); and the conference "The complexity of the prison system: psychological distress in critical parts of the system" (19 December);

– signing a new Memorandum of Understanding between the Guarantor of the rights of the person of Veneto and the President of the Juvenile Court of Venice, on 8 March. It aimed to promote and facilitate the nomination of voluntary guardians for unaccompanied foreign minors (the protocol substitutes the previous version dated 29 June 2017, and transposes the amendments introduced by lgs.d. 22 December 2017, No. 22);

– supporting the "Terreferme Project. Foster Programme for Unaccompanied Minors", a pilot project of UNICEF and CNCA aiming at defining a foster family network to support second-line reception paths for minors who are currently living in immigration reception structures in Palermo (May);

– participating in the conference "Building the future day by day" "Il futuro si costruisce giorno per giorno", which concluded the European project "Prepare for leaving care". The Guarantor of the rights of the person of Veneto was the Italian partner of this project;

– joining and supporting the project "C.R.E.S.C.E.R.E." ("Building Relationships and Developing Experiences Shared with Empathy, Responsibility and Enthusiasm" 2009–2021), a longitudinal study that monitors a sample of children and families living in the Province of Padova and the Municipality of Rovigo during their transition from childhood to adolescence and towards adulthood. The annual seminar of the project "Growing up unequal: challenges and hope for the future" was promoted by the Zancan Foundation and was held in Padova on 6 December;

– promoting and implementing information seminars in the various penitentiary institutions in the Veneto region, with the aim of promoting a new and different culture of penalty among prisoners and prison workers. This culture effectively respects the dignity and fundamental rights of the persons with restricted liberty and effectively oriented towards the reintegration of the condemned person into the community, bearing in mind the conclusions reached by the National Assembly on the execution of sentences (*Stati Generali*).

Alongside initiatives taking a proactive approach to the protection human rights, traditional activities that are considered complementary to the former were also performed: accepting and managing reports, applications, complaints and requests for consultancy or guidance in the field of protecting the rights of physical and legal persons against public administrations and activities promoting, and protecting and facilitating the pursuit of rights for minors and the rights of persons subject to restricted personal liberty.

In 2018, the Authority published a report on the presence of detained persons in various penitiary institutes in Veneto, last updated data on 30 June 2018. The document was written from reports published by the Ministry of Justice and offers an analyis of the adult incarcerated population in the region: the total number of people, their gender, age, and nationality, the current capacity and the regulated capacity of every prison insitution.

VII. Regional Commission for Equal Opportunities between Men and Women

The Commission was established by r.l. 30 December 1987, No. 62, and it is the regional consultative body on gender policies for the actual implementation of the principles of equality and equal opportunities enshrined in the Constitution and Regional Statute. The Commission was established at the Veneto Regional Council and is chaired by Elena Traverso.

> The main task of the Commission is to carry out investigations and research into the condition of women in Veneto, with particular reference to issues involving employment, labour and professional training and to disseminate information on these areas. At the same time, the Commission respects its commitment to being present on the ground and to developing new synergies with all the actors and forces involved to promote and support the realisation of equal opportunities in the social, political and economic life of the population of Veneto. It may offer opinions on the current state of implementation of laws and on bills, as well as drawing up proposals of its own. The Veneto Equal Opportunities Commission carries out its mission in contact with other Commissions at the local, regional and national level and maintains a constant exchange with all women's organisations in the region.

Among the activities and the awareness initiatives promoted and supported by the Commission during 2018, the following are of note:

- conference "New electoral law and female representation ", organised in collaboration with the Equal Opportunities Council of Veneto network to further investigate and promote the new electoral law to the Chamber of Deputies and the Senate of the Republic, Venice, 14 January;
- *"Corsa Rosa"* "Pink Run" a charity walk for women promoted by UISP, Mestre, 4 March;
- Federmanager convention "Welfare and Conciliation" to demonstrate the levels of professionalism of women with reference to the Industry 4.0 plan, focusing on the topic of life/work balance, Verona, 8 March;
- "Maternity Festival", three days dedicated to understanding, spreading awareness and reflecting upon the importance of the first part of a baby's life, from conception to two years, Padova, 13–15 April;
- conference "Smart Working for smart sustainable cities", Florence, 17–18 October.

VIII. Regional Observatory on Immigration

The Observatory is a service within the Region of Veneto "Migratory Flows" organisational unit and is managed by Veneto Lavoro. Its establishment was included in the three-year plan 2007–2009 comprising measures and initiatives in the field of immigration, and was confirmed in subsequent three-year plans, pursuant to Article 3 of r.l. 9/1990 (Measures in the immigration sector).

The Observatory is a technical-scientific instrument aiming to monitor, analyse and disseminate data and information on migratory flows and integration at the regional and national level. To this end, it: collaborates with the other regional observatories which are affected in various ways by the migration phenomenon; assures the proper functioning and constant input for databases, the monitoring of immigration dynamics, further study on various thematic aspects, housing conditions, the social and educational integration of minors, schooling and training; it ensures updated reconnaissance of specialised laws, proposing training sessions to facilitate acquaintance with these laws and their correct implementation.

At the moment of writing this *Yearbook*, the fifteenth annual report on foreign immigration in Veneto (with data for 2018) is not yet available. For the latest published report, see *Yearbook 2018*, p. 137.

IX. Regional Archive «Pace Diritti Umani - Peace Human Rights»

The Regional Archive was created pursuant to r.l. 18/1988 and reconfirmed by the subsequent r.l. 55/1999. The Archive is managed by the University of Padova Human Rights Centre, It is one of the main instruments through which the Region of Veneto promotes the culture of human rights, peace, development cooperation and solidarity in Italy and abroad.

> The Archive works to collect, elaborate and publish documents, thematic databases and informational resources on topics regarding regional law, particularly through the regular updating of the portal "Archivio Pace Diritti Umani" (http://unipd-centrodirittiumani.it/en/), available in Italian and English, and the distribution of knowledge on human rights through multimedia tools and social networks. In addition, it oversees publication of books, teaching aids, in-depth studies and multimedia and offers technical and scientific support to the actors most closely involved in the promotion and practice of the culture of peace, especially as concerns initiatives promoted by teachers, education staff, schools and civil society organisations. In 2018, the Archive published and distributed 16 editions of the "peace human rights" newsletter in Italian and in English to a long and qualified mailing list.

In 2018, the Archive updated the databases available on its website, notably the Italian translations of the database of international legal instruments on human rights, humanitarian law, criminal law and refugee law; the associations and NGOs active in the field of human rights and development cooperation in Veneto; and the collection of national and international documents and publications for persons with disabilities. In addition to its usual activities of updating, providing in-depth studies and information, the Archive contributed to promoting the scientific journal of the University of Padova Human Rights Centre, *Peace Human Rights Governance (PHRG)*. The Archive also contributed to the publication and promotion of the 2017 edition of the *Italian Yearbook of Human Rights* in Italian and in English and the institutional presentation of this publication at the *Great School* of *Saint John* the *Evangelist* in Venice (20 November).

Furthermore in 2018, the Archive collaborated with national and international organisations and experts in organising a series of initiatives at the University of Padova, especially multimedia and documentary aspects. The following initiatives are noteworthy: the conference "Ministry of Peace: a governmental choice" (12 February); the meeting "Human Rights Defenders. The refugee city project and the role of local authorities and civil society organisations" (17 May); the student initiative "Face to Face with tomorrow. Meet Your Future" (31 May); the info day on the civil peace corps (19 September), the International Conference "Cities, Territories and the Struggles for Human Rights: a 2030 Perspective" (26–27 November), promotional activity for the *General course* "Human Rights and Inclusion" at the University of Padova for the academic year 2018/2019, the multimedia event celebrating Human Rights Day 2018 (10 December).

PART III

Italy in Dialogue with International Human Rights Institutions

The United Nations System

I. General Assembly

The General Assembly, which is the main deliberative body of the United Nations, comprises six Committees, each of which is made up of all 193 United Nations Member States. Human rights issues are handled mainly within the Third Committee (the Social, Humanitarian and Cultural Committee). The responsibilities of this Committee include issues such as torture and other cruel, inhuman and degrading treatment or punishment; the advancement of women; the rights of refugees and displaced persons; the promotion and protection of the rights of children; the rights of indigenous peoples; the elimination of racism, racial discrimination, xenophobia and related intolerance; the right of peoples to self-determination; and social development.

In December 2018, the 73rd General Assembly adopted 53 human rights resolutions (32 of which by consensus) that had already been debated and approved by the Third Committee in October and November, on a wide range of issues; from the rights of migrants to digital privacy, from protection against discrimination on the basis of sexual orientation and gender identity to special country situations.

In particular, the approval of two *Global Compacts* for refugees (Resolution A/RES/73/151, adopted with 181 votes in favour, including Italy, 2 against and 3 abstentions) and for safe, orderly and regular migration (Resolution A/RES/73/195, adopted with 152 votes in favour, 5 against and 12 abstentions, including Italy).

Since 31 July 2018, Italy's Permanent Representative to the United Nations in New York has been Ambassador Mariangela Zappia; the Deputy Permenant Representative is Ambassador Stefano Stefanile; First Counsellor Simona De Martino and First Secretary Ilario Schettino were responsible for following the activities of the Third Committee.

A. Resolutions on Human Rights - Italy's Voting Behaviour

As in the past, in 2018, Italy's action in support of human rights prioritised the following thematic areas: promotion of the rule of law and strengthening of democracy; the fight against torture, xenophobia, racism and all forms of discrimination, with specific attention to religious discrimination and intolerance; the rights and protection of children; the abolition of the death penalty; combating violence against women and female genital mutilation.

More specifically, Italy presented the resolution: Strengthening the United Nations crime prevention and criminal justice programme, in particular its technical cooperation capacity (A/RES/73/186). This resolution falls within the definition of Goal 16: promote peaceful and inclusive societies for sustainable development, provide access to justice for all and build effective, accountable and inclusive institutions at all levels.

Italy sponsored 37 resolutions and was asked to pass an open vote on 21 resolutions (11 votes in favour, 5 against, 5 abstentions), the outcome of which is shown below.

Subject	Resolution	Main sponsor of the Resolution	Information regarding Italy	Outcome of the Plenary Session
	A/RES/73/140 Volunteering for the 2030 Agenda for Sustainable Development	Brazil et al.	Co-sponsor of the Resolution	Adopted by consensus
Social Development	A/RES/73/141 mplementation of the outcome of the World Summit for Social Development and of the twenty-fourth special session of the GA	Egypt	Co-sponsor of the Resolution Voted in favour	188 in favour, 3 against, no abstentions

Subject	Resolution	Main sponsor of the Resolution	Information regarding Italy	Outcome of the Plenary Session
	A/RES/73/142 Inclusive development for and with persons with disabilities	Antigua and Barbuda et al.	Co-sponsor of the Resolution	Adopted by consensus
	A/RES/73/143 Follow-up to the Second World Assembly on Ageing	Canada et al.	Co-sponsor of the Resolution	Adopted by consensus
	A/RES/73/145 Literacy for life: shaping future agendas	Chile et al.	Co-sponsor of the Resolution	Adopted by consensus
Advancement of women	A/RES/73/146 Trafficking in women and girls	Belarus et al.	Co-sponsor of the Resolution	Adopted by consensus
	A/RES/73/147 Intensification of efforts to end obstetric fistula	China et al.	Co-sponsor of the Resolution	Adopted by consensus
	A/RES/73/148 Intensification of efforts to prevent and eliminate all forms of violence against women and girls: sexual harassment	Belize et al.	Co-sponsor of the Resolution	Adopted by consensus
	A/RES/73/149 Intensifying global efforts for the elimination of female genital mutilation	China et al.	Co-sponsor of the Resolution	Adopted by consensus

Subject	Resolution	Main sponsor of the Resolution	Information regarding Italy	Outcome of the Plenary Session
Refugees, displaced persons and humanitarian issues	A/RES/73/150 Assistance to refugees, returnees and displaced persons in Africa	Mozambique	Co-sponsor of the Resolution	Adopted by consensus
	A/RES/73/151 Office of the United Nations High Commissioner for Refugees	Belgium et al.	Co-sponsor of the Resolution Voted in favour	181 in favour, 2 against, 3 abstentions
Report of the Human Rights Council	A/RES/73/152 Report of the Human Rights Council	Mozambique	Abstention	121 in favour, 4 against, 60 abstentions
Promotion and protection of children's rights	A/RES/73/153 Child, early and forced marriage	Algeria et al.	Co-sponsor of the Resolution	Adopted by consensus
	A/RES/73/154 Protecting children from bullying	Brazil et al.	Co-sponsor of the Resolution	Adopted by consensus
	A/RES/73/155 Rights of the child	Albania et al.	Co-sponsor of the Resolution	Adopted by consensus
Rights of indigenous peoples	A/RES/73/156 Rights of indigenous peoples	Armenia et al.	Co-sponsor of the Resolution	Adopted by consensus

Subject	Resolution	Main sponsor of the Resolution	Information regarding Italy	Outcome of the Plenary Session
Elimination of racism, racial discrimination, xenophobia and related intolerance	A/RES/73/157 Combating glorification of Nazism, neo-Nazism and other practices that contribute to fuelling contemporary forms of racism, racial discrimination, xenophobia and related intolerance	Russian Federation	Abstention	129 in favour, 2 against, 54 abstentions
	A/RES/73/262 A global call for concrete action for the total elimination of racism, racial discrimination, xenophobia and related intolerance and the comprehensive implementation of and follow-up to the Durban Declaration and Programme of Action	Egypt and China	Abstention	120 in favour, 11 against, 41 abstentions

Subject	Resolution	Main sponsor of the Resolution	Information regarding Italy	Outcome of the Plenary Session
The right to self-determination	A/RES/73/158 The right of the Palestinian people to self-determination	Bolivia et al.	Co-sponsor of the Resolution Voted in favour	172 in favour, 6 against, 11 abstentions
	A/RES/73/159 Use of mercenaries as a means of violating human rights and impeding the exercise of the right of peoples to self-determination	Cuba	Voted against	129 in favour, 53 against, 10 abstentions
Promotion and protection of human rights Implementation of human rights instruments	A/RES/73/161 World Braille Day	Antigua and Barbuda et al.	Co-sponsor of the Resolution	Adopted by consensus
	A/RES/73/162 Human rights treaty body system	Australia et al.	Co-sponsor of the Resolution	Adopted by consensus
	A/RES/73/163 Human rights and extreme poverty	Belize et al.	Co-sponsor of the Resolution	Adopted by consensus
	A/RES/73/165 United Nations Declaration on the Rights of Peasants and Other People Working in Rural Areas	Bolivia	Abstention	121 in favour, 8 against, 54 abstentions

Subject	Resolution	Main sponsor of the Resolution	Information regarding Italy	Outcome of the Plenary Session
	A/RES/73/166 The right to development	China et al.	Abstention	148 in favour, 11 against, 32 abstentions
	A/RES/73/167 Human rights and unilateral coercive measures	Cuba and China	Voted against	133 in favour, 53 against, 3 abstentions
	A/RES/73/169 Promotion of a democratic and equitable international order	Cuba	Voted against	131 in favour, 53 against, 7 abstentions
Human rights issues, including alternative approaches to improve enjoyment of human rights and fundamental freedoms	A/RES/73/170 Promotion of peace as a vital requirement for the full enjoyment of all human rights by all	Cuba	Voted against	135 in favour, 53 against, 1 abstention
	A/RES/73/171 The right to food	Cuba	Co-sponsor of the Resolution Voted in favour	188 in favour, 2 against, nessuna abstention
	A/RES/73/172 Extrajudicial, summary or arbitrary executions	Albania et al.	Co-sponsor of the Resolution Voted in favour	125 in favour, nessun against, 60 abstentions

Subject	Resolution	Main sponsor of the Resolution	Information regarding Italy	Outcome of the Plenary Session
	A/RES/73/173 Promotion and protection of human rights and fundamental freedoms, including the rights to peaceful assembly and freedom of association	Afghanistan et al.	Co-sponsor of the Resolution Voted in favour	154 in favour, 0 against, 35 abstentions
	A/RES/73/174 Terrorism and human rights	Belize, Egypt and Mexico	Co-sponsor of the Resolution	Adopted by consensus
	A/RES/73/175 Moratorium on the use of the death penalty	Albania et al.	Co-sponsor of the Resolution Voted in favour	121 in favour, 35 against, 32 abstentions
	A/RES/73/176 Freedom of religion or belief	Albania et al.	Co-sponsor of the Resolution	Adopted by consensus
	A/RES/73/177 Human rights in the administration of justice	Australia et al.	Co-sponsor of the Resolution	Adopted by consensus
	A/RES/73/178 Missing persons	Azerbaijan et al.	Co-sponsor of the Resolution	Adopted by consensus
	A/RES/73/179 The right to privacy in the digital age	Austria et al.	Co-sponsor of the Resolution	Adopted by consensus

Subject	Resolution	Main sponsor of the Resolution	Information regarding Italy	Outcome of the Plenary Session
	A/RES/73/180 Situation of human rights in the Democratic People's Republic of Korea	Albania et al.	Co-sponsor of the Resolution	Adopted by consensus
	A/RES/73/181 Situation of human rights in the Islamic Republic of Iran	Australia et al.	Co-sponsor of the Resolution Voted in favour	84 in favour, 30 against, 67 abstentions
Situation of Human rights and reports of Rapporteurs and Special Representatives	A/RES/73/263 Situation of human rights in the Autonomous Republic of Crimea and the city of Sevastopol, Ukraine	Australia et al.	Co-sponsor of the Resolution Voted in favour	65 in favour, 27 against, 70 abstentions
	A/RES/73/182 Situation of human rights in the Syrian Arab Republic	Saudi Arabia	Co-sponsor of the Resolution Voted in favour	111 in favour, 15 against, 55 abstentions
	A/RES/73/264 Situation of human rights in Myanmar	Austria et al.	Co-sponsor of the Resolution Voted in favour	136 in favour, 8 against, 22 abstentions
	A/RES/73/187 Countering the use of information and communications technologies for criminal purposes	Russian Federation	Voted against	94 in favour, 59 against, 33 abstention

Subject	Resolution	Main sponsor of the Resolution	Information regarding Italy	Outcome of the Plenary Session
	A/RES/73/188 United Nations African Institute for the Prevention of Crime and the Treatment of Offenders	Morocco	Co-sponsor of the Resolution	Adopted by consensus
Crime prevention and Criminal Justice	A/RES/73/189 Strengthening and promoting effective measures and international cooperation on organ donation and transplantation to prevent and combat trafficking in persons for the purpose of organ removal and trafficking in human organs	Armenia et al.	Co-sponsor of the Resolution	Adopted by consensus

Subject	Resolution	Main sponsor of the Resolution	Information regarding Italy	Outcome of the Plenary Session
	A/RES/73/190 Preventing and combating corrupt practices and the transfer of proceeds of corruption, facilitating asset recovery and returning such assets to legitimate owners, in particular to countries of origin, in accordance with the United Nations Convention against Corruption	Antigua and Barbuda et al.	Co-sponsor of the Resolution	Adopted by consensus
International Drug Control	A/RES/73/192 International cooperation to address and counter the world drug problem	Antigua and Barbuda et al.	Co-sponsor of the Resolution	Adopted by consensus

Source: United Nations, General Assembly

II. Human Rights Council

The Human Rights Council is the subsidiary body of the General Assembly responsible for for addressing human rights violations, promoting worldwide respect of all human rights and fundamental freedoms for all, without distinction of any kind.

Established in 2006 under General Assembly resolution 60/251, the Council is an inter-governmental body made up of 47 United Nations Member States elected by the General Assembly for an initial period of three years, extendable for not more than two consecutive terms. It meets in Geneva, in three ordinary sessions per year, for an overall period of at least ten working weeks. Furthermore, although it is a body of Government representatives, the Council is open to the contributions of nongovernmental organisations which enjoy advisory status with the ECOSOC, which may participate in the meetings and submit written documents.

The Council has established several different "mechanisms" for monitoring human rights (resolution A/HRC/RES/5/1 of June 2007), including: the Universal Periodic Review (UPR), the Special Procedures (which include mandates by Country and thematic mandates), the Advisory Committee and a Complaints Procedure.

In 2018, the Council held:

– three ordinary sessions: 37th (26 February-23 March); 38th (18 June-6 July); 39th (10–28 September);
– one special session on the deteriorating situation in the Occupied Palestinian Territories, including East Jerusalem (28th session, 18 May);
– three sessions of UPR: 29th (15–26 January); 30th (7–18 May), 31st (5–16 November).

Since July 2018, Italy has been represented at the Human Rights Council by Ambassador Gian Lorenzo Cornado, Permanent Representative of Italy to the International Organisations in Geneva, by First Counsellor Daniela d'Orlandi and by First Secretary Massimo Baldassarre.

A. Italy's Behaviour at the Human Rights Council in 2018

In 2018, Italy participated in the ordinary sessions of the Human Rights Council as an Observer State (hence, without the right to vote). On 12 October 2018, Italy was elected as a member of the Council for the three-year period 2019–2021 by the General Assembly with 180 votes.

Over the course of 2018, the Human Rights Council adopted 85 resolutions (23 fewer than 2017): 42 resolutions during the 37th session; 20 during the 38th session; and 23 during the 39th session. Of these resolutions, 54 were adopted with the consensus of all Member States, whereas a majority vote by Council members was necessary for 31 of them, showing a slightly higher level of disagreement than in the previous year, when majority voting was required for 32 % of the resolutions adopted.

The following paragraph analyses Italy's behaviour at the Human Rights Council in 2018, with a particular focus on Italy's diplomatic efforts in the negotiation and presentation of resolutions.

On this issue, 67 % of the resolutions adopted by the Council were negotiated with direct participation (sponsoring) or with diplomatic support (co-sponsoring) from Italy. Indeed, of the 85 resolutions adopted, Italy sponsored 11 (compared to the 9 of 2016) and co-sponsored 46 (compared to the 54 of 2017). 4 of the 11 resolutions sponsored by Italy are thematic and refer to right to religion and belief, to cultural rights, rights of children and adolescents, education and training of human rights (promoting Goal 4 of the SDGs: Ensure inclusive and equitable quality education and promote lifelong learning opportunities for all). The other 7 resolutions refer to the situation of human rights in the Democratic People's Republic of Korea, Myanmar, Burundi, Syria and Belarus.

The table below summarises the resolutions approved by the Council in 2018 and shows that, of the resolutions that Italy either sponsored or co-sponsored, 74 % were adopted by consensus by the Council, whereas 26 % were adopted by majority vote.

Human Rights Council: resolutions sponsored by Italy in 2018

Resolution	Other sponsors of the resolution	Outcome of the voting process
A/HRC/RES/37/9 Freedom of religion or belief	Bulgaria et al.	Adopted by consensus
A/HRC/RES/37/17 Cultural rights and the protection of cultural heritage	Cyprus et al.	Adopted by consensus
A/HRC/RES/37/20 Rights of the child: protection of the rights of the child in humanitarian situations	Bulgaria et al.	Adopted by consensus
A/HRC/RES/37/28 Situation of human rights in the Democratic People's Republic of Korea	Bulgaria et al.	Adopted by consensus

Resolution	Other sponsors of the resolution	Outcome of the voting process
A/HRC/RES/37/29 The human rights situation in the Syrian Arab Republic	United Kingdom, Qatar et al.	27 in favour, 4 against, 16 abstentions
A/HRC/RES/37/32 Situation of human rights in Myanmar	Bulgaria et al.	32 in favour, 5 against, 10 abstentions
A/HRC/RES/38/14 Situation of human rights in Belarus	Austria et al.	19 in favour, 6 against, 21 abstentions
A/HRC/RES/38/16 The human rights situation in the Syrian Arab Republic	United Kingdom et al.	26 in favour, 5 against, 15 abstentions
A/HRC/RES/39/3 World Programme for Human Rights Education	Slovenia et al.	Adopted by consensus
A/HRC/RES/39/14 Situation of human rights in Burundi	Austria et al.	23 in favour, 7 against, 17 abstentions
A/HRC/RES/39/15 The human rights situation in the Syrian Arab Republic	United Kingdom et al.	27 in favour, 4 against, 16 abstentions

Source: United Nations, Human Rights Council

Human Rights Council: resolutions co-sponsored by Italy in 2018

Resolution	Sponsors of the resolution	Outcome of the voting process
37th (26 February-23 March)		
A/HRC/RES/37/1 The deteriorating situation of human rights in Eastern Ghouta, in the Syrian Arab Republic	United Kingdom	29 in favour, 4 against, 14 abstentions

Resolution	Sponsors of the resolution	Outcome of the voting process
A/HRC/RES/37/2 The right to privacy in the digital age	Germany et al.	Adopted by consensus
A/HRC/RES/37/4 Adequate housing as a component of the right to an adequate standard of living, and the right to non-discrimination in this context	Germany et al.	Adopted by consensus
A/HRC/RES/37/5 Mandate of the Independent Expert on the enjoyment of human rights by persons with albinism	Togo	Adopted by consensus
A/HRC/RES/37/6 The role of good governance in the promotion and protection of human rights	Poland et al.	Adopted by consensus
A/HRC/RES/37/8 Human rights and the environment	Costa Rica, Switzerland et al.	Adopted by consensus
A/HRC/RES/37/12 Mandate of the Special Rapporteur in the field of cultural rights	Cuba	Adopted by consensus
A/HRC/RES/37/13 Question of the realization in all countries of economic, social and cultural rights	Portugal	Adopted by consensus
A/HRC/RES/37/14 Rights of persons belonging to national or ethnic, religious and linguistic minorities	Austria, Mexico and Slovenia	Adopted by consensus

Resolution	Sponsors of the resolution	Outcome of the voting process
A/HRC/RES/37/15 High-level intersessional discussion celebrating the centenary of Nelson Mandela	Togo	Adopted by consensus
A/HRC/RES/37/16 Right to work	Egypt, Greece et al.	Adopted by consensus
A/HRC/RES/37/18 Promoting human rights through sport and the Olympic ideal	Greece et al.	Adopted by consensus
A/HRC/RES/37/19 The negative impact of corruption on the right to be free from torture and other cruel, inhuman or degrading treatment or punishment	Denmark	Adopted by consensus
A/HRC/RES/37/22 Equality and non-discrimination of persons with disabilities and the right of persons with disabilities to access to justice	Mexico and New Zealand	Adopted by consensus
A/HRC/RES/37/24 Promotion and protection of human rights and the implementation of the 2030 Agenda for Sustainable Development	Denmark, Chile et al.	Adopted by consensus
A/HRC/RES/37/26 Prevention of genocide	Armenia	Adopted by consensus
A/HRC/RES/37/27 Terrorism and human rights	Egypt and Mexico	Adopted by consensus
A/HRC/RES/37/30 Situation of human rights in the Islamic Republic of Iran	Sweden et al.	21 in favour, 7 against, 19 abstentions

Resolution	Sponsors of the resolution	Outcome of the voting process
A/HRC/RES/37/31 Situation of human rights in South Sudan	United States et al.	Adopted by consensus
A/HRC/RES/37/39 Technical assistance and capacity-building for Mali in the field of human rights	Togo	Adopted by consensus
A/HRC/RES/37/40 Cooperation with Georgia	Georgia	19 in favour, 5 against, 23 abstentions
A/HRC/RES/37/41 Technical assistance and capacity-building to improve human rights in Libya	Togo	Adopted by consensus
A/HRC/RES/37/42 Contribution to the implementation of the joint commitment to effectively addressing and countering the world drug problem with regard to human rights	Colombia, Switzerland et al.	Adopted by consensus
38th (18 June-6 July)		
A/HRC/RES/38/1 Elimination of all forms of discrimination against women and girls	Mexico and Colombia	Adopted by consensus
A/HRC/RES/38/5 Accelerating efforts to eliminate violence against women and girls: preventing and responding to violence against women and girls in digital contexts	Canada	Adopted by consensus

Resolution	Sponsors of the resolution	Outcome of the voting process
A/HRC/RES/38/6 Elimination of female genital mutilation	Togo	Adopted by consensus
A/HRC/RES/38/7 The promotion, protection and enjoyment of human rights on the Internet	Sweden, Brazil et al.	Adopted by consensus
A/HRC/RES/38/8 Human rights in the context of HIV and AIDS	Brazil et al.	Adopted by consensus
A/HRC/RES/38/9 The right to education: follow-up to Human Rights Council resolution 8/4	Portugal	Adopted by consensus
A/HRC/RES/38/11 The promotion and protection of human rights in the context of peaceful protests	Switzerland and Costa Rica	Adopted by consensus
A/HRC/RES/38/12 Civil society space: engagement with international and regional organizations	Ireland et al.	35 in favour, 0 against, 11 abstentions
A/HRC/RES/38/13 Business and human rights: improving accountability and access to remedy	Norway et al.	Adopted by consensus
A/HRC/RES/38/18 The contribution of the Human Rights Council to the prevention of human rights violations	Norway et al.	28 in favour, 9 against, 8 abstentions
A/HRC/RES/38/19 The incompatibility between democracy and racism	Brazil et al.	Adopted by consensus

Resolution	Sponsors of the resolution	Outcome of the voting process
39th (10–28 September)		
A/HRC/RES/39/1 Promotion and protection of human rights in the Bolivarian Republic of Venezuela	Peru et al.	23 in favour, 7 against, 17 abstentions
A/HRC/RES/39/2 Situation of human rights of Rohingya Muslims and other minorities in Myanmar	Pakistan, Austria et al.	35 in favour, 3 against, 7 abstentions
A/HRC/RES/39/6 The safety of journalists	Austria et al.	Adopted by consensus
A/HRC/RES/39/7 Local government and human rights	Republic of Korea et al.	Adopted by consensus
A/HRC/RES/39/8 The human rights to safe drinking water and sanitation	Spain and Germany	44 in favour, 1 against, 2 abstentions
A/HRC/RES/39/10 Preventable maternal mortality and morbidity and human rights in humanitarian settings	Colombia et al.	Adopted by consensus
A/HRC/RES/39/11 Equal participation in political and public affairs	Czech Republic et al.	Adopted by consensus
A/HRC/RES/39/13 Human rights and indigenous peoples	Mexico and Guatemala	Adopted by consensus
A/HRC/RES/39/16 Human rights situation in Yemen	Canada et al.	21 in favour, 8 against, 18 abstentions
A/HRC/RES/39/17 National human rights institutions	Australia	Adopted by consensus

Resolution	Sponsors of the resolution	Outcome of the voting process
A/HRC/RES/39/18 Enhancement of technical cooperation and capacity-building in the field of human rights	Thailand et al.	Adopted by consensus
A/HRC/RES/39/19 Technical assistance and capacity-building in the field of human rights in the Central African Republic	Togo	Adopted by consensus
A/HRC/RES/39/23 Assistance to Somalia in the field of human rights	United Kingdom and Somalia	Adopted by consensus

Source: United Nations, Human Rights Council

Human Rights Council: resolutions not sponsored by Italy in 2018

Resolution	Sponsors of the resolution	Outcome of the voting process
37ª (26 February-23 March)		
A/HRC/RES/37/3 Integrity of the judicial system	Russian Federation	23 in favour, 2 against, 22 abstentions
A/HRC/RES/37/7 Promoting human rights and the Sustainable Development Goals through transparent, accountable and efficient public services delivery	Azerbaijan, Kenya et al.	Adopted by consensus
A/HRC/RES/37/10 The right to food	Cuba	46 in favour, 1 against, no abstentions

Resolution	Sponsors of the resolution	Outcome of the voting process
A/HRC/RES/37/11 The effects of foreign debt and other related international financial obligations of States on the full enjoyment of all human rights, particularly economic, social and cultural rights	Cuba	27 in favour, 16 against, 4 abstentions
A/HRC/RES/37/21 Human rights and unilateral coercive measures	Venezuela	28 in favour, 15 against, 3 abstentions
A/HRC/RES/37/23 Promoting mutually beneficial cooperation in the field of human rights	China	28 in favour, 1 against, 17 abstentions
A/HRC/RES/37/25 The need for an integrated approach to the implementation of the 2030 Agenda for Sustainable Development for the full realization of human rights, focusing holistically on the means of implementation	South Africa	Adopted by consensus
A/HRC/RES/37/33 Human rights in the occupied Syrian Golan	Pakistan	25 in favour, 14 against, 7 abstentions
A/HRC/RES/37/34 Right of the Palestinian people to self-determination	Pakistan	43 in favour, 2 against, 1 abstention
A/HRC/RES/37/35 Human rights situation in the Occupied Palestinian Territory, including East Jerusalem	Pakistan	41 in favour, 3 against, 2 abstentions

Resolution	Sponsors of the resolution	Outcome of the voting process
A/HRC/RES/37/36 Israeli settlements in the Occupied Palestinian Territory, including East Jerusalem, and in the occupied Syrian Golan	Pakistan	34 in favour, 4 against, 8 abstentions
A/HRC/RES/37/37 Ensuring accountability and justice for all violations of international law in the Occupied Palestinian Territory, including East Jerusalem	Pakistan	27 in favour, 4 against, 15 abstentions
A/HRC/RES/37/38 . Combating intolerance, negative stereotyping and stigmatization of, and discrimination, incitement to violence and violence against, persons based on religion or belief	Pakistan	Adopted by consensus
38th (18 June-6 July)		
A/HRC/RES/38/2 Human rights and international solidarity	Cuba	31 in favour, 14 against, 1 abstention
A/HRC/RES/38/3 Enhancement of international cooperation in the field of human rights	Venezuela	28 in favour, 14 against, 3 abstentions
A/HRC/RES/38/4 Human rights and climate change	Bangladesh, The Philippines and Vietnam	Adopted by consensus
A/HRC/RES/38/10 Human rights and the regulation of civilian acquisition, possession and use of firearms	Ecuador and Peru	Adopted by consensus

Resolution	Sponsors of the resolution	Outcome of the voting process
A/HRC/RES/38/15 Situation of human rights in Eritrea	Djibouti and Somalia	Adopted by consensus
A/HRC/RES/38/17 The Social Forum	Cuba	Adopted by consensus
A/HRC/RES/38/20 Technical assistance to the Democratic Republic of the Congo and accountability concerning the events in the Kasai region	Togo	Adopted by consensus
39th (10–28 September)		
A/HRC/RES/39/4 Promotion of a democratic and equitable international order	Cuba	28 in favour, 14 against, 15 abstentions
A/HRC/RES/39/5 The use of mercenaries as a means of violating human rights and impeding the exercise of the right of peoples to self-determination	Cuba	30 in favour, 15 against, 2 abstentions
A/HRC/RES/39/9 The right to development	Venezuela	30 in favour, 12 against, 5 abstentions
A/HRC/RES/39/12 United Nations Declaration on the Rights of Peasants and Other People Working in Rural Areas	Bolivia et al.	33 in favour, 3 against, 11 abstentions
A/HRC/RES/39/20 Technical assistance and capacity-building in the field of human rights in the Democratic Republic of the Congo	Togo	Adopted by consensus

Resolution	Sponsors of the resolution	Outcome of the voting process
A/HRC/RES/39/21 Technical assistance and capacity-building for Yemen in the field of human rights	Tunisia	Adopted by consensus
A/HRC/RES/39/22 Technical assistance and capacity-building to improve human rights in the Sudan	Togo	Adopted by consensus

Source: United Nations, Human Rights Council

Furthermore, in 2018, Italy participated in the 28th special session on the deteriorating situation in the Occupied Palestinian Territories, including East Jerusalem (18 May). Italy was not one of the countries that requested the convocation of the session, nor was it a sponsor of the final resolution, adopted with 29 votes in favour, 2 against and 14 abstentions.

B. Universal Periodic Review

Italy was subjected to its first Universal Periodic Review (UPR) in 2010 (7th session): on that occasion, 92 recommendations were addressed to Italy, of which it fully accepted (supported) 78, partially rejected (noted) 2 and fully rejected 12. Detailed information on the outcome of the first Universal Periodic Review for Italy is demonstrated in the 2011 edition of the *Italian Yearbook of Human Rights* (p. 169–173).

> In 2014, Italy was subjected to its second cycle of the UPR (20th session), during which, 186 recommendations were addressed to Italy, of which it fully supported 176 and noted 12. Detailed information on the outcome of the second Universal Periodic Review for Italy is displayed in the 2015 edition of the Italian *Yearbook* of Human Rights (p. 161–164).

C. Special Procedures

In 2018, the Human Rights Council did not establish any special procedures. Consequently, there were 44 thematic mandates and 10 country mandates in operation at the Council.

It should be noted, in particular, that in 2018 Maria Grazia Giammarinaro held the position of Special Rapporteur on trafficking in persons, especially women and children.

In 2018, Italy was subject to a visit (Special Rapporteur on contemporary forms of slavery, including its causes and consequences), a thematic report (Special Rapporteur on the situation of human rights defenders) and six communications.

Visit of the Special Rapporteur on contemporary forms of slavery, including its causes and consequences, Urmila Bhoola (3–12 October 2018).

The objective of the mission was to assess the situation of labour exploitation of migrants in the agricultural sector. To fulfil this objective, the Special Rapporteur met with representatives of governmental authorities, employers' organisations, trade unions, and exploited workers, visiting reception centres in Calabria, Apulia and Lazio and the informal settlements of Borgo Mezzanone (Foggia) and San Ferdinando (Calabria).

Although the Italian legal framework provides protection of the human rights of migrant workers (particularly law No. 199/2016, the so-called anti-*Caporalato* Law, and the National Action Plan against Human Trafficking and Labour Exploitation and National Action Plan for Business and Human Rights) and this protection is extended by national and provincial collective agreements, the Special Rapporteur estimates there are over 400,000 agricultural workers at risk of being exploited and around 100,000 risk inhuman and degrading conditions. The Caporalato system creates the conditions for exploitation of workers, as it leads to dependency on a middleman not only regarding access to the labour market but also to access other services, such as transport, food and water. This situation gives these middlemen (who are often members of criminal organisations or illegal trade unions) considerable power and control over the workers they recruit, as many workers have no choice but to continue working in slavery-like conditions. Other forms of coersion include: physical and sexual violence, threats of violence, withholding wages and documents, threats against family member in their countries of origin in cases of refusal to continue to work illegally.

Therefore, the Special Rapporteur recommends that Italy:

— Establish local public employment centers which are tasked with matching supply and demand of workers in the agricultural sector. In this way, the intervention of intermediaries will be avoided and the transparency of recruitment processes increased;

- Ensure public transportation systems in rural areas, particularly during harvesting seasons in order to avoid dependency on intermediaries;
- Create stronger incentives for reporting labour exploitation, inter alia by increasing the protection of victims and ensuring access to complaint mechanisms, to justice and to an effective remedy regardless of the workers' migration status;
- Strengthen the Labour Inspectorates by allocating additional resources in order to ensure that inspections are effective, free from corruption and by also guaranteeing the safety and security of inspectors;
- Ensure access to basic services including adequate healthcare, housing and sanitation to everyone living in the Italian territory, regardless of their migration status, in accordance with international human rights standards;
- Ratify P029 (Protocol of 2014 to the Forced Labour Convention) and the International Convention on the Protection of the Rights of All Migrant Workers and Members of Their Families;

Special Procedure Visits to Italy (2002–2018)

Date	Mandate of the Special Procedures	Report
3–12 October 2018	Modern forms of slavery, including its causes and consequences	Report to be published
12–13 October 2017	Trafficking in persons, in particular women and children	Report to be published
10–16 May 2017	Extrajudicial, summary and arbitrary executions	A/72/335
1–5 June 2015	People of African descent	A/HRC/33/61/Add.1
2–5 December 2014	Human rights of migrants	A/HRC/29/36/Add.2
7–9 July 2014	Arbitrary detention	A/HRC/30/36/Add.3

Date	Mandate of the Special Procedures	Report
11–18 November 2013	Freedom of opinion and expression	A/HRC/26/30/Add.3
12–20 September 2013	Trafficking in persons	A/HRC/26/37/Add.4
30 September-8 October 2012	Human rights of migrants	A/HRC/23/46/Add.3
15–26 January 2012	Violence against women	A/HRC/20/16/Add.2
3–14 November 2008	Arbitrary detention	A/HRC/10/21/Add.5
9–13 October 2006	Contemporary forms of racism	A/HRC/4/19/Add.4
20–29 October 2004	Freedom of opinion and expression	E/CN.4/2005/64/Add.1
7–18 June 2004	Human rights of migrants	E/CN.4/2005/85/Add.3
11–14 March 2002	the independence of judges and lawyers	E/CN.4/2002/72/Add.3

Report of the Special Rapporteur Special Rapporteur on the situation of human rights defenders, Michel Forst, at the 73rd session of the General Assembly (A/73/215).

Michael Forst included Italy in the World Report on the Situation of Human Rights Defenders (attached to the report for the General Assembly 73rd session). According to the report, Human Rights Defenders in Italy generally enjoy a safe and enabling environment for their activities. Italy has also expressed support for defenders, particularly those at risk, working abroad.

Although the general environment is favourable and there are no formal restrictions on forming civil society organisations, the right to freedom of association of Human Rights Defenders, particularly those of the rights of people on the move and minority rights, are often, in practice, restricted. Demonstrations have been often met with excessive force from police. Also, defenders and journalists dealing with environmental rights or other political or socially sensitive issues (e.g. corruption and investigating organised crime) are often at risk of threat or reprisals, aboveall from non-State actors.

The Special Rapporteur recommends that the State further strengthen its protective mechanisms for human rights defenders at risk, in consultation with at-risk journalists and at-risk defenders

Communications of Special Procedures regarding Italy, 2018

In 2018, Italy received six communications from 16 thematic Special Procedures (that is, from around a third of the total number of Special Procedures operating within the Human Rights Council in 2018.

1) 20 March, the *Special Rapporteur on the promotion and protection of the right to freedom of opinion and expression* brough to the attention of the Italian Government information concerning "operational protocol for the « Fight Against the Diffusion of Fake News through the Web on the Occasion of the Election Campaign for the 2018 Political Elections", announced by the Minister of the Interior on 18 January 2018, expressing concerns about its potential impact on freedom of opinion and expression.

The protocol aims to fight the diffusion of "false, exaggerated, or biased" news reports or "openly defamatory" content: these terms, moreover, are vague and are not clearly and unambiguously defined. Furthermore, the Protocol would link the diffusion of "fake news" to criminal law against defamation, that imposes significant sanctions for "injuring the reputation of an absent person via communication with others". The lack of clarity concerning how the Protocol would operate, coupled with the threat of criminal sanctions, raises the danger that the Government could become arbiters of truth in the public and political domain. Accordingly, the Protocol could disproportionately suppress a wide range of expressive conduct essential to a democratic society, including criticism of the government, news reporting, political campaigning and the expression of unpopular, controversial or minority opinions.

In light of these concerns, the Special Procedures urge the Government to consider alternative measures such as the promotion of independent fact-checking mechanisms, State support for independent, diverse and adequate public service media outlets, and public education and media literacy, which have been recognized as less intrusive means to address disinformation and propaganda.

2) 21 September, *Special Rapporteur on adequate housing as a component of the right to an adequate standard of living, and on the right to non-discrimination in this context* brought to the attention of the Italian government to have received information concerning an increasing number of forced evictions. Data in the latest report of the Ministry of the Interior show the gravity of the situation: 59,600 eviction injunctions granted in 2017, of which over 52,500 for back rents; 29,000 evictions (on average 130 evictions a day), carried out with police intervention. Many people were evicted by force, without access to alterative accommodation. This situation has been caused principally by the financial crisis that affected families of low or middle income, who were not able to sustain the costs of their homes, combined with the lack of temporary social housing: data from the Ministry of the Interior show that there are only 900 temporary social housing with almost 650,000 families on the waiting list.

The situation could be aggravated by circular 11001/123/111 (1) Uff. II-Ord. and Sic. of the Cabinet of the Minister of the Interior (Gabinetto del Ministro dell'Interno. Circolare del 1° September 2017 - Misure in materia di occupazioni arbitrarie di immobili), published 1 September 2017, in order to accelerate the evictions of people who occupy buildings without legal title or in precarious security conditions. The evictions could concern occupations of vacant buildings, nomad camps or other structures inhabited by poor people, citizens, refugees and migrants.

In light of these concerns, the Special Rapporteur requests the Government to indicate: what measures are in place to ensure that banks (given that the report had highlighted the case of a threatened eviction of a large immigrant family in the Padua Province, ordered by a credit institution) and local authorities do not carry out forced evictions or demolitions in violation of the international and domestic human rights obligations; what legal procedures and remedies are available, including notice periods, and access to legal aid and to adjudicative bodies, for the residents to challenge eviction; and information in detail on steps taken by the Government to ensure affordability of houses including through subsidies, social housing or other measures.

3) 19 October: joint comunication the Working Group of Experts on People of African Descent; the Special Rapporteur on

contemporary forms of racism, racial discrimination, xenophobia and related intolerance; the Special Rapporteur on extrajudicial, summary or arbitrary executions; the Special Rapporteur on the human rights of migrants; the Special Rapporteur on minority issues; and the Special Rapporteur on the promotion and protection of the right to freedom of opinion and expression the climate of hostility, intolerance, racial hatred and xenophobia in Italy, fuelled by political authorities' rhetoric against migrants and refugees, and minorities, including people of African descent or origin and Roma communities. This situation has led to an increase in racist and hate-motivated attacks and shootings as well as the exacerbation of racially discriminatory practices against individuals of the abovementioned groups, including impacts on their enjoyment of economic and social rights.

During the 2018 electoral campaign, xenophobic and racist rhetoric, especially around migration, was rampant throughout the country. According to the data given by the Special Procedures, between 8 February and 2 March 2018, monitoring of the tweets, images, videos and posts of 1,419 electoral candidates revealed 787 cases of offensive, racist and discriminatory messages. These posts were attributable to 129 candidates, 77 of whom were elected to office. 43.5 per cent of these cases were attributable to political leaders within a party, 50 per cent to Parliamentary candidates, and 6.5 per cent to candidates for the Presidency of the Lazio and Lombardia regions. 51 % of cases were attributable to candidates of the League, 27 % to candidates of Brothers of Italy, 13 % to Forza Italia, 4 % to Casa Pound, 3 % to Italy for the Italians ("Italia agli Italiani") and 2 % to the Five Star Movement ("Movimento 5 Stelle"). 91 % of these hate messages reportedly targeted migrants; 11 % related to religious groups (particularly Muslim groups); 6 % targeted the LGTBI community; 4.8 % targeted Roma communities, and 1.8 % targeted women. 7 % of these messages incited violence towards these groups. Incitement to hatred and discrimination linked to immigration capitalized on and reinforced socio-economic, political and national security anxieties.

The hostile political environment described above has exacerbated resentment towards migrants, refugees, and racial and ethnic minorities, in particular people of African descent or origin and the Roma community, leading to an increase in racially motivated incidents and violent attacks. On 31 July 2018, the Office of the High Commissioner for Refugees expressed its concern after recording at least 12 violent attacks in a period of 50 days targeting people belonging to these groups.

While no comprehensive information has been provided to the Special Procedures regarding the status of all investigations and prosecutions for the above cited cases, information received indicates that in some cases of violent acts against minorities and migrants, some accused have been charged with less serious offences than possible under the law, and that there has been a tendency to delink the charges from hate-motivated crimes.

In light of these concerns, the Special Procedures request that the government provide further information on: measures taken to address the rise in cases of incitement to hatred, discrimination and violence against migrants, people of African descent, Roma, Sinti, Caminanti and other minorities and marginalized groups; measures taken to fight against discrimination, racism, racial discrimination, xenophobia and related intolerance and on the adoption and implementation of a national plan of action in this regard; sanctions taken against government officials and other politicians for inciting discrimination, hatred and violence through their public statements; measures in place to facilitate hate crime reporting and accompany the victims of such crimes through judicial proceedings.

> 4) 22 October: joint comunication from the *Special Rapporteur on violence against women, its causes and consequences and the Working Group on the issue of discrimination against women in law and in practice* on the potential serious retrogression in the advancement of the rights of women and their protection from domestic and gender-based violence in the city of Rome and throughout Italy.

The communication focuses on draft Decree 735, which was presented on 10 September 2018 by the Justice Commission of the Senate (the so-called the "Pillon Decree"). The Decree would introduce provisions that could entail a serious retrogression fuelling gender inequality and gender-based discrimination and depriving survivors of domestic violence of important protections. In its Articles 1–4 and 7–8, the Decree would introduce compulsory mediation in all separation cases where a child is directly or indirectly involved, elevating mediation to a condition in order to access judicial remedies. This provision would be very detrimental if applied to cases of domestic violence. Article 48 of the Council of Europe Convention on preventing and combating violence against women and domestic violence (the Istanbul Convention) requires States to "prohibit mandatory alternative dispute resolution processes, including mediation and conciliation, in relation to all forms of violence" within the scope of the Convention. If adopted, the Decree would seem to be in direct contravention of this article.

Furthermore, Articles 9, 11, 12, 14, 17 and 18 of the Decree would introduce for the first time in the Italian domestic legal system two legal assumptions, which would have negative consequences on the party in situation of most vulnerability: the assumption of the falsity and unfounded basis of reports of abuse and physical and psychological violence; and the assumption of the presence of parental alienation syndrome, a highly contested theory, without any need of supporting factual or legal evidence.

The Special Procedures express their deep concern that the "Pillon Decree" and the crackdown on women's spaces may be reflections of a trend, also expressed in statements of Government officials and other elements of the platforms of the ruling Government parties, of backlash against the rights of women and attempts to reinstate a social order based on gender stereotypes and unequal power relations and structures between men and women and contrary to Italy's international human rights obligations.

Therefore, the Special Procedures invite the government to provide additional information regarding any efforts to review, evaluate and amend the "Pillon Decree" to ensure its compatibility with Italy's obligations under European and international human rights law.

5) On 1 November, the Special Rapporteur on the rights of persons with disabilities sent a communication to Italy concerning the restriction of the legal capacity of Mr. Dominique Da Prat, Italian citizen, who has been denied the right to choose his own administrator and the right to manage his own financial affairs, which could constitute a violation of Article 12 and the right to be free from exploitation, violence and abuse, in violation of Article 16 of the Convention of the Rights of Persons with Disabilities. Therefore, the Special Rapporteur invites the Government to provide details on measures taken to review its legislation on legal capacity, and on the measures taken to ensure the monitoring and accountability of administrators.

6) 12 November: Joint Communication of the Special Rapporteur on the promotion and protection of the right to freedom of opinion and expression; the Special Rapporteur on the rights to freedom of peaceful assembly and of association; the Special Rapporteur on the situation of human rights defenders; the Independent Expert on human rights and international solidarity; the Special Rapporteur on the human rights of migrants; the Special Rapporteur on contemporary forms of racism, racial discrimination, xenophobia and related intolerance; the Special Rapporteur on contemporary forms of slavery, including its causes and consequences; the Special Rapporteur on torture and

other cruel, inhuman or degrading treatment or punishment; the Special Rapporteur on trafficking in persons, especially women and children; and the Special Rapporteur on violence against women, its causes and consequences.

The communication concerned the smear campaign and criminalization of activities of migrants' rights defenders, including civil society organisations, private individuals and journalists who criticise the Italian Government's migrantion policies and its attempts to block their work. As a result, civil society organizations have witnessed a drastic reduction in public and private donations, which is allegedly impacting on their operability both at sea (search and rescue operations) and on land (providing protection and life-saving assistance to migrants), increasing migrants' vulnerabilities to trafficking and other forms of exploitation

A further matter of concern is the Decree on Immigration and Security No.113/2018 (*Decreto immigrazione e sicurezza*). Under this decree, the humanitarian protection is repealed and replaced by five other types of residence permits which do not provide the same level of protection. Particularly vulnerable migrants such as victims of trafficking and of other forms of exploitation no longer benefit from special protection measures, increasing their risk of being exposed to trafficking or to other forms of exploitation.

In light of these concerns, the Special Procedures request the government indicate: a) detailed information on the factual and legal bases for the charges brought against individuals and civil society organizations for "abetting irregular migration" and explain how such charges are compatible with international human rights law and standards, in particular the treaty obligations undertaken by Italy under the ICCPR; b) how the refusal by the Italian authorities to allow NGO vessels carrying rescued persons to dock at Italian ports, or the refused or delayed permission to disembark, are in line with international obligations in relation to the protection of the right to life, such as under Article 6 of the ICCPR; c) how the Government is planning to fulfil its obligations to prevent the loss of life of migrants in the Mediterranean Sea and abide by the principle of non-refoulement in coordinating the search and rescue operations involving the Libyan coastguard; d) what measures have been taken to ensure that migrant rights defenders in Italy are able to carry out their legitimate work, including through the use of their right to freedom of opinion and expression, freedom of association, in a safe and enabling environment without fear of threats or acts of intimidation and harassment of any sort; e) provide information regarding procedures or mechanisms in Parliament to review and ensure the compatibility of the Decree-Law 113/2018 with Italy's obligations under international human rights law.

Date	Mandate of the Special Procedures	Communication Subject
12 November	freedom of opinion and expression freedom of peaceful assembly and association human rights defenders international solidarity	Smear campaigns and the criminalisation of migrant rights defenders rescuing migrants, including members of civil society organizations, private individuals and journalists criticizing Italian migration polices, as well as attempts to obstruct their work, allegedly carried out by Italian authorities.
	migrants racism slavery torture human trafficking violence against women	Concerns regarding the negative impact on the human rights of migrants based on the proposed law on immigration and security, further criminalising solidarity and leaving many migrants in irregular situations.
1 November	disability	Restriction of the legal capacity of Mr. Dominique Da Prat, Italian citizen, who has been denied the right to choose his own administrator and the right to manage his own financial affairs, which could constitute a violation of Article 12 and the right to be free from exploitation, violence and abuse, in violation of Article 16 of the Convention of the Rights of Persons with Disabilities.
22 October	violence against women discrimination against women in law and in practice	Potential serious retrogression in the advancement of the rights of women and their protection from domestic and gender-based violence in the city of Rome and throughout Italy.

Date	Mandate of the Special Procedures	Communication Subject
19 October	people of African descent extrajudicial executions freedom of opinion and expression migrants minorities racism	Climate of hostility, intolerance, racial hatred and xenophobia in Italy, fuelled by political authorities' rhetoric against migrants and refugees, people of African descent or origin and Roma and Sinti communities.
21 September	housing	Information received concerning an increasing number of forced evictions; particular attention to the alleged intention to forcibly evict the Mokthari family from their home.
20 March	freedom of opinion and expression	Concerns regarding the operational protocol for the Fight Against the Diffusion of Fake News through the Web, announced by the Minister of the Interior on 18 January 2018, due to its potential impact on freedom of opinion and expression.

III. High Commissioner for Human Rights (OHCHR)

The Office was established by the General Assembly in December 1993 with Resolution 48/141.

The High Commissioner has a very broad mandate which includes the prevention of violations of human rights, ensuring the respect of all human rights, coordinating all United Nations activities involving human rights and strengthening national systems for protecting human rights and the rule of law. In this context, one of the crucial strategic activities for the High Commissioner's Office is supporting the establishment and development of independent human rights commissions at the national level. In order to fulfil its mandate, the Office of the High Commissioner has consolidated its presence "on the ground", establishing 13 regional offices and 13 national offices, sending experts on integrated United Nations peace missions or dispatching independent fact-finding operations, as well as mainstreaming the human rights component in United Nations teams' activities at Country or Programme level, and in those of specialised agencies of the United Nations (such as UNDP).

In September 2018, Michelle Bachelet (Chile) took the role of High Commissioner for Human Rights.

The Office of the High Commissioner is funded one-third by the regular budget of the United Nations, approved by the General Assembly every two years; the remaining two-thirds of the budget are voluntary contributions, mostly from States and additionally from international organisations, foundations, commercial enterprises, and private citizens.

In her inaugural speech at the 39th ordinary session of the Human Rights Council (10 September 2018), on migration, the High Commissioner encouraged the European Union to establish search and rescue operations for people crossing the Mediterranean and to guarantee access to asylum procedures and to human rights protection. The High Commissioner also highlighted that the Italian Government has been denying entry to NGO rescue ships, underlining that this kind of political posturing and other recent developments have devastating consequences for many already vulnerable people. Commenting on various European States' practices in this field, the High Commissioner announced her intention to send staff to Italy to assess the reported sharp increase in acts of violence and racism against migrants, persons of African descent and Roma.

In 2018, Italy contributed to the budget of the High Commissioner's Office with funds of about $2,500,000 (around 1.36 % of all voluntary contributions received by the office in 2018, ranking 16th among donors), the highest contribution since 2008 (see graph below).

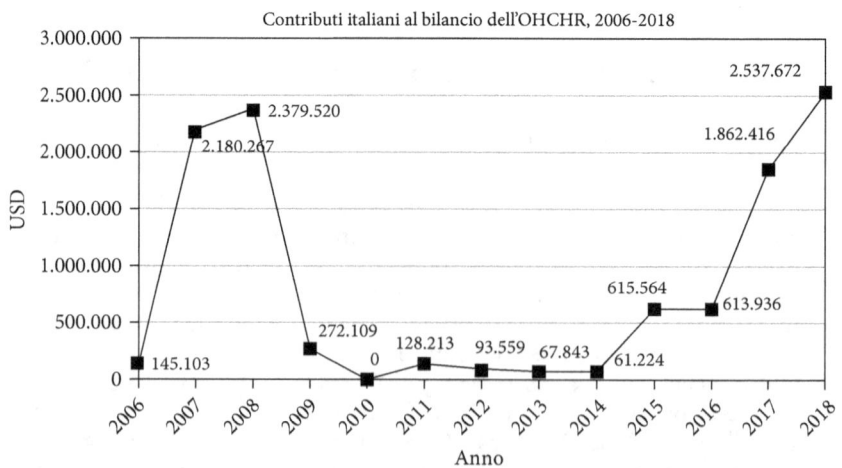

Source: OHCHR, Voluntary contributions to OHCHR in 2018

IV. High Commissioner for Refugees (UNHCR)

> This Office was established by the United Nations General Assembly on 14 December 1950, with resolution A/RES/428(V).
>
> The mandate of the Agency is to coordinate international action for the protection of refugees and the resolution of their problems all over the world. Its primary mission is to protect the rights and welfare of refugees and to ensure that all of them can exercise their right to request asylum and seek safe shelter in another State, with the option to return voluntarily to their home Country, integrate locally or to resettle into a third Country. The remit of the UNHCR also includes assistance to stateless persons.
>
> On 1 January 2016, the General Assembly of the United Nations appointed Filippo Grandi (Italy) High Commissioner for Refugees, for a five-year mandate.

The UNHCR has had its own office in Rome since 1953. The Italian office participates in the procedures to determine refugee status in Italy and performs other duties regarding international protection, training, dissemination of information on refugees and asylum-seekers in Italy and in the various crisis areas all over the world, raising public awareness and fund-raising with Governments, companies and individual donors. Since 2006, the Italian UNHCR Office has performed as the Regional Representative for Albania, Cyprus, Greece, Malta, Portugal, San Marino, and the Holy See, besides Italy. In 2018, the UNHCR Spokesperson in Italy was Carlotta Sami.

According to the data provided by the UNHCR, in 2018, 23,370 migrants arrived in Italy by sea, a reduction of 80 % compared to 2017 (119,369). 22 % came from Tunisia, followd by Eritrea (14 %), Iraq, Sudan and Pakistan (7 % each), Nigeria, Algeria and Côte d'Ivoire (5 % each), Mali and Guinea (4 % each). The majority of people who arrived by sea were men (72 %), followed by unaccompanied or separated minors (15 %), women (10 %) and accompanied minors (3 %).

Libya remains the main country of departure for people arriving in Italy by sea, although departures from this country fell significantly compared to the previous year. In 2018, 56 % of the new arrivals by sea (12,977 people) had crossed Libya, compared to 91 % (108,409 people) in 2017. The percentage of departures from Tunisia increased from 4 % in 2017 to 25 % in 2018; the remaining 20 % come from other countries, among which 12 % of people arriving by sea in 2018 were from Turkey, and also from Greece (5 %) and from Algeria (3 %).

In 2018, Italy contributed to the UNHCR budget by allocating approximately $65 million, (around 1.68 % of overall voluntary contributions for the office in 2018, ranking 12th among donors) showing an increase by about $15 million compared to the previous year (see chart below).

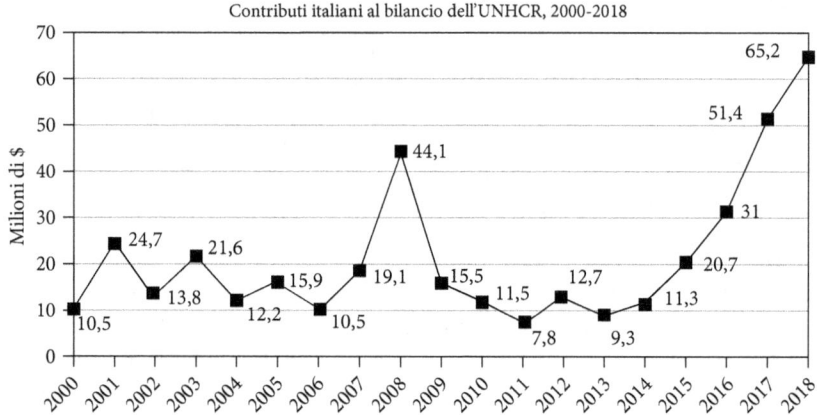

Contributi italiani al bilancio dell'UNHCR, 2000-2018

Source: UNHCR

V. Human Rights Treaty Bodies

Over the years, the United Nations has established a comprehensive Human Rights Code (*International Bill of Human Rights*), whose backbone are the following nine conventions: International Convention for the Elimination of All Forms of Racial Discrimination (ICERD, 1965); International Covenant on Civil and Political Rights (ICCPR, 1966); International Covenant on Economic, Social and Cultural Rights (ICESCR, 1966); Convention against all Forms of Discrimination against Women (CEDAW, 1979); International Convention against Torture (CAT, 1984); Convention on the Rights of the Child (CRC, 1989); International Convention on the Protection of the Rights of All Migrant Workers and Members of Their Families (ICRMW, 1990); Convention on the Rights of Persons with Disabilities (CRPD, 2006); International Convention for the Protection of All Persons from Enforced Disappearance (CPED, 2006).

Italy has ratified eight conventions and relevant optional protocols (as shown in the following table). However, it has not yet signed the ICRMW.

Convention	Ratification law	Declarations/ reservations	Recognition of Specific Competences of the Committee
ICERD	l. 13 October 1975, No. 654	Yes (Article 4)	Individual Comunications (Article 14): Yes
ICESCR	l. 25 October 1977, No. 881	No	-
OP	l. 3 October 2014, No. 52	No	-
ICCPR	l. 25 October 1977, No. 881	Yes (Article 15.1 and 19.3)	Individual Comunications (Article 41): Yes
OP - 1	l. 25 October 1977, No. 881	Yes (Article 5.2)	-
OP - 2	l. 9 December 1994, No. 734	No	-
CEDAW	l. 14 March 1985, No. 132	Yes (general)	-
OP	Deposito ratifica: 22/09/2000	No	Enquiry Procedure (Articles 8 and 9): Yes
CAT	l. 3 November 1988, No. 498	No	Individual Comunications (Article 22): Yes Interstate Comunications (Article 21): Yes Enquiry Procedure (Article 20): Yes

Convention	Ratification law	Declarations/ reservations	Recognition of Specific Competences of the Committee
OP	l. 9 November 2012, No. 195	No	Visits by the Subcommittee on Prevention of Torture (Article 11) Yes
CRC	l. 27 May 1991, No. 176	No	-
OP - AC	l. 11 March 2002, No. 46	Declaration binding pursuant to Article 3: 17 years	-
OP - SC	l. 11 March 2002, No. 46	No	-
OP - IC	l. 16 November 2015, No. 199	No	Individual Comunications: Yes Enquiry Procedure (Article 13): Yes
CRPD	l. 3 March 2009, No. 18	No	-
OP	l. 3 March 2009, No. 18	No	Enquiry Procedure (Articles 6 and 7): Yes
CPED	l. 29 July 2015, No. 131	No	Enquiry Procedure (Article 33): Yes

Legend: OP = Optional Protocol
OP - AC = Optional Protocol to the Convention on the Rights of the Child on the Involvement of Children in Armed Conflict
OP - SC = Optional Protocol to the Convention on the Rights of the Child on the sale of children, child prostitution and child pornography
OP-IC = Optional Protocol to the Convention on the Rights of the Child on a Communications Procedure

In addition to recognising human rights in legally binding treaties, the UN has created monitoring mechanisms for each treaty. These committees or conventional bodies (Treaty Bodies) are composed of 10 to 23 independent experts selected on the basis of their probity and experience recognised in the field of human rights. In 2018, Mauro Politi was a member of the Human Rights Committee (civil and political) while Alessio Bruni was a member of the Committee against Torture.

> The main function of the Committees is to examine the periodic reports on the implementation of the internationally established standards in the Contracting Country. States are obliged to present these reports periodically (usually every 4 or 5 years). The Committees can carry out monitoring functions through three other mechanisms: field surveys; examination of inter-State communications; examination of individual communications. The Committees provide their interpretation of the content of the provisions on human rights by publishing *General Comments* (for a more in-depth analysis of these functions, see *Yearbook 2011*, p. 180–182).
>
> Italy is monitored by eight Committees, as indicated in the following table. In 2018, Italy presented the first report on the International Convention for the Protection of All Persons from Enforced Disappearance and has not yet received concluding remarks.

Italy's cooperation with UN Treaty Bodies

Committee	Total reports presented	Last report presented	Latest concluding remarks	Reporting status
CERD	20	February 2015	December 2016	XXI report: due in 2019
CESCR	5	August 2012	October 2015	VI report: due in 2020
CCPR	6	October 2015	March 2017	VII report: due in 2022
CEDAW	7	October 2015	July 2017	VIII report: due in 2021
CAT	6	October 2015	November 2017	VII report: due in 2021
CRC	6	July 2017	-	V and VI joint report: presented and awaiting discussion
CRPD	1	November 2012	September 2016	II, III and IV joint report: due in 2023
CED	1	April 2018	-	I report: presented and awaiting discussion

A. Committee on Economic, Social and Cultural Rights

In 2018, the Committee held two sessions: 63rd (12–29 March) and 64th (24 September-12 October). In the 63rd session, the Committee analysed the reports of Bangladesh, Central African Republic, Mexico, New Zealand, Niger and Spain; in the 64th session, those of Argentina, Cape Verde, Germany, Mali, South Africa and Turkmenistan. During the year, no *General Comments* were adopted.

The last periodic report of Italy was discussed by the Committee in September 2015, during its 56th session (see *Yearbook 2016*, p. 159–162). Italy is required to present its sixth report in 2020.

B. Human Rights Committee (Civil and Political Rights)

In 2018, the Committee held three sessions: 122nd (12 March-6 April), 123rd (2–27 July) and 124th (8 October-2 November). During the 122nd session, the reports of El Salvador, Guatemala, Hungary, Lebanon and Norway were analysed; in the 123rd, the reports of Bahrain, Lao People's Democratic Republic, Liberia and Lithuania; in the 124th those of Belarus, Belize, Bulgaria, Guinea and Sudan. During the year, *General comment* No. 36 on Article 6 of the International Covenant on Civil and Political Rights.

The last periodic report on Italy was discussed by the Committee in March 2017, during the 119th session (see *Yearbook 2018*, p. 173–178). Italy is required to present its seventh report in 2022.

C. Committee against Torture

In 2018, the Committee held three sessions: 63rd (23 April-18 May), 64th (23 July-10 August) and 65th (12 November-7 December). During the 63rd session, the reports of Belarus, Czech Republic, Norway, Qatar, Senegal, Tajikistan were analysed; in the 64th, the reports of Chile, Mauritania, Russian Federation, Seychelles; in the 65th, those of Canada, Guatemala, Maldives, The Netherlands, Peru, Vietnam. During the year, no General Comments were adopted.

The last periodic report on Italy was discussed by the Committee in November 2017, during the 62nd session (see. *Yearbook 2018*, p. 178–182). Italy is required to present its seventh report in 2021.

D. Committee on the Elimination of Racial Discrimination

In 2018, the Committee held three sessions: 95th (23 April-11 May), 96th (6–30 August) and 97th (26 November-14 December). During the 95th session, the reports of Kyrgyzstan, Mauritania, Nepal, Peru, Saudi Arabia and Sweden were analysed; in the 96th, the reports of Bosnia Herzegovina, China, China (Hong Kong), China (Macau), Cuba, Japan,

Latvia, Mauritius and Montenegro; in the 97th session, those of Albania, Honduras, Iraq, Norway, Qatar and Republic of Korea. During the year, no General Recommendations were adopted.

> The last periodic report of Italy was discussed by the Committee in December 2016, during its 91st session (see *Yearbook 2017*, p. 174–177). Italy is required to present its twenty-first report in 2019.

E. Committee on the Elimination of Discrimination against Women

In 2018, the Committee held three sessions: 69th (19 February-9 March), 70th (2–20 July) and 71st (22 October-9 November). During the 69th session, the reports of Chile, Fiji, Luxembourg, Malaysia, Marshall Islands, Republic of Korea, Saudi Arabia and Suriname; in the 70th session, the reports of Australia, Cook Islands, Cyprus, Liechtenstein, Mexico, New Zealand, Palestine and Turkmenistan; in the 71st, those of the Bahamas, Congo, Lao People's Democratic Republic, Mauritius, Nepal, Republic of North Macedonia, Samoa, and Tajikistan. During the year, *General recommendation* No. 37 on Gender-related dimensions of disaster risk reduction in the context of climate change was adopted.

> The last periodic report of Italy was discussed by the Committee in July 2017, during the 67th session (see *Yearbook 2018*, p. 183–189). Italy is required to present its eighth report in 2021.

F. Committee on the Rights of the Child

In 2018, the Committee held three sessions: 77th (15 January-2 February), 78th (14 May - 1 June) and the 79th (17 September-5 October). During the 77th session, the reports of Guatemala, Marshall Islands, Palau, Panama, Seychelles, Solomon Islands, Spain and Sri Lanka; in the 78th session, the reports of Angola, Argentina, Lesotho, Montenegro and Norway; in the 79th, those of El Salvador, Lao People's Democratic Republic, Mauritania and Niger. During the year, no General Comments were adopted.

> Italy presented its latest report in July 2017 (see *Yearbook 2018 p. 189–190*) but has not yet discussed it.

G. Committee on the Rights of Persons with Disabilities

In 2018, the Committee held two sessions, the 19th (14 February-9 March) and the 20th (27 August-21 September). During the 19th session, the reports of Haiti, Nepal, Oman, Russian Federation, Seychelles, Slovenia, and Sudan were analysed; in the 20th session, those of Algeria, Bulgaria, Malta, The Philippines, Poland, Republic of North Macedonia and South Africa. During the year, two *General comments* were adopted: No. 6 on equality and non-discrimination (Article 5) and on Participation with persons with disabilities in the implementation and monitoring of the Convention (Article 4.3 and 33.3).

> The last periodic report of Italy was discussed by the Committee in August 2016, during its 16th session (see *Yearbook 2017*, pp. 178–182). Italy is required to present the combined second, third and forth periodic report in May 2023.

H. Committee on Enforced Disappearances

In 2018, the Committee held two sessions, the 14th (22 May-1 June) and the 15th (5–16 November), during which the concluding observations regarding Albania, Austria and Honduras (14th session), Japan, Mexico and Portugal (15th session) were adopted.

Italy presented its latest report in April 2018, but has not yet discussed it.

Latest report presented by Italy

Reporting round	I report
Date for the presentation of the Report	22/12/2017 (presented 9/04/2018)
Report	CED/C/ITA/1

The report shows the legislative framework, policies and programmes adopted by Italy to implement the regulations contained within the Convention.

I. Committee on Migrant Workers

In 2018, the Committee held two sessions, the 28th (9–20 April) and the 29th (3–12 September), during which the concluding observations regarding Algeria, Guyana, and Saint Vincent and the Grenadines (28th session), Madagascar and Mozambique (29th session). During the year, no *General Comments* were adopted.

Italy has not ratified the International Convention on the Protection of the Rights of All Migrant Workers and Members of Their Families and therefore is not monitored by the Committee.

VI. Specialised United Nations Agencies, Programmes and Funds

A. *International Labor Organization (ILO)*

Established by the Treaty of Versailles in 1919, the ILO became the first specialised agency of the United Nations in 1946.

The ILO is devoted to promoting decent and productive work for men and women in conditions of freedom, equality, safety and dignity. Its chief objectives are: to promote rights at work, to encourage decent employment opportunities, to enhance social protection and to strengthen dialogue on work-related issues. The ILO is the only United Nations agency which has a tripartite structure: representatives of Governments, employers and workers jointly elaborate the policies and programmes of the Organisation. 185 States are members of the ILO.

Since its foundation, the ILO has adopted 189 conventions. Of these, the ILO has identified 8 which it defines as "fundamental" or "core" (No. 29 on Forced Labour, 1930; No. 87 on Freedom of Association and Protection of the Right to Organise, 1948; No. 98 on the Right to Organise and Collective Bargaining, 1949; No. 100 on Equal Remuneration for Men and Women Workers for Work of Equal Value, 1951; No. 105 on the Abolition of Forced Labour, 1957; No. 111 on the Elimination of All Forms of Discrimination in Employment, Occupation, Vocational Training and Terms and Conditions of Employment, 1958; No. 138 on the Minimum Age for Admission to Employment or Work, 1973; and No. 182 on the Elimination of the Worst Forms of Child Labour, 1999) and 4 defined as "priority" (or "governance": No. 81 on Labour Inspection, 1947; No. 122 on Employment Policy, 1964; No. 129 on Labour Inspection [Agriculture], 1969; and No. 144 on Tripartite Consultation [International Labour Standards], 1976).

Italy has been a member of the ILO since 1919 (amongst the founding members); it withdrew from the Organisation in 1937 but joined again permanently in 1945. The ILO is present in Italy with its offices in Rome, which have been operating since 1920, and the International Training Centre, established in Turin in 1965.

Italy has ratified 113 conventions adopted by the ILO (of which 82 are in force and 31 denounced), including the 8 fundamental ones, the 4 priority ones and 101 of the 177 technical conventions.

In order to monitor the application of conventions ratified by States, in 1926, the ILO established the *Committee of Experts on the Application of Conventions and Recommendations*, a body made up of twenty eminent jurists and social professionals, who are independent of Governments and appointed on individual merits. The monitoring mechanism requires each Member State to submit periodic reports on the steps they have taken, in law and in practice, to apply each of the conventions it has ratified. At the same time, Governments are required to submit copies of their reports to employers' and workers' organisations, which are entitled to make comments and supply further information. Government reports are initially examined by the Committee of Experts, which can make two different kinds of comments: *observations* and *direct requests*. The observations contain comments on fundamental questions raised by the application of a particular convention by a State, and are published in the Committee's annual report. On the other hand, direct requests relate to more technical requests or requests for further information; they are not published in the report but are communicated directly to the Governments concerned.

> Upon conclusion of its considerations, the Committee presents an annual report to the *International Labour Conference*, the most representative body of the ILO, comprising representatives from all the ILO Member States and including all its observations and recommendations, which are carefully examined by the *Conference Committee on the Application of Standards*, a tripartite standing committee made up of Government, employer and worker delegates. This Committee selects a number of observations from the report for more in-depth discussion. The Governments referred to in these comments are invited to respond before the Conference Committee to provide information on the situation in question. In many cases, the Conference Committee adopts conclusions recommending that Governments take specific steps to remedy a problem or to invite the ILO to come on a mission to their Country or to request technical assistance.

In 2018, Italy received a direct request regarding No. 29 Forced Labour Convention, 1930.

- *Article 1, 2 and 25: trafficking in persons.* The Committee, recalling its concluding observations adopted 24 July 2017 by the Committee on the Elimination of Discrimination against Women of the United Nations concerning the low prosecution and convinction level in cases of trafficking, requests the Government to strengthen its efforts to ensure that all perpetrators involved in trafficking in persons are subject to investigations and prosecutions and that sufficiently effective and dissuasive penalties are applied in practice. The Committee also requests the Government to continue to provide information on the application in practice of the abovementioned provisions of the Criminal Code, as amended by legislation decree 24 of March 2014, including the number of prosecutions, convictions, and the specific penalties applied. Finally, the Committee requests the Government to provide information on the implementation of the NAP for 2016–18, as well as efforts to provide protection and assistance to victims of trafficking.

- *Article 1 and 2: Exploitation of foreign workers in an irregular situation.* While acknowledging the difficult situation facing Italy following the entry of high number of migrants, the Committee encourages the Government to pursue its efforts to prevent foreign migrants from falling victim to exploitative situations (*"caporalato"*, forced labour) regardless of their legal status, and to ensure that they can assert their rights, including by means of accessing the competent authorities. The Committee requests the Government to continue to provide information on the application in practice of section 603bis of the Criminal Code, as modified by law No. 199, 29 October 2016, *"Provisions to combat undeclared work, labour exploitation in agriculture and realign wages in the agricultural sector"*, and the measures taken to offer assistance to victims of exploitation under this provision.

In 2017, Italy contributed 3.75 % of the regular budget of the ILO, with a sum of around 17 million Swiss Francs. For the two-year period 2016–2017, Italy allocated a further voluntary contribution to the regular budget of 232,000 dollars, as one of eight donating countries, with Belgium, Denmark, Germany, Luxembourg, the Netherlands, Norway and Sweden.

B. United Nations Educational, Scientific and Cultural Organisation (UNESCO)

The human rights which fall under the responsibility of UNESCO are the right to education, the right to benefit from scientific progress, the right to participate freely in cultural life and the right to information, including freedom of opinion and expression. In connection with these, the right to freedom of thought, conscience and religion, the right to seek, receive and impart information and ideas through any instrument and across borders, the right to protection of the moral and material interests resulting from any scientific, literary or artistic production are pertinent, as are the right to freedom of assembly and association, the right to education, the right to enjoy the benefits of scientific progress, the right freely to participate in the cultural life, and the right to information, including the freedom of opinon and expression.

Italy has been a member of UNESCO since 1948. Since October 2018, the post of Permanent Representative to UNESCO has been filled Amb. Massimo Riccardo. Since its establishment, UNESCO has adopted 28 conventions, 20 of which have been ratified by Italy.

In the field of education, it should be noted that in 1991, the 26th General Conference of UNESCO established the International Programme for University Cooperation (IUC - International University Cooperation). The Programme works to foster the creation of a network of centres of excellence (UNESCO Chairs) able to implement advanced teaching and research programmes in disciplines related to UNESCO policies, with particular reference to the issues of peace and human rights, democracy and intercultural dialogue. There are over 700 UNESCO Chairs created all over the world; in 2017 in Italy there are 25 Chairs (as in 2016), 3 of which deal specifically with human rights, reporting the wording in the denomination: Chair "Human Rights, Democracy and Peace", established in 1999 at the University of Padova; Chair "Human Rights and Ethics of International Cooperation", established in 2003 at the University of Bergamo; Chair "Bioethics and Human Rights", established in 2009 at the Pontifical Athenaeum "Regina Apostolorum", European University of Rome.

In the field of bioethics, two committees operate at UNESCO: the International Bioethics Committee (IBC) and the Intergovernmental Bioethics Committee (IGBC).

The IBC was established in 1993, particularly thanks to the efforts of Director-General of UNESCO at that time, Federico Mayor. It is a body made up of 36 independent experts coming from different geographical and disciplinary backgrounds. Its mission is to follow progress in life science and its applications in order to ensure respect for human dignity and human rights and to promote reflection on the ethical and legal issues raised by research in the life sciences and their applications. To this end, over the years the IBC has published a number of recommendations and other documents, the most significant of which is the Universal Declaration on Bioethics and Human Rights, adopted by the UNESCO General Conference in 2005. The Committee meets once a year when convocated by the Director-General of UNESCO.

The IGBC was created in 1998 pursuant to Article 11 of the IBC Statute. It is comprised of 36 Member States who are elected by the UNESCO General Conference and meets at least once every two years to examine the proposals and recommendations of the IBC and to forward these proposals, accompanied by its own opinions, to the other UNESCO Member States.

As in previous years, in 2018, Italy contributed about 4.5 % of the regular budget of UNESCO (which covers the regular expenses for the maintenance of the staff and for the main activities of the Organisation), with an equal amount of approximately $14.4 million, ranking in seventh place among the main contributors of the Organisation. In 2018, Italy was not among the countries that have made voluntary extra-budget donations (with which the multiannual cooperation programmes managed by UNESCO are financed).

UNESCO Machinery

Italy was not involved with any of the organisation's monitoring mechanisms in 2018.

C. Food and Agriculture Organisation of the United Nations (FAO)

The FAO was established in 1945 in Ville de Quebec, Canada, and has its headquarters in Rome. José Graziano da Silva (Brazil) has been the Director-general of the Organisation since 1 January 2012. The Organisation budget for the biennium 2018–2019 has amounted to $2.6 billion.

> As of 30 March 2019, Italy was the eighth biggest contributor to the FAO with over $10 million in contributions. Italy collaborates with the FAO through the FAO/Italy Cooperation Programme, whose main components, financed by Italian voluntary contributions, are the traditional programme; the Italian Trust Fund for food security and the decentralised cooperation programme.

D. World Health Organization (WHO)

The primary objective of the Organisation, established in 1948, is the attainment by all peoples of the highest possible level of health, understood not as the absence of disease but as a state of complete physical, mental and social well-being.

In Italy, there is a WHO office (Venice), while 28 collaborating centres are currently accredited (in terms of the number of this type of structure, Italy is the second in Europe and ninth in the world). The latter, specialised institutions to which the WHO does not grant any funding, are identified by the WHO Director General and are part of a worldwide network of organisational support in the various medical-scientific fields. In Italy, their activity is coordinated by the Ministry of Health.

On 17 September 2018, the Health Ministers and high-level representatives of 53 WHO Member States for Europe met in Rome with partner organisations and representatives of Civil Society for the WHO Regional Committee for Europe. On this occasion, the European Health Report 2018 was officially launched.

E. United Nations Development Program (UNDP)

The United Nations Development Programme (UNDP) was established by the General Assembly in 1965 and has the role of central agency for the coordination and funding of development cooperation of the United Nations system.

NDP action pursues the general objective of "human development", understood as not only economic growth but also as social development, based on gender equality and respect for human rights. UNDP conducts research and analysis, preparing studies and reports. Of the most significant, worth noting are the Annual Report on Human Development and the report on the state of achievement of the Sustainable Development Goals.

In 2018, Italy contributed about $5.9 million to the UNDP's regular budget, keeping it in 16th place among the major contributing countries. During this year, Italy allocated another $75.7 million for specific projects and programmes coordinated by the UNDP.

On 24 September 2018, during an official ceremony held at the office of the Permanent Representative of Italy to the United Nations, Eni (National Hydrocarbons Authority) and the UNDP signed a memorandum of understanding aimed at improving access to sustainable energy in Africa and at achieving the Sustainable Development Goals.

F. United Nations Environment Program (UN-Environment)

UN-Environment is the leading global environmental authority that defines the global environmental agenda, promotes the coherent implementation of the environmental dimension of sustainable development within the system of nations. Its mission is to coordinate and promote the creation of a global partnership for the development of projects and activities to protect the environment so that nations and peoples can improve their quality of life without compromising that of future generations.

Erik Solheim has been the Director General since 13 May 2016. The Representative at the UN-Environment and also the Head of Mission of the Italian Embassy in Nairobi is Amb. Alberto Pieri, as of September 2018, succeeding Amb. Mauro Massoni.

G. United Nations Program for Human Settlements (UN-HABITAT)

United Nations Program for Human Settlements, UN-HABITAT is invested with the mission to foster sustainable urbanisation from the social and environmental point of view with the ultimate aim of guaranteeing everyone the right to decent housing.

The current General Director is Maimunah Mohd Sharif (Malaysia); the representative at the UN-HABITAT and also the Head of Mission of the Italian Embassy in Nairobi is Amb. Alberto Pieri, as of September 2018, succeeding Amb. Mauro Massoni.

UN-HABITAT works in close collaboration with local authorities, including Municipalities, Provinces and Regions, thanks above all to the special report established with UNACLA, the UN Advisory Committee on Local Authorities. The latter is made up of mayors and representatives of umbrella organisations of local authorities chosen by the UN-HABITAT Director-General on the basis of their competence and commitment in implementing the UN agenda on human settlements.

H. United Nations Children's Fund (UNICEF)

UNICEF is the permanent fund of the United Nations which is assigned the mandate to protect and promote the rights of children, girls and adolescents with the aim of improving their living conditions. Since 1 January 2018, the Executive Director is the American Henrietta H. Fore.

In Italy, the UNICEF Research Centre is located at the Istituto degli Innocenti in Florence. Since 1974, the Italian Committee for UNICEF has been working in Italy; it is a non-governmental organisation whose activities are overseen by a cooperation agreement signed with UNICEF International. Francesco Samengo has been President since 25 July 2018 (outgoing President: Giacomo Guerrera).

UNICEF has launched a vast programme in Italy for migrant and refugee minors, particularly minors who are not accompanied by a family member. The aim of this programme is to provide measures of assistance from first reception to their transferal to smaller, more stable structures, from monitoring human rights standards to school and cultural inclusion in the local community.

I. *International Organization for Migration (IOM)*

Established in 1951, the IOM is the major inter-governmental organisation which deals with migrant issues. Its mission is to promote orderly migration based on respect for human dignity; to this end, it collaborates with Governments and civil society. From June 2018, the Director-General of the Organisation is António Manuel de Carvalho Ferreira Vitorino (Portugal), who succeeded William Lacy Swing (USA).

> The IOM Coordination Office for the Mediterranean countries is based in Rome and the main activities of the IOM offices in Italy concern: providing assistance to vulnerable groups and minors, migration and employment, migration and health, migration, climate and development, reuniting families, supporting voluntary return, and relocation and resettlement.

The activities of the IOM regarding Italy in 2018 include the publication of *Migration and Transnationalism in Italy* (February) which collects and analyses data on migration to and from Italy, considering the transnational dimension of migration and focusing on Italian migration to foreign countries and the links between migration, integration and development. One of the most significant conclusions of the briefing was that the migration of Italian citizens is rarely discussed in current debate despite its magnitude, almost 5 million Italians living abroad in 2017. The size of Italian emigration is comparable to that of the foreign population regularly residing in Italy (around 8.4 % of the total resident population in 2017). According to the briefing, migrant entrepreneurship in Italy maintained a sustained pace of growth even during the economic crisis when Italian firms stagnated (+26 in the last five years). Nevertheless, it is characterized by a high turnover and the prevalence of individual companies (79 % of the total firms registered in 2016). Overall, migrants' contributions are enabled when they have secured a strong status in the societies they belong to and fully participate in social, economic and political processes conducive to their engagement in transnational activities, which produce value for themselves and for the societies they bridge. As such, integration precedes migrants' engagement in development.

Another briefing published by the IOM in 2018, *Migrant Children in Italy* (December 2018), focuses on unaccompanied foreign minors and describes the activity of the IOM in the field of assisting minors at disembarkation points, family reunification and family tracing. Data analysed in the briefing shows that in the past few years, Italy has been the main entry point for unaccompanied minors: between January 2016 and September 2018 45,000 unaccompanied minors arrived by sea. IOM in Italy provides technical advice to Italian authorities in support of the implementation of the legislative provisions in favour of unaccompanied minors. In order to guarantee the respect of the best interest of the child in all situations, IOM Italy assisted more than 2,200 UASC arriving by sea, contributing to the correct identification of many of them; built the capacity of more than 300 professionals that assisted migrant children; traced the families of more than 300 UASC; conducted more than 2500 DNA tests to support family reunification; and relocated about 160 UASC to other European countries.

From January 2018 to March 2019, the IOM was involved in implementing the AVRR (Assisted Voluntary Return & Reintegration from Italy) project, put into practise by the Department for civil liberties and immigration of the Ministry of the Interior and financed by the European Commission through the Asylum, Migration and Integration Fund (AMIF) – a fund set up to cope with the increase in voluntary return requests from migrants who are irregularly present in Italian territory and with little possibility of becoming regular.

In the summer of 2018, the IOM signed a memorandum of understanding with the Municipality of Palermo, the *Associazione Casa dei giovani* and the CISS on "Coordinated Interventions in the field of human trafficking". The main goal of the initiative was to strengthen the multi-agency system with various different operators working to combat human trafficking in order to better protect victims, especially child-victims.

On 4 October, the Ministry of Foreign Affairs and International Cooperation, via the Africa Fund, provided an overall fund of 2.5 million euros to support the work of the IOM in Niger and Egypt in two projects: "Direct Assistance to Abandoned Migrants", aiming to strengthen the presence of the IOM in the north-western region of Niger on the border with Algeria, to provide assistance to migrants and facilitate voluntary repatriation to their home countries; and "Support and Increase Healthcare Access for migrants and vulnerable Egyptian host community members".

Council of Europe

The Council of Europe (CoE, 47 Member States) was established on 5 May 1949 and is the first and most advanced regional system for the promotion and protection of human rights. The Permanent Representative of Italy to the Council of Europe for the period September 2016 to February 2019 is Amb. Marco Marsilli. The Italian official Gabriella Battaini-Dragoni holds the position of Deputy Secretary-General of the Organisation. Since 2011, Italy has been home to an external office of the CoE in Venice, whose international legal status was recognised in June 2017 following the signing of a Memorandum of Understanding between Italy and the Council of Europe. The activities of this office focus on the integration of minorities, gender equality, participation of citizens in democratic processes, the role of women in the Euro-Mediterranean context, the integration of the Roma and the Day of Remembrance.

The Office participates in many projects with local academic institutions, including the Venice International University, the European Inter-University Centre for Human Rights and Democratisation – EIUC/Global Campus for human rights and Venice Ca' Foscari University. It hosts training courses on human rights and democracy with special reference to southern shore Mediterranean countries.

In 2018, Italy made a contribution worth €35,261,058 to the activities of the CoE, €27,515,762 of which was allocated for the regular budget (In 2017, the total contribution was € €34,984,652, € €27,486,110 of which was allocated for the regular budget). In 2018, the voluntary contributions provided by Italy amounted to €590,432 (€590,318 in 2017).

> The following pages will illustrate the activities of the Parliamentary Assembly and the Committee of Ministers with reference to Italy; those of seven bodies established by a treaty: the European Court of Human Rights, the Committee for the Prevention of Torture, the European Committee of Social Rights, the Advisory Committee on the Framework Convention for the Protection of National Minorities, the Group of Experts on Action against Trafficking in Human Beings Group of Experts on Action against Violence against Women and Domestic Violence and Lanzarote Committee on the

Protection of Children against Sexual Exploitation and Sexual Abuse; and of four bodies established by the Committee of Ministers: Commissioner for Human Rights, the European Commission against Racism and Intolerance, the European Commission for Democracy through Law and the Group of States against Corruption.

As is coherent with the multi-year initiative calendar of vaious monitoring bodies of the Council of Europe, only some of these were able to analyse the human rights situations in Italy in 2018. The main issues tackled concerned corruption (Group of States against Corruption), human trafficking, especially child trafficking for labour exploitation (Group of Experts on Action against Trafficking in Human Beings), the conditions of migrants in "hotspots" and Repatriation Centres (Committee for the Prevention of Torture), discrimination against Roma and Sinti comunities, and sexual and reproductive health in Italy (both come under the scope of the European Committee of Social Rights) from which relevant observations and recommendations have emerged. From an Agenda 2030 perspective which takes the Sustainable Development Goals into account, these issues mainly concern Goal 3 (Ensure healthy lives and promote well-being for all at all ages), Goal 5 (Achieve gender equality and empower all women and girls), particularly Target 5.6 (Ensure universal access to sexual and reproductive health and reproductive right), Goal 8 (decent work and economic growth), particularly Target 8.7 (Take immediate and effective measures to eradicate forced labour, end modern slavery and human trafficking and secure the prohibition and elimination of the worst forms of child labour [...]), Goal 10 (Reduce inequality within and among nations) and Goal 16 (peace, justice and strong institutions), particularly Target 16.2 (End abuse, exploitation, trafficking and all forms of violence against and torture of children) and 16.5 (Substantially reduce corruption and bribery in all their forms).

I. Parliamentary Assembly

In the Parliamentary Assembly of the Council of Europe (PACE), made up of delegations from the national parliaments of the Member States of the CoE, 18 members of the Senate and the Chamber of Deputies sit for Italy; there are an equal number of alternate members.

PACE is a forum for discussing the main issues underlying the Organisation's mandate and it has advisory functions in relation to all international conventions drawn up in this context. It elects the judges of the European Court of Human Rights, the Commissioner for Human Rights, the Secretary General of the CoE and their deputy.

The following are the members and alternate members (a) of Italian PACE in 2018 (for Italian delegates in post before the political elections of 4 March 2018, see *Yearbook 2018*, p. 202): Deborah Bergamini, Marina Berlinghieri (a), Anna Maria Bernini, Francesco Berti (a), Simone Billi, Maria Elena Boschi, Maurizio Buccarella, Pino Cabras (a), Sabrina De Carlo, Fabio Di Micco, Fassino Piero (a), Claudio Fazzone (a), Gianluca Ferrara (a), Roberto Paolo Ferrari (a), Carlo Fidanza, Emilio Floris, Paolo Grimoldi, Barbara Guidolin (a), Francesco Laforgia (a), Alvise Maniero, Gianni Marilotti (a), Gaspare Antonio Marinello, Augusta Montaruli (a), Andrea Orlando, Gianluca Perilli, Daisy Pirovano, Roberto Rampi, Alberto Ribolla (a), Maria Rizzotti (a), Tatjana Rojc (a), Gianfranco Rufa (a), Rosellina Sbrana (a), Filippo Scerra, Francesco Scoma (a), Simona Suriano (a), Manuel Vescovi.

From January to June 2018, the role of President of the CoE Parliamentary Assembly was filled by an Italian member of Parliament elected during the previous legislature: Michele Nicoletti (then substituted by Swiss Member of Parliament Liliane Maury Pasquier). Alvise Maniero, who is President of the Italian delegation to PACE, is also Vice-President of the Parliamentary Assembly. During this time, no Italian Member of Parliament was President or Vice-President of any Parliamentary Commissions.

Two reports were published by Italian members of PACE in 2018, presented by outgoing Members of Parliament to the relevant committees, on the basis of which PACE subsequently adopted resolutions: the report of Elena Centemero on *Empowering women in the economy* (report presented 8 June 2018, resolution 2235 adopted 29 June 2018) and of Manlio Di Stefano on the humanitarian situation of refugees in the countries neighbouring Syria (presented 7 June 2018, resolution 2224 adopted 26 June 2018).

Among the documents adopted by PACE in 2018, Resolution 2218 on *Fighting organised crime by facilitating the confiscation of illegal assets* (adopted 26 April 2018, *rapporteur:* Mart van de Ven) refers specifically to Italy. In this report, the Parliamentary Assembly mentions the country among others (Ireland, The Netherlands and the United Kingdom) that have adopted specific regulations to facilitate the confiscation of illegal assets, particularly reducing the burden of proof from the authorities regarding the criminal origins of unexplained wealth. This can be through the use of factual presumption or even, under certain conditions, the reversal of the burden of proof. As observed by PACE, these "civil confiscations" have passed all checks by the highest courts in the States concerned and by the European Court of Human Rights, and have been found to comply with human rights standards.

II. Committee of Ministers

On the subject of human rights, the Committee of Ministers (CM) relies on the work of the Steering Committee for Human Rights, an intergovernmental body composed of representatives of the 47 Member States which performs, among other things, *standard-setting* and *follow-up*.

> The CM adopts recommendations regarding the Member States and on matters for which a common policy is agreed upon – in accordance with its role in the implementation of the European Social Charter (Article 29) – with the aim of asking some States to adapt their laws and public policies with the provisions contained in the Charter. In addition, it is ultimately responsible for monitoring the Framework Convention on National Minorities (Article 26). In this context, it adopts specific resolutions by Country based on the opinions of the Advisory Committee of the Framework Convention (see, this Part, Council of Europe, VIII).
>
> With regard to its role in relation to the European Court of Human Rights, the CM has the function of supervising the execution of judgments of the Court, ensuring that Member States act in accordance with the rulings issued by the same. The Committee terminates each case by adopting a final resolution. Finally, the CM may apply to the Court for a ruling on issues related to difficulties of interpretation of the judgments of the Court itself which would impede their implementation and if it finds that a Member State fails to comply with a final judgment, it may refer the issue to the Court.

In 2018, the CM adopted 3 final resolutions on the execution of the ECtHR judgments by Italy: CM/ResDH(2018)328 on the case *Coppola and others;* CM/ResDH(2018)361 on case *Grossi and others and other 4 cases;* CM/ResDH(2018)353 on the case *Ledonne and other 161 cases.*

Concerning the ongoing monitoring of the implementation of ECtHR judgments against Italy, the Committee of Ministers adopted three decisions in 2018.

On 7 March 2018, during its 1310th session, the CM adopted a decision on the *Khlaifia and others* case (CM/Del/Dec(2018)1310/H46-9) related to the condition of reception of immigrants in irregular situations in Italy and expulsion methods (see *Yearbook 2016*, pp. 255). Regarding individual measures, the Committee noted that the applicants are no longer suffering the effects of the violations found by the ECtHR. Regarding general measures decided by the Court of Strasbourg, the CM noted that this judgment raises complex problems relating to the lack of a legal basis and judicial review in respect of the deprivation of liberty of migrants placed in reception centres, together with the absence of remedies enabling such persons to complain before a national authority about the conditions of their reception. Furthermore, the Deputies express their regret that the information provided so far does not address these key issues and asked them to provide as soon as possible details s on the legislative framework governing the operation of "first aid and assistance centres", the average length of stay of persons placed in such centres before and after their identification and the practice followed with regard to the freedom of movement of these persons after their identification. Moreover, the Committee called on the authorities to indicate, within the same period, what measures have been adopted or envisaged to ensure that persons placed in such centres are not arbitrarily deprived of their liberty. Finally, the CM noted with interest the monitoring activity of the National Ombudsman over places of deprivation of liberty and the possibility for persons deprived of their liberty to submit complaints concerning the reception conditions; in this context, invited the authorities to clarify the powers of that authority to redress the individual situation of complainants and to provide, where appropriate, examples of measures adopted for this purpose.

On 7 June 2018, during its 1318th sessione, the CM adopted a decision on the *Talpis* case (CM/Del/Dec(2018)1318/H46-12, related to an episode of discrimination within a case of domestic violence (see *Yearbook 2018*, p. 309). In this decision, as regards individual measures, the Committee invited the authorities to ensure that the criminal proceedings against the aggressor were concluded promptly and to provide information on their outcome. As regards general measures, the CM welcomed the numerous measures taken by the Italian authorities following the ratification of the Istanbul Convention, that demonstrate the country's determination to tackle violence against women and discrimination based on sex, underlining the positive results achieved by these measures. Furthermore, the Committee firmly encourages the Italian authorities to continue their efforts to provide a comprehensive response to the many aspects of the complex problem of the violence against women, also addressed in the monitoring mechanism framework for the implementation of the Convention, in order to progress further. The Committee invites the Italian authorities to provide detailed information, preferabily for the period 2013–2018, to allow the CM Members to fully evaluate the efficiency of the implementation of the normative framework with particular reference to the criteria used by the competent authorities to respond to preventative and protective measures requests, the average time taken to respond to these requests and the number of measures awarded; the average length of the investigations and criminal procedures concerning incidents of domestic and sexual abuse, the number of interrupted procedures and the number of convictions and acquittals that have acquired the force of res judicata concerning the presented complaints.

On 20 September 2018, during its 1324th session, the CM adopted a decision on the *Ledonne* case group (CM/Del/Dec(2018)1324/H46-11) concerning the excessive length of judicial proceedings (see *Yearbook 2017*, p. 194). In this decision, in regards to individual measures, the Committee proposed to close the supervision of 162 cases related to this topic, adopting resolution CM/ResDH(2018)353. Regarding general measures, the Committee notes overall promising trends for the last few years in the average length of criminal proceedings and in the backlog clearance of criminal cases before the courts of first instance, juvenile courts and the Court of Cassation. It welcomes the recent criminal justice reform to tackle this long-standing problem of excessive length of criminal proceedings, especially the measures adopted to streamline appeals proceedings in the appeals court, where the situation is still problematic. Finally, the Committee encourages the Italian authorities to ensure the success of the reform by closely monitoring its impact on the length of proceedings and the size of the backlog, with a focus on the courts of appeal, and provide precise, comprehensive and detailed data on the impact of the reform.

On 4 July 2019, the CM adopted resolution CM/ResChS(2018)5 on the decision of the European Committee of Social Rights to the collective complaint towards Italy presented by the *Unione Italiana del Lavoro U.I.L. Scuola-Sicilia* (113/2014, see *Yearbook 2015*, p. 215; *Yearbook 2016*, p. 185). In the resolution, the CM takes note of the decision of the the European Committee of Social Rights which states that the Italian authorities did not act in violation of Articles 12(1) and 12(3) of the European Social Charter (revised) (see this Part, 2.5).

On 26 September 2018, the CM adopted resolution CM/ResCSS(2018)10 on the application of the European Code of Social Security (related to the period 1 July 2016–30 June 2017) with particular reference to the following parts of the Code: V (Old-age benefit), VI (Employment injury benefit), VII (Family benefit), and VIII (Maternity benefit). Based on the report provided by the Italian Government and on the report produced by the ILO Committee of Experts on the application of ILO conventions and recommendations, the CM lists a series of observations and requests additional information from the Italian authorities.

In particular, concerning Part V, the Committee invites the Government of Italy to re-establish the right of all persons protected under Part V to a reduced social insurance pension after 15 years of contributions and to explain in its next report to what extent the derogation with respect to discontinuous workers (a) serves the purpose of Article 29(2)(a) and (b) permits to close the gap between insured workers before and after 1 January 1996. Concerning Part VI, the CM requests confirmation that the National Institute for Insurance against Employment Injuries (INAIL) provides all types of medical care benefits mentioned in Article 34(2)(b), (c) and (e) of the Code without any cost-sharing by the victims of employment injuries. Concerning Part VIII, Article 51 of the Code, the Committee requests that the Italian authorities indicate in its next report the qualifying period required for entitlement to maternity benefit. Concerning Article 71(3) of the Code, the CM asks the Italian authorities to clarify who is in charge of actually paying maternity benefit and explain whether the INPS will ensure payment of maternity benefit to the beneficiary in case of the employer's failure to pay. Concerning Part XI (standards to be complied with by periodical payments), the CM asks the Government to confirm in its next report that the wages of level I and III metalworkers are the appropriate proxies for the reference wages of unskilled and skilled workers determined by using ISCO 08 Major groups 9 (elementary occupations) and 7 (craft and related trades workers), and to explain the above-mentioned differences, particularly if the replacement rate of benefits recalculated on the basis of the SES reference wage would not attain the percentage prescribed by the Code.

On 18 April 2018, the CM declared that Italian professor Ms Emma Lantschner was elected to the list of experts eligible to serve on the Advisory Committee on the Framework Convention for the Protection of National Minorities. (CM/ResCMN(2018)4)).

III. European Court of Human Rights

The European Court of Human Rights (EctHR) guarantees the respect of the commitments laid down in the ECHR and its protocols by Member States of the CoE.

The Italian judge who currently sits at the Court is Guido Raimondi, appointed President of the ECtHR in September 2015. On 22 January 2019, PACE elected Raffaele Sabato to the role, who will take up the position in May 2019. Of the 639 members of the Registry, which provides legal and administrative support to the Court in exercising its functions, 24 are Italian.

The statistical data provided by the Court and updated in December 2018 shows that the total number of complaints pending against Italy amounted to 4,050, corresponding to about 7.2 % of the total. In a worse situation are Romania with 8,500 appeals pending, corresponding to 15.1 % of the total, Russian Federation (11,750, 20.9 %), Turkey (7,100, 12.6 %), and Ukraine (7,250, 12.9 %). For Italy, 24.10 % of cases concern the right to a fair trial (Article 6 ECHR) followed by 18.25 % of cases concerning the ban on torture and inhuman or degrading treatment (Article 3 ECHR).

In 2018, the Court received 1,374 valid individual complaints about a violation of rights contained within the ECHR from Italy (1,409 in 2016, 1,885 in 2017). In the same period, 1,674 complaints were declared inadmissable or removed; 14 were judgments as to substance, 11 of which found at least one violation of the Convention. Overall, the Court found the following violations: 2 with regard to inhuman and degrading treatment according to Article 3 ECHR; 1 for excessive duration of procedure according to Article 6 ECHR; 1 concerning the enforcement of a judgment according to Article 6 ECHR; 1 for the principle *nulla poena sine lege* according to Article 7 ECHR; 4 in the field of private and family life according to Article 8 ECHR; 1 for lack of effective remedy according to Article 13 ECHR; 3 in the field of protection of property according to Article 1, Protocol 1 ECHR.

Furthermore, 499 appeals were communicated to the relevant Country in view of a hearing on their merits. The Court also received 36 requests for urgent measures pursuant to Article 39 of the Court's regulations, mostly regarding the suspension of deportation proceedings for as many applicants, only 2 of which were granted by the ECtHR.

An analysis on the Court's judgments concerning Italy in 2018 is presented in Part IV, Italy in the Case-law of the European Court of Human Rights.

IV. Committee for the Prevention of Torture

The European Committee for the Prevention of Torture and Inhuman or Degrading Treatment or Punishment (CPT) was established by the 1987 Convention of the same name, conceived as complementary to the regulations under Article 3 of ECHR which sets forth an absolute ban on torture. The CPT is a body composed of independent experts and has one member for each State Party to the Convention for the Prevention of Torture (all the CoE countries are party to it). The members of the Committee are elected by the Committee of Ministers. Elisabetta Zamparutti was elected as Italian member from 7 October 2015 until 19 December 2019.

The Committee's main function is to verify, by means of inspections, the treatment of persons deprived of their liberty in order to strengthen, if necessary, their protection from torture and inhuman or degrading treatment or punishment (Article 1). CPT is not an investigative body, but a preventive body. At the end of each visit, the Committee draws up a detailed report and sends it to the State involved, to which it requests an answer in relation to any critical issues raised in it. The action of the CPT is based on the principles of cooperation with national authorities and confidentiality. Therefore, its reports and the responses of the Governments are initially reserved and only subsequently, at the request of the country concerned, may they be made public together with the replies and observations provided by the national authorities.

In 2018, the Committee conducted 18 visits in the following countries: Albania, Andorra, Bulgaria, Czech Republic, France, Georgia, Germany, Greece, Hungary, Lituania, Norway, Russian Federation, Republic of Moldova, Romania, Slovak Republic, Spain (Catalunia), Turkey and United Kingdom. During the year, the CPT published 19 reports on visits previously carried out in the following CoE Member States: Albania, Azerbaijan (6 reports), Bulgaria, Croatia, Cyprus, Hungary, Italy, Lithuania, Poland, Portugal, Serbia, Turkey, Ukraine and United Kingdom (Northern Ireland).

In total, the CPT conducted 14 visits to Italy (seven periodic visits and seven ad hoc visits). The last one took place between 12–22 June 2019 to examine the situation of people detained in high or maximum-security regimes (the so-called "41-*bis* regime") and other isolation and segregation methods. The Committee will adopt the report for this visit during 2019.

On 10 April 2018, the CPT published the report to the Italian Government alongside the observations of the Italian authorities, on the visit to Italy carried out from 7 to 13 June 2017 (see *Yearbook 2018*, p. 153). The main purpose of the CPT's visit to Italy in June 2017 was to examine the situation of foreign nationals deprived of their liberty in the so-called "hotspots" and immigration detention centres in a context of large-scale arrivals from North Africa. To this end, the CPT's delegation visited the "hotspots" in Lampedusa, Pozzallo and in Trapani (Milo), as well as a mobile "hotspot" unit at Augusta port. Furthermore, it was able to observe a disembarkation procedure at Trapani port. The delegation also visited the closed removal centres (centri di permanenza per i rimpatri, CPR) in Caltanissetta, Ponte Galeria (Rome) and Turin, as well as the holding facilities at Rome Fiumicino Airport.

The delegation received very good co-operation from both the national authorities and staff at the establishments visited. They held meetings with officials of the Ministry of the Interior, officials of the law enforcement authorities (Guardia di Finanza, Polizia di Stato, Central Directorate of Immigration and Border Police) the Italian Coast Guard, the Head of the Italian Ombudsperson for the rights of persons detained or deprived of their liberty, Mauro Palma, representatives of the UNHCR and numerous NGOs. In general, the CPT emphasises that it recognises the significant challenges faced by the Italian authorities in the context of the influx of new arrivals and acknowledges the significant efforts made by the Italian authorities in carrying out rescue operations at sea and in providing shelter and support to the hundreds of thousands of refugees, asylum seekers and migrants currently present in Italy. The delegation was impressed by the way in which the Italian authorities were handling the situation on a daily basis in the places visited, and the CPT clearly stated the need for a co-ordinated European approach and support to address the phenomenon of mass migratory arrivals.

While the Committee's overall assessment of the findings is largely positive as regards "hotspots", it did note a number of specific issues that call for improvement, particularly with respect to closed removal centres.

With regard to the "hotspots", The CPT recommends that the Italian authorities install the necessary infrastructure, and particularly showers at the mobile "hotspot" unit at Augusta port. In the meantime, the facility should only be used to accommodate new arrivals for very short periods of time. Concerning living conditions, the CPT recommends that the Italian authorities increase structurally the bed capacity of the

Lampedusa "hotspot" in the light of the above remarks. Other questions of quality and capacity of the infrastructure on these placese, the CPT report concentrates on the following: recommendation that the necessary repairs be undertaken swiftly at Lampedusa "hotspot"; recommendation that the Italian authorities introduce a range of activities for foreign nationals at the Lampedusa "hotspot" and provide for a common room; request for information about the refurbishment works carried out at the Trapani "hotspot"; the request to remove the metal fencing on top of the accommodation blocks as a step towards reducing the carceral aspect of the centre. In general, the Committee recommends that the Italian authorities make further efforts, in particular regarding the Lampedusa "hotspot", to ensure that foreign nationals only remain at the "hotspots" for the shortest possible period of time. Concerning health-care services in the "hotspots", The CPT invites the Italian authorities to consider providing foreign nationals diagnosed as suffering from scabies with oral anti-scabetic treatment, as required, in all "hotspots" and that the Italian authorities introduce individual medical files for each newly arrived person at the Pozzallo "hotspot".

Referring to *legal safeguards*, the CPT delegation identified a series of deficiencies and requests that the Italian authorities take action to remedy them; notably in order to reduce the risk of *refoulement* of foreign nationals with prima facie genuine protection needs. Foreign nationals should not be returned from the "hotspots" without judicial oversight. The Italian authorities should provide adequate judicial control of the legality of all cases of deprivation of liberty of foreign nationals in the "hotspots", including by way of legislative amendments. In particular, the Committee recommends that the Italian authorities ensure that: newly arrived foreign nationals are able to fully understand the information provided to them and the consequences of their declarations; all foreign nationals held with a view to their removal have an effective right of access to a lawyer as from the very outset of their deprivation of liberty (including through the provision of free legal aid) and an effective right to appeal; that various anomlaies found by the delegation are addressed, concerning the foreign national's understanding of information requested in the "*fogli notizie*" document and its subsequent signing, and that all foreign nationals be provided with a copy of the foglio notizie and, when they have manifested their intention to apply for asylum, an official attestation of that fact. Finally, the CPT suggests that in all "hotspots" officers working in direct contact with foreign nationals inside the "hotspots" should not carry truncheons and firearms, as it unnecessarily impacts negatively on the overall relaxed atmosphere at the "hotspots" and encourages the Italian authorities to introduce a dedicated mobile phone/ Internet space also at the Lampedusa "hotspot".

On the question of *non-accompanied minors* inside the "hotspots", the CPT encourages the Italian authorities to ensure that unaccompanied minors are swiftly transferred to dedicated open shelter facilities and that a guardianship procedure is initiated as soon as possible after their arrival, as the support available for their specific needs is only limited in the "hotspots". In general, the CPT welcomes the recent legislative improvements and requests to receive confirmation that this new multidisciplinary age assessment procedure is now being applied in all Italian "hotspots".

Concerning Closed Removal Centres (CPRs), the Committee requests that the Italian authorities provide updated information about the plans (including the locations, capacity and timeline) for the (re-)opening of the additional CPR dedicated to immigration detention facilities and open new facilities across the country in the near future. This would lead to a capacity of around 1,600 places (as opposed to the 359 places at the time of the visit).

On the question of ill-treatment in the CPRs, after finding some episodes of inter-detainee violence and intimidation during the visit, the CPT recommends that the management and staff of CPR Caltanissetta and CPR Turin exercise increased vigilance and make use of all the means at their disposal to prevent this type of violence. Furthermore, custodial staff in both centres should be reminded about their responsibility to protect detained persons from other detainees who wish to cause them harm, including by intervening when necessary.

Concerning *conditions of detention*, the CPT recommends that the Italian authorities take further steps to improve the material conditions at CPR Caltanissetta and in CPR Ponte Galeria, including by urgently repairing the sanitary annexes, and, subsequently, to maintain them in an adequate state of repair. Detained persons should also be provided with clean mattresses, clean blankets and appropriate facilities to wash their clothes and blankets. Moreover, the Committee recommends that the Italian authorities develop a regime of activities for foreign nationals deprived of their liberty in all closed removal centres (CPR). This should include access to appropriate means of recreation (e.g. board games, table tennis, other sports, arts and crafts, etc.) and access to reading material in the most frequently spoken foreign languages, as well as allowing non-governmental organisations to organise activities. For persons staying for more than a few months, the authorities should develop a broader range of purposeful activities (vocational and work).

Numerous recommendations of the CPT concern the situation of health-care services in the CPR. In particular, and in the light of the deficiencies observed during the visit, the CPT encourages the Italian authorities to take the necessary measures to ensure that, in all CPRs in Italy, the record drawn up after a medical examination of a foreign national (whether newly-arrived or not) contains: i) a full account of objective medical findings based on a thorough examination (supported by a "body chart" for annotating traumatic injuries), ii) a full account of statements made by the person concerned which are relevant to the medical examination (including a description of his/her state of health and any allegations of ill-treatment), and iii) the doctor's observations in the light of i) and ii), indicating the consistency between any allegations made and the objective medical findings. In addition, the results of every examination, including the above-mentioned statements and the doctor's observations, should be made available to the foreign national and his/her lawyer. Moreover, the authorities should ensure that whenever injuries are recorded which are consistent with allegations of ill-treatment made by the foreign national concerned (or which, even in the absence of an allegation, are clearly indicative of ill-treatment), the record is systematically brought to the attention of the competent prosecutor, regardless of the wishes of the person concerned. Furthermore, The CPT recommends that the Italian authorities ensure that, at CPR Turin, medical examinations are always conducted out of the hearing and – unless the doctor concerned requests otherwise in a particular case – out of the sight of custodial staff.

On the subject of *legal safeguards*, the Committee maintains that the Italian authorities need to put in place additional guarantees to ensure that the hearings are conducted in conditions that allow for confidentiality (i.e. without the presence of police officers or security staff) and that the lawyers have been in direct contact with the persons concerned prior to the hearings. Therefore, the CPT asks to receive the comments of the Italian authorities on this point. Furthermore, according to the CPT, efforts should be pursued to ensure that all foreign nationals understand the information about their situation and their rights. Appropriate steps should be taken to enable ex officio lawyers to consult the file and meet with their clients before the judicial hearing, if necessary, with the aid of an interpreter. The CPT wishes to receive clarification of the procedures and safeguards available to rejected asylum seekers in detention, which guarantee respect of the principle of non-refoulement. With reference to all CPRs visited, the Committee recommends that the Italian authorities institute a central incidents register for any health-related incident and to introduce a confidential access to an appropriate complaints procedure.

Acknowledging that in the CPR the relationship between detainees and staff is essentially positive, the CPT recommends that steps be taken to ensure an increased presence of staff in the detention areas in all closed removal centres, and particularly at CPR Turin, and encourage greater interaction and communication between staff and detainees.

Among the principle *security-related issues* observed by the delegation, the CPT reiterates that in immigration detention centres must avoid, as far as possible, any impression of a carceral environment, which was an impression found by the delegation in the CPR Caltanisetta and CPT Turin. The CPT invites the Italian authorities to reconsider their emphasis on security measures at these two centres, recommends that the Italian authorities review the security restrictions in place at CPR Ponte Galeria. According to the CPT, clear rules should be adopted to regulate the placement, duration, conditions and safeguards surrounding the use of segregation units or cells in CPR establishments.

Concerning unaccompanied minors, the CPT recommends that police officers be reminded to accurately record the foreign nationals' statement of their age. In case of uncertainty about whether a particular irregular migrant is a minor (i.e. under 18 years of age), the person in question should be treated as such until proven otherwise. The Italian authorities should also take the necessary follow-up action by way of ordering an age assessment. As requested for the "hotspots", the Committee requests confirmation that the new multidisciplinary age assessment procedure is also being applied in all CPR establishments.

Finally, with reference to the situation in the *holding facilities* at Rome Fiumicino Airport, the CPT recommends that the Italian authorities ensure that any foreign national who is deprived of his/her liberty at Rome Fiumicino holding facilities in excess of 24 hours be transferred to a more suitable holding facility in the vicinity which offers access to natural light and outdoor exercise. The Committee requests more detailed information about the plan presented by the Italian authorities to construct a new structure in Terminal 3 of the airport, and invites the authorities to take into account the comments in the report regarding suitable detention conditions when designing the new facility. Finally, the CPT recommends that effective steps are taken without delay to ensure that meals are always provided three times a day –and at appropriate times which should be recorded- to all foreign nationals held at the facility; it requests confirmation that a satisfactory solution has been put in place.

V. European Committee of Social Rights

The European Committee of Social Rights (ECSR) was established pursuant to Article 25 of the European Social Charter of 1961 in order to determine whether the legislation and practice of States Parties comply with the provisions of the European Social Charter, its Protocols and the European Social Charter (revised) (ESC-R). Currently, the Committee is composed of 15 independent experts elected by the Committee of Ministers for a six-year mandate renewable only once. The Italian expert Giuseppe Palmisano has been re-elected for the period 2016–2022 as the President of the Committee.

Italy ratified the European Social Charter in 1965 and the revised European Social Charter in 1999, accepting 97 of its 98 paragraphs. The only non-accepted provision is Article 25 ESC-R, which protects the right of workers in the case of the insolvency of their employer. In 2002, the CM decided that, every five years, countries must also inform the European Committee of Social Rights on the status of rights protected under provisions that they have not accepted. Italy's most recent communication on this issue dates back to 2014 (see *Yearbook 2016*, p. 183); the Committee's next assessment of Article 25 ESC-R is scheduled for 2019.

As concerns the analysis of provisions it has accepted, from 1967–2015 the Italian Government submitted 20 annual reports on the application of the 1961 Charter and 15 on that of the revised Charter. Based on these, the Committee adopted its conclusions each year on the status of protection of social rights in Italy. Their most recent Conclusions on Italy were published in January 2018. The document concerns the sixteenth report, submitted in 7 March 2017 that covers the provisions of the Revised Charter in the thematic group 2, "Health, social security and social provision (Articles 3, 11, 12, 13, 14, 23, 30 ESC-R) with reference to the period of 1 January 2012 - 31 December 2015 (see *Yearbook 2018*, p. 220–226).

For the year 2018, Italy was included in a group of eight States (alongside Belgium, Bulgaria, Finland, France, Greece, Ireland and

Portugal) that were exempt from reporting on the provisions subject to assessment in the framework of the Conclusions 2018, in accordance with the changes to the reporting system adopted in 2014. These countries were invited, instead, to provide information on the follow-up given to the decisions on the merits of collective complaints, provided for in the 1995 Protocol, in which the Committee had found violations of the European Social Charter (revised). For Italy, the following six decisions were discussed:

1) *European Roma Rights Centre (ERRC) v. Italy* (complaint 27/2004, decision on the merits of 7 December 2005);
2) *Centre on Housing Rights and Evictions (COHRE) v. Italy* (complaint 58/2009, decision on the merits of 25 June 2010);
3) *International Planned Parenthood Federation-European Network (IPPF-EN) v. Italy* (complaint 87/2012, decision on the merits of 10 September 2013);
4) *Confederazione Generale Italiana del Lavoro (CGIL) v. Italy* (complaint 91/2013, decision on admissibility and the merits of 12 October 2015);
5) *Associazione Nazionale dei Giudici di Pace (ANGdP) v. Italy* (complaint 102/2013, decision on the merits of 5 July 2016);
6) *"La Voce dei Giusti" v. Italy* (complaint 105/2014, decision on the merits of 18 October 2016).

The first two decisions concern the rights of Roma and Sinti in Italy, particularly their living conditions in camps and the circumstances surrounding their eviction (see *Yearbook 2011*, p. 218–220), and therefore the Committee jointly assessed the measures taken. Considering the decisions taken on the merits of the complaints and the information presented by the Italian Government about measures taken over the years to remedy the violations found in the present complaint, the Committee gave the following assessment of the *follow-up.*

Concerning living conditions in camps, segregation and access for families to adequate housing (Article E, read in conjunction with Articles 31(1), 31(3), 16, 19(4).c ESC-R), Committee asks for up-to-date information in the next report on the results obtained in the implementation of the various projects under way, with the aim of overcoming segregation and helping these populations to gain access to satisfactory living conditions (see *Yearbook 2014*, p. 28–30). It also asks for up-to-date figures on the supply and demand of social housing for Roma and Sinti. The information will be submitted in October 2019, in the meantime the Committee considers that the situation has not been brought into conformity with the European Social Charter (revised).

A similar assessment concerning the clearing of camps (Article E, read in conjunction with Articles 31(2) and 16 ESC-R) was given. The Committee requests up-to-date information to be included in the next report on the increase or decrease in the number of evictions involving RSC communities and the legal safeguards applying to them. It considers in the meantime that the situation has not been brought into conformity with the Charter.

Regarding marginalisation and social exclusion of these communities (Article E, read in conjunction with Article 30 ESC-R), the Committee notes that the information provided is not sufficient to conclude that there has been a general improvement in the situation. Furthermore, most of the measures described in the report are still at an initial stage. The Committee therefore will reassess the situation with regard to the marginalisation and social exclusion of Roma and Sinti with the next report, maintains its assessment that the situation has not been brought into conformity with the Charter.

On the queston of hate speech (Article E ESC-R read in conjunction with Article 19(2) ESC-R), after noting the measures taken by the Italian authorities to combat this issue, the Committee requests clarification about the measures taken, particularly with regard to racist misleading propaganda against Roma and Sinti indirectly allowed or directly emanating from the authorities. It considers in the meantime that the situation has not been brought into conformity with the Charter.

Referring to expulsion from the country (Article E ESC-R read in conjunction with Article 19(8)), the Committee takes note of the termination of the "security measures" linked with the state of emergency, which had given rise to the expulsion of a number of Roma from the country. It also notes that measures are being considered to limit or resolve cases of statelessness. In the light of these developments and the decision 9687/2013 of the Court of Cassation, it considers that the situation has been brought into conformity with the Charter.

The third and fourth decisions are related to the organisation of sexual and reproductive health services in Italy, particularly the insufficient number of non-objecting doctors in services carrying out voluntary terminations of pregnancy (see *Yearbook 2015*, p. 216). The Committee therefore decided to assess jointly the measures taken.

On the question of discrimination against women wishing to terminate their pregnancy and violation of their right to health because of problems with access to abortion services (Article 11(1) and Article E, read in conjunction with Article 11(1) ESC-R), the Committee noted with reservation the improvements presented by the Italian authorities' report. It observed that, with regard to the decrease in the numbers of terminations of pregnancies carried out, the decrease could also reflect problems with access to these services. The Committee therefore asks for information in the next report on the measures taken to reduce the remaining disparities at local level that continue despite the apparent improvements in the general situation, and the results obtained.

In relation to discrimination against non-objecting gynaecologists and failure to protect such doctors from moral harassment (Article 1(2) ESC-R and 26(2) ESC-R), the Committee notes that the situation has clearly improved with regard to the average workload of non-objecting practitioners. It notes a series of problems concerning the difference between the diffusion and effective presence of these doctors throughout the country and the lack of information provided about any awareness-raising or prevention measures concerning harassment in the Government's report. In light of these deficiencies and until further information is provided in Italy's next report, the Committee considers that the situation has not been brought into conformity with the Charter with regard to this issue.

Concerning the assessment of the follow-up of the fifth collective complaint, with regard to the lack of social protection for persons who performed the duties of Justice of the Peace (violation of Article E ESC-R read in conjunction with Article 12(1) ESC-R, see *Yearbook 2017*, p. 208), the Committee takes note of the new legislative measures adopted that introduce compulsory social coverage for lay judges who are not already covered by other social insurance schemes. It takes note, however, of the restrictions which apply in the event of sickness or maternity and asks for clarification in the next report as to whether this means that no maternity or sickness benefit is paid to lay judges who are not covered by other social insurance schemes, including in cases of incapacity arising from sickness or accident having a causal link with the exercise of the office of judge. Pending receipt of this information, it considers that this situation has not been brought into conformity with the European Social Charter (revised).

The follow-up assessment concerning the sixth collective complaint regarding teachers in the third category on aptitude lists suffered indirect discrimination with regard to access to specialist training in support teaching for disabled students (violation of Article E ESC-R read in conjunction with Articles 10(3) lett. a), b) ESC-R, see *Yearbook 2018*, p. 225–226).

The Committee notes that the information provided by the Italian Government about legislative developments does not explain to what extent the new provisions actually facilitate access to authorisation and hence to specialist training in teaching support for teachers in the third category. Furthermore, no changes seem to have been made as regards the recognition of occupational achievements so as to take better account of the career paths of the teachers in question and the experience they may have acquired. Therefore, the Committee considers that the situation has not been brought into conformity with the Charter.

On 24 January 2018, a further decision by the Committee was published regarding a collective complaint presented by the *Unione Italiana del Lavoro U.I.L. Scuola-Sicilia* (complaint 113/2014). The complainant trade union accused Italy of violating Articles 12 ESC-R (1) and (3) (the right to social security), and 25 ESC-R (the right of workers to the protection of their claims in the event of the insolvency of their employer) read in combination with clause non-discrimination contained in section E of the Revised European Social Charter, and under the Italian regulations on social protection (Interministerial decree No. 83473, 1 August 2014) excludes workers of training bodies in Sicily from the assistance paid by the Wage Guarentee Fund (*Cassa integrazione guadagni*) by derogation. After analysing the complaint of the trade union and the responses on the merits provided by the Italian Government, the Committee decided that in the case in examination there had been no violation of Article 12(1) ESC-R (unanimous decision) and Article 12(3) (9 votes in favour, 5 against). Therefore, the Committee did not consider it necessary to make a separate assessment of Article E of the Charter, in conjunction with the latter. The part of the complaint concerning Article 25 ESC-R was excluded from the decision on admissibility on the basis that Italy, as previously mentioned, did not accept this provision of the revised Charter (see *Yearbook 2016*, p. 185).

In 2018, six new collective complaints were presented against Italy.

The first was presented by the *Associazione Professionale e Sindacale (ANIEF)* (159/2018). The complainant alleges a violation of the following articles of the European Social Charter (revised): 1(1) and 1(2) (right to work), 4(1) and 4(4) (right to a fair remuneration), 5 (right to organise), 6(4) (right to collective bargaining), 24 (right to protection in the event of dismissal) and E (non-discrimination). The trade union organisation alleges that, as a result of a change in the case-law of the Council of State end 2017, people with a primary school teaching certificate (diploma magistrale) obtained before 2001/2002 are henceforth excluded from the reserve lists from which teachers in primary school and preschool are recruited. The Committee declared the complaint admissible on 2 July 2018.

The second and third collective complaints were presented, respectively, by the *Confederazione Generale Sindacale* (CGS) and the *Federazione dei Lavoratori Pubblici e Funzioni Pubblici* (FLP) (161/2018) and by the *Nursing Up* organization (169/2018). Both concern articles: 5 ESC-R (right to organise), 6(2) ESC-R (right to bargain collectively), 21 ESC-R (right to information and consultation), 22 ESC-R (right to take part in the determination and improvement of the working conditions and working environment) and E ESC-R (non-discrimination). In both cases, complainants allege that the National Collective Labour Agreement (NCLA) related to staff from the public health sector of 21 May 2018, excludes representative trade unions from any subsequent participation in collective bargaining because of their refusal to sign the agreement. The Committee declared the complaint No. 161 admissible on 11 September 2018 and the complaint No. 169 admissible on 18 March 2018.

The fourth complaint was presented by the *Sindacato autonomo pensionati Or.S.A.* (167/2018) concerning Article 12(3) ESC-R (right to social security). The complainant union alleges that the provisions introduced by legislative decree No. 65/2015 (urgent provisions for pensions, welfare and severance pay guarantees) and the Stability Law 2014 (Law No. 147/2013) have limited - or even ruled out - the equalisation of pensions with mechanisms resulting in a substantial drop in statutory retirement pensions in breach of the above-mentioned provisions. The Committee declared the complaint admissible on 22 January 2019.

The fifth complaint was presented by the *Unione sindacale di base (USB)* (170/2018) and concerns the following articles: 1 (right to work), 4 (right to a fair remuneration), 5 (right to organise), 6(4) (right to collective bargaining), 12 (right to social security), 24 (right to protection in the event of dismissal) and E (non-discrimination) ESC-R.

In the complaint, the trade union complains about the abuse of 'socially useful workers' contracts by municipalities and public bodies in Sicily and Campania contributing to make the situation of these public sector employees more precarious in violation of the aforementioned provisions of the Charter.

A sixth complaint was presented by the Sindacato Autonomo Europeo Scuola ed Ecologia (SAESE) (166/2018). On 16 March 2019 the Committee declared the complaint inadmissible, which related to Article 11 ESC-R (right to protection of health). The complainant union alleged that the Fornero Act, (law 201/2011), which extends the minimum retirement age for public and private sector workers, violates the above-mentioned provision.

VI. Commissioner for Human Rights

The Commissioner for Human Rights is an independent non-judicial institution established by the Committee of Ministers' Resolution (99)50 of 7 May 1999. On 1 April 2018, Dunja Mijatovic (Bosnia-Herzegovina) was elected Commissioner for Human Rights of the Council of Europe by the PACE. Mijatovic had served as the OSCE Representative on Freedom of the Media (see this Part, Organisation for Security and Cooperation in Europe, III), succeding Nils Muižnieks (Latvia, 2012–2018), and will be in the role until April 2024.

> The Commissioner's duties are to promote effective respect for human rights, to support the 47 Member States in implementing the relevant CoE standards and to promote education and awareness of human rights. Its main activity is to conduct a permanent dialogue with Governments of the Member States, including visits to their respective territories. At the end of the mission, the Commissioner draws up a report that includes both an analysis on human rights and the improvement thereof; this report is published and spread widely. In addition, the Commissioner conducts follow-up visits to evaluate the progress made regarding the implementation of the previous recommendations and relevant reports are also rendered public.
>
> In 2018, the outgoing Commissioner Muižnieks conducted visits and missions in the former Yugoslav Republic of Macedonia, Slovak Republic and Serbia and the new Commissioner Mijatovic conducted visits in Albania, Armenia, Estonia, Germany, Greece, Romania and missions in Turkey, Poland and Berlin (in order to participate in an event on "Technology and the next frontier in human rights"). During the year in question, furthermore, the office of the Commissioner published reports on visits conducted (in 2017

and 2018) in the following countries: Estonia, Greece, Romania and Sweden and sent letters requesting information to the following countries: Belgium, Bosnia-Herzegovina, Bulgaria, Croatia, Russian Federation (2), France, Malta (2), Poland, United Kingdom (2), Spain and Ukraine.

The Commissioner for Human Rights conducted five visits in Italy. The last one was held from 3–6 July 2012 and aimed to examine a series of critical issues, focusing on the excessive duration of judicial process and protection of the rights of Roma and Sinti communities, migrants and asylum seekers. The subsequent report was published on 18 September 2012 (CommDH (2012)26) (see *Yearbook 2013*, p. 255–262). Although their last visit and report took place five years ago, the Commissioner has kept up a dialogue with the Italian authorities through various letters requesting clarifications, especially related to policies on Roma minorities and the management of migrants, refugees and asylum seekers (see, for example, *Yearbook 2017*, p. 209–210 and *Yearbook 2018*, p. 227–228). There were no specific initatives by the Commissioner (visits, reports, letters) about Italy in 2018.

> Among the Commissioner for Human Rights' work in 2018, the online publication of various *Human Rights Comments,* short posts in which the Commissioner analyses and summarises relevant human rights situations in Europe, is particularly noteworthy. Over the year, 7 *comments* were published (10 in 2017, 11 in 2016). Three of these refer specficially to the human rights situation in Italy.
>
> *The right of older persons to dignity and autonomy in care (18 January 2018).* In this comment, the outgoing Commissioner Muižnieks writes about the difficulties faced by older persons upon implementing their human rights. Italy is mentioned in reference to the issue of Advance Care Planning and "living wills", which are especially pertinent for older persons with degenerative illnesses. The Commissioner underlines that, even though the Council of Europe has recognised the importance of these documents, their application varies greatly from State to State. Therefore, the debate in Italy that brought about the so-called "Living Will law" (l. 219/2017) was welcomed by the Commissioner.
>
> *Europe's duty to internally displaced persons (29 May 2018).* The new Commissioner took the opportunity of the 20th Anniversary of the United Nations Guiding Principles on Internal Displacement (1998) to remind States of the need to give serious attention to the needs of those who find themselves interally displaced. The comment in question reiterates the main responsibilities of States on the issue and gives recommendations on the steps to take, while also summarising the current situation of internally displaced persons (IDPs) in Europe. By the end of 2017, there were close

to 4 million IDPs in Europe, mostly resulting from conflicts and instability (Ukraine, Turkey, Bosnia-Herzegovina etc.). The Commissioner cites the case of displacement emanating from the earthquakes in 2016 as an example of a large number of people who find themselves internally displaced within Europe due to natural disasters and climate change.

Paris Principles at 25: Strong National Human Rights Institutions Needed More Than Ever (*12 December 2018*). The reflections in this comment also come out of an important anniversary; the adoption of the so-called "Paris Principles" by the UN General Assembly on *20 December 1993* (A/RES/48/134). In this comment, the Commissioner highlights the importance of independent national human rights institutions (NHRIs) as protection measures against the recent attacks on democracy, the rule of law and respect for human rights that are going on in many European countries and observes with concern that several NHRIs in Europe have experienced blows to their independence and effective operations over the past few years, attacks that have taken several forms, from head-on criticism and threats, to more subtle damaging tactics. To strengthen theses insitutions at the European levelm the Commissioner presents a series of recommendations generally aimed at ensuring these institutions are well-structured and act compliantly with the "Paris Principles", also within the Global Alliance of NHRIs (GANHRI). Italy is mentioned in this comment as one of the few European Countries that still do not have an NHRI (alongside Malta and Switzerland). For these countries, the Commissioner recommends them to establish an NHRI without delay, and are fully-compliant with the Paris Principles.

VII. European Commission against Racism and Intolerance

The European Commission against Racism and Intolerance (ECRI), established in 1993, is a monitoring body of the Council of Europe specialised in combating any form of racism, xenophobia, anti-semitism and intolerance in a human rights perspective. The members of ECRI remain in office for five years. They are selected for their moral authority and their recognised experience in the field of combating racism, xenophobia, anti-semitism and intolerance; they act on an individual basis and independently. The Commission is composed by a member and, if a Government so wishes, a deputy member for each State of the Council of Europe. In 2018, the Italian expert was Vitaliano Esposito. Constance Hermanin was an alternate member. An Italian official, Stefano Valenti, was responsible for the External Relations of the Commission Secretariat, part of the Directorate-general Human Rights and the Rule of Law of the Council of Europe

> The mandate of the ECRI covers all measures to combat violence, discrimination and prejudice against people (or groups of people) on the basis of racial, linguistic, religious, national, or ethnic preconditions. The Commission carries out an in-depth analysis of the situation regarding racism and intolerance in each of the Member States of the CoE and write suggestions and proposals by drawing up reports. The report is on the basis of an analysis of documentary sources, site visits and a confidential dialogue with national authorities and civil society organisations. ECRI also directs general policy recommendations to all Member States and promotes cooperation with relevant actors, in particular NGOs, mass media and youth associations.
>
> In 2018, the Commission published reports of the fifth monitoring cycle for Croatia, Liechetestein, Malta, Republic of Moldova, San Marino, Spain and Sweden. Furthermore, the Commission presented the conclusions on the priority recommendations to the following countries in the context of the fifth cycle reports already published: Albania, Austria, Czech Republic, Estonia, Greece, Hungary, Norway and Poland. In 2018, also conducted visits, within their respective monitoring cycles, in: Russian Federation, Finland, Ireland, Latvia, the Netherlands, Romania and Slovenia.
>
> In 2018, the Commission also published the revised and updated version of two General Policy Recommendations, No. 2, on Equality Bodies to combat racism and intolerance at national level (original recommendation adopted in 1997), a,d No. 7, national legislation to combat racism and racial discrimination (original recommendation adopted in 2002). Both documents were approved in their revised versions on 7 December 2017 and published 27 February 2018

The last ECRI report on the situation of racism and intolerance in Italy related to the fifth monitoring cycle was adopted on 18 March 2016 and published on 7 June 2016 (CRI(2016)19). This report followed an ECRI delegation visit to Italy from 13 and 18 September 2015 and was summarised in the *Yearbook 2017* (p. 212–217). The next report will concern the implementation of the two priority recommendations addressed to Italy in the context of the fifth monitoring cycle: 1) provide all information, protection and support necessary to live in harmony with their own sexual orientation and gender identity to all students; 2) guarantee full independence and autonomy to the UNAR and extend their competences to all field where discrimination may occur.

VIII. Advisory Committee on the Framework Convention for the Protection of National Minorities

The Committee is a monitoring body instituted pursuant to Article 26 of the Council of Europe Framework Convention for the Protection of National Minorities. It is composed of 18 independent experts with recognised expertise in the field of the protection of national minorities. It is composed of 18 independent experts with recognised expertise in the field of protection of national minorities who sit on the Committee in their individual capacity for a period of four years. In 2018, there were no Italian experts on the Advisory Committee. On 18 April 2018, the Committee of Ministers elected Emma Lantschner to the list of experts eligible to serve on the Advisory Committee in respect of Italy with resolution CM/ResCMN(2018)4.

> The Advisory Committee serves to assist the CM in evaluating the implementation of the Framework-Convention in States Parties, through the examination of periodic State Reports. The results of this evaluation are expressed in a detailed opinion which serves as a basis for the preparation of the CM's conclusive resolutions on the Country in question. Follow-up meetings are generally organised by the Advisory Committee with a view to bringing together all actors – governmental and non-governmental – interested in the implementation of the Convention and to examine ways of implementing the results of the monitoring procedure. The CM concludes each monitoring cycle of the Framework-Convention by adopting a resolution.
>
> In 2018, within the framework of the respective monitoring cycles, the Consultative Committee of the Framework-Convention conducted visits to the following countries: Albania, Georgia, Ireland, Lithuania, Montenegro, the Netherlands, and Switzerland; has adopted, but not yet published by virtue of the confidentiality principle, *opinions* on the Russian Federation and Latvia, and has published opinions on the situation of national minorities in Bosnia-Herzegovina, Kosovo, Romania, Slovenia, Switzerland and Ukraine. It held follow-up meeting with representatives of Finland and Sweden.

The opinion of the Advisory Committee on Italy concerning the fourth monitoring cycle of the Framework Convention, based also on the visit conducted by the latter in Italy between 29 June and 3 July 2015, was adopted on 19 November 2015 (ACFC/OP/IV(2015)006) and published on 12 July 2016 together with the comments provided by the Italian Government on the observations made by the Advisory Committee (see *Yearbook* 2017, p. 218–221). The resolution of the Committee of Ministers concluding this monitoring cycle was adopted on 5 July 2017 ((CM/ResCMN(2017) 4), see *Yearbook 2018*, p. 207–208). The presentation of the report of Italy's activities is scheduled for April 2019, and will initiate the fifth monitoring cycle of the Framework-Convention.

IX. European Commission for Democracy through Law

The Commission, also known as the Venice Commission, is the Council of Europe's advisory body on constitutional issues; it was established in 1990 and receives financial support by a law of the Region of Veneto.

> The Commission is composed of independent experts with extensive experience in the area of democratic institutions or excellence in the legal and political domains. Members are designated for four years by the participating countries which, as well as the 47 Member States of the CoE, include Algeria, Brazil, Chile, Israel, Kazakhstan, Kyrgyzstan, Mexico, Morocco, Peru, South Korea, Tunisia and United States. Belarus is an associate member, while Argentina, Canada, the Holy See, Japan and Uruguay participate in the work of the Commission as observer countries. The European Commission, Palestinian National Authority, South Africa and the Association of Constitutional Courts using the French Language have a special co-operation status.
>
> Since 2009, Gianni Buquicchio has been President of the Venice Commission. Two Italian experts participate in the Commission's activities as alternate members: Marta Cartabia e Cesare Pinelli.
>
> Among its activities, the Commission put forwards studies and opinions on subjects covered by its competence, also at the request of other bodies such as the Parliamentary Assembly of the CoE, and promotes in-depth seminars. In 2018, the Venice Commission adopted 29 opinions with regard to the adoption of laws or bills of law on matters of constitutional importance in the following countries: Albania (2 opinions), Former Yugoslav Republic of Macedonia/ North Macedonia (3), Georgia (3), Hungary (3), Kazakhstan (2), Kosovo, Luxembourg, Malta (2), Montenegro, Republic of Moldova (3), Romania (2), Serbia, Tunisia, Turkey, Ukraine (2) and Uzbekistan. No opinions or documents were adopted concerning Italy in 2018.

X. Group of experts on Action against Trafficking in Human Beings

The Group of Experts (GRETA) was established pursuant to Article 36 of the Council of Europe Convention on Action against Trafficking in Human Beings and is charged, together with a Committee made up of the representatives in the CM of the States Parties to the Convention (Committee of the Parties), with monitoring the implementation of the obligations contained in the Convention.

The Group is made up of 15 independent experts known for their recognised competence in the fields of human rights, assistance and protection of victims of trafficking in human beings or having professional experience in the areas covered by the Convention. On 9 November 2018, the Italian national Francesco Curcio was elected as the latest member of GRETA, who will stay in the role until 31 December 2022.

> The monitoring procedure is divided into 4-year rounds. The Group of Experts starts the dialogue with the Party under evaluation by sending out a questionnaire, which may be followed by requests for further information. If the Group of Experts deems it necessary, additional information may be requested from civil society organisations or gathered by organising a visit to the Country concerned. The draft report is sent to the relevant Government for comments. On receiving them, GRETA prepares its final report and conclusions and transmits it to the Country concerned and to the Committee of the Parties, which can adopt recommendations on the basis of the contents of the document. Each Party to the Convention appoints a contact person to cooperate with the Group of Experts.

> In 2018, the Expert Group published the evaluation reports on the implementation status of the Convention in: Azerbaijan, Estonia, Former Yugoslav Republic of Macedonia/ North Macedonia, Hungary (following an ad hoc visit pursuant to Urgent Procedures - Rule 7 of the GRETA Rules of procedure), Luxembourg, the Netherlands, Serbia, Slovenia, Spain, Sweden and Ukraine. They conducted in-depth visits to the following countries: Andorra, Finland, Germany, Hungary, Italy, Iceland, Liechtenstein, Lithuania, San Marino, Switzerland and Turkey.

The first evaluation cycle on the implementation of the Warsaw Convention by Italy concluded with the recommendation of the Committee of the Parties (CP(2014)16), adopted on 5 December 2014, which confirmed the recommendations previously made by the Group of experts (GRETA(2014)18, see *Yearbook 2015*, p. 225–229). Furthermore, on 30 January 2017, GRETA published the report on an urgent visit by a delegation in Italy from 21–23 September 2016 to address the issue of Italy's removal of possible victims of trafficking through forced repatriation flights to Nigeria, as part of joint removal operations organised and coordinated by the FRONTEX European Agency (see *Yearbook 2017*, p. 222–225).

On 7 December 2018, GRETA adopted its final report on the second evaluation round of the implementation of the Warsaw Convention in Italy (GRETA/2018/28, published on 25 January 2019). The report is based on the reply provided by the Italian authorities to the questionnaire sent by the Group of Experts in 2017 (GRETA/2017/23) and on the observations emerging from the evaluation visit conducted by a GRETA delegation between 29 January and 2 February 2018 in order to examine developments and improvements of the situation compared to the 2014 and 2017 reports.

During the visit, the GRETA delegation held consultations with officials from the Department for Equal Opportunities of the Italian Presidency of the Council of Ministers, the Ministry of the Interior, the Ministry of Foreign Affairs and International Co-operation, the Ministry of Justice, the Ministry of Labour and Social Policies, the Ministry of Health, the Ministry of Agricultural, Food and Forestry Policies, the National Anti-Mafia and Anti-Terrorist Directorate, the State Police, the Carabinieri Corps, the *Guardia di Finanza*, the National Association of Italian Municipalities, the National Commission for the Right to Asylum, the Territorial Commission for Recognition of International Protection in Rome, and the National Statistics Institute. The GRETA delegation also met Ms Filomena Albano, Italian Ombudsperson for Children and Adolescents. The visit also foresaw trips to Sicily and Tuscany where the delegation met representatives of public bodies and civil society involved in local anti-trafficking networks. Finally, the GRETA delegation visited shelters for victims of trafficking and held separate meetings with drop-in centres providing services to possible victims of trafficking, run by NGOs and an emergency reception centre (CAS) for asylum-seeking women in Torre Angela, near Rome.

In general, GRETA notes that progress has been made in some areas compared to the previous evaluation round. The national legal framework against human trafficking has evolved since the first evaluation, and new regulations have been adopted to strengthen the protection of unaccompanied children, including child-victims of trafficking. The adoption of a national anti-trafficking action plan (2016–2018) (see the in-depth analysis in this edition) is seen as a positive development, focusing particularly on measures to improve knowledge on trafficking of human beings, strengthen prevention in countries of origin and combating trafficking for forced labour. According to GRETA, the institutional framework for combating human trafficking has also evolved, with the setting up of the Steering Committee, an inter-institutional forum for planning, implementation and financing of measures to combat human trafficking. GRETA welcomes the efforts made to provide training on human trafficking to an increasing range of relevant professionals, following a multi-agency approach, and with the active involvement of international organisations. It notes that while a National Referral Mechanism for the identification and referral to assistance of victims of trafficking has been drafted as part of the National Action Plan, this remains to be implemented. GRETA welcomes the adoption of Guidelines for the identification of victims of trafficking among applicants for international protection.

The Group of Experts notes significant process in the area of assistance to victims of trafficking. The setting up of the "Single programme for the emergence, assistance and social integration of victims of trafficking and exploitation", replaced the previous dual assistance approach based on short-term and long-term projects. Further, GRETA welcomes the considerable increase in the budgetary funding allocated to anti-trafficking projects, the increase in the number of accommodation places for victims of trafficking, and the setting up of more reception centres for unaccompanied children. Among the other positive developments recognised by the report is the increase in the number of persons granted some form of international protection on the grounds of having been trafficked. Finally, GRETA also commends the specialisation of law enforcement officers and prosecutors to deal with human trafficking cases, as well as Italy's engagement in international co-operationagainst human trafficking.

Despite the progress achieved, the GRETA report highlights some issues that continued to give rise to concern. Some of these request the Italian Authorities to take further immediate action.

For the purpose *of preparing, monitoring and evaluating* anti-trafficking policies, GRETA urges the Italian authorities to develop and maintain a comprehensive and coherent statistical system on trafficking in human beings by compiling reliable statistical data on measures to protect and promote the rights of victims as well as on the investigation, prosecution and adjudication of human trafficking cases. Statistics regarding victims should be collected from all main actors and allow disaggregation concerning sex, age, type of exploitation, country of origin and/or destination. This should be accompanied by all the necessary measures to respect the right of data subjects to personal data protection, including when NGOs working with victims of trafficking are asked to provide information for the national database.

On the issue of preventing trafficking of human beings for the purpose of labour exploitation, GRETA urges the Italian authorities to intensify their efforts in the following fields:

- training labour inspectors throughout the country, as well as other inspecting agencies, law enforcement officers, prosecutors and judges, on combating trafficking of human beings for the purpose of labour exploitation and the rights of victims;
- expanding the capacity of labour inspectors so that they can be actively engaged in the prevention of trafficking of human beings, including in private households and in small businesses in the hotel, catering and restaurant sectors;
- monitoring the frequency and effectiveness of labour inspections and ensuring that sufficient human and financial resources are made available to labour inspectors to fulfil their mandate, including in remote locations at risk of trafficking of human beings in the agricultural sector;
- separating immigration enforcement functions from labour inspectorate roles and ensuring that labour inspectors prioritise the detection of persons working in irregular situationswho are vulnerable to trafficking of human beings;
- reviewing the regulatory systems concerning migrants working as home care workers and ensuring that inspections can take place in private households with a view to preventing abuse of domestic workers and detecting cases of human trafficking;
- strengthening the monitoring of recruitment and temporary work agencies and reviewing the legislative framework for any gaps that may limit protection or preventive measures;
- supporting ethical trading initiatives, and effective enforcement of due diligence obligations to monitor supply chains, particularly in the fruit and vegetable sectors;
- raising awareness amongst the general public as well as, in a targeted manner, amongst migrant workers, about the risks of trafficking of human beings for the purpose of labour exploitation;
- establishing effective mechanisms to allow irregularly present migrant workers to lodge complaints in respect to labour standards against employers and obtain effective remedieswithout the risk

of the sharing of their personal data or other information with immigration authorities for the purposes of immigration control and enforcement.

Concerning trafficking in children, GRETA urges the Italian Authorities to:
- strengthen their efforts to prevent trafficking in children for different types of exploitation by raising public awareness about the risks and different manifestations of child trafficking (including early, child and forced marriages, exploitation of begging and forced criminality);
- sensitise and train teachers, educational staff and child welfare professionals across the country about trafficking of human beings and its different forms, and ensuring that sensitisation programmes on the matter of trafficking are put in place in schools;
- mainstream the prevention of trafficking in the training of all staff working with unaccompanied and separated children, ensuring the best interests of the child;
- prevent unaccompanied or separated children from going missing and ensure that they can benefit from protection of their rights and effective care arrangements, including safe and specialised accommodation, access to education and health care, so that they are not exposed to risks of trafficking;
- take action to address situations of violence of unaccompanied and separated children at the Italian/French border, including through international cooperation and positive measures to prevent trafficking, identification of possible child victims of trafficking at the borders, effective access to assistance and protection and timely appointment of guardians.

Regarding the necessary steps to take to improve the proactive identification of victims of trafficking of human beings, GRETA urges the Italian authorities to:
- strengthen the multi-agency involvement in victim identification by introducing into practice a National Referral Mechanism which defines the procedures and roles of all frontline actors who may come into contact with victims of trafficking, and providing guidance and training on its application to all relevant professionals;

- increase efforts to proactively identify victims of trafficking for the purpose of labour exploitation, by reinforcing the capacity and training of labour inspectors and other relevant agencies and involving trade unions and NGOs;
- take steps to proactively identify victims of trafficking for other forms of exploitation, such as forced criminality, forced begging, forced marriage and organ removal;
- provide NGOs involved in the identification of victims of trafficking amongst asylum seekers with sufficient resources to enable them to fulfil their tasks and enable effective co-operation with NGOs, including those engaged in rescue at sea operations;
- ensure identification of possible victims of trafficking in human beings at all border crossings in accordance with the OHCHR's Recommended Principles and Guidelines on Human Rights at International Borders.

Furthermore, GRETA recommends the Italian authorities to:

- adopt as a matter of priority a National Referral Mechanism for child victims of trafficking in human beings which takes into account the special circumstances and needs of child victims, involving child specialists and ensuring that the best interests of the child are the primary consideration in all proceedings relating to child victims of trafficking in human beings and children at risk;
- ensure that relevant actors take a proactive approach and increase their outreach work to identify child victims of trafficking in human beings for different forms of exploitation, by paying particular attention to unaccompanied and separated children and children from Roma communities;
- ensure that child victims of trafficking in human beings across the country, regardless of whether they seek asylum or not, benefit from the assistance measures provided for under the Convention, including appropriate accommodation, effective access to free legal assistance and psychological support;
- take further steps to address the problem of children going missing while in the care of the State and ensure that there are clear instructions as to which institution holds the lead responsibility for tracing missing children and for taking appropriate measures to notify all relevant authorities in order to ensure that children are traced and provided with appropriate protection;

- monitor the effectiveness and quality of the voluntary guardianship system;
- ensure long-term assistance for the integration of child victims of trafficking.

As written in the previous report, GRETA once again urges the Italian authorities to review the legislation in order to ensure that the recovery and reflection period is specifically defined in law as provided for in Article 13 of the Convention, and that all possible foreign victims of trafficking are offered a recovery and reflection period and all the measures of assistance envisaged in Article 12, paragraphs 1 and 2, of the Convention during this period.

GRETA is concerned by the failure to implement Article 15 of the Convention and once again urges the Italian authorities to take steps to facilitate and guarantee access to compensation to victims of Trafficking in Human Beings, and in particular to:

- review the criminal and civil procedures regarding compensation from perpetrators with a view to improving their effectiveness;
- enable victims of trafficking to exercise their right to compensation, by informing them, in a language they can understand, of the right to compensation and the procedures to be followed, and building the capacity of legal practitioners to support victims to claim compensation;
- include victim compensation in training programmes for law enforcement officials, prosecutors and judges;
- enable victims of trafficking who have left Italy to benefit from the possibility of claiming compensation;
- set up a State compensation scheme effectively accessible to victims of trafficking in human beings, regardless of their nationality and immigration status, and review the maximum amount of 1,500 euros of compensation paid by the State in order to ensure that it corresponds to the actual harm suffered by victims;
- make full use of the existing legislation on the freezing and forfeiture of assets to secure compensation to victims of trafficking.

The Group of Experts urges the Italian authorities to continue to take steps to ensure that the return of victims of trafficking in human beings is conducted with due regard to their rights, safety and dignity, including the right to non-refoulement (Article 40(4) of the Convention), and in the case of children, by fully respecting the principle of the best interests of the child. Recalling the judgment of the European Court of Human Rights in *Hirsi Jamaa and others v. Italy* (see *Yearbook 2013*, p. 257–259) GRETA urges the Italian authorities to ensure that individualised assessments of risk are undertaken in all cases prior to any forced returns or expulsions, including during operations in Libyan territorial waters. In this context, the authorities should continue to develop co-operation with countries of origin and transit of victims in order to ensure comprehensive risk and security assessment (Article 16(7) of the Convention) and safe return of the victims, as well as their effective reintegration on return. Full consideration should be given to the UNHCR's Guidelines on the application of the Refugees Convention to trafficked persons.

Reiterating a recommendation that was addressed at the Italian authorities in the last evaluation cycle, GRETA once again urges the Italian authorities to ensure compliance with Article 26 of the Convention of Warsaw (non-punishment provision) through the adoption of a provision on the non-punishment of victims of trafficking for their involvement in unlawful activities, to the extent that they were compelled to do so, and/or by developing relevant guidance. Public prosecutors should be encouraged to be proactive in establishing if an accused person is a potential victim of trafficking and to consider trafficking in human beings as a serious violation of human rights. While the identification procedure is on-going, potential victims of trafficking should not be punished for immigration-related offences.

Among the other recommendations that require immediate action, GRETA urges the Italian authorities to take measures to ensure that trafficking in human beings offences are investigated and prosecuted effectively, leading to proportionate and dissuasive sanctions; and to review the Code of Conduct for NGOs undertaking activities on migrants' rescue operations at sea with a view to enabling the identification of victims of trafficking amongst migrants and refugees at sea and in ports.

XI. Group of States against Corruption

The Group of States against Corruption (GRECO) was established in 1999 in order to monitor the compliance of CoE Member States with the anti-corruption standards and rules of the Organisation. These benchmarks are contained in the legal instruments adopted by the

Council of Europe on actions against corruption – the Criminal Law Convention on Corruption with its Additional Protocol and the Civil Law Convention on Corruption – as well as the recommendations and resolutions adopted by the Committee of Ministers (in particular resolution (97)24 on the 20 Guiding Principles for the Fight against Corruption).

> The Group comprises 49 States (47 Member States of the CoE plus Belarus and the United States). GRECO's main objective is to improve the capacity of its members to fight corruption by monitoring their compliance with Council of Europe anti-corruption standards through a dynamic process of mutual evaluation and peer pressure. It helps to identify shortcomings in national anti-corruption policies, prompting the necessary legislative, institutional and practical reforms. GRECO also provides a platform for sharing best practices. The GRECO monitoring system takes place in periodic cycles and includes: a "horizontal" evaluation procedure involving all the members and ending with the elaboration of recommendations on the necessary reforms in the legislative and institutional field; and a "compliance" procedure whose purpose is to assess the measures taken by Member States to implement these recommendations.
>
> Italy has been a member of GRECO since 30 June 2007 and has undergone three evaluation rounds to date. The first two rounds were dealt with jointly and concluded in 2013 with the adoption by the Group of States of an addendum to the compliance report (see *Yearbook 2014*, p. 253). On 23 June 2014, on the basis of information previously provided by the Italian Government, GRECO adopted the compliance report (Greco RC-III(2014)9E) on the measures adopted by the Italian authorities to implement the 16 recommendations received in the course of the third monitoring round regarding two themes: I) incrimination for corruption and II) transparency of party funding (see *Yearbook 2015*, p. 229–232). In 2016, GRECO adopted two reports on Italy: the second compliance report, relative to the third monitoring cycle, adopted and published on 2 December 2016, and the evaluation report on Italy after the fourth evaluation round (GrecoEval4Rep(2016)2), adopted on 28 October 2016 and published in January 2017 (see *Yearbook 2017*, p. 225–228).

In December 2018, GRECO adopted its fourth evaluation round compliance report regarding Italy (GrecoRC4(2018)13) focusing on corruption prevention in respect to members of parliament, judges and prosecutors. The compliance report is based on the situation report presented by the Italian authorities on 1 August 2018 on measures taken to implement the 12 recommendations that GRECO addressed to the Italian Government in the previous evaluation report.

After assessing the developments by the Italian authorities regarding these issues, GRECO concluded that only three recommendations addressed in the last evaluation round had been implemented satisfactorily. Of the remaining reccomendations, five had been partly implemented and four had not been implemented.

Concerning the recommendations about corruption of members of Parliament, GRECO acknowledged that there was a period of political change, extending from the end of 2016 to mid-2018, that led, in turn, to delays in implementation of recommendations. During the previous legislature, in May 2016, an Advisory Committee on the Conduct of Deputies was established to provide support in implementing a Code of Conduct for the Chamber of Deputies, focusing on the requirements for reporting and implementation. Some initiatives were taken to systematise and streamline rules and compliance proceedings regard conflicts of interest, but none of those were discussed and have yet to be resumed by the new legislation. Furthermore, GRECO considers the development of a mandatory public register for lobbyists in the Chamber of Deputies an important step, but maintains that additional measures can be taken, focusing more on the parliamentary dimension of lobbying. Furthermore, the Senate is yet to develop its own rules on lobbying similar to those of the Chamber to promote a philosophy of integrity among its members. GRECO therefore concludes that the overall developments in this area have been partly implemented.

Implementation records regarding the recommendations made to the judiciary were much more positive. The triennium 2016–2018 witnessed a much-awaited reform of the justice sector to substantially improve the efficiency of both civil and criminal law trials, efforts for which the Italian authorities were commended by the Group of States. Time and experience with the newly introduced changes will show whether further adjustments are still necessary to accomplish the ambitious and multifaceted underlying goals of the justice reform. GRECO also showed interest in the anti-corruption measures contained with the "Bribe Destroyer" bill (bill No. 1189 at the time of publication of the GRECO report, transformed into l. 3/2019). According to GRECO, good effort has been made to establish dedicated mechanisms to open up channels for the discussion of ethical dilemmas shared by magistrates and to deliver advisory tools in relation to integrity-related matters. The action initiated to strengthen the current financial disclosure regime of magistrates has been welcomed by the Group of States. It notes that positive steps were taken to strike the necessary balance between hierarchical organisation of prosecution offices and internal autonomy of individual prosecutors. The important changes introduced regarding the matter of honorary judges, notably, by enhancing their professional training, supervision and assessment were considered important by GRECO, which highlighted that a similar comprehensive approach has yet to follow in fiscal jurisdiction. Finally, GRECO recognises that the adoption of stricter regulation regarding the participation of magistrates in political life will require support in the newly elected Parliament.

In view of the above, GRECO notes that further significant material progress is necessary to demonstrate that an acceptable level of compliance with the recommendations within the next 18 months can be achieved. However, bearing in mind the notable action already taken by the authorities in the justice sector and on the understanding that the Italian authorities will further pursue their efforts to meet GRECO's outstanding recommendations in the newly started legislature, GRECO concludes that the current low level of compliance with the recommendations is not "globally unsatisfactory". Additional information regarding the implementation of recommendations not yet implemented must be submitted to GRECO by 30 June 2020.

XII. Group of Experts on action against Violence against Women and Domestic Violence

The Group of Experts (GREVIO) is the body responsible for monitoring the implementation of the Council of Europe Convention on Preventing and Combating Violence against Women and Domestic Violence (Istanbul Convention) by the Parties which have ratified it.

> GREVIO's main purpose is to draw up and publish reports evaluating legislative and other measures taken by the Parties to give effect to the provisions of the Convention. If necessary, in the event of serious and persistent acts of violence covered by the Convention, GREVIO may initiate a special inquiry procedure. It can also adopt general recommendations on themes and concepts of the Convention.
>
> GREVIO currently has 10 members (with increases in the number of ratifications of the Istanbul Convention, this can go up to 15) with multidisciplinary expertise in the area of human rights, gender equality, violence against women and domestic violence or in the assistance to and protection of victims. The first ten members of GREVIO were elected by the

Committee of the Parties at its first meeting of 4 May 2015. Among them is the Italian expert Simona Lanzoni.

In 2018, after receiving the respective national reports on the state of implementation of the Istanbul Convention, the GREVIO published the first evaluation reports on the implementation of the Istanbul Convention in the following countries: Albania, Austria, Denmark and Monaco.

The evaluation process of the Group of Experts on Italy started in February 2018 with the administration of the questionnaire. The first state report from the Italian authorities on the implementation of the provisions of the Istanbul Convention was submitted on 22 October 2018. In this regard, many reports and additional contributions were submitted to GREVIO by civil society organisations, including the following: AIDOS, End FGM, Be Free, Italian Forum for Disability, Relive, UNIRE and others, groups of experts and specialist professionals in the field of women's and children's rights. The first evaluation visit to Italy is planned for March 2019, and the evaluation report will be published in January 2020.

XIII. Lanzarote Committee

The Committee of the Parties to the Convention on the Protection of Children from Sexual Exploitation and Abuse (or "Lanzarote Committee", named after the city in which this legal instrument was adopted), is the body established by the Council of Europe in order to monitor the implementation of this Convention.

> The Committee is composed by the representatives of the current and potential States party to the Convention and has the function of assessing the situation for children's protection against sexual violence at national level on the basis of information provided by national authorities in response to two periodic questionnaires (a general questionnaire and a thematic questionnaire) and in other sources. The Italian member of the Committee is Tiziana Zannini of the Department for Equal Opportunities of the Presidency of the Council of Ministers.
>
> The Committee also functions as the facilitator of the collection, analysis, and exchange of information, experiences and best practices to increase the capacity to prevent and combat sexual abuse and violence against children. In this context, the Committee organises capacity building activities aimed at the exchange of information and the organisation of hearings on specific challenges raised by the implementation of the Convention.

On 31 January 2018, the Committee published its second collective report for the first thematic monitoring round on the implementation of the Convention. The first report focused on judicial standards and mechanisms to collect data on the protection of children against sexual abuse in the circle of trust, while the second report focuses on strategies (structures, measures and processes in place) to prevent and protect children. The report was based on replies sent to the questionnaire by the authorities of the 26 States that have ratified the Convention (among which Italy) and specifically looks into strategies regarding the involvement of relevant stakeholders, awareness-raising, education and training and assesses the processes in place to screen and deny access to children to persons convicted of sexual offences against them. Stock is also taken of the measures and programmes to assist persons who fear they might committ sexual offences and prevent the possible risk of repetition of offences.

European Union

I. European Parliament

The European Parliament (EP), together with the Commission and the Council of the European Union, exercises a fundamental role in the promotion and protection of human rights within the overall framework of EU activities.

> Among the permanent EP Committees prominent in human rights issues, the following are highlighted: the Subcommittee on Human Rights (Chair: Pier Antonio Panzeri) within the Committee on Foreign Affairs (Italian members: Goffredo Maria Bettini, Mario Borghezio, Fabio Massimo Castaldo, Lorenzo Cesa, Pier Antonio Panzeri; substitute Italian members: Brando Benifei, Raffaele Fitto).
>
> Other Committees with significant involvement in human rights issues are the Committee on Civil Liberties, Justice and Home Affairs (Italian members: Caterina Chinnici, Laura Ferrara, Cécile Kashetu Kyenge, Barbara Matera, Alessandra Mussolini, Giancarlo Scottà; substitute Italian members: Fabio Massimo Castaldo, Ignazio Corrao, Innocenzo Leontini, Elly Schlein, Barbara Spinelli, Daniele Viotti); the Committee on Constitutional Affairs (Vice Chair: Barbara Spinelli; other Italian members: Mercedes Bresso, Fabio Massimo Castaldo; substitute Italian member: Roberto Gualtieri); the Committee on Legal Affairs (Vice Chair: Laura Ferrara; other Italian member: Enrico Gasbarra; substitute Italian members: Isabella Adinolfi, Mario Borghezio, Sergio Gaetano Cofferati); the Committee on Employment and Social Affairs (Italian members: Laura Agea, Tiziana Beghin, Brando Benifei, Mara Bizzotto, Elena Gentile; substitute Iitalian members: Silvia Costa, Rosa D'Amato, Alessandra Mussolini, Flavio Zanonato); the Committee on the Environment, Public Health and Food Safety (Italian members: Marco Affronte, Simona Bonafè, Alberto Cirio, Elisabetta Gardini, Giovanni La Via, Massimo Paolucci, Piernicola Pedicini, Damiano Zoffoli; substitute Italian members: Renata Briano, Nicola Caputo, Caterina Chinnici, Herbert Dorfmann, Eleonora Evi, Eleonora Forenza, Elena Gentile, Danilo Oscar Lancini, Aldo Patriciello); the Committee on Development (Italian members: Ignazio Corrao, Elly Schlein; substitute Italian members: Cécile Kashetu Kyenge, Piernicola Pedicini, Patrizia Toia the Committee on Women's Rights and Gender Equality (Vice Chair: Barbara Matera; other

Italian members: Isabella Adinolfi, Daniela Aiuto, Pina Picierno; substitute Italian members: Eleonora Forenza, Alessandra Mussolini, Elly Schlein, Marco Zullo) and the Committee on Petitions, of which more below.

In 2018, the Sakharov Prize for Freedom of Thought was awarded to Oleg Sentsov, Ukrainan director and writer; as an open opposer of the Russian annexation of the Crimea, he was arrested on 10 May 2014 accused of planning terrorist attacks against the "de facto" Russian domain in Crimea.

Among the European Parliament's actions adopted in 2018 with themes regarding both human rights and specific initiatives carried out by Italy, the following activities are reported: resolution on the European Parliament decision of 18 April on discharge in respect of the implementation of the budget of the European Asylum Support Office for the financial year 2016 (P8_TA(2018)0140), the resolution of 3 May 2018 on the protection of children in migration (P8_TA(2018)0201), the resolutions of 25 October 2018 on the employment and social policies of the euro area (P8_TA(2018)0432) and on the rise of neo-fascist violence in Europe (P8_TA(2018)0428), the esolution of 13 November 2018 on minimum standards for minorities in the EU (P8_TA(2018)0447) and the resolution of 13 December 2018 on Egypt, notably the situation of human rights defenders (P8_TA(2018)0526).

Commission for petitions

The task of the Commission is to examine the petitions submitted by citizens (a right enshrined in the CFREU under Article 44, as well as Articles 24 and 227 TFEU), and to endeavor to resolve any breaches of their rights under EU law. Italian members of the Commission are Alberto Cirio, Andrea Cozzolino and Eleonora Evi; substitute Italian members are Laura Agea and Michele Giuffrida.

On 17 and 18 December, a delegation of the Committee on Petitions conducted a fact-finding visit to the area of Valledora in Piedmont regarding petition 0909-20163, which criticises the serious environmental deterioration of this area, which at one time was predominantly agricultural. It is now home to landfills for household and industrial waste covering a total of 4 million m^3.

II. European Commission

The European Commission plays a central role in the development and implementation of European Union policies on human rights both within the Union and regarding third countries.

Of the 28 Commissioners, particularly important are: Frans Timmermans, First Vice-President responsible for the quality of legislation, inter-institutional relations, the rule of law and the Charter of Fundamental Rights; Dimitris Avramopoulos, Commissioner for Migration, Home Affairs and Citizenship; Marianne Thyssen, Commissioner for Employment, Social Affairs, Skills and Labour Mobility; Christos Stylianides, Commissioner for Humanitarian Aid and Crisis Management; and Věra Jourová, Commissioner for Justice, Consumers and Gender Equality.

The primary financial resources for the European Union activities on human rights is the European Instrument for Democracy and Human Rights (EIDHR) that supports projects of the European Inter-University Centre for Human Rights and Democratisation (EIUC) and the European Master in Human Rights and Democratisation (E.MA).

Further details on the Commission's action can be found in the section on EU Legislation in 2018 (see Part I, Reception of International Human Rights Law in Italy, III, B.).

III. Council of the European Union

Within the Council there are the Human Rights Working Group (COHOM), the Working Party on Fundamental Rights, Citizens' Rights and Free Movement of Persons (FREMP), the Working Group "Asylum" and the Working Group of Public International Law (COJUR), within which a sub-group devoted to the International Criminal Court operates (COJUR-ICC).

There were no decisions that contained specific references to Italy concerning human rights in 2018.

IV. Court of Justice of the European Union

Following the entry into force of the Treaty of Lisbon, which made the Charter of Nice legally binding, the Court of Justice plays an ever more vital role for the promotion of human rights within the scope of EU law.

Since 8 October 2018, Lucia Serena Rossi has been a member of the court as a judge and Giovanni Pitruzzella as an advocate-general (in the previous months of 2018, these roles were filled by Antonio Tizzano, as a judge and Vice-President, and Paolo Mengozzi, as an advocate-general).

According to the data provided by the CJEU, in 2018, Italy ranked second in the number of preliminary rulings (Article 267 TFEU) taken before the Court (68 out of 568), preceded only by Germany (78 rulings).

For a selection of the jurisprudence of the CJEU concerning Italy in 2018, see Part IV, Italy in the Case-law of the Court of Justice of the European Union).

V. European External Action Service

The European External Action Service (EEAS) assists the High Representative of the Union for Foreign Affairs and Security Policy in upholding the CFSP/CSDP and ensuring the consistency of EU external actions in their functions both as President of the Foreign Affairs Council and as Vice-President of the Commission. Since November 2014, Federica Mogherini has been the High Representative.

The activities and intiatives of the EEAS involve a widespread network of European Delegations across the world. Among those promoted throughout 2018 that focus on Italy's contribution, on 14 November, two projects were launched to support the right to health, to hygiene and to access to safe water in Sudan. The projects were promoted as part of the Italian Agency for International Cooperation, the Italian Embassy in Sudan and the EU delegation in Sudan with funds of 14 million euros.

VI. Special Representative for Human Rights

Appointed by EU Council decision 2012/440/CFSP of 25 July 2012, the mandate of the European Union Special Representative for Human Rights involves enhancing dialogue with all relevant stakeholders concerning EU human rights policy, including international organisations, States and civil society organisations. Stavros Lambrinidis was appointed on 1 September 2012 as the first incumbent. The first mandate has been extended until 28 February 2019. From 1 March, he will be replaced by Eamon Gilmore (Ireland).

No significant actions concerning Italy took place in 2018.

VII. Fundamental Rights Agency (FRA)

An advisory body established in 2007, the FRA is the main technical instrument available to the EU with the task of supporting European and national institutions in the promotion and protection of human rights. Since 16 December 2015, Michael O'Flaherty (Ireland) has been Director of the Agency. Since July 2015, Filippo di Robilant (vice president as of 29 September 2017) has been on the FRA Management Board for Italy. The latter was also appointed to the Executive Board in May 2017.

The research element of FRA's work consists mainly of the gathering and comparative analysis of data concerning the fundamental rights situation in the various EU Member States, including Italy. In this area, a brief summary is given below of some of the reports drawn up by the FRA in 2018, followed by some comments on the most significant facts that emerged concerning Italy:

Being black in the EU (November 2018). This report outlines selected results from FRA's second large-scale EU-wide survey on migrants and minorities (EU-MIDIS II) and examines the experiences of almost 6,000 people of African descent in 12 EU Member States.

The data presented in the report shows that in Italy, regarding the prevalence of racial hatred in the last five years, 48 % of people of African descent report experiencing racially fuelled abuse hatred. 70 % of people stopped by the Police in the 12 months prior to the survey are sure that the last time they were stopped by the police there was a racial motivation for it. Only 9 % of respondents who felt like a victim of racial discrimination had reported their most recent incident. Around 19 % of respondents know that an Institution for Equality exists in the country and around 27 % say that they know there are anti-discrimination laws in force. The perception of racially-based discrimination for finding employment is high with around 46 % of respondents. 42 % of respondents from 18–24 years old are neither working or studying nor doing professional training sessions. 31 % of respondents report that it had been impossible to privately rent an apartment in Italy due to their racial or ethnical heritage, while 20 % were asked to pay a higher rent due to their racial and ethnical differences.

From institutions to community living for persons with disabilities: perspectives from the ground (December 2018). This report presents the main insights gained during fieldwork on the drivers of and barriers to deinstitutionalisation for those residing in institutional settings, with a vision to realising the right of persons with disabilities to live independently in the community according to the Convention on the Rights of Persons with Disabilities. The report focuses mainly on the local level, it gives voice to a diverse set of actors.

Refering to Italy, the report relates to the second National Action Plan for the Promotion of rights and the Integration of persons with disabilities and recognises that professionals appreciate inclusion of action points referring specifically to policies, services and organization models to support independent life and the inclusion in the community of people with disabilities. The survey participants noted that the high level of relocation of expertise on these aspects in Italy creates a barrier to the uniform application of these policies on a national level. On political commitment, the participants cite law 122/2016 as signalling a unified commitment to deinstitutionalisation, moving away from voluntary pilot projects towards a firm national commitment to close institutions and create community-based services. According to the study's participants, regional and local pilot projects in Italy play an important role in informing, encouraging and developing national policy. Moreover, participants from across stakeholder groups at the national and local level identified so-called 'territorial networks' as one of the main drivers of the deinstitutionalisation process. Bringing together social cooperatives, private companies and other associations involved in providing services, participants credited these networks with facilitating a holistic approach to deinstitutionalisation.

Among the various barriers for implementation of this process, the study participants cited the financial crisis as a key factor in the lack of resources allocated for implementation to the deinstitutionalisation process in Italy. Other more specific factors identified by participants in Italy were that the annularity of funding sometimes makes it difficult to plan longer term deinstitutionalisation projects, and that there was vested interest at the political level within service providers. On the issue of barriers to deinstitutionalisation due to a lack of guidance from responsible bodies at the national level and the local level, the document cites the Guidelines for the presentation of projects in the area of independent living and inclusion in the community of persons with disabilities as an example.

In April 2018, the FRA, in collaboration with the Office for the Ombudsperson for Children and Adolescents prepared and published a note related to the principal changes on the subject of legal protection of unaccompanied foreign minors in Italy following the adoption of law 7 April 2017, No. 47 (Provisions on the protection of unaccompanied foreign minors). According to this note, the approach that was introduced by the new law could become a promising practise at the EU level since it establishes a flexible guardianship system that can respond to changing needs that is less costly than a system based on professional guardians and, more importantly, involves actively the society in the destination country. At the same time, however, this system may also involve significant risks, in particular for its management, the support to and the oversight of a high number of persons who decide to become volunteer guardians.

VIII. European Ombudsman

The European Ombudsman, an institution established in 1992 by the Treaty of Maastricht and provided for in Articles 24 and 228 TFEU, examines the complaints lodged by European citizens about maladministration in the institutions and bodies of the European Union. The Ombudsperson is elected by the EP, and their duties are performed with complete independence. Emily O'Reilly, previously the National Ombudsperson of the Republic of Ireland, currently holds this position.

According to the report on the activities of the European Ombudsman concerning 2017 (published on 16 May 2018), over the period considered, the Office processed 2,201 complaints, of which 123 were from Italy. Again in 2017, it launched 447 investigations (of which 41 for complaints from Italy), a total of 363. In the same year, 14 investigations were initiated by the Ombudsperson on their own initiative.

IX. European Data Protection Supervisor

Established by Regulation 45/2001, the European Data Protection Supervisor is responsible for ensuring the right to the protection of individual privacy in the handling of personal data by EU institutions and bodies, as specified in Articles 7–8 of the Nice Charter. It is an independent body elected by the Parliament and the Council of the EU and the Supervisor in 2019 was Giovanni Buttarelli, who was previously Secretary-General to the Italian Data Protection Authority.

No significant actions concerning Italy took place in 2018.

Organization for Security and Cooperation in Europe (OSCE)

Through a multi-dimensional approach to security, the OSCE (57 participating States) deals with conflict prevention, crisis management and post-conflict rehabilitation. Among its specific mechanisms and bodies are the Office for Democratic Institutions and Human Rights (ODIHR), the High Commissioner on National Minorities, the Representative on Freedom of the Media and the Special Representative and Coordinator for Combating Trafficking in Human Beings. The Italian diplomat Lamberto Zannier was Secretary General of the OSCE until July 2017. He was succeeded by Thomas Greminger (Switzerland).

With a unanimous decision of the OSCE Participating States, Italy was elected to hold OSCE's rotating Chairmanship for 2018. Therefore, during this period, the country coordinated the decision-making process and will set the priorities for the Organization's activities in the field of Security and Cooperation in Europe, assisted by Austria (Chairmanship 2017) and Slovakia (Chairmanship 2019).

The main priorities for Italy for this year were based on the following:

— giving full political support to the efforts to seek a solution to the Ukraine crisis, on the basis of the Minsk agreements and in the Normandy format;
— dedicating utmost attention to the role of OSCE in "protracted" conflicts (Nagorno-Karabakh, Transnistria, Georgia: Abkhazia and Ossetia);
— focusing greater attention on the challenges and opportunities arising in the Mediterranean, including migrations;
— taking a pro-active approach to OSCE's three security "dimensions" (politico-military, economic and environmental, human rights) and on the new transnational threats (terrorism, cyber security, combating illegal trafficking, from drug trafficking to the trafficking of cultural property);
— strengthening dialogue on political/military questions to re-establishing a climate of trust among Participating States, stimulating a discussion on the evolution of security in Europe and on the ways of re-establishing an adequate level of "cooperative security";

- enhancing dialogue on issues such as promoting economic progress and security through innovation, human capital, good governance and the transition towards renewable energy;
- promoting the universality and indivisibility of all fundamental rights, in addition to combating all forms of discrimination and intolerance and fighting human trafficking.

The Head of the Italian mission at the OSCE is currently Amb. Alessandro Azzoni. 13 members of the Chamber of Deputies and the Senate sit in the OSCE Parliamentary Assembly. The head of the Italian parliamentary delegation is Paolo Romani. The other 12 Italian parliamentarians are: Marietta Tidei (vice president of the OSCE Parliamentary Assembly), Ferdinando Aiello, Luigi Compagna, Cristina De Pietro, Sergio Divina, Emma Fattorini, Federico Fauttilli, Claudio Fava, Francesco Monaco, Guglielmo Picchi (Vice- President of the first committee), Emanuele Scagliusi and Francesco Scalia. From 1 January 2016, the Italian official Roberto Montella is the Secretary General of the OSCE Parliamentary Assembly.

Italy is one of the major contributors to this organisation. In 2018, the Italian contribution to the budget was around €14.3 million (about 10.4 % of the total budget), equal to those of France and the United Kingdom, lower only to the contribution of the USA (12.4 %). Italy also contributed 13 % of the extra budgetary expenses with a commitment of €5.5 million, ranking in third place. In 2018, Italy was in third place for number of officials involved in the Secretariat, in OSCE institutions and in field missions (61).

Some of the activities organised or promoted by the Italian Presidency of the OSCE in 2018 are as follows (other specific initiatives are expanded in the following sections, which are dedicated to those respective mechanisms):

- meeting of the political directors of the Organisation, held in Rome on the priorities of the Italian Presidency, the three security dimensions and the proposals for reforming the Organisation (8 October 2018);
- training course for personnel of the Kosovan forces of law and order, to strengthen competencies on the fight against corruption through experience and good practise exchange for the Guardia di Finanza (Finance division of the police) and the Service for Criminal (from 16 to 19 October);

– Conference on "fight against intolerance and discrimination, focusing on religious discrimination: towards a comprehensive response from the OSCE region" (Roma, 23 October).

In the framework of the function of the Organisation Presidency, on 7 December 2018, the Italian Government organised and hosted the 25th OSCE Ministerial Council in Milan. Many documents were adopted during the summit, including a Declaration on the improvement of security and cooperation in the Mediterranean, decisions on the prevention and fight against violence against women, child and unaccompanied minors trafficking, a declaration on the contribution of young people to the efforts for peace and security, and a declaration in support of the negotiation process in Transistria. A decision to promote the security of journalists of the region with specific attention to the human dimension to the OSCE security approach was adopted.

Finally, the Center of Excellence for Stability Police Units (CoESPU) of Vicenza organised the fifth edition of the international training initiative based on a simulation activity to combat human trafficking along migratory routes following a multi-agency approach based on human rights

The main monitoring activity by OSCE mechanisms regarding Italy in 2018 was the evaluation of the parliamentary elections of 4 March by the ODIHR (see, in this Part, Organization for Security and Cooperation in Europe, I). From a Agenda 2030 for sustainable development perspective, the recommendations addressed to the Italian authorities in this field to improve efficiency, transparency and inclusivity in the State's electoral process contribute to the implementation of two Sustainable Development Goals: 10 (reduce inequality within and among contries) and 16 (peace, justice and strong institutions), particularly Target 16.3 (Promote the rule of law at the national and international levels and ensure equal access to justice for all) and 16.6 (Develop effective, accountable and transparent institutions at all levels).

I. Office for Democratic Institutions and Human Rights (ODIHR)

The ODIHR is the main institution of the OSCE which has been assisting Member States in the implementation of their commitments on the human dimension since 1991. Ingibjörg Sólrún Gísladóttir (Iceland) has been in the role of Director of the Office since 19 July 2017.

On 6 June 2018, the ODIHR adopted its final report on the national parliamentary elections of 4 March 2018. The report is based on the conclusions of the Election Assessment Mission (EAM) deployed to Italy between 20 February and 8 March on the invitation of the Permanent Delegation of Italy to the OSCE, and on the recommendations of the Needs Assessment Mission (NAM) deployed in December 2017.

Generally, according to the ODIHR, the elections of 4 March were competitive and pluralistic, providing voters with a wide range of candidates. While the campaign was conducted with respect for fundamental freedoms, it was confrontational and at times characterised by discriminatory stereotyping and intolerant rhetoric targeting immigrants, including on social media. While certain aspects of the legislation and training in key election day procedures should be reviewed and consolidated to enhance consistency and equal treatment of all voters, the elections were conducted in a professional manner and reflected a high degree of public confidence in their administration. In this regard, according to the ODIHR, the criteria for the selection of poll workers should be clearly defined and unified to further improve the work of Polling Election Offices. Furthermore, the law should be amended to include the mandatory training for poll workers with a view to ensureconsistent implementation of voting and counting procedures. The system of appointing PEO chairpersons and members for both regular and out-of-country constituency polling stations should be reviewed, and necessary measures should be taken in order to avoid absences of appointed poll workers on election days. To further enhance the transparency of the tabulation process, preliminary results by polling stations should be published as soon as they are received. Official results by polling stations should be published once they have been validated.

According to the observations in the ODIHR report, the legal framework regarding democratic elections is fragmented, and significant changes were introduced only a few months prior to the elections. The new election law was adopted without public consultation, through a hasty, constitutionally challenged procedure. The legal amendments include changes to the electoral system, the delineation of constituencies and a new system of campaign finance. Most of the previous ODIHR recommendations remain to be addressed and certain deficiencies persist in the law.

To overcome the deficiency related to the inequality of vote, consideration should be given to granting equal voting rights for elections to the Senate to all citizens who reached the age of majority. The ODIHR considered that it would be appropriate to codify existing regulations into electoral legislation so as to ensure legal certainty and coherence. Legal reform should be undertaken well in advance of the next elections and involve open consultations with all relevant stakeholders. As a priority, the State should consider adhering more closely to the electoral quota for all constituencies across the country, including in the out-of-country constituency, in line with international good practice concerning the equality of the vote, without prejudice to the protection of minorities.

According to the ODIHR, there are no clear rules for verifying the signatures collected to register a candidate list, which should be clarified to avoid possible errors. The authorities should consider clarifying the definitions and criteria required for classification of party logos. Furthermore, legislation should be reviewed to allow for independent candidacies, in line with international commitments. Given almost identical functions of the two chambers of parliament, consideration should be given to eliminate the different age requirements for candidates.

Even though the new election law introduced rules that the candidates on the lists in multi-mandate constituencies should alternate based on their gender, subject to refusing the list, women did not feature prominently in the campaign, neither as candidates nor as participants at campaign events. In the new parliament, 34 per cent of members are women.

Concerning voters with disabilities, the election administration took active measures to promote their participation, providing additional assistance to vote if needed and allowing them to vote in any accessible polling station within the same municipality. However, these special arrangements are not provided for persons with intellectual disabilities, at odds with international obligations. As a priority, election legislation should be harmonized with the objectives of the Convention of the Rights of Persons with Disabilities to ensure the full voting rights of all persons with disabilities, including the right to request assistance to vote. The ODIHR found that a number of special polling stations had been established in hospitals, prisons and pre-trial detention centres, and mobile voting was permitted for homebound voters.

Even though the electoral campaign was low key, the ODIHR described the tone of the campaign as antagonistic and confrontational. While the campaign was generally peaceful, it was marred by some violent incidents, including a shooting by a far-right activist at immigrants which resulted in six of them being injured.

Regarding campaign financing, despite improvements regarding a general ban on anonymous donations, a lower threshold for disclosing the source of donations, and reviewed sanctions for infringements of political finance rules, according to the ODIHR, some areas of concern remained. These were a lack of adequate powers and resources to carry out a pro-active and efficient oversight, investigation and enforcement of political finance regulations, as well as timing of disclosure of campaign income and expenditure. The institution suggested that to enhance transparency, consideration could be given to disclosing campaign finance reports prior to election day as well as extending the rules related to reporting and disclosure requirements to all donors and to non-affiliated third parties. As a priority, consideration could be given to enhancing the oversight system, including by providing a leading oversight body with a mandate, adequate powers and resources to carry out a pro-active and efficient supervision, investigation and enforcement of political finance regulations.

On the issue of the media, the ODIHR noted that despite repeated appeals from international bodies, defamation and slander remain criminal offences in Italy. Criminal provisions for such should be strictly proportionate to the actual harm caused. Regarding the coverage of the campaign, broadcasters covered the campaign extensively, providing citizens with access to differing political views and enabling them to make an informed choice. Both public and private broadcasters organised talk shows and extensive interviews with candidates, although there was no debate between party leaders. The public broadcaster RAI complied with the legal obligation to allocate up to three minutes of free coverage to each contesting party, however the time was allotted outside of the primetime, significantly limiting their potential audience. According to the ODIHR's assessment, consideration could be given to allocate direct access broadcasting time to contestants at the time when such addresses are likely to reach the widest possible audience. Among the weaknesses of the media and communications sector during during elections, the ODIHR mission noted the need to strengthen the independence of the broadcast media regulator AGCOM. In particular, the independence of the broadcast media regulator could be further strengthened by revising the system of appointment of its members.

Concerning the review of complaints related to the election results, which is monitored by the newly elected parliament, there are still some deficiencies in the legislation that may limit the legal right to appeal, such as the lack of possibility to appeal election results to a competent court as the final authority and of adequate time limits for deciding on election- related complaints. According to the ODIHR, to ensure the implementation of the right to an effective and timely remedy, legislation should provide adequate time limits for deciding on election-related complaints at all levels. Information about submitted complaints and requests should be made publicly available.

Among the other work promoted by ODIHR in 2018 regarding Italy, a training course was organised for civil society representatives and legal professionals who work with hate crime victims. The course took place in Milan on 11 and 12 April and was part of the wider project "Building a Comprehensive Criminal Justice Response to Hate Crime".

II. High Commissioner on National Minorities

The office of the High Commissioner on National Minorities is the institution responsible for identifying, and as far as possible addressing, situations of inter-ethnic tension in the OSCE area. As well as serving as a conflict-preventing mechanism, the High Commissioner can also support quick solutions which can defuse processes of escalating violence. On 19 July 2017, the Italian diplomat Lamberto Zannier, former Secretary-General of the OSCE from 2011 to 2017, became the High Commissioner on national minorities.

Some of the initatives of the High Commissioner in 2018 regarding Italy were as follows:

- the two-day event in Udine, organised in cooperation with the OSCE Chairmanship (15–16 July) to celebrate the tenth anniversary of the Bolzano/Bozen recommendations on National Minorities in Inter- State Relations (2008). Representatives of the OSCE Member States, international organisations, and the academic world all took part in the event, reflecting on the way in which States are able to tackle the judicial and political concerns that arise from the situation of minorities within and across national borders.

— organising a round table on conflict prevention with the Permanent Representative of Italy in New York, with the participation of various regional organisations, including the Arab League, the EU, the Organization of American States, the OSCE and the Shanghai Cooperation Organization.

III. Representative on Freedom of the Media

Established in 1997 with a view to ensuring a high level of compliance with the rules and standards on freedom of expression and freedom of the media accepted by the States Parties to OSCE, the Representative on Freedom of the Media acts as an early warning instrument in cases of violation of the right to freedom of expression, with particular attention to any obstacles or impediments to the activities of journalists. From March 2010 to July 2017, this position was held by Dunja Mijatovic (Bosnia and Herzegovina). On 18 July 2017, Harlem Désir (France) was appointed as the new OSCE Representative on Freedom of the Media.

On 14 September 2018, the OSCE Representative sent a letter to the Minister of Foreign Affairs and International Cooperation Moavero Milanesi to express concern about the seizure of the mobile phone and computer of a *La Repubblica* journalist, Salvo Palazzolo, as part of an investigation related to a case of an alleged leak of information and violation of confidentiality of a judicial procedure after the journalist published a report on the via D'Amelio bombing, an attack by the Sicilian Mafia in which magistrate Paolo Borsellino was killed with five policemen in 1992.

According to the OSCE Representative, the seizure and search of the journalist's mobile phone and computer undermined the protection of sources of the journalist and the right of the press not to disclose confidential sources, which is essential for the exercise of reporting on issues of public interest. To support his argument, the Representative cites the interpretation of Article 19 ICCPR contained in General Comment No. 34 of the UN Human Rights Committee which clearly indicated that freedom of expression includes the protection of journalistic sources and the recommendation made in 2015 by the UN Special Rapporteur on freedom of opinion and freedom of expression, David Kaye, which stated that any restrictions on confidentiality must be genuinely exceptional and subject to the highest standards, and implemented by judicial authorities only.

IV. Special Representative and Coordinator for Combating Trafficking in Human Beings

The Office of the Special Representative and Coordinator for Combating Trafficking in Human Beings is responsible for assisting OSCE States to progressively meet their commitments in this area under the 2003 Action Plan. It also serves as the body co-coordinating all OSCE activities combating trafficking. From September 2014, Madina Jarbussynova (Kazakhstan) is the OSCE Special Representative and Coordinator.

The activities of this office in 2018 regarding Italy include, on 12 April, in a ceremony that took place just before the International Conference "Trafficking of Human Beings from a Human Rights Perspective", organised by the Department for Equal Opportunities, the City of Venice and the OSCE, The Special Representative and Co-ordinator for Combating Trafficking in Human Beings signed an agreement with the Municipality of Venice to reinfornce cooperation to protect victims and fight against organised criminal networks involved in human trafficking.

On 11 October, the Office of the Special Representative and Cooperdinator and the Italian OSCE Chairmanship organised a workshop in which a team of paramedic staff shared good practicies on the most efficient way to tackle migratory routes in a multi-agency approach combining effective investigative measures with victim protection.

Humanitarian and Criminal Law

I. Adaptation to International Humanitarian and Criminal Law

Italy is part of all the main international conventions concerning the law of armed conflicts and international criminal law. With the l. 4 December 2017, No. 200, Italy ratified and implemented an amendment to the Rome Statute establishing the International Criminal Court, adopted in 2015, concerning the elimination of Article 124 of the same Statute. The latter provision, better known as "opting out clause", provisionally provided that each State may declare that it does not accept, for a period of seven years from the entry into force of the Statute against it, the jurisdiction of the Court with respect to war crimes committed by their own citizens or on their territory. 2018 celebrated the 20th Anniversary of the Rome Statute, signed in 1998. 2018 was also the year that The Philippines deposited a notification of withdrawal from the International Criminal Court. The decision was communicated on 17 March 2019. The Philippines is the second State to withdraw from the Rome Statute (Article 127) after Burundi in 2017.

Italy has not yet ratified the amendments to the Rome Statute adopted in 2010 during the Review Conference of Kampala (Uganda) and related to the statutory provisions on war crimes and crime of aggression.

On 6 December 2017, the Assembly of States Parties elected Italian Judge of the International Criminal Court, Rosario Salvatore Aitala, whereas on 10 March 2018 Cuno Tarfusser (Italy) completed his mandate, which had started in March 2009.

In connection with the armaments sector, the obligation to present periodic reports on the state of implementation of the provisions of the various conventions is particularly important. In this regard, in 2018, Italy presented its annual report required by Article 7 of the Oslo Convention on the banning and limitation of deployment of conventional arms; the annual report required by Article 7 of the

Convention against anti-personnel mines; the report requested by the Protocol on Mines, Booby-Traps and Other Devices and concerning the Protocol on Explosive Remnants of War, required by the Convention on Prohibitions or Restrictions on the Use of Certain Conventional Weapons; the annual report required by the Convention of Oslo on Cluster Munitions (April 2018).

On 7 July 2017, the Treaty on the Prohibition of Nuclear Weapons. It was opened for signature on 20 September 2017, as of April 2018, 70 States had signed and 23 had ratified it. Italy voted against the resolution which the United Nations General Assembly decided to convening a working group to develop the treaty, did not participate in the drafting process and is not one of the States that has signed the Treaty.

II. Italian Contribution to "Peacekeeping" and to Other International Missions

With the entry into force of the l. 21 July 2016, No. 145 regarding the participation of Italy in international missions, the procedures for authorisation and financing of the missions follow two distinct procedures: the procedure for the launch of new missions pursuant to Article 2 (resolution of the Council of Ministers, transmission to the Chambers, parliamentary authorisation by means of guidelines) and the procedure for the extension of the same for the following year, included in the so-called parliamentary session on the progress of the authorised missions (Articles 3 and 4). Article 3 of the law also provides that, by 31 December of each year, the Government present to the Chambers, an analytical report on the missions in progress for discussion and subsequent parliamentary deliberations.

On 28 November 2018, the Council of Ministers discussed the analytic report concerning the international missions carried out between 1 January-30 September 2018 (Doc. XXVI, No. 1). This resolution aimed to authorise the continuation of these missions for the final three-months of 2018, pursuent to Article 3 of law 21 July 2016 and Italy's participation in a new international mission, pursuant Article 2, paragraph 1, of the same law (DOC. XXV, No. 1). This is a training mission for the Iraqi security forces that NATO decided to initiate in July 2018 during the Brussels Summit (NATO Mission in Iraq - NM-l). Both the resolutions of the Council of Ministers were approved on 13 December 2018 by

Commissions III (Foreign and European Affairs) and IV (Defence) of the Chamber of Deputies.

The resolutions of the Chamber of Deputies (No. 6-00382) and of the Senate of the Republic (Doc. XXIV, No. 93 and No. 94) were approved, respectively, on 17 January 2018 and 15 January 2018. They authorised the continuation of the ongoing international missions and development cooperation initiatives to support peace and stabilisation processes, contained in Annex I of the Council of Ministers resolution of 28 December 2017 for the period 1 January- 30 September 2018. Only a few missions were extended for the whole year of 2018: EULEX Kosovo (European Union Rule of Law Mission in Kosovo), UNMIK (United Nations Mission in Kosovo), participation of military personnel to the programme of police forces in Albania; EUPOL COPPS (European Union Police Mission for the Palestinian Territories) in Palestine; Assistance and Support bilateral mission to the Libyan military Coast Guard; European Union Border Assistance Mission in Libya, EUBAM. Compared to the 2017 resolution, the following are not present:

– Military personnel to the bilateral mission for sanitary support in Libya, designated Operation Ippocrate;
– Military personnel to strengthen the provision of NATO Interim Air Policing in Iceland;
– Military personnel to strengthen the provision of NATO Interim Air Policing in Bulgaria.

The following list shows the military and police missions to which Italy participated with its own personnel in 2018. The total annual average number of armed forces' contingents used in the theatres operating in 2018 is 6,428 units. For the period January – September 2018, €747,619,047 were allocated for the performance of outgoing missions and to start new armed forces missions. A total allocation of €1,132,505,294 is expected for the full year of 2018.

Country/ geographical area of mission	Mission
Asia	Global Coalition Against Daesh
Afghanistan	NATO Resolute Support Mission (RSM)

Country/ geographical area of mission	Mission
Africa	United Nations Mission for the Referendum in Western Sahara-MINURSO
	European Union Training Mission Central African Republic-EUTM RCA
	NATO Support Mission in Tunisia to develop their interforce defence capacities
Albania	Bilateral Coorperation Mission of Italian Police Forces in Albania and Balkan countries
Bosnia-Herzegovina	European Union Mission ALTHEA
Cyprus	United Nations Peacekeeping Force in Cyprus (UNFICYP)
Egypt	Multinational Force and Observers in Egypt (MFO)
United Arab Emirates / Bahrain/ Qatar/ Tampa, USA	Military personnel in the United Arab Emirates, Bahrain, Qatar and Tampa for needs connected to missions in the Middle East and Asia
Kosovo/Balkans	European Union Rule of Law Mission in Kosovo (EULEX Kosovo)
	United Nations Mission in Kosovo (UNMIK)
	Joint Enterprise Operation (NATO)
	United Nations Military Observer Group in India and Pakistan (UNMOGIP)
Libya	United Nations Support Mission in Libya (UNSMIL)
	Support and Assistence Bilateral Mission for the Libyan military Coast Guard
	European Union Border Assistance Mission in Libya (EUBAM Libia)

Country/ geographical area of mission	Mission
	Bilateral Assistance and Support Mission in Libya
Lebanon	Bilateral Training Mission for Libyan Armed Forces
	United Nations Interim Force in Lebanon (UNIFIL)
Mali	United Nations Multidimensional Integrated Stabilization Mission in Mali (MINUSMA)
	EUCAP Sahel Mali
	European Union Training Mission Mali (EUTM Mali)
Mediterranean	EUNAVFOR MED Operation SOPHIA
	NATO Sea Guardian in the Mediterranean Sea (ex Active Endeavour)
Niger	Bilateral support mission in the Republic of Niger
	EUCAP Sahel Niger
	Temporary International Presence in Hebron (TIPH2)
Palestine	Bilateral Training Mission for Palestinian Secrurity Forces
	European Union Police Mission for the Palestinian Territories (EUPOL COPPS)
	European Union Border Assistance Mission in Rafah (EUBAM Rafah)
Palestine/Egypt	EUNAVFOR Operation Atalanta
Somalia/Horn of Africa	European Union Training Mission Somalia (EUTM Somalia)
	EUCAP Somalia (ex EUCAP Nestor)

Country/ geographical area of mission	Mission
	Bilateral training mission of the Somalian and Djiboutian police forces
	Personnel based in the national military base in the Republic of Djibouti for needs connected with international missions in the Horn of Africa and surrounding areas
Strengthening national and NATO provisions	NATO: provisions for the defence of the South-East borders of the Alliance, (NATO Support to Turkey)
	"Mare Sicuro": National naval air provisions in the Mediterranean Sea, which includes the bilateral mission supporting the Libyan Coast Guard
	NATO: provisions for surveillance of the South-west Alliance Air space
	NATO: provisions for presence in Latvia (Enhanced Forward Presence)
	NATO Support in Tunisia
	NATO Air Policing for surveillance of the Alliance Air space

Part IV

National and International Case-Law

Human Rights in Italian Case-law

Continuing the work started in the previous editions of the *Yearbook*, Section IV presents an overview of the case-law of the Italian courts in 2018 and highlights the theme of internationally recognised human rights. The focus is on the case-law of the Constitutional Court and the Court of Cassation and on the aspects of case-law of the international courts that are closest to Italian judicial practice and have specific competence on human rights: the European Court of Human Rights (ECtHR) and the Court of Justice of the European Union (CJEU). The section also contains a brief presentation of rulings passed by these two courts referring to Italy and human or fundamental rights.

As always, the intent is not to provide an exhaustive examination, but rather to cite and note the guidance and the new paths that were recorded in 2018 within Italian and European judicial practice regarding human rights standards, following an approach that aims at consolidating information given in previous editions.

Given the relative low number of judgments to present, the parts on the rulings of the ECtHR and CJEU are subdivided into topics. They follow criteria fundamentally linked to the sequence of articles of the respective instruments, while the section on Italian case-law follows the 12-part subdivision seen in the first edition of the *Yearbook* and continued in the following years.

The action of judicial bodies working at national and international level can also be analysed from a SDGs perspective. The Agenda 2030 analytic and strategic framework can help identify both strengths and weakenesses of the protection judicial system for fundamental rights, and naturally provides an important incentive to redefine the thematic articulation which has so far been used in this review.

The Court's work is mainly covered by the SDG framework in Goal 16: Peace, justice and strong institutions.

Targets 16.3 (Promote the rule of law at the national and international levels and ensure equal access to justice for all), 16.7 (Ensure responsive, inclusive, participatory and representative decision-making at all levels) and 16.10 (Ensure public access to information and protect fundamental freedoms, in accordance with national legislation and international agreements) are particularly relevant for our analysis.

These goals feature prominently in sections 1.1., 1.3., 1.9., 1.11. and 1.12. of the Part on Italian case-law. The first section shows some decisions have clarified the relationship between the Italian legal system and the international legal system, particularly regarding EU law. The balance between multi-level justice actors that has been progressively built within the European framework has taken many forms over the years, and recently, in the light of the entry into force of the CFREU and some protocols to the ECHR, it is going through a significant change, generally towards reevaluating the State's role compared to that of a supranational court. This trend may have a serious impact of the international interest in human rights and in the long term, could weaken the capacity of singular judicial systems to resist social pressure towards the surpression of these rights. Section 1.3. presents some cases related to the guarantee of the right of free association, especially in the field of politics and trade unions. Section 1.9. mainly focuses on some cases that concerned the right to privacy and the right to view personal data; while section 1.11. provides an update on the application on the regulations introduced in Italy almost twenty years ago to protect citizens facing excessively long durations of judicial procedures. Section 1.12. summarises various questions on the application of criminal law, ranging from problems relating to the definition of certain crimes to questions raised about criminal procedure and the ways of implementing criminal sentences. It focuses on the application of recent regulations concerning compensation for detention in inhuman or degrading conditions. The topics addressed are often linked to the legal response to challenges posted to Italian society and institutions by organised criminal gangs (to which there must be a firm response that fully respects the rights of individuals and the principles of the Rule of Law). These are connected to Goals 16.4 (By 2030, significantly reduce illicit financial and arms flows, strengthen the recovery and return of stolen assets and combat all forms of organized crime) and 16.5. (Substantially reduce corruption and bribery in all their forms).

Criminal problems and more are detailed in section 1.10., which focuses on the rights of children and adolescents. The subject is specifically identified given its relevance not only to the overall guarantee of human rights, but also, with the interpretative parameters derived from the

Convention on the Rights of the Child (1989) and other international instruments concerning children (including the Istanbul Convention on domestic violence and the Lanzarote Convention on Protection of Children against Sexual Exploitation and Sexual Abuse) are referred to in the motivations of the Italian Courts. Goals that refer specifically to the condition of children include 16.2. (End abuse, exploitation, trafficking and all forms of violence against and torture of children).

Other sections can be linked to other areas of interest covered by the SDGs, other than the abovementioned Goals. For example, section 1.2. presents various cases connected to the issue of legal recognition in Italy by judicial institutions (same-sex marriage, same-sex adoption, assisted suicide, and similar) which raise legitimate differences from State to State and can only be resolved by referring to supranational principles such as human rights (including the principle of the best interest of the child. Goal 16.9 (By 2030, provide legal identity for all, including birth registration) is relevant in this area out of the SDGs. The Goal is also important in reference to the cases presented in section 1.8 (immigration), concerning the granting of Italian citizenship to foreign nationals who are long-tem residents in Italy or even born in Italy, as well as the issue of statelessness. The issue of migration is linked with Goal 10.7 (Facilitate orderly, safe, regular and responsible migration and mobility of people, including through the implementation of planned and well-managed migration policies), intrinsically connected with the reduction of inequality (SDG 10). The issue of inequality and combating discrimination is also the basis of sections 1.5, 1.6 and 1.7, concerning respectively to the field of ethnic and religious discrimination, rights of persons with disabilities and social rights. In this regard, various Goals can be cited, including Goal 16.B (Promote and enforce non-discriminatory laws and policies for sustainable development) 16.2 (End abuse, exploitation, trafficking and all forms of violence against and torture of children), and also Goals 10.2. (By 2030, empower and promote the social, economic and political inclusion of all, irrespective of age, sex, disability, race, ethnicity, origin, religion or economic or other status), 10.3. (Ensure equal opportunity and reduce inequalities of outcome, including by eliminating discriminatory laws, policies and practices and promoting appropriate legislation, policies and action in this regard) and 10.4. (Adopt policies, especially fiscal, wage and social protection policies, and progressively achieve greater equality). Regarding the issue of inclusion in education of persons with disabilities, Goal 4.5.

(By 2030, eliminate gender disparities in education and ensure equal access to all levels of education and vocational training for the vulnerable, including persons with disabilities, indigenous peoples and children in vulnerable situations) is particularly noteworthy. Concerning workers' conditions (including those who must also look after family members with disabilities), the SDGs dedicated to "Promote sustained, inclusive and sustainable economic growth, full and productive employment and decent work for all." are particularly applicable. These include Targets 8.5 (By 2030, achieve full and productive employment and decent work for all women and men, including for young people and persons with disabilities, and equal pay for work of equal value), 8.7 (Take immediate and effective measures to eradicate forced labour, end modern slavery and human trafficking and secure the prohibition and elimination of the worst forms of child labour, including recruitment and use of child soldiers, and by 2025 end child labour in all its forms), and 8.8 (Protect labour rights and promote safe and secure working environments for all workers, including migrant workers, in particular women migrants, and those in precarious employment).

Many of the causes illustrated in Section 1.4., which focuses on asylum and international protection, are at the meeting point between social rights and problems related to civil liberties. The criteria fixed by Italian, European and international regulations to ensure protection for people coming from humanitarian crises can be used for differentiated interpretations and applications, also given the overlap of legislative reforms that are not always attributable to a coherent *ratio* inspired by the protection of people and their rights. Italy at the end of 2018 is a prime example.

Finally, though not expressly identified in a specific section – not because it is irrelevant, but due to its transversal and pervasive nature – multiple and intersecting forms of discrimination against women mirroring deep and unresolved social injustices are present in many cases. For these reasons, the reference to Goal 5 (Achieve gender equality and empower all women and girls) is also relevant, in its various forms.

The contribution to environmental sustainability in a framework of sustained economic development provided by the judicial instruments has always been underestimated by the parameters of the analyses used up to this point. The action of the judiciary in opposing the indiscriminate exploitation of environmental resources can hardly be overlooked, in particular earth and water, in light of climate change (SDG 6, 7, 8, 9,

11, 12, 13, 14, 15). In rethinking the collection and analysis of Italian case-law for the next issues of this *Yearbook,* this lack of analysis will be be taken into account to bridge the gap.

I. Aspects of the Relationship between the Italian Justice System and European Case-law

A. Questions of Constitutionality and Preliminary Referral to the CJEU: "Dual Preliminarity"

Some judgments of the Court of Cassation, including Court of Cassation, Civil Division, sec. II, 16 February 2018, No. 3831 focused on the issue raised by the ruling of the Constitutional Court 269/2017 concerning the so-called "dual preliminarity" in the case of suspected violations of human rights.

In a digression by the Constitutional Court within a routine decision, the judges gave various considerations which aimed to reframe the relationship between EU law and the Italian legal system when conflicts emege between the Italian and European systems with regard to fundamental rights, recognised by both the CFREU and the Consititution (as well as the ECHR). The Constitutional Court has pronounced that in the cases where an Italian law appears to be in conflict with EU law relating to the CFREU, national judges should always submit questions of constitutionality, irrespective of whether the CFREU recognises directly effective provisions; the preliminary referral to the CJEU as a second line, once the Constitutional Court has given its judgment. The decision of the Constitutional Court must harmonise the parameters of the Constitution with those coming from EU law and from the ECHR itself. Moreover, the Italian judge can proceed in reverse order, first referring to the CJEU and then submitting the question of constitutionality. The new structure laid out by the Constitutional Court in its *obiter dictum* seems to overturn the previous established procedure, according to which the existence of conditions for a preliminary referral excluded – except in exceptional cases – the intervention of the Constitutional Court, due to the principle of primacy of EU law above national law. It seems that the new stance aims to make laws more coherent, since disapplying national law when it is contrary to a European provision does not rescind the regulation from national law, while declaring it unconstitutional has the effect of removing the regulation from the State's legislation. The new system leaves some points uncertain and, above all, envisages situations in which conflicts may emerge between the evaluation of the Constitutional Court and of the CJEU, or by the judge who must apply or disapply the contested legislation. If the CJEU pronounced the incompatibility of EU law with Italian law that has already been recognised constitutionally legitimate by the Constitutional Court, the Italian judge would be obliged to disapply a law that the Constitutional Court had declared legitimate, just as they could directly disapply a law in the case that there were no doubts about the opposition of the law with the CFREU. Establishing a potential conflict between the Constitutional Court and the CJEU, not on extraordinary issues of crucial importance, but on a wide range of problems relating to the application of the CFREU, risks complicating the relationship between the two legal systems, which deserve to be carefully regulated.

The Court of Cassation judgment No. 3831/2018 cited above (see also, in this Part, XII.A) observes that Italian law punishes insider trading with both administrative (imposed by the CONSOB) and criminal sanctions (so-called "double track"), but it also obliges the individuals to provide the CONSOB with a series of information that could be used against them in criminal proceedings; this would seem to violate the right to a defence (particularly the right to be forced to self-incriminate), guaranteed by the Constitution, international human rights law, and by Article 47 CFREU. In compliance with the supposed new orientation of the Constitutional Court, the Court of Cassation brought up the question of constitutionality, warning that on this point other judges - or the Court of Cassation itself - could proceed differently, disapplying Italian legislation in the matter due to the contradiction with Article 47 CFREU, or the CJEU could decide contrarily to that indicated by the Constitutional Court.

B. Obligation to Abide by the Final Judgements of the ECtHR: Article 46 ECHR Does not Impose the Revocability of Final Judgements in Civil and Administrative Matters

The judgment *Zhou v. Italy*, No. 33773/11, 21 January 2014, of the ECtHR (see *Yearbook 2015*, p. 327) had pronouced that the Italian authorities had violated the right to private and family life of the defendant, announcing a state of abandonment and the successive adoption (ordered by a judge in 2010) of her son without sufficient efforts to maintain family ties. After the judgment, the mother and the guardian of the child asked in court that the judgment of the ECtHR be carried out, namely the rebuilding of maternal bond which after the adoption had been broken and appealing the extraordinary repealing of the judgment which originally allowed for the adoption.

The incompatibility with the ECHR as ascertained by the Court of Strasbourg is not foreseen in the reasons listed in Article 395 civil procedure code for purpose of revision. The Venice Court of Appeal, apprised of the case, raises the question of constitutionality of the cited Article 395. The impossibility of reopening the adoption procedure would result in a violation of the State's duty to comply with the ECtHR judgment, as established by Article 46 ECHR, and therefore constitutes a violation of Article 117(1) of the Constitution.

The question echoes the issue already tackled by the Constitutional Court in judgment 123/2017 (see *Yearbook 2018*, p. 196–7). In that ruling, the Constitutional Court concluded that the ECtHR case-law imposes on States that the reopening of processes that constituted a violation of the ECHR only when they are criminal cases, not for civil or administrative matters. In these cases, the individual is not facing supposed punishment by the State, but as opposed to other individuals who were unable to participate in procedures before the ECtHR and would not see their legal position change after the *res judicata* of a national judgment. This stance has been repeated recently by the ECtHR (cited in case *Moreira Ferreira v. Portugal (no. 2)* [GC], no. 19867/12, 11 July 2017). The Constitutional Court (judgment 93/2018), therefore concludes that the question of constitutionality is groundless.

> Also concerning administrative justice, the established contradiction between ECHR legislation and the decisions of the Italian courts does not necessarily imply the unconstitutionality of legislation that, as in these cases, does not provide for the reopening of administrative cases that have been closed with a definite ruling, or even the reopening of the terms to propose appeals. Judgment 6/2018 of the Constitutional Court tackled a series of cases which cast doubt on the constitutionality of Article 69(7), lgs.d. 165/2001, a regulation that establishes that the jurisdiction concerning the employment relationship of public employees, for the events that took place after 30 June 1998, passes from the administrative court to the civil court, setting 15 September 2001 as the deadline to propose any remaining questions to the Regional Administrative Court. With respect to these provisions, various issues have emerged, including those which brought about judgments *Mottola* and *Staibano* of the ECtHR (see *Yearbook 2015*,

p. 318; *Yearbook 2016*, p. 172–173; see also, in this Part, Italy in the Case-law of the European Court of Human Rights, II). Specifically, the ECtHR held that this convened the right to access to a hearing (Article 6 ECHR) and the forfeiture of the right to propose to any administrative or civil judges a question on the subject of work reported before June 1998 for anyone who missed the 2001 deadline. The joint sections of the Court of Cassation held that the disputes closed by the Council of State with a rejection of the request on the basis of the action of such forfeiture should be reopened in the light of the rulings of the ECtHR and raised a question of constitutionality with regard to the lack of a provision in the Italian legal system which provides for such an eventuality. The judgment of the Constitutional Court in the first place declared the question inadmissable by the joint sections of the Court of Cassation, since it is not for this body to review the decisions of the Council of State (according to Article 111(8) of the Constitution, "Appeals to the Court of Cassation against decisions of the Council of State and the Court of Accounts are permitted only for reasons of jurisdiction"). It also confirms that the lack of any remedy in the cases in question does not in itself constitute a violation of the Constitution (pursuant to Article 6 ECHR), despite the *Mottola* and *Staibano* established case-law. The peremptory nature of the deadline set by the law was neither unreasonable nor unexpected, even if case-law on the subject has not always been consistant.

With judgment 24/2018, the Constitutional Court clarified – in line with EU case-law – that a law introducing pejorative changes in the matter of remuneration does not constitute a violation of the principle of legality and fair trial, or an interference by the legislative power over the prerogatives of the judicial order, contrary to Articles 6 and 13 ECHR (standards set in relation to Article 117(1) of the Constitution). Specifically, the law in question was a provision eliminating some automatic pay rises favouring State Councillors and had already been ruled on the basis of various extraordinary appeals to the Head of State, some of which are still pending. The appeals to the Head of State do not constitute jurisdictional proceedings and their conclusions are administrative, non-jurisdictional acts; these procedures therefore do not represent a limit to the operation of a retroactive act *in peius*, and can be adequately justified by considerations of public interest.

II. Dignity of the Person, Right to Identity

A. *Right to Know One's Origins*

The Court of Cassation (Court of Cassation, Civil Division, sec. I, judg. 20 March 2018, No. 6963) pronounced that an adopted person has the right to know their origins even if it was an anonymous birth (see *Yearbook 2018*, p. 264). This includes the right to know biological family members which extends not only to parents but also siblings and other close family members, with their consent, which must be obtained with the maximum privacy. The Court came to this conclusion through an innovative interpretation of l. 184/1983, undoubtedly steered by the Constitution and international legislation, on the rights of the child to a family. The right envisions that an adopted person can see information on their biological parents after their 25th birthday. The law can also be extended to biological brothers and sisters, however, in those cases, the right of the adopted person to know their family origins in full depends on the siblings' consent, as the Court recognises the clashing right to not disclose their biological link with the concerned.

B. Assisted Suicide

Court of Assize of Milan submitted the question of legitimacy of Article 580 of the criminal code to the Constitutional Court, which punishes the crime of instigating or assisting suicide, also applicable to those who aid suicide, without contributing or reinforcing determination to suicide (that is, through material assistance). The case which gave birth to the question of constitutionality was widely debated at a political level and in the media. It involved a politician who, accusing himself of the crime in question, he hoped to bring up the ethical, political and judicial aspects of the right of self-determination of the individual to end their own life. This right may require the collaboration of a second person (acting as material help for carrying out the suicide) if the individual is not self-sufficient. The fact that Article 580 of the Criminal Code considers the help given in these circumstances as a crime, which would constitute a violation of Articles 2, 13 (personal freedom) and 117(1) of the Constitution, the latter in relation with Articles 2 and 8 ECHR.

According to the Constitutional Court (ord. 207/2018), the text of Article 580 of the Criminal Code leaves no doubts about the punishment of assisted and instigated suicide: in this case, an interpretation according to the Constitution of the provision in question is not possible. However, the law itself is not constitutionally unfounded. It aims to protect people in fragile situations who "could be easily induced to leave life prematurely, if the law allowed anyone to cooperate in carrying out their suicidal choice". Regarding the fact that the criminal law interferes with individual self-determination, the Court, recalling the noteworthy case *Pretty* and other successive decisions from the ECtHR, evokes that the right to intangibility of choices concerning their own private life can come under legitimate restrictions by the State, in particular when it is necessary in a democratic society to protect other rights and freedoms and the measures presented are proportionate to the goal. The Constitutional Court recognises that more situations in contemporary society are emerging in which assistance to suicide is an option for people suffering from terminal illnesses, a source of intolerable suffering, who is kept alive with life support treatments, but is nevertheless fully capable of taking free and informed decisions. This is the situation captured by law 22 December 2017, No. 219 (regulations on informed consent and provisions on advanced care planning). The law develops the right to informed consent, a combination of the right to personal freedom (Article 13 of the Constitution) and the right to freedom of treatment (Article 32 of the Constitution). The latter entails the non-punishment of doctors who carry out the wishes of patients to refuse health treatment and reduce their own suffering by suspending treatment to the patient, including vital support treatment, to prevent a prolonged death process, as underlined by the Court. This does not equate to the doctor actively determining the death of the patient by quickly putting an end to the suffering of the person, even if this is the will of the persons who, with this choice, would avoid placing them in a situation incompatible with human dignity. Therefore, there is a lack of legislation recognising that caring for a patient in the above-described conditions is exempt from the law in force concerning assisted suicide, inspired by a patient's right to self-determination in choice of treatment that includes palliative care. The Court does not hold that annuling the criminal provision on assisted suicide due to unconstitutionality is a viable solution, as it would allow anyone to offer assisted suicide services to people in vulnerable situations. A law that completes what is regulated by law 2019/2017 is therefore required. Following the example of the Canadian and British Supreme Courts, the Constitutional Court made a reasoned order to update its decision of 24 September 2019, giving Parliament twelve months to adopt a new law concerning assisted suicide that regulates the various ethical and legal aspects illustrated within the judgment, in order to foster a collaborative dialogue between the Court and Parliament.

C. Registration of Surnames for Civil Unions

Lgs.d. 19 January 2017, No. 5 provides that the public records of the individuals in a civil union must keep their surnames from before the civil union. In other words, the individuals in a civil union, according to law 76/2016 that introduced this legal system, can choose a shared family surname, like for a hetrosexual marriage, but does not entail changing the individual's public record, unlike what happens in hetrosexual marriages. This different treatment raises a doubt, in the judgment of the Court of Ravenna, on the Constitutionality of the cited provision, in particular, by contrast, with Articles 2, 3 and 22 (right to a name) of the Constitution and with Article 117(1), in conflict with the principle of freedom of personal and family life guaranteed by Articles 7 CFREU and 8 ECHR.

According to the Constitutional Court (judg. 212/2018), the disputed law is constitutionally legitimate. This is a reasonable consequence of the fact that law 76/2016 establishes that the individuals in a civil union can choose a shared family surname, but adds that this choice is valid only "for the duration of the civil union". This clarification aims to distinguish between the civil union and marriage legal systems and seems to be coherent with the law that does not allow the update of the individuals' public record. Regarding the contravention of Article 22 Constitution, the appeal is inadmissable since the right to a name is protected by the Constitution with respect to political interference, although these reasons are not discernible by the ruling judge in the present appeal.

D. Right to Health and Compulsory Vaccinations

The Region of Veneto doubts the constitutional legitimacy of l.d. 6 June 2017, No. 73, as well as conversion law 31 July 2017, No. 119 (with amendments) of the same decree. The disputed instruments regulate the ways of administrating ten types of vaccines (six compulsary, four recommended), and foresees heavy sanctions and a ban of unvaccinated children in infant schools and infant education services for non-compliance. The Region of Veneto has contested the law many times about its legitimacy. The criticisms focus particularly on its compulsary nature of the vaccines, regarded as contravening the principle of freedom of treatment (Article 32 of the Constitution) and the right to private and family life (Article 8 ECHR; also citing the Convention on the Rights of the Child and the Convention of Oviedo of the Council of Europe, which establishes the principle of informed consent for medical treatment). Furthermore, the State law is contrary to the provisions that have been in place for some time in the Region of Veneto, which focus on the consent of the parents, rather than the imposition of vaccinations regardless of the decision of the family. The appeal by the Region was deemed admissible, since the issue concerns a national law that affects a matter – in this case health – of regional competence and impacts on the applicability of existing regional rules.

The judgment 5/2018 of the Constitutional Court completely rejects the criticisms concerning law 119/2017. With respect to individual autonomy for health, the Court recalls that the constitutional values involved in the problem of vaccinations are not limited to freedom of treatment, but also concern the protection of collective health, the interest of the child and the need to protect them from potentially prejudicial choices by parents. At an international level, various States have legislated to provide a range of measures, from imposing compulsary (sometimes criminal) sanctions to promoting awareness campaigns for voluntary vaccinations by families, with many initiatives in between. The same can be said for access for unvaccinated children to school. Furthermore, both in Italy and other countries, legal choices about compulsory vaccinations have varied across the years, taking into consideration new medical evidence or due to health emergencies that required the adoption of different restrictive measures. Therefore, on this point, States have a wide margin of discretion. According to judges, the choice of the State legislator cannot be censured in terms of reasonableness or disproportionality, since Parliament based its decision on reports from competent medical authorities that generally showed that purely persuasive measures are inefficient.

E. Transcription of Foreign Documents and Alleged Oppostition to Public Order: Same-sex Marriage and Adoption

The Court of Cassation (joint sections, judg. 27 June 2018, No. 16957) ruled on the contoversies related to the transcription of same-sex marriages that took place in other countries where this form of marriage is fully recognised. It has ruled that that they come under the judisdiction of an ordinary judge, and not the judisdiction of an administrative court. In this regard, the same Court, (Court of Cassation, Civil Division, sec. I, judg. 14 May 2018, No. 16969) reiterated the principle that same-sex marriage that has taken place abroad according to the law of the State cannot be transcribed in Italy as marriage, but rather as a civil union pursuant to l. 76/2016. This also applies if the marriage took place before the law in question came into force. The Supreme Court excluded that this represented discriminatory treatment to the detriment of the couple (on this point, see *Yearbook 2017*, p. 252–255; *Yearbook 2018*, p. 267–268).

In other cases, the Court of Cassation had to rule on the implications of recognising same-sex marriage regarding the children of these couples.

A French couple of women (one of whom also had Italian citizenship), who were married in France and were residents both in France and Italy, had both adopted the child of the other, both children having been born through assisted fertilisation. The adoptions were fully recognised by the French judge. The spouses had asked the Civil State Authorities of the Italian municipality of their residence to transcribe both their marriage contract in France and the adoption papers, and were refused both. Similarly, a request to add the name of the adoptive spouse to the name of one of the biological children of the couple was rejected by a different municipality. After the Court judgment that confirmed the local authorities' refusal, justifying it as contrary to Italian public order of the institution of same-sex marriage, the Court of Appeals held that the act of transcribing an adoption registered in France was not contrary to international public order, since their recognition was functional and establishes the superior interest of the child to participate in family life and to maintain family ties with both parental figures. In response to this verdict, the mayors of the municipalities in question brought the case to the Court of Cassation. The Supreme Court tackled the issue from the persepctive of international private law (l. 218/1995), focusing on the potential clash between foreign laws on same-sex marriage and adoption and Italian laws. Complying with the notion of "public order" to limit the effects of foreign judgments in Italy should be extremely restricted and strictly bound by the principles established by the Constitution and by the CFREU, not to those connected to the Italian legislation that presides over particular areas of law, for example over the law on civil unions or assisted fertilisation. Regardless, law 76/2016 on civil unions expressly leaves out adoptions from its legal framework, leaving specific reference to the abovementioned supreme principles, particularly the principle of the best interest of the child. Only in the case that a foreign ruling is demonstrably against the best interest of the minor it can not be recognised in Italy as contrary to public order. In the present case, the minors would go into a family formed of couple of two women who are firmly united and, preliminary rulings aside, there seem to be no reservations about the suitability of the family environment to support the upbringing of these children. It is understood therefore that the public order cannot be used to oppose the transcription of the adoption of the children of the spouses that were registered abroad (Court of Cassation, Civil Division, sec. I, judg. 31 May 2018, No. 14007 – on this point, see also *Yearbook 2018*, p. 267-268).

> Accordingly, various courts have ruled on similar cases (see, among others: Tribunal of Rome, sez. I, judgment 11 May 2018; Court of Appeal of Venice, sez. III, judgment 28 June 2018; Tribunal of Bologna, judgment 7 July 2018; Court of Appeal of Perugia, judgment 22 August 2018; Tribunal of Milan, sez. VIII, judgment 15 November 2018; Tribunal of Genoa, sez. IV, judgment 8 November 2018).

F. Homosexual Couples and Access to Assisted Reproduction Procedures: Questions of Constitutionality of Article 5, L. 40/2004

The Tribunal of Pordenone raised a question on the constitutionality of Article 5 of l. 40/2004 on assisted reproduction, since the law stipulates that access to these procedures is reserved for heterosexual couples. A female couple who had been living together for many years and were married with a civil union, appeared before the judge. They were already parents to two twins, born after assisted reproduction procedures in Spain, but were then denied the services by the local health facility in Italy, due to the aforementioned law. According to the judge, the question of constitutionality is posed in relation to Article 2 (different treatment for parenting between heterosexual families and the social formation of the civil union couple), 3 (disparity of treatment due to sexual orientation and economic conditions – the latter is relevant given that it is possible to access assisted reproduction techniques by going abroad and facing huge expenses), 31 and 32 (reproduction and health rights), and 117(1) of the Constitution (the latter in reference to Article 8 ECHR: right to private and family life, and to Article 14 ECHR, protection from discrimination). As a constitutionally adequate interpretation of the disputed law is not possible, nor does its disapplication since the matter does not fall under EU law, recourse to the Court is justified.

III. Political Rights and Freedom of Association; Citizenship; Freedom of the Press

A. Exclusion of Electoral List Due to Reference to Fascist Ideology

The Regional Administrative Court of Lombardy excluded a list named *"Fasci italiani del lavoro"* from the mayoral and council elections for the Municipality of Sermide and Felonica (Mantua) who had received just over three hundred votes (10 % of the electorate) in the 2017 local elections, without prejudice to the Mayoral and Council elections. The members of the list appealed to the Council of State against this decision. The Council of State (sec. III, judg. 29 May 2018, No. 3208) rejected the appeal. The judges held that both the name and political platform refers explictly to the dissolved Fascist party, whose suppression and prohibition of reconsitution is established by the XII temporary and final provision of the Constitution. This rule is not limited to repressing the conduct that reconstitutes the fascist party, but extends to prohibiting any act that may favour this result. The Council of State did not follow the Regional Administrative Court in confirming the election results, as between the winning list and the second place, the difference in the number of votes was lower than the total number of votes received by the excluded list. Although its not possible to say which competing list the citizens who voted for the excluded list would have voted for, it is undeniable that moving 10 % of the votes would have had a significant impact on the final outcome. The elections must therefore be annulled and the proclamation of all elected municipal officials must be declared invalid.

B. Rights of Members of the Armed Forces to Form Trade Unions

The Council of State and the TAR of Veneto raised the question of constitutional legitimacy in relation to Article 1475 Military Code (lgs.d. 66/2010), which states that "the military cannot establish trade unions or join other trade unions". In 1999, the Constitutional Court ruled on this point, with regard to the legislation on military discipline in force at the time and with reference to Articles 3, 39 and 52 of the Constitution. The Court, in judg. 120/2018, was asked to rule on the same point, while integrating the standards laid down by the ECHR, interposed in the judgment of constitutional legitimacy under Article 117(1) of the Constitution. In particular, Article 11 ECHR (freedom of assembly and association) must be considered. The ECtHR had two ways to tackle a problem similar to that of the Constitutional Court in the cases *Matelly v. France,* 10609/10, 2 October 2014 and *Adefdromil v. France,* 32191/09, 2 October 2014. In these rulings, the ECtHR clearly stated that the definitely exclusion of the members of the armed forces from any possibility of joining trade unions violates Article 11 ECHR. Following this decision, the French Parliament approved an ad hoc bill allowing professional organisations within the armed forces.

Furthermore, the Court fully considers the European Social Charter (in its "revised" form after the Protocol of 1996 – ESC-R) as an adequate source to provide standards submitted when ruling on the constitutional legitimacy of Italian laws. According to the Constitutional Court, the ESC-R "does not have direct effect, and cannot be applied immediately to the work of a common judge but requires the intervention of this Court, which considers the question of constitutional legitimacy for the violation of Article 117(1) of the Constitution, by national laws considered in contrast with the Charter". Therefore, Article 5 of the ESC-R recognises the rights of trade unions and leaves the adoption of bills that regulate the extension of these rights to the members of police and military forces to the States themselves. However, there is nothing in the Charter that justifies the total exclusion of a category of workers from enjoying trade union rights. The European Committee on Social Rights adopted (27 January 2016) and published (4 July 2016) a decision on the *Conseil Européen des Syndicats de Police (CESP) v. France* case (complaint No. 101/2013). This decision, while having no binding effect on the judgments on the ECtHR (and not referring to Italy), confirms the incompatibility of a total ban of trade union organisations within the military with international instruments. In conclusion, the Constitutional Court recognises the consitutional illegitimacy of the legal normative of the military code which stops members of the military from founding trade union organisations. This type of representation should be set by a law, which can establish limits to the trade union activities, including a ban on strikes. However, the ban on members of the armed forces from joining trade unions that are not founded within the military is not against the Constitution. This prohibition is justified by the specific need for internal cohesion and neutrality of military personnel.

IV. Asylum and International Protection

A. Questions of Constitutionality of L.d. 13/2017 Rejected by the Court of Cassation

With a series of decisions, the Court of Cassation has rejected as manifestly unfounded or irrelevant a series of questions of constitutionality (previously proposed before a trial judge and rejected) concerning l.d. 13/2017 (so-called "Minniti Decree", after the then-Minister of the Interior), concerning the procedures for recognising international protection status. The Court of Cassation (sec. I, judg. 5 July 2018, No. 17717 and 5 November 2018, No. 28119) considers that there are urgent and necessary conditions that justify the emission of the decree in question, even though the same decree set new procedural regulations into force six months from its adoption concerning cases of international protection (and therefore gave rise to the need to set out necessary organisation measures). Judgment No. 17717 also rejected that doubts raised on the constitutionality of the decree that establishes procedures in the Council Chamber for appeals against the decisions on the application for international protection instead of a public hearing, considering that many other procedures for personal status are decided in this way, which does not prevent the full participation of the interested party via a legal representative.

Another controversal point introduced by the 2017 decree was the exclusion of appeal mechanism for judges' decisions on complaints against resolutions of territorial committees (decisions of the Court can only be challenged if there is a violation of the law). The judgments Court of Cassation, Civil Division, sec. I, 30 October 2018, No. 27700; 5 November 2018, No. 28119 and 30 December 2018, No. 32319 concluded that the lack of appeal was justified in the first place because the right to an appeal is not fully covered by constitutional law and the various other procedures do not provide for it; secondly because procedures before a territorial commission, where the asylum seeker will be interviewed by personnel who have the competency to receive the application, exhausts much of the investigation necessary to decide the case. The Court of Cassation finds the challenge of constitutional legitimacy of the legislation manifestly unfounded: the legislation reduces the suspensive scope of the decision of the territorial commission that rejects the application, rendering it immediate after the adoption of the rejection appeal decree by the Court. In Court of Cassation, Civil Division, judg. 13 December 2018, No. 32319, the ruling underlines how the question has already been resolved regarding compliance with EU law by the judgment of the CJEU in the case C-422/18 (see, in this Part, 3.1). Other controversial issues (for example, the fact that without the suspension, the applicant would be forced to follow the course of the eventual subsequent phase of the procedure from outside Italy) are resolved by relying on the discretion of the executive branch when intervening in matters of national migration policy

B. Appeals against Refusal to Recognise International Protection

The Court of Cassation recalled (in two not entirely compatible judgments) that any possible procedural failures in the territorial commission's conduct concerning recognising international protection status – specifically the fact that the asylum seeker was heard by only one out of four members of the commission – cannot be identified during an appeal before the Court, which can only rule on the merit of the applicant's right to international protection (Court of Cassation, Civil Division, sec I, judg. 19 December 2018, No. 32862) (except, however, when a reduced commission is considered a specific cause of infringement of fundamental rights: Court of Cassation, Civil Division, sec. VI, judg. 17 July 2018, No. 19040). The next development of the judicial procedure phase is video recording the interview in front of the territorial commission; if video recording is not possible, it is necessary for the Court to arrange the hearing of the interested party (even if the application seems unfounded), while providing a transcript of the interview cannot substitute a video.

The procedures for the international protection status of the applicant requires the active participation of the territorial commission and the judge to validate and integrate information provided by asylum seekers, drawing from sources that are unaccessible to the applicant (see, among the many, Court of Cassation, Civil Division, sec. VI, judg. 6 February 2018, No. 2875). The asylum seeker has to provide information on which to base their application for asylum and cannot only cite generic information about the situation or about widespread human rights violations that characterise certain areas (in many cases, the situation of Libya is mentioned), but instead must clearly show the elements of disorder connected to them being at risk (see, for example, Court of Cassation, Civil Division, sec. VI, judgments 6 February 2018, No. 2861; 29 October 2018, No. 27336; sec. I, judg. 6 December 2018, No. 31676).

The Tribunal of Venice (judg. 27 July 2018, No. 4243) admitted the appeal presented by a Nigerian woman due to the denial of international protection by the territorial commission in 2017 and recognises her right to refugee status. The applicant had told the Territorial Commission that she had fled Nigeria as she was being persecuted by a sect who had ordered her to "sacrifice" herself when she turned twenty-five years old. The Territorial Commission did not believe her story credible, nor did it consider other parts of the story relevant or compatible with the specific case of human trafficking for sexual exploitation. The Court ascertains that the woman had been tricked into leaving Nigeria by a friend who was already in Italy and working as a shop owner where the woman would have been able to work. In reality, when the woman arrived in Libya, she was forced into prostitution. These events had all the characteristics of human trafficking, which systematically affect women coming from certain areas of Nigeria. The status of victim of human trafficking justifies a recognition of refugee status, as a person that has been persecuted due to belonging to a "social group" and at risk of being oppressed because of their gender.

On the basis of Italian legislation in force until the adoption of l.d. 113/2018, an asylum seeker coming from an area of the State where they were at risk of persecution had the right to international protection even if that risk was not present in other parts of the same country. The Court of Cassation clarifies that if the area the person comes from is not affected by the dangerous situation that is present in other areas of the country, the person cannot claim the right to international protection and may be repatriated (Court of Cassation, Civil Division, sec. I, judg. 7 November 2018, No. 28433) (d.l. 113/2018 itself resolved the problem, establishing that in both cases repatriation is legitimate).

Committing a serious crime before entering Italian territory is grounds for rejecting an asylum application (including humanitarian protection), even if the alleged crime is supposedly politically motivated. The mere existence of an investigation (rather than a pronounced sentence) does not in itself block the application procedure; the Territorial Commission and the judicial authority allow themselves a certain degree of discretion in the classification of a crime as "serious" (Court of Cassation, Civil Division, sec. VI, judg. 30 October 2018, No. 27504).

Subsidiary protection can be recognised to a person who is not directly threatened by an internal or international armed conflict in a determined country, only if the level of indiscriminate violence threatens the life or safety of civilians in that State. Consequently, an international asylum seeker from Bangladesh cannot claim subsidiary protection if they are not able to establish a specific vulnerability to the current conflict, as the situation of indiscriminate violence currently present in the State is not enough to jeopardise the safety of an individual within the State (Court of Cassation, Civil Division, sec. VI, judg. 31 May 2018, No. 13858).

C. Humanitarian Protection

The Court of Cassation clarified with a series of Joint Section judgments that the appeals concerning the condition of international asylum seekers (including the decisions on the resolution of competent European States to deal with the issue of international protection), as well as decisions on residency permits for victims of labour exploitation, concerning fundamental human rights, are within the scope of the ordinary courts and not the administrative court (Court of Cassation, Civil Division, joint sections, ord. 30 March 2018, No. 8044; 13 September 2018, No. 22412; 27 November 2018, No. 30658; 28 November 2018, No. 30757; 11 December 2018, No. 32044).

Humanitarian protection can be recognised on the basis on an assessment considering the serious and actual limitations to human rights in the asylum seeker's country of origin. The disputed achievement of a good level of integration in Italian society is not a reason to recognise a residency permit for humanitarian protection, since national legislation, as recognised many times by ECtHR case-law, can justify an interference of the private and family life of foreign citizens (particularly migrants in an irregular situation) for reasons of public interest – in particular for an ordered management of immigration procedures. On the other hand, proving the existence of a general situation of human rights violation in the country of repatriation is not enough, rather it is necessary to assess whether these conditions influence the asylum seeker specifically and how it affects the exercise of their fundamental rights (Court of Cassation, Civil Division, sec. I, judg. 23 February 2018, No. 4455; sec. VI, judg. 28 June 2018, No. 17072).

V. Discrimination – General Issues

A. Discrimination Based on Nationality or Ethnic Origin

An insurance company regularly gave higher automobile insurance policies for foreign citizens than for Italian citizens, violating, among others, a specific recommendation of the UNAR concerning automobile insurance policies for civil responsibility. The Court of Bologna (sec. I, ord. 7 March 2018) held that this practice constituted discriminatory behaviour under Article 43 of lgs.d. 286/1998 (Single Text on Immigration). Having a different nationality does not affect a policy holder's capability to drive, nor does it therefore increase the risk for the insurance company. Different classifications of insurance premiums based on the country of birth of the driver represents discrimination in providing insurance based on one's nationality. The Court orders the termination of the discriminatory conduct.

The Tribunal of Milan (sec. I, ord. 6 June 2018) rules on the discriminatory character of a series of declarations between 2015 and 2016 made on national radio by the mayor of Albettone (Vicenza) who, on various occasions, insulted African migrants, Roma communities and muslim persons. Two associations of lawyers (*Avvocati per Niente* and *ASGI*) asked the Court to intervene pursuant to Articles 44 of lgs.d. 286/1998 and 28 lgs.d. 150/2011, requesting the verification of their discriminatory character and compensation for non patrimonial damages for these associations, which work to defend migrants and Roma communities. The Court admitted the request, underlining that the anti-discrimination laws within Italian legislation aim not only to protect people from violations of the right to equal treatment, but also from undesirable behaviour and abuse that can potentially create a "intimidating, hostile, humiliating or offensive climate" (lgs.d. 215/2003, Article 2) for reasons of racial, religious, or national differences. According to the Tribunal of Milan, this is the most concise form of anti-discrimination protection as it targets underground forms of discrimination that victims often do not report due to fear or feeling of submission. The attempts to retract the statements and at a friendly settlement made by the mayor in question were not held as credible, just as the judge sustained that the fact the Municipality supported an international cooperation project in Benin was immaterial, since discrimination on the basis of ethnicity or race is prohibited, without territorial limits. After ascertaining dicriminatory nature of the behaviour and ordering its immediate cessation, the judge sentenced the mayor to pay 6,000 euros in compensation to both of the applicant associations.

The municipality of Lodi had introduced a regulation requesting that citizens of countries outside Europe whose children wanted to continue to use subsidised canteen and transport services to both fill in a declaration to indicate any property owned abroad and a certification of the possible availability of any property issued by the competent body of a foreign State, translated into Italian and legalised by the Italian Consular Authoritiy. By doing this, the Municipality made significant changes to the access subsidised social services, intervening in issues that were not within the scope of the local authorities. The severe procedures were applied only to citizens of non-European countries, where the lgs.d. 286/1998 and other legislative provisions in force in Italy generally provide for the equal rights of the non-EU foreign citizen with Italian and EU citizens. The municipal regulation is therefore a form of direct discrimination against non-European citizens who, not being able to assert the simple substitutive declaration of an act available with the public administration, must request the required certificates from their own State administrations and the local Italian embassy. The Municipality of Lodi published guidelines for the implementation of the disputed regulation which established that this procedure was not applicable to those with refugee status or to those from countries identified as in a situation of war or where getting the requested certificates was deemed impossible. Apart from the first, these criteria are generic and arbitrary, and therefore it is unsure that they can reasonably be fulfilled. This unreasonability is precluded to the Municipality, but also to the government authority and the legislator itself; any amendment to the form provided for the substitutive declarations which makes the access of non-European citizens to subsidised social benefits more burdensome risks being unreasonable and results in a discriminatory behaviour based on nationality. In conclusion, the Tribunal of Milan held that the behaviour of the Municipality of Lodi was discriminatory, and prescribed with an order of 13 December 2018 an amendment to the access regulation for subsidised social benefits so that an application can be presented both by non-European citizens and EU citizens in the same way. It also sentenced the Municipality to pay the legal costs incurred by the two associations that presented the complain.

In 2016, the Ministry of Justice published a public call for applications for 800 judicial assistants, which was strictly reserved for Italian citizens. A candidate with Albanian citizenship, long-term resident in Italy, with the association *L'altro diritto onlus*, complained that the public call was discriminatory (the complaint of the woman, who had applied anyway and had been excluded after the written test, was declared inadmissible due to lack of standing). The court carries out a thorough examination of EU legislation and case-law concerning the access of foreign citizens to public roles. It should be noted that according to EU law, European citizens are generally entitled to have access to public employment in the Member States, as are their family members who are nationals of non-European countries or entitled to permanent residence, as well as non-EU nationals who hold long-term or permanent residence permits, refugees and those

Discrimination – General Issues

under subsidiary protection. In Italy, it is within the competency of the Council Presidency to determine by decree which public administration roles can require Italian citizenship; this was done in 1994, with a d.p.c.m. which gives citizens access to entire sectors of public administration (for example, to any role of the Ministries of Justice, Foreign Affairs, Interior, etc.). These provisions are contrary to EU law and must therefore be disapplied. The criteria established by EU law, which are also valid for Italy, are based on the specific function that the worker must carry out. The role can be legitimately reserved for citizens of the State if the functions actually involve the exercise of rights conferred by public law or coercive powers on a regular basis. The duties of the judicial assistant do not fall within this ambit, since if they foresee an activity closely connected with that of the judges, they do not involve management or coercion. Therefore, the public call of the Ministery which excludes foreigners from applying for the role of judicial assistant is discriminatory on the basis of nationality. The Court of Florence ascertains the discriminatory behaviour of the Ministery and sentenced it to pay 30 thousand euros in compensation to the association *L'altro diritto* (Tribunal of Florence, sec. labour, ord. 26 June 2018).

B. Allowances in Favour of Victims of Racial Laws

The Council of State (sec. IV, judg. 12 October 2018, No. 5896) clarifies that Italian legislation equating ex-combatants with victims of racial laws (laws 336/1970 and 541/1971) does not only apply to those who were deemed "belonging to the Jewish race" according to infamous provisions of Royal Decree No. 1728 of 17 November 1938 (according to which, in particular, the children of parents of Italian nationality, of which only one "of Jewish race" who belonged to a religion other than Judaism or who had not formally joined an Jewish community were not considered Jews). Any person of Jewish origin can ask for access to the provisions within the law, which aims to financially compensate the prejudices suffered by Italian citizens for the application of racist laws or other measures within the fascist ideology. In this controversial case, the competent commission at the Presidency of the Council of Ministers had rejected a request to access the fund for former victims of racism, based on the fact that the applicant was not defined as belonging to the Jewish race, even though she had to follow her Italian mother, adopt her surname and abandon her Jewish father during the Second World War. The Council of State observes that using these racist judicial categories nowadays to identify who can benefit from compensation for victims of racial laws would constitute a negative perpetuation to the person concerned of the juridical effectiveness of aberrant antisemitic laws (see also *Yearbook 2012*, p. 260-261).

VI. Rights of Persons with Disabilities

A. Redundancy

An employee of a company carrying out maintenance work at a cement plant developed a disability that rendered it unsuitable for him to work in an environment saturated with dust. Believing that he could not work at another facility, one far from where the noxious dust was produced, if the company did not undergo a complex restructuring, the company decided to dismiss the worker. The territorial judges had declared this dismissal illegitimate and the company therefore proposed the question to the Court of Cassation, since the ban on dismissing the person with a handicap involved an excessive interference in the right of the employer of organise their own business. The Supreme Court proceeded with a reading of Directive 2000/78 of 27 November 2000, implemented in Italy with lgs.d. 216/2003. The transposition instrument was reformed by introducing the obligation for the employer to prepare reasonable solutions to allow people with disabilities to access work and carry out their work without discrimination, according to l.d. 28 June 2013, No. 76 (Article 9 (4-*ter*)), converted with l. 99/2013 (the new Article 3 (3-bis) was introduced following the Italy's conviction in an infringement procedure: see *Yearbook 2014*, p. 335).

Even though European Directives are not binding in itself for private companies, and the facts occurred before the 2013 reform, it remains the task of the Italian Court to apply the regulations in line with the concept of "handicap" established by the EU since 2000. According to EU law, the concept of disability entails a limitation which results in particular from physical, mental or psychological impairments which in interaction with various barriers may hinder the full and effective participation of the person concerned in professional life on an equal basis with other workers". Without being able to enter into the merits of how the worker could effectively be re-employed in the company without imposing a disproportionate burden on the employer, the Court of Cassation confirms that the relocation of the worker was a viable option and that therefore his dismissal was illegitimate (Court of Cassation Civil Division, sec. Labour, judg. 19 March 2018, No. 6798).

B. Maternity Benefits and Leave to Assist People with Disabilities

The Constitutional Court returns once again to the matter of extraordinary leave to assist family members with disabilities (see *Yearbook 2014*, p. 285-286). The case dealt with by judg. 158/2018 concerns two women who had been denied the INPS indemnity provided for by Article 24(3), l.d. 151/2001 (single text of the provisions protecting and supporting maternity and paternity leave) in the event of a risky pregnancy, based on the fact that both of them have already been granted extraordinary leave (envisaged by Article 42 of the same l.d. 151/2001) to assist respectively the spouse and another child with disabilities. The provision in question establishes that the workers who have been at work in the two months before the start of the period of maternity leave can benefit from this support, with some exceptions (for example, leave to care for a sick child), which does not include leave to assist a family member with disabilities. Therefore, the law would require female workers to suspend assistance to the family member and return to work in order to have access to maternity allowance. The Constitutional Court holds that this is in violation with the constitutional provisions that protect maternity and childhood (Articles 31 and 37 of the Constitution). The referring judges also pointed to the contradiction with ECHR and CFREU regulations, interposed under Article 117 (1), which prohibit any discrimination based on gender and disability. In conclusion, Article 24(3) of lgs.d. 151/2001 must be interpreted as meaning that, other than the exceptions to the regulations that in order to enjoy maternity leave, the worker must not be absent from work for more than 60 days, the case in which the pregnant woman has taken special leave to assist a cohabiting spouse or a child with disabilities must be included, pursuant to Article 4(1), l. 104/1992.

C. Ability of Persons with Disabilities to Take an Oath in Order to Acquire Italian Citizenship

The law on the acquisition of Italian citizenship (law 91/1992) establishes that the applicant for citizenship must take an oath of loyalty to the Republic and respect the Constitution and the law. The Constitutional Court has recognised the unconstitutionality of the rule as it does not provide that the person unable to meet this requirement due to a serious and ascertained disability condition is exempted from the oath (see *Yearbook 2018*, p. 278). The Court of Modena (sec. II, judg. 12 January 2018) confermed this decision, proceeding to grant citizenship to a person who is completely disabled and affected by infantile cerebral palsy. The judge operated in the sense indicated at the request of the support administrator, excluding the automatic exemption from the oath.

D. Inclusion in Education

With judgment 11 October 2018, No. 5851, the Council of State, sec. VI, established that a support teacher assigned to a student with visual impairment, for whom special competence in braille language is required, cannot be replaced by a support teacher with generic competences, even when assisted, in turn, by an expert in accessible technologies and accessible teaching. The school authorities defended themselves by declaring that they had failed to find a support teacher with the specialised expertise in Braille. This fact, however, according to the Council of State, cannot legitimately be used to violate the right of students with disabilities to receive an education in their own language. In particular, in the absence of an already-competent teacher, it is the task of the school adminstration to provide specialised training to an appointed teacher.

The Council of State (sec. V, judg. 7 February 2018, No. 809) recognised that the claim of a student with a disability to use school transport constitutes a subjective right guaranteed by the law and that cannot be disregarded for purely budgetary reasons by the responsible institution, while any rules hindering its implementation would be contrary to the Constitution. Access to school transport is to be considered as a component of the right of the disabled person to full school integration. Law does not only concern compulsory education, but also high school post-14 years. In the specific case, the authority required to provide transportation for students with disabilities is the Campania Region. The subjective nature of the claim in question does not exclude the jurisdiction of the administrative judge to handle the dispute: it is a dispute over a provision of public administration.

In various judgments, administrative judges found a violation of the law and annulled the relative resolutions of the school administration, as well as sentencing the Ministry of Education to pay compensation for the damages suffered to penalised pupils, for the lack of or late hiring of a support teacher, or appointing them for only part of the school hours of a student with disabilities (see, for example, the Lazio Regional Administrative Court, Rome, sec. III, judg. 19 October 2018, No. 10132). The same Lazio Regional Administrative Court, Rome, sec. III (judg. 23 May 2018, No. 5740) holds that the number of hours of assistence must be the same as those of the students' school attendence. The Council of Administrative Justice for the Sicily Region (CGA, judg. 30 October 2018, No. 614), while recognising the decision to reduce the hours of support teaching does not respect the right to education of the student with disabilities, annuls the sentence of the school administration to compensation the damage, since it does not attribute fault on the part of the administration. The judgment of not guilty was based on the novelty and complexity of the issue and on the organizational difficulties encountered to ensure full coverage, and places the administration in a sort of "state of necessity" and forcing it to give partial coverage.

> The scope of the administrative or ordinary judges to rule on the right of students with disabilities to assistance in the school environment remains a situation of uncertainty, despite the recent rulings of the Court of Cassation (see *Yearbook 2015*, p. 265-266). The Council of Administrative Justice for the Sicily Region (CGA, judg. 3 May 2018, No. 258), in response to the failure to appoint a personal support teacher to a student with disabilities, stated that the fundamental right to education of the disabled person is conditioned by the administration's obligation to implement these measures, without which that right cannot be fully respected. Considering the complex mix of legitimate rights and interests that the subjective position is based on, it is reasonable to concentrate the scope to deal with these problems in their entirety with administrative judges. The Veneto Regional Administrative Court focuses on the same issue, sec. I, judg. 19 October 2018, No. 976.
>
> Article 5(2) of d.p.r. 81/2009 (regulations for the organisation and human resources in schools) establishes that in all schools, the first classes where there is a student with disabilities cannot typically have more than 20 students. The Tuscany Regional Administrative Court (Florence, sec. I, judg. 26 March 2018, No. 439) clarifies that this regulation cannot bring about the exclusion of a person with disabilities from their choice of school (the minor had been excluded from enrolling in two separate schools, both times because the classes could not respect the 20 students limit. The limit should be the case in ideal situations, but the general principle favouring the inclusion of the student with disabilities always prevails, which is true for any regulation in Italian law on the matter. In other words, the 20 student per class limit does not justify the exclusion of the student with disabilities from enrolling in school courses. The Lazio Regional Administrative Court, among others, concluded the same, Rome, sec. III, judg. 28 February 2018,

No. 2250. In this case, a child with serious disabilities was exluded from enrolling in a first-year primary school class to the advantage of another child, whose disabilities were on the same scale but who lived closer to the school.

The administrative judge cannot state the number of hours of assistance with a support teacher that a child with disabilities is entitled to without an individualised educational plan drawn up by the school. The Sicily Regional Administrative Court, Palermo (sec. III, judgments 23 March 2018, No. 644, 2 October 2018, No. 2030 and 2031) therefore only gives the school administration a deadline of thirty days to draw up a plan, after which the manager of the Region of Sicily School Administration Office must intervene as an ad hoc commissioner.

VII. Social Rights

A. Laws with Retroactive Effect on Pensions

Constitutional Court judgment 12/2018 deals with the problem of the frequent adoption of laws with retroactive effects negatively impacting on legitimate expectations of some citizens and subject to ongoing legal proceedings. The issue concerned the Stability Law for 2011, which introduced an authentic interpretation decision for a 1990 provision, applicable to workers in some previously-nationalised banks. Over the years, the Court of Cassation had released an interpretation of the rule that was overall more favourable for the pensioners of these banks, and more burdensome for INPS, the authoritiy that was required to pay social security benefits which previously were charged to specific funds. The 2011 law imposed a more advantageous in interpretation of the normative for the INPS, requiring the courts to resolve any contentious proceedings that were still pending contrary to precedent consolidated in case-law. According to the referring judges, this regulatory intervention was in contrast with the principle of a fair trial (Article 6 ECHR) which, among other things, requires the executive and legislative powers not to interfere with the action of the courts by introducing rules with retroactive effect.

The Constitutional Court carried out an in-depth review of the ECtHR case-law regarding retroactive regulations that interfere with juridicial decisions, the nature of which was already clear given the case-law – an issue that has often come up over the years concerning the matter of pensions (see, for example, *Yearbook 2018*, p. 280-281).

The ECtHR does not believe that Article 6 ECHR always renders illegitimate any authentic interpretations with retroactive effect that force the Courts to resolve matters in a certain way, when the outcome would have probably been the different without the interference of law makers. Such interference can indeed be justified, by asserting "imperative reasons of general interest". Conversely, if the retroactive law appears to be closely linked to a specific pending dispute on which it would decisively affect, the principle of non-interference by the legislator on the judicial sphere (a pillar of the rule of law) must prevail. In the specific case, very clear elements contained in the technical report accompanying the Stability Law for 2011, as well as the timing of the case, lead to the conclusion that the rule was used primarily to prevent the Court from deciding in a manner that is consistent with the interpretations consolidated in case-law and that would be unfavorable to INPS. Therefore, the Constitutional Court concludes that the authentic interpretation rule (with retroactive effect) contained within the Stability Law of 2011 does not comply with the Constitution, since it is incompatible with Article 6 ECHR (which is interposed with Article 117(1) of the Constitution) underpinning the rule of law principle.

> Also regarding pension legislation with retroactive effect, the Court of Cassation (Court of Cassation Civil Division, sec. Labour, judg. 30 January 2018, No. 2286) returns to the long-standing problem of "Swiss pensions" (see *Yearbook 2018*, p. 280-281). The Court reiterated that a conflict exists between the Italian law introduced in 2006 (that denied the expectations of more favourable pensions accrued by some Italian workers who had paid pension contributions in Switzerland in the previous decades) and the principles of a fair trial and the separation of powers, as well as the right to property, which has been demonstrated by some judgments of the ECtHR. However, the Court also stated that the issue is irrelevant from an EU law perspective and does not allow the disapplication of Italian law due to conflicts with the Treaties or derived EU law, but may justify the opening up of a question of constitutionality pursuant to Article 117(1) of the Constitution. The contradiction between Italian law and the ECtHR case-law was addressed by the Constitutional Court in 2017 and ruled without prejudice in favour of the Italian law, despite its retroactive effects, on parameters that the Court of Strasbourg case-law itself considers plausible. It should be noted that, since the question arises with respect to decisions implemented before 2009, the Court considers the reference to the rights guaranteed by the CFREU to be irrelevant.

B. Changes to the Pension System: Blocking the Revaluation of Medium-high Pensions

In 2018, the Constitutional Court reiterated the point that, as already ruled in judgments 70/2015 (see *Yearbook 2016*, p. 233-234) and 250/2017 (see *Yearbook 2018*, p. 281), that the measures to block the revaluation of pensions of more than six times the minimum amount are not in violation with the Constitution, as they introduce a partial and temporary sacrifice, and are therefore adequate and proportional (judg. No. 96/2018).

C. Grants on the Birth of a Child to Foreign Citizens

INPS denied the benefit of a grant on the birth of a child to foreign citizens, which is paid upon birth to families living with less than a certain wage. Law 190/2014 reserves this benefit for Italian or EU citizens, as well as citizens of a non-European country with a long-term residence permit – the applicants did not fulfil the final criteria. The fact that there was no discriminatory treatment on the part of INPS (but in the implementation of a law) removes any possible remedy under Article 44, lgs.d. 286/1998 and Article 28, lgs.d. 150/2011 (anti-discrimination action): any discriminatory nature must in fact be the subject of a ruling of constitutional legitimacy or, as in the present case, of an assessment using parameters established by EU law.

The grant on the birth of a child, regardless of the title given by the establishing law, falls within the scope of "social security" measures as identified by EU law. According to EU law (in particular Directive 2011/98 on the residency stay of non-European migrants, Article 12), these measures must be applied without discrimination to all workers, including migrants, without checking the type of residence permit issued by the State (naturally as long as the residency permit allows the person to legitimately work) (on this point, see also *Yearbook 2018*, p. 323). It follows therefore that the provision of law 190/2014, which effectively denies access to the "baby bonus" to those with a long-term residence permit, excluding foreigners who meet the established income and family criteria but who hold a temporary residence permit, is contrary to the abovementioned European Directive on equal treatment in the social security. It must, therefore, be disapplied (Tribunal of Monza, sec. labour, ord. 1 August 2018).

VIII. Immigration

A. *Italy-Libya Memorandum of Understanding of 2017: its Nature as an International Treaty*

Some Members of Parliament of the XVII legislature filed with the Constitutional Court a complaint on conflict of attribution of responsibility between State powers. The complaint disputed the failure of the Government to present the "Memorandum of Understanding on cooperation in development, combatting irregular migration, human trafficking and strengthening border security between the State of Libya and the Italian Republic" to Parliament for authorisation. The Memorandum was signed in Rome on 2 February 2017 by the Prime Minister of Italy and the Libyan Prime Minister of the national reconciliation cabinet. In the applicants' opinion, such an agreement does not fall within the criteria of "implementation" or just "technical" agreements laid out in the Treaty on Friendship, Partnership and Cooperation between the two States, signed in Bengasi in 2008, ratified and enacted on the basis of l. 6 February 2009, No. 7. Rather, this would be a highly political and innovative instrument with respect to the 2008 Friendship Treaty, setting specific objectives on monitoring of migration, border control, asylum rights, and security issues, which characterise Italian foreign policy commitments. It therefore should have been voted for in Parliament, according to procedures set out in Article 80 of the Constitution. The fact that the Memorandum was not subjected to a vote in the Chamber constitutes a violation of Parliament's attribution of responsibility.

The Constitutional Court declared the question of constitutionality inadmissable, since the legitimacy to act in such a case belongs to the assemblies (the Chamber and Senate) and not to individual parliamentarians (Constitutional Court, Ord. 163/2018).

B. *Orders to Exclude Immigrants from Municipal Areas*

With a "necessity and urgency" decree as foreseen in exceptional circumstances by the Public Administration Code, ruled legitimate by the administrative judge, the mayor of the Sicilian municipality of Valguarnera Caropepe set a series of stringent limitations on the possibility of granting in renting homes, specifically to prevent the settlement of migrants, refugees or asylum seekers, possibly also within

SPRAR projects. The reasons for the provision were health, hygiene, building and urban planning based. The act was challenged before the administrative judge by the Ministry of the Interior.

The Sicily Regional Administrative Court, Catania, sec. IV (judg. 6 August 2018, No. 1671) notes that the order intervenes on a matter (migratory flows monitoring), outside competences of the local authority and entrusted to State authorities in particular by Legislative Decree 142/2015. The reasons given for health and hygiene or urban planning (the only competencies of the mayor) could not justify the order, since none of the migrants or refugees were residing in the municipal territory at the time of issuing the order, which aimed to prevent any possible settlement. The Regional Administrative Court observes that the order, affecting the possibility of leasing buildings owned in the municipal area lacking a certificate of habitability (among others), all of which are municipal competencies, also affects private property rights and the exercise of economic activity, protected by Articles 41 and 42 of the Constitution. It is also for this reason that the order should be considered null and void. Furthermore, it has a clear discriminatory nature pursuant to Article 43 of lgs.d. 286/1998, Article 2 of the Constitution and international standards on discrimination based on race or ethnicity, in particular Article 21 CFREU, Article 14 ECHR and Article 1 Protocol 12 ECHR, and Article 2 of the International Convention on the Elimination of All Forms of Racial Discrimination. Discriminatory measures must be challenged before the ordinary courts, and not before the Regional Administrative Tribunals. In this case, however, the administrative judge can rule on the discriminatory nature of the measure adopted by the mayor, since the applicant is not a private victim of the order, but the Ministry of the Interior. The discriminatory measure must be considered null and void from the outset, and not merely voidable. The prohibition of discrimination established by the Constitution and the aforementioned international norms prohibits the exercise of any public power that results in a discriminatory act that is contrary to human dignity. Therefore, the Regional Administrative Court ordered the transfer of proceedings to the public procurator's office for the possible prosecution of abuse of office aggravated by racial discrimination, or discriminatory acts for racial or ethnic reasons.

It should be noted that similar orders were adopted by other administrations, aiming at blocking possible settlements of reception facilities for migrants. These were then revoked, rendering the judgments that had been instituted in the Regional Administrative Courts by the Ministry of the Interior impossible to proceed with (see, for example, Lombardy Regional Adminstrative Court, Brescia, sec. I, judg. 22 January 2018, No. 68).

C. Issuing, Refusing to Issue or Withdrawing a Residence Permit

The Council of State (sec. III, judg. 28 May 2018, No. 3184) confirms the decision of the Regional Adminstrative Court, that had considered the denial of the residence permit legitimate. It had been ordered by the Pordenone Police Headquarters against an Albanian citizen, given the applicant was found guilty of crimes concerning the production and illicit trafficking of drugs. These crimes are considered legitimate reasons to block the renewal of a residence permit under Article 4 lgs.d. 286/98 (Single Text on immigration). The Council of State points out that, in order to justify the denial when there are strong family ties in the Italian territory, the conviction for drug offenses must be accompanied by other circumstances. These circumstances must show that the individual is a danger to society, and that they have not integrated into society. Concerning family ties with persons lawfully residing in Italy, there can be a generic reference in the judgment, thereby without violating the obligation to state reasons.

D. Access to Italian Citizenship: Ample Discretion of Administrations in Granting

The granting of Italian citizenship is a measure with respect to which the public authority enjoys the widest discretion in examining the opportunities for foreigners to successfully integrate into the society of the State. The ample discretion left to adminstrative bodies means a definite refusal can only be challenged when it is based on insufficient investigations, non-existent facts or on illogical, inconsistent or unreasonable grounds (see, for example, Council of State, sec. III, judg. 19 March 2018, No. 1736; Lazio Regional Adminstrative Court, Rome, sec. I, judgments 19 March 2018, No. 1736; 12 April 2018, No. 4002; 16 May 2018, No. 5469; 28 June 2018, No. 7212; 23 July 2018, No. 8318; 20 November 2018, No. 11253; 5 December 2018, No. 11796).

Citizenship can be legitimately denied to foreigners who are connected to organisations and movements that jeopardise national security, even if the person concerned has never been criminally charged in relation to any activities of such groups. Being involved in criminal proceedings and having acquaintances within groups that pose a risk to State security or public order are two distinct reasons that can justify the rejection of an Italian citizenship claim (see, for example. Lazio Regional Adminstrative Court Rome, sec. I, judgments 24 May 2018, No. 5775; 20 November 2018, No. 11249). Furthermore, when refusal is based on security reasons, the reasoning for the refusal must not be provided in an in-depth and analytical manner, in order to protect those who have carried out necessary checks (Lazio Regional Adminstrative Court, Rome, sec. I, judgments 6 September 2018, No. 5262; 12 December 2018, No. 12063).

The integration of the foreigner in Italian society is another assessment that is at the discretion of the administration, which also includes the probability that such integration will take place. This can be deduced from the labour, economic, or family situation and the irreproachability of applicant's behaviour (see Lazio Regional Adminstrative Court, Rome, sec. I, judgments 18 June 2018, No. 6824; 26 July 2018, No. 8466; 6 September 2018, No. 5262; 1 October 2018, Nos. 9659, 9678; 15 October 2018, No. 9993; 19 November 2018, No. 11192). Even having a criminal record for the applicant receiving stolen goods from the son (which did not lead to a sentence because the fact was considered irrelevant by the juvenile judge) can legitimately justify rejecting an application for Italian citizenship (Lazio Regional Adminstrative Court, Rome, sec. I, judg. 4 October 2018, No. 9735). The lack of a sufficient wage is also a legitimate reason to reject an application, since the citizen would be asked to pay taxes to finance public spending (Lazio Regional Adminstrative Court, Rome, sec. I, judg. 4 October 2018, No. 9739).

Acquiring Italian citizenship through marriage constitutes a subjective right, which cannot be disregarded unless there are circumstances related to State security (Article 6(1) lett. c, l. 91/1992): in this case, it is up to the discretion of the public administration, supervised by the administrative judge (Lazio Regional Adminstrative Court, Rome, sec. II, judg. 21 November 2018, No. 11321). The fact that the married couple are no longer living together, or that there are ongoing legal separation proceedings cannot have any negative influence on the granting of citizenship to the foreign partner, since Article 5, l. 91/1992 refers to the existence of a spouse with no further criteria necessary (Tribunal of Modena, sec. II, judg. 6 November 2018, No. 1827).

The Lazio Regional Adminstrative Court (Rome, sec. I, judg. 28 August 2018, No. 9048) notes that the two-year period within which the State must respond to the request for Italian citizenship does not prevent the administration from rejecting the application, even after this period has elapsed - the silence-assent rule does not therefore apply. However, if a foreign citizen appeals against the administration's lack of response, raising the question of illegitimacy and subsequently closing the appeal due to the lack of interest in the dispute given the application's approval with delay in the meantime, the State cannot avoid paying the legal fees for this appeal by citing the large number of applications for citizenship (Council of State, sec. III, judg. 5 June 2018, No. 3411).

E. Statelessness

Ruling on the case of a person with Cuban origins, the Tribunal of Brescia (sec. III, judg. 17 February 2018, No. 508) stated – recalling the case-law of the Court of Cassation – that in Italian law, statelessness includes both cases in which a person is formally deprived of any citizenship, and also where there is a substantial loss of citizenship. This is what happens to Cuban citizens who, according to Cuban law, if the individual does not return to their own country for more than 24 months, they acquire the status of "emigrants", followed by the loss of residence at home, where the individual may only stay for periods not exceeding three months, with limitations of their other civil rights (see also *Yearbook 2014*, p. 207). It follows that a Cuban citizen who, as defined by the State authorities, has the status of "emigrant" can be given the status of stateless person.

F. Expulsions, Refoulement

The Supreme Court (Court of Cassation civile, sec. I, judg. 2 October 2018, No. 23957) reiterated a point that has been clarified in previous judgments (see, for example, *Yearbook 2014*, p. 218; *Yearbook 2016*, p. 2016), that the right to private and family life, in particular the right to maintain the personal and family relationships that a foreign citizen has developed in Italy, must be assessed on a case-by-case basis by the judge and can justify an opposition to expulsion measures. The expulsion of the irregular foreign citizen, beyond the cases of a threat to public order and State security, cannot be ordered if its effects disproportionately violate their right to private and family life.

G. Social Rights of Immigrant Citizens

The Constitutional Court, with judgment 166/2018, ruled on a doubt of consittutionality concerning l.d. 112/2008, which established that to access the lease support fund for people in serious economic hardship, immigrants must have been in Italy for at least ten years or in the same region for at least five. A citizen from El Salvador, resident in Italy since November 2011, did not meet the legal requirements and therefore was unable to receive contributions to her rent, despite having a residence permit for work reasons and a very low income. The Court observes that the measures were introduced in 1998 as a multi-use instrument to support those in need to meet essential market-based housing costs and to avoid the risk of eviction. In the view of the Court, the criteria of long-term residence, introduced in 2008, constitutes unreasonable discrimination against citizens of non-EU countries. The term of ten years, in particular, in contrary to Directive 2003/109/CE, which establishes equality between citizens and long-term residents, provided that the latter can be obtained after five years of residence in the Member State territory. The term of five years is unreasonable and disproportionate, considering the measure is typically intended to compensate for transient situations of people moving to the national territory by accessing the free rental market. More specifically, given the scarcity of allocated resources, it is a benefit reserved for cases of severe poverty, without any correlation with the duration of residence in the regional territory. The regulation is therefore to be considered constitutionally illegitimate.

> Similarly, with judg. 106/2018, the Constitutional Court ruled on the unconstitutionality of regulations introduced by a regional law of Liguria. The regional law aimed to assign public housing, and had replaced the originally requirements envisaged for immigrant citizens (to carry out work and hold a residence card or two-year residence permit), with that of regular residence in Italy for at least ten consecutive years. The abovementioned Directive 2003/109/EC equates European citizens with long-term resident immigrants, or those who have been residing regularly in a Member State for at least five years, for the purpose, among other things, of enjoying social services and benefits, including the allocation of housing for public residential building. Therefore, the regional law that extends these residency criteria to 10 years is contrary to the Directive and unconstitutional due to a violation of Article 117(1) of the Constitution.

The Court of Cassation (sec. labour, judg. 2 October 2018, No. 23763) stated that foreign nations residing regularly in Italy in a continuous and non-episodic way, even if not in possession of a long-term residence permit, are entitled to a civil disability pension when all the legal requirements are fulfiled. There can be no discrimination between Italian citizens and immigrants based on the duration of their stay in Italy in relation to social benefits covering the basic human needs of the person (see *Yearbook 2014*, p. 283-284).

IX. Right to Private and Family Life. Right to Property

A. *Right of the Press and the Right to Be Forgotten*

An interviewer attempted to speak to a famous Italian singer, who reacted with disappointment. The images were televised on RAI with a sarcastic comment, and five years later, the same clip was used within the same TV show, in a satirical part on the most unpleasant and obnoxious characters of the transmission, once again without the singer's consent. The singer asked RAI to be ordered to pay compensation for damage to his image, complaining in particular that the right to be forgotten had not been respected during the second airing of the clip. The territorial courts did not accept the request, holding that the privacy of a public figure did not prevail over the right to report and, in particular, the right to satire, and that the reference to the right to be forgotten was not relevant.

The Supreme Court (Court of Cassation, Civil Division, sec. I, Ord. 2 March 2018, No. 6919) carried out an in-depth analysis of both the conflict between the right to privacy and the right to report, and of the scope of the so-called "right to be forgotten", using precedents laid out in national and European case-law (ECtHR and CJEU). Concerning the right to be forgotten, the Court of Cassation identifies five situations which justify the prevailance of the right not to see news or images relating to one's own person again, over right to report, after some time and in a different context to the original news or image. The right to report prevails in a series of situations: if the use of the image or news contributes to a debate of public interest; if the effective interest in the use of the news or image, prevails over other interests, in particular commercial or audience, of those who reuse the material. These are to be assessed considering their contribution to culture, education, rights protection, police, justice, etc.; if the public profile of the person concerned, in a political or economic situation, compromises their own privacy; if the methods of using the news or image show an objective interest in the broadcasting of the news to the public, through source verification; finally, if the person concerned is notified before broadcasting and is given the opportunity to reply. The Court held that none of these criteria were met in considering the rebroadcasting of the interview clip. In particular, even if the broadcast of the service at the time had been of public interest, the rebroadcasting years later aimed only at denigrating him, alluding to an alleged decline in popularity and therefore violates his right to privacy and the so-called right to be forgotten. There are also no connotations of satire (an expression of the right of criticism in a particularly corrosive and hyperbolic form for social or political denunciation) to be found, since the comments had no intention of social criticism but groundless offense.

> On the right to be forgotten, the Court of Cassation (Court of Cassation, Civil Division, sec. III, ord. 5 November 2018, No. 28084) decided to postpone the appeal concerning the publication in a newspaper of information regarding the conviction of the applicant for the murder of his wife, a crime committed several decades before and for which the culprit had served 12 years in prison. The so-called right to be forgotten does not refer to the digital storage of data and its re-use or memorisation in search engines or social media platforms - a problem of enormous importance which only recently emerged in the national and European case-law guidelines. The question raised concerns the right not to see repeated publication of past news that was legitimately widespread but that, after a few years, the lack of "freshness" of the news means it is not still in the public interest. According to the Court of Cassation, the solution requires additional reflection, in light of the entry into force of the EU Regulation on personal data (EU Regulation 2016/679, in particular Article 17). For this reason, the section decided to send the documents to the joint sections to get a suitable ruling to guide future decision of the national courts.

Regarding personal data, the Court of Cassation's ruling (Court of Cassation, Civil Division, sec. I, judg. 29 August 2018, No. 21362) concerning the data storing of persons subjected to criminal investigations is worth mentioning. The amount of time and methods of storing such data, even when an investigation ended in no charges against the person investigated, should be governed by a specific regulation, implementing the general provisions of the Privacy Code (lgs.d. 196/2003). In reality, this regulation was only introduced in 2018, following d.p.r. 15/2018, which fixes a maximum of twenty-years to store data, except for a series of restrictions and precautions, as well as the principle that requires to separate the data collected for criminal purposes from administrative. The regulation specifies that after a maximum of ten years, data is accessible only to a small group of judicial police officers.

The applicant, a professional who had been investigated in relation to a crime, but whose role had been dismissed, complained that the information relating to his involvement in criminal investigations after several years was still available in the data processing centre, and was accessible to others professionals in his sector, causing him reputational damage. According to the Court of Cassation, in light of the recent d.p.r., the complaint was not imcompatible with the applicable regulation, since the duration terms indicated had not expired. However, all precautions must be applied to the complainant to protect the personal data collect in detail by the regulations.

On the right to report, the judgment (Court of Cassation, Civil Division, sec. I, 9 July 2018, No. 18006). that confermed the sentence on RAI to pay damage compensation (set at an equitable basis at 25 thousand euros) to a professional interviewed for a news broadcast without informing the applicant about the use of a hidden camera. The Supreme Court holds that this way of collecting news is contrary to a journalist's code of ethics, which prohibits exerting pressure to get information. If information is received through fradulent means, the right to report, which allows the use of personal data for journalistic purposed without the interested party's consent (lgs.d. 196/2003, Article 137(2)), cannot be invoked.

B. Collection of Biometric Data to Check Workers' Attendence in Companies

A separate waste collection company had introduced a system for recognising the biometric features of its employees' hands to clock in at work. The Data Protection Authority sanctioned the company for not communicating this personal data collection system. The competent court admitted the appeal of the company, holding that the technology involved did not involve personal biometric data and therefore its installation did not require communication to the Data Protection Authority. The system only collected the biometric data of the employees' hands to generate an ID number memorised by the ID badge of each worker. When the worker uses their ID badge, the system recognised the digital code, not the biometric data. On this basis, the territorial judge excluded that the action concerned personal data aiming to identify a person: what is actually tracked is the badge. This opinion is not shared by the Supreme Court (Court of Cassation, sec. II, judg. 5 October 2018, No. 25686).

According to current regulations (Privacy Code lgs.d. 196/2003), the concept of data processing concerns any type of data, and personal data is what allows, even indirectly, to identify a physical person. It is irrelevant that biometric data relating to employees' hands are collected only once in order to generate a numeric code, and not stored. It is sufficient that a code, associated with a personal identification tag, allows the worker to be traced. The sanction imposed by the Authority for failing to inform the interested parties, to verify the risks in advance and to notify the Authority of the personal data processing is therefore legitimate.

C. Privacy and Access of Workers to Evalutation Data of Companies

The Court of Cassation, Civil Division (sec. I, judg. 14 December 2018, No. 32533) intervened in an appeal presented by a bank employee who, subject to a disciplinary sanction, asked his boss to see the contents of the Human Resources assessment produced on him. This was requested via the Italian Data Protection Authority. The bank denied the request, raising the case before the Court of Rome, then before the Court of Cassation. The company resisted the request for access presented by the employee and confirmed by the Authority, asserting that to respond to this request it would have made documents available that are strictly for internal use only, and that revealed the bank's organizational methods, which were then covered by the right to privacy. The Court of Cassation rejects the appeal of the bank and confirms that the right of access of a worker to their own personal data extends to assessments on their activity within company organisations. The protection of privacy concerns all data on the dignity of the person, including those accumulated in assessment procedures. From the company's point of view, it would be possible to protect their confidentiality by omitting passages that do not directly refer to the assessment of the worker.

D. Defamation on Facebook – Obligation to Investigate even When Social Networks Refuse to Collaborate

The judge for the preliminary investigations dismissed procedings against unknown persons for defamation that took place via Facebook posts. The American management of Facebook was not available to collaborate with the investigations, who communicated that they were not able to reveal the IP addresses that the comments (considered defamatory) came from. In light of this, the public prosecutor's office and Court held that further investigations were not possible. The victim appealed to the Court of Cassation against the dismissal, which instead established that Facebook's advanced secrecy cannot be considered sufficient reason to dismiss a case without attempting other investigations to identify the perpetrator (Court of Cassation, Criminal Division, sec. V, judg. 12 July 2018, No. 42630).

E. Publication of Private Data on School Notice Boards

A school published a ranking list to attend educational courses offered to the students, by posting the list in a public place in front of the school complex, which indirectly detailed the health problems of a child (a family member of the student). In the view of the territorial judges, supported by the Court of Cassation's decision that dismissed the appeal of the Minister of Education (Court of Cassation, Civil Division, sec. III, judg. 26 June 2018, No. 16816), the revelation, however indirect, of the health situation of a minor, constitutes a violation of the right to privacy, including family members, given that the information was divulged to persons outside the circle of people required to know. Compensation for damage is therefore due for the illegal disclosure of sensitive data to the family of the child (the amount of compensation is reduced, since the injured party did not promptly request the removal of the list).

F. Legislation Retroactively Affecting Quarrying Regime

In 2015, the Sicily Region introduced a law renewing previous legislation of 2013 concerning fees that quarry owners must pay to the Region and Municipality where the quarry is located. The administrative court was asked to judge on the case regarding the fees in question, holding that the mentioned laws violated legislation on private property (given that they introduced a tax that was disproportionate to the economic value of the extraction operations, and had subsequently raised the amount with retroactive effect). With judgment 89/2018, the Constitutional Court, on the one hand, denies that the measure introduced constitutes a tax, but rather a fee aimed at partially covering the distruption that the quarry brings to the community and the territory. It also denies that between the introduction of the fee in 2013 and its increase in 2015, there was no indication of the raise in tax, forming a reliance on the amount payable that should to be protected pursuant to the joint provisions of Articles 6 and 13 ECHR. Although retroactive application of stricter laws only concerning criminal matters are prohibited by the Constitution, the legislator must try to avoid working reactively *in peius* in all sectors. However, in this case, the tax raise was not considered disproportionate or unforeseeable.

X. Children's Rights

A. *Crime of Paedo-pornography*

The joint divisions of the Criminal Court of Cassation (judg. 31 May 2018, No. 51815) ruled on a controversial point of the interpretation of Article 600-*ter* (1), No. 1, regarding the illegal production of pornographic material with minors under 18 years old. The doubt concerned whether it was necessary to link the mere existence of the crime to the danger of spreading the material produced. Widespread case-law orientation considered it necessary to ascertain that the child pornography material was produced for diffusion, however limited; if, instead, the images or other child pornography material were limited to the perverse use of the author of the fact (apart from possession of child pornography: Article 600-*quater*), the crime did not exist. This interpretation was found incompatible with a series of European and international regulations, including the Lanzarote Convention for the protection of minors against sexual exploitation and abuse. Furthermore, technological communication developments and the explosion of social media make it impossible to distinguish between material produced for private use and material available on IT networks. The joint sections therefore conclude to integrate the crime of producing any kind of image, video or other child pornography material that uses minors, (even with their consent), exploiting their personality to reduce it to a tool of sexual satisfaction, regardless of the danger of spreading the material. The forms of so-called "domestic pornography" are excluded, limited to cases in which intimate images are used in a strictly private form between peers (adolescents over 14 years) on the basis of mutual consent and with no doubt of abuse or exploitation. Finally, according to the joint sections, the proposed new interpretation does not entail a pejorative reform of criminal law for citizens. It is based on previously prevailing interpretations, which in turn were based on the danger of spreading the material produced. Considerations regarding the immediate availability on the computer networks of images and videos would have led to the same conclusion in concrete cases.

B. Right to Paternity Allowance for Adoptive Freelance Fathers

With judgment 385/2005, the Constitutional Court ruled on the unconstitutionality of some provisions of lgs.d. 151/2001 (Single text for legislative provisions on protecting and supporting maternity and paternity – amended in 2015) which excluded maternity allowance payments in favour of the adoptive father if it had been renounced by the adoptive mother. In a case concerning a similar situation (a couple of lawyers adopted three children and the mother refused the allowance she should have received, on the assumption that her husband would have benefited from it, however, the National Insurance and Welfare fund refused the request), the Court brought up once again the question of constitutionality, holding that the 2005 decision of "additive judgment of principles" could not be applied in the case in question, since only a new law could have eliminated the different treatment between the adoptive mother and father; according to the referring judge, it was therefore necessary for the Court to rule again, setting out the same principle with respect to the new case.

Judgment 105/2018 of the Constitutional Court clarifies that, when a judgment of constitutionality adds a principle that is integrated with the law and states it sufficiently precisely, the Courts must directly apply this principle even before it is written into legislative reform provisions. In this case in question, the 2005 judgment had clarified that maternity protection institutions were not intended to protect women (as in the past) but to defend the best interest of the child; therefore, any differential treatment between parents, whether biological or adoptive, is unreasonable. In conclusion, the Court considers the new question of constitutionality inadmissable, brought up in reference to regulations that have been previously recognised as contrary to the Constitution and directs the judge to directly apply the principle of protecting the best interest of the child, established by previous judgments.

C. State of Neglect and Adoption

In several decisions, the Court of Cassation reiterates the position that the opening of a case of abandonment and removal of a child from the parents must only take place in extreme cases and after all appropriate measures to keep the family together have gone ahead without success.

This is based on the CRC and the case-law of the ECtHR, as well as Article 1 of l. 184/1983. The fact that parents have been sentenced to long detention periods could however constitute a reason to begin child adoption processes, when the detention period correlates with a crucial growth phase. The Court of Cassation rejected the appeal of a couple at the centre of a particularly serious and high-profile news story (Court of Cassation, Civil Division, sec. I, judg. 19 January 2018, No. 1431), in the application of this principle. The two had organised a series of acid attacks against an ex-partner and complained about the immediate adoption of their newborn baby as a form of indirect punishment. The Court of Cassation reiterates the reasons given by the merits judge to take the child away from the couple (whose troubled personality was also highlighted) and to exclude adoption by the child's grandparents.

According to another ruling of the Court of Cassation, the biological parents' disagreement with the adoption is enough to prevent the adoption of the child, even if the child already lives with the adopting parents and not the biological partents, unless it has been objectively shown that the original family situation has disintegrated to such an extent as to break any emotional bonds with the child (Court of Cassation, Civil Division, sec. I, judg. 16 July 2018, No. 18827).

D. Judicial Hearing of Children in Custody and International Abduction Procedures

In *de potestate* procedures (adoption, fostering, etc.), the minor must not only be heard by the judge but is a necessary part in the process, given that they are in conflict of interests with the parents or guardians. This also applies when the issue is raised by one of the parents for the protection of the same child. Article 336 of the Civil Code establishes that the minor is represented by a lawyer and a special trustee must be appointed (which can be the same legal defender). The decree adopted without adversary procedure being integrated with the child's legal defender is therefore repealed (Court of Cassation, Civil Division, sec. I, judg. 6 March 2018, No. 5256).

The Supreme Court (Court of Cassation, Civil Division, sec. VI, judg. 1 August 2018, No. 20375) investigated a case of international child abduction. A couple of Argentinian citizens, separated in Italy with the custody of their son to the mother, returned to Argentina where the separation was not recognised. After some years she returned to Italy, where her ex-husband accused her of international child abduction. The Italian Juvenile Court, without convocating the father, ruled that returning to Argentina would be be harmful to the minor and confirms custody to the mother. The appeal of the father was brought before the Supreme Court, which stated that the decision of the Italian judge, while claiming to be in the child's best interests, had been taken without listening to the child – a condition of legitimacy for these matters pursuant to Article 315-*bis* of the Civil Code and the European Convention on the Exercise of Children's Rights – and therefore the decision must be dismissed. In these cases, only particularly grave reasons can justify the omitted listening of the child, which were not present in the Italian Juvinile Court judgment.

E. Joint or Exclusive Custody of Children of Separated Couples: Conditions of Joint Custody

In procedures concerning the personal separation of spouses, children are not considered parties to the proceedings. Their judicial hearing is therefore not generally accompanied by the appointment of a special representative in court. Despite this, the Court of Cassation (Court of Cassation, Civil Division, sec. I, judg. 11 May 2018, No. 11554) stated that, when custody of the child is in discussion, the judge must assess whether it is necessary to appoint a special representative for the minor, considering the judge-verified incapacity of the parents, to protect the interest of the child. However, in another decision, the Supreme Court observes that the conflict between parents during separation procedures is not a sufficient indicator to nominate a special representative (Court of Cassation, Civil Division, sec. I, judg. 11 May 2018, No. 11554).

According to the Supreme Court, also in cases of non-married couples, the decree providing for child custody and maintenance to only one of the parents can be challenged before the Court of Cassation (even if it is a temporary provision, subject to change), because it is a decision-making act which, for the time it is carried out, corresponds to "something judged". That said, the choice not to share custody must be explained in detail and take various reasons into account, including undoubtedly the opinion of the minor, especially if they are a teenager. The geographic distance between the parents' houses, while it may influence the decision, is not itself a sufficient reason to give exclusive custody to one parent (Court of Cassation, Civil Division, sec. I, judg. 24 October 2018, No. 30826).

On the subject of shared custody, the Court of Cassation (Court of Cassation, Civil Division, sec. I, judg. 24 May 2018, No. 12954) stated that the best interest of the child principle is the fundamental criteria to which the judge must adhere in the event of parental conflict, in light of the pre-eminent right of the child to a healthy and balanced growth. The pursuit of this objective can therefore also entail adopting measures containing or restricting the parents' individual rights to freedom, where their externalisation is detrimental for the child, compromising their physical and mental health and development. In this case, it was the child's participation, alongside her father and his wife, to the religious services of the Jehovah's Witnesses church - a religion he had joined after the relationship with the child's mother. The mother complained that the child did not want to participate in this ceremony and a psychological expert affirmed that the practise had caused her mental discomfort. It should be noted that the appeal to the Court of Cassation did not raise the question of the possible repression of the right to religious freedom of the persons involved.

F. Right to Maintain Grandparent/Grandchild Relationships

The Court of Cassation (Court of Cassation, Civil Division, sec. I, judg. 25 July 2018, No. 19780), reiterating the principles of protection of child to grow up in stable families of the CRC, of the CFREU and the ECHR (the Court of Cassation highlighted the significant case of *Beccarini and Ridolfi* ruled on by the ECtHR – see *Yearbook 2018*, p. 319-320), established that the right to maintain significant relationships with grandparents also extends to the spouse or de facto partner of the parent, if that they have established a positive relationship with the minor. Furthermore, the grandparents' right is not unquestionable: it is up to the judge to ascertain whether the grandparent/grandchild relationship deserves to be maintained, exclusively considering the interest of the minor. This is especially true when the presence of the grandparents supports the positive education experience of the parents (see Court of Cassation, Civil Division, sec. VI, judg. 12 June 2018, No. 15238). The aforementioned judgment No. 19780 is also significant since for the Court of Cassation it confirms the appeal of the Court of Appeal's degree on right to access and visiting. A "definite" nature must recognised to this right, albeit until new facts and rulings emerge on disputes between parties: on one hand, the minor, on the other the adults who argue the right to custody or to visit (on the contentious nature of proceedings concerning parental authority (in this case, the procedure concerned the ruling on the state of adoption) and circumstances in which biological parents must be present for judgment, see also Civil Court of Cassation, sec. I, judg. 10 July 2018, No. 18148).

G. Family Abuse and Corrective Abuse

The Court of Cassation excluded that some episodes of denigration by a teacher to a student with a stutter could constitute family abuse (Article 572 of the Criminal Code), but considered that any form of even mild moral, verbal or physical violence, even if allegedly for educational purposes, constitutes a crime of corrective abuse (see *Yearbook 2017*, p. 286). Since the crime in question is typically a dangerous offence, the harm caused by the illegal conduct of the teacher to the health of the student can be only probable, on the basis on an assessment of common experience (Court of Cassation, Criminal Division, sec. III, judg. 11 July 2018, No. 45736). Regarding habitual violent behaviour within the family (in the case in question, committed by an adult on the youngest children of his co-habiting partner), the educative intention is irrelevant in declassifying the crime of family abuse (Article 572 of the Criminal Code) to the lesser crime of corrective abuse (Article 571 of the Criminal Code) (Court of Cassation, Criminal Division, sec. 3, judg. 6 November 2018, No. 17810).

An employee of a structure for elderly people who continuously harasses clients commits the crime of family abuse as referred to in Article 572 of the Criminal Code (which also applies to pseudo-family situations such as a community for the elderly). However, the crime does not necessarily imply responsibility for the abandonment of the incapacitated person (Article 591 of the Criminal Code), for which it is necessary to prove that the victim is in danger (Court of Cassation, Criminal Division, sec. VI, judg. 25 January 2018, No. 12866).

The crime of abuse in a pseudo-family context can also refer to an educator at a nursery school (the case in question concerned specifically an infant school), who upon knowledge of abuse of the children followed by other educators, fails to report the abuse in order to protect herself and her group of children. The same omissive behaviour can be noted in municipal representatives who, upon hearing about abuse, does not report it to the authorities. This person is an accessory to the crime (Court of Cassation, Criminal Division, sec. VI, judg. 1 February 2018, No. 10763).

The crime of family abuse does not require episodes of violence to taken place when family members are living together, but can take place between non-cohabiting persons (Court of Cassation, Criminal Division, sec. VI, judg. 5 December 2018, No. 6506. However, there must be a family or similar relationship between the individuals. In this regard, the Court of Cassation considers that between two persons, occasional and non-conhibiting partners, the existence of a family relationship can be excluded, even if they have a child together (Court of Cassation, Criminal Division, sec. III, judg. 9 January 2019, No. 345); on the other hand, it concludes that a de facto couple, even if they have been living together for only one month, can constitute a justify the accusation of family abuse against a violent partner, since the existence of a joint life plan has been proven (in particular with the start of civil union proceedings) (Court of Cassation, Criminal Division, sec. III, judg. 17 December 2018, No. 56673). Family abuse constitutes a more serious conduct than sanctioned in Article 612-*bis* (persecutoy acts – stalking). After many years of harassment of partners and children, an individual can be charged not only with abuse, but also with stalking in relation to violent or threatening behaviour after living together (Court of Cassation, Criminal Division, sec. VI, judgments 19 June 2018, No. 42918; 9 October 2018, No. 55737).

A situation similar to a family is interpersonal dynamics and hierarchies formed within a company or professional studio that broadly reflect those that characterise a family. The harassment that occurs there can therefore be sanctioned as family abuse. The Court of Cassation, for example, holds that this could be the case of a notary office, in which the owner had tormented and humiliated his employee/sister-in-law for years. Other examples are family-run businesses and domestic work (Court of Cassation, Criminal Division, sec. VI, judg. 7 June 2018, No. 39920). Without this definition, mobbing is the best description of cases of victimisation of an employee. The dismissal from a company motivated by the fact that the worker has been convicted of family abuse is not justified. A different assessment may be legitimate, however, if the conviction were reflected within the work relationship (Civil Court of Cassation, sec. Work, judg. 10 September 2018, No. 21958). The Court of Cassation, Criminal Division, specified that behaviour that forced minors to witness violence against their mother within the family constitutes family abuse (so-called witnessed violence), providing that the characteristics of the crime exist – habitual behaviour and causing psychophysical suffering (Court of Cassation, Criminal Division, sec. VI, judg. 23 February 2018, No. 18833).

It should be noted that, with reference to the crime of slight physical injuries (Article 582(2) of the Criminal Code: these are injuries that cause damage lasting no longer than twenty days), the Constitutional Court (judg. 236/2018) established that the provisions attributing jurisdiction to the Justice of the Peace instead of the ordinary court were illegitimate, unless the victim was the descendant of the perpetrator, but not the biological child. This unequal treatment, which had evidently eluded the legislator who intervened several times in the matter, constitutes a difference in treatment and is also unreasonable. Over the years, the legislator introduced some amendments to Article 577 of the Criminal Code to widen the range of protected subjects in case of domestic violence, extending the aggravating circumstance for murder, injuries and other crimes committed against the spouse and children, even in cases of violence committeed against adopted children, one of the parties in a civil cohabitation, a permanently cohabiting person or person personally linked with the guilty party. Furthermore, the legislation adopted in Italy in 2013 following the ratification of the Istanbul Convention against domestic violence introduced the possibility of adopting precautionary measures, such as emergency removal from the family home to fight feminicide and other crimes against vulnerable family members. However, legislation concerning the powers of the Justice of the Peace were not accurately amended by the reforms (lgs.d. 274/2000, and successive amendments). Consequently, the judge of peace found themselves dealing with the crime of slight physical injuries committed against the biological child and not the ordinary court, while the Court was competent if the victim was the adopted child. This was recognised as discriminatory and unreasonable by the Court. The most important practical implication of this regime was that the judge of peace, when proceeding for the crime of slight physical injuries, unlike the Court, could not adopt personal precautionary measures that the court can. These precautions, such as removal from the family home, have proved very effective in preventing more serious crimes. The adoption of l. 11 January 2018, No. 4 (Amendments to the Civil Code, Criminal Code, Criminal Procedures Code and other provisions in favour of ophans due to domestic crimes) did not resolve the problem. Consequently, the Constitutional Court only has to ascertain the illegitimacy of the disputed provision of lgs.d. 274/2000 and exclude the jurisdiction of the judge of peace (in favour of the Court) for the offense referred to in Article 582 (2) of the Criminal Code and with regard to cases in which the victim is the descendant or natural ascendant of the guilty party, and in all other cases in which the family community members are involved, identified by the current Article 577 of the Criminal Code.

H. Foreign Minors and Residence Permit for Parents

The Court of Cassation (Court of Casasation, Civil Division, sec. I, judgments 21 February 2018, No. 4197; 4 June 2018, No. 14238) reiterates its interpretative guidelines on Article 31 of the Single Text on immigration (lgs.d. 286/1998) relating to recognising residence permits for "serious reasons" to the benefit of a foreign minor of unknown age.

Ruling on appeals filed against acts of the Juvenile Court that did not allow the parents of non-Italian citizens to stay in Italy (in one case the father, in the other both parents of three children, since the adults were charged or convicted of various crimes concerning copyright, counterfeiting and handling of stolen goods) the Court of Appeals, confirmed the decision of the Court of First Instance. Article 31 of lgs.d. 286/1998, recognises the right of the child to live with their family, to private life and protection, as well as the principle of the best interest of the child (citing the Convention on the Rights of the Child.). It specifies that allowing parents to remain with children cannot apply when the adult's behaviour is contrary to the best interest of the child. On one hand, the law does not require there to be exceptional situations or situations linked to the health of the child (illness, disability etc.) when giving a reason for extending a residence permit in Italy: instead it refers to situations of vulnerability, to be assessed on a case by case basis. On the other hand, behaviour that is contrary to the best interest cannot be abstractly traced back to particular types like, for example, committing a crime that foresees the revocation of a residence permit or expulsion. The Court of Cassation recalls its own case-law (judg. 21799/2010 – see *Yearbook 2011*, p. 285) to conclude that, in the cases considered, the territorial court expressed itself irrefutably, without in practical terms balancing the needs of public order and national security and the "serious reasons connected with the child's psychophysical development" required by law, without prioritising the latter.

I. Responsibility in Supervising Institutions for Harassment to a Student

An appeal was filed for damages against the Ministery of Education, the Province of Rome and the National Agency for the Deaf. The appeal concerned the lack of supervision of the work of a support teacher, appointed to provide assistance to a girl at a special institution for deaf children, who had sexually harassed another child. The man was found guilty in a Criminal Court and must also respond in Civil Court for damages caused to the child and family. The appeal in question reaffirms the responsibility of the institutions that made it possible for the teacher, later charged, to be present at the victim's school. The National Agency for the Deaf, which manages the school, defended itself by claiming that the teacher had been hired through a cooperative on supply and therefore did not work directly for the agency, adding that his presence in the school had not given him to opportunity for harassment, and it could have also taken place in other circumstances. The Province and the Ministry also observed that the teacher was not their employee, and they therefore could not be held responsible for the damage caused by his criminal behaviour. The Tribunal of Rome (sec. XII, judg. 11 January 2018, No. 613) holds that the civil responsibility referred to in Article 2049 of the Civil Code does not require there to be a formal employment relationship between the person responsible for supervision and the offender: a clear, factual relationship is sufficient. As for the opportunity offered by the job at the school, the Court holds that there is no doubt that his presence as a teacher provided the necessary opportunity to carry out the harassment. The three institutions are therefore required to pay the child's family approximately 100 thousand euros in compensation (compared to the 600 thousand requested by the applicants).

XI. Due Process and the Pinto Act

A. Compensation of Legal Costs Divided between the Parties

L.d. 12 September 2014, No. 132, converted in law 10 November 2014, No. 162, provided that Article 92 of the Civil Procedure Code was reformed; the judge provided that compensation of legal costs could be divided between the two parties in civil judgments in only two cases, other than when there is a mutual loss (that is when the judgment rejects the opposing questions of both parties): when the issue dealt with is an absolute novelty; or when it involves a change in case-law with respect to a decisive point of the dispute. According to various Courts, this limitation on judge's decisions on Court fees is contrary to Articles of the Constitution, of the ECHR and of the CFREU on due process (Articles 3, 24, 25, 102, 104, 111 of the Constitution; 6, 13, 14 ECHR and 21 and 47 CFREU). In the opinion of the referring courts, there may be various other reasons that justify the costs of the proceedings not being entirely covered by the losing party. Specifically, in some cases of labour, social security or family reunification disputes, there was an evident disproportion in terms of economic capacity between the parties involved.

The Constitutional Court ruled on a point on judg. 77/2018, which was also recalled in judg. 190/2018. According to this regulation, the fact that losing party in a civil trial is required to pay the legal fees also for winning party is not exempt from exceptions, and Article 92 of the Civil Procedure Code, before the 2014 reform, attributed the decision on dividing compensation between the parties of the costs arising out of a Court case to the judge's decretion, while justifying the existence of "serious and exceptional" reasons, on the basis of 2005 and 2009 reform laws. The 2014 reform attempted to reduce the number of instrumental appeals brought before the Court. The substantial ban on compensating is one way that the legislator attempted to discourage the large number of civil judicial procedures, alongside measures of mediation, assisted negotiation, referral to arbitration, and attempts at reconciliation. The new 2014 reform is unreasonable insofar as it does not take into account various other circumstances which, although quite similar to those typified by the change in case-law and the novelty of the question, are nevertheless irrelevant for the purposes of compensation. For example,

Constitutional Court judgments that change the regulatory framework during a proceeding could (like a change in case-law) justify dividing compensation between the successful and unsuccessful parties, but this fact is completely irrelevant as it is not included in the scope of Article 92 of the reformed Civil Procedure Code. However, the fact that the losing party is a worker, against an employer, does not in itself justify dividing the costs of litigation between the two parties. Within the limits indicated, the Constitutional Court concludes that the Article 92 of the Civil Procedure Code is unlawful.

B. *Standards of Authentic Interpretation*

The Constitutional Court (judg. 167/2018) intervened on the complex question brought up by a 2006 regulation which charged a fund (financed by airport operators) for a part of the firefighting services in Italian airports (in addition to extra boarding charges for all airport passengers). On the contributions owed by the airport companies, which were clearly fiscal (levies established by law, intended to perform a public function, such as fire prevention services), a wide dispute took place. The State interferred with law 208/2015 (Stability Law of 2016), introducing an authentic interpretation regulation of the 2006 provisions, which defined the airport companies' contribution as "payment for a service" and not a "tax". As a result of this alternative definition, all tax commission and Reginal Administration Courts were rendered null and void. The joint sections of the Court of Cassation, where the dispute was heard, raise the question of the consitutionality of the 2015 authentic interpretation given a violation of Articles 3, 24, 25, 102, 111 of the Constitution (there was no doubt that the contributions requested were taxes and therefore the authentic interpretation rule - which takes the competence for the disputes away from the Tax Court - was not justified). They also argued a violation of Article 6 ECHR (interposed regulations) since the law in question interfered with an ongoing procedure, took competency away from the Tax Court for pending proceedings, generally favoured the procedural position of the State and most likely involved the unreasonable duration of the processes. According to the Court, despite the different definition of 2015, the burden on airport companies is undoubtedly a tax and not a charge. The authentic interpretation regulation is therefore unconstitutional, in contrast with Article 3 of the Constitution (reasonability), purporting to change the fiscal definition of the regulation which is objectively self-evident.

C. Reasonable Duration of Criminal Proceedings – Issues of Constitutionality

The Stability Law of 2016 (l. 208/2015) introduced Article 5-*sexies* to the Pinto Law (l. 89/2001) which has influenced the payment of fair compensation due by the State for excessive duration of a judicial proceeding. It links the payment to presenting a documented declaration of non-collection or of specific further legal action by the person entitled to the service: this payment is due within six months of such declaration. According to the Liguria Regional Adminstrative Court, this legislation conflicts with both the articles of the Constitution that protect due process and Article 6 ECHR. The measure allegedly makes the payment of money owed by the State to private individuals and deriving from a judgment ascertaining an excessive duration of a process more difficult than other credits claimed towards the public administration, namely with regard to credits established after 2016, for which a term of six months would add to the ordinary four-month limit. In practice, the compliance judgment for non-payment could only be proposed after ten months, instead of the four months that are generally foreseen.

The Constitutional Court (Judg. 185/2018) rejects the exception of unconstitutionality, proposing a constitutionally oriented interpretation of the contested provision. Firstly, the need to produce a documented declaration is neither excessively burdensome nor more burdensome than claiming amounts owed by other public administrations. Secondly, the end of six months, that was introduced by the 2015 law and that is applied to all creditors including those who got a judgment before 2016 (contrary to the claims of the appellant court) is not added to the ordinary 4 months, but substitutes it. In view of the high number of indeminites that the administration must pay under Pinto judgments, the legislator decided to give more time to the State to carry out the liquidation to avoid further executive proceedings by the creditors. Article 5-*sexies* introduces a reasonable mechanism that allows the payment of the amount due following the judgment of excessive duration of proceedings. It allows cooperation between the administration and citizens, and imposes a longer waiting time than for an ordinary judgment without questioning the fullnesses and effectiveness of the credit.

The Constitutional Court with judgment 88/2018 intervened on another controversial point of the Pinto Law. Article 4 of l. 89/2001 establishes the term of six months from the final assessment of the provision that defined the procedure for requesting fair compensation before the competent Court of Appeal. With a unanimous interpretation, the Constitutional Court considers this rule makes the proposal of fair compensation claim inadmissible until there is a final judgment. Therefore, there are numerous cases of applicants who, since they had presented the request for fair compensation before the definitive judgment, their application was denied and they had lost all possibility of receiving relief provided by law, with alleged violation of the principles of fair trial (Articles 3, 24 and 111 of the Constitution), and of Article 117(1) of the Constitution related to the standard of Articles 6 and 13 ECHR (reasonable duration of procedures and effective judicial protection). The question had already been dealt with by the Constitutional Court with judgment 30/2014 (see *Yearbook 2015*, p. 289), which had requested a legislative intervention to make the use of effective remedy possible during ongoing procedures that already exceed the limits of reasonableness. However, the 2015 reform did not change the disputed provision; instead it introduced provisions (of dubious efficiency) aimed at speeding up processes, without considering that requesting and receiving fair compensation before the "natural" conclusion of the process is in itself a significant incentive to make the procedure faster. Contrary to its 2014 judgment, the Constitutional Court with judgment 88/2018 both recognises the unconstitutionality of existing regulatory framework and requesting effective intervention from the legislator and, with an additive ruling, states that Article 4 of l. 89/2001 is unconstitutional since it does not provide for the possibility of requesting fair compensation for unreasonable duration of proceedings pending judgment of an ongoing procedure.

XII. Criminal issues

A. Double Sanctions for Fiscal Evasion: the Problem of the "Double Track" Sanctions

With judg. 43/2018, the Constitutional Court ruled on the case in which the referring judge considered the regime of sanctions laid down by Italian law in the case of tax evasion (income and VAT) incompatible with the principle of *ne bis in idem* established by Article 4 Protocol 7, ECHR (adopted in 1984 and entered into force in Italy in 1990). The defendant for the crime of failure to file a tax return (according to Article

5, lgs.d. 74/2000) had already been sentenced to pay an administrative sanction for the same, according to Articles 1(1) and 5(1) of lgs.d. 471/1997. This sanction, is while formally adminstrative, could well be characterised in substance as criminal, given that it consists of a payment of 120 % of the amount evaded. It is true that the law provides for the suspension of this payment when verified in the tax office until criminal trial is resolved; however, this does not eliminate the circumstance that a criminal trial has begun on the same crime that has already been tried and sanctioned with a fiscal judgment of a substantially criminal nature. Article 649 of the Criminal Procedures Code, which excludes a second judgment on a matter that has already been definitively decided by a previous judgment, is not sufficient to prevent a second trial since it only applies to two formally criminal sentences. Hence the request to the Constitutional Court for a declaration of unconstitutionality of Article 649 of the Criminal Procedure Code or of an adequate reading that extends its scope to final sentences imposing a sanction which, although formally administrative, is equivalent to a "penalty", according to the ECtHR case-law.

The Constitutional Court carries out an extensive discussion of the question, also highlighting the differences between the regime specified by the ECtHR and the one in force in EU law. Concerning ECtHR case-law, the Constitutional Court holds that in recent years, it has relaxed the rigid nature of its previous decisions. With particular reference to the *A and B v. Norway* case [GC], No. 24130/11 and 29758/11, 15 November 2016, the Court of Strasbourg acknowledged the legitimacy of national laws which, especially in fiscal matters, allow the unfolding of a "double track" sanction, as long as the two proceedings are strictly connected and in particular, if the second judgment, in determining the sanction, can adequately take the sentence imposed in the first judgment into account. Considering these developments in ECtHR case-law, the Constitutional Court assigns the task of evaluating, in this specific case, whether the two proceedings are sufficiently connected to not violate the principle of *ne bis in idem* to the judge, or whether this parameter developed by the ECtHR is inapplicable. In this second case (which seems the least likely), the question of constitutionality of Article 649 of the Criminal Procedure Code could be considered reasonable. The Constitutional Court holds, therefore, that the legislator should intervene to avoid this or other situations of friction between the Italian legal system and the ECHR.

It is worth noting that the question also arises in reference to to EU law, which refers to the same regulations as the ECHR and sets forth the principle of *ne bis in idem* pursuant to Article 50 CFREU (see further, in this Part, 3.3).

> The theme of "double track" sanctions, in the terms defined by the Constitutional Court with the indications coming from the CJEU and the ECtHR, was also confronted by the Court of Cassation in many judgments that applied the aforementioned principles (in anticipation of a complete legislative arrangement) to a series of specific circumstances. The following decisions are noteworthy: Court of Cassation Civil Division, sec. II, judgments 16 February 2018, No. 3831 (on the latter, see above, in this Part, 1.1); 6 December, No. 31632, 31634, 31635; sec. V, judg. 30 October 2018, No. 27564.

B. Compulsary Revocation of Driving Licences following Drug Offences

Some courts have raised the question of constitutional legitimacy concerning Article 120 of the "New Road Code" (lgs.d. 285/1992, reformed in 2009), in the part which establishes that the chief magistrate must revoke the driving licence of anyone who charged with drug offences. On one hand, the law is considered contrary to the irretroactivity of criminal law (Article 7 ECHR), since the "sanction" of revoking a licence can concern facts that precede the regulation's entry into force (in 2009); on the other hand, is contrary to the principle of reasonability, proportionality and non discrimination (Article 3 of the Consitution), as it provides for the compulsory revocation, without the possibility for the chief magistrate to adjust the measure considering the vast and diversified range of drug related offenses. Judgment 22/2018 of the Constitutional Court holds that the revocation of the licence due to the absence of the minimum moral requirements required for driving licence holders is not to be considered a criminal sanction. It is not aimed as a punitive, retributive or deterrent measure, but aims to verify whether the individual is lacking moral reliability linked to sentencing laws on drug crimes. The reference to Article 7 ECHR is therefore not relevant, since the revocation of the license is not a punishment. However, the criticism based on the discriminatory and disproportionate nature of the measure is striking, above all considering that the chief magistrate is not allowed any discretion in revoking the licence, whether the crime is minor in nature or took place a long time previously. It should be added that while the judge "can" order the withdrawal of the license – as a punitive measure - in case of conviction for drug crimes, the chief magistrate "must" revoke the licence. In conclusion, where the law says that the chief magistrate "shall ensure" the revocation, the Constitutional Court holds that the Article 120 of the new highway code must read in the sense that the chief magistrate "can" revocke the driving license, in case of drug trafficking crimes.

C. Additional "Fixed" Sentence for Fraudulent Bankruptcy

> The fraudulent "Parmalat" bankruptcy has been linked to a certain number of people; an additional sentence is applicable to those involved of ten years ban on any commercial activity and on assuming any managerial role, pursuant to the additional measures laid out in Article 223 of the bankruptcy law (Royal Decree 16 March 1942, No. 267). The fixed duration of the additional measure was criticised by the referring judge, since it is contrary to the principles of proportionality of penalties and violates Article 8 ECHR. The additional sentence, which was established in a fixed measure, affects the private and professional life of the convict, without allowing the judge any room for discretion. The Constitutional Court agrees with the fact that the rigid nature of the additional sentence is incompatible with constitutional principles but holds that the bankruptcy law allows a constitutional interpretation of the provision, that must be understood as indicating ten years as the maximum duration of the additional sentence, in line with what the same law foresees for other forms of bankruptcy. This allows the judge to define the measure in relation to each specific case (Constitutional Court, judg. 222/2018).

D. Torture and Inhuman Treatment

The Court of Cassation ruled on some significant problems concerning the application of legislation adopted in Italy following the *Torreggiani* case (see *Yearbook 2014*, p. 307-308); Article 35-*ter* of prison regulations (l. 354/1975), introduced by l.d. 92/2014 establishing a compensation procedure in favour of detainees who are victims of inhuman treatment.

In a first ruling, the Supreme Court held that 8 euros per day of detention in inhuman and degrading conditions is a fair quantification of damages and therefore finds the request to raise a question of constitutionality manifestly unfounded. The compensation provided does not claim to constitute effective compensation for the damage caused - in short, the measure is not the same as that provided for cases of unjust imprisonment, and its adequacy has been recognised by the ECtHR (Court of Cassation, Civil Division, sec. I, judg. 2 July 2018, No. 17274).

The Court of Cassation, Civil Division (sec. III, judg. 6 December 2018, No. 31556) intervened on a complaint of a detainee whose compensation request was denied by the parole officer having spent 556 days in a cell of less than three square metres, insufficient heating and other deficiencies. The parole officer found the evidence produced on the treatment's inhuman or degrading character insufficient, which were partly based on reports on the prison where he was detained and more *Antigone* and other associations reports on the Italian prison system. The prison administration contradicted these reports with their own documents. According to the Court of Cassation, which follows the same approach adopted by the ECtHR, the burden of proof for fulfilling obligations deriving from the ECHR and national laws on procedures on implementing criminal convictions lies with the State and not the prisoner. The situation that arises between the State (who holds punitive power) and the prisoner (who holds the fundamental right not to suffer inhuman or degrading treatment) is unbalanced. It requires the prison administration to have the burden of proving that the damage claimed by the applicant did not occur because of the prison's deliberate act or its own negliegence. To this end, the parole officer can use the additional powers relative to the information provided by the parties, which is typical in a council chamber procedure. The applicant must demonstrate the damage and its connection with the detention conditions, being able to also use the results of investigations and evaluations conducted by specialised bodies, for example, the *Antigone* association reports. The State cannot only generally oppose the accusations, but must also provide evidence – using the wide range of data at its disposal – that the the prisoner's condition did not result from a general situation of inhuman or degrading treatment in this specific case. In the absence of such evidence, the prisoner's allegations must be considered founded. The prisoner only has to prove the conditions of detention and its duration, without providing, for example, the detention certificate, since such a document can be easily found by the parole officer (Court of Cassation, Civil Division, sec. I, judg. 6 March 2018, No. 5255).

The Supreme Court dealt with another matter (Court of Cassation, Civil Division, Joint Sections, judg. 8 May 2018, No. 11018) concerned the right to receive compensation for each day spent in conditions that do not comply with the criteria set out in Article 3 ECHR (as stated above, the compensation was set at 8 euros a day). The Criminal Court of Cassation (Joint Sections, judg. 26 January 2018, No. 3775) reiterated the principle that the right to use Article 35-*ter* of the prison procedure system lapsed on 28 June 2014, when the reform entered into force; the situations of inhuman or degrading treatment to which the complaint refers, however, may have also previously, as which the 2014 regulation established the legal reference, the right to not to be subject to this treatment existed before. The Court of Cassation, Civil Division adds that the payment of compensation received is, as a general principle, in ten years (not five, as established in the right to compensation for damage for an unlawful act). It is calculated with respect to each day of detention in inhuman conditions. The requirements will operate from the entry into force of the new indemnity regime only for the cases when detention finished before 2014 (although the application must have been filed within six months of 28 June 2014).

> The Court of Cassation, Civil Division, sec. I, judg. 20 February 2018, No. 4096 specifies that the conditions that must be met to consider a situation of prison overcrowding as imhuman or degrading exist when a single cell is less than three square metres (excluding in-cell sanitary facilities, fixed cabinets and beds), with no tables or chairs. The "strong presumption" of inhuman treatment that is established under these conditions may be rebutted if the prison administration claims, as in this specific case, that the if some compensatory factors are met: the short duration of the period in reduced space, sufficient communal spaces and the overall appropriate nature of the detention facility (see also Court of Cassation, Civil Division, sec. V, judg. 7 June 2018, No. 53731). In particular, according to the Court of Cassation, Civil Division, sec. I, judg. 24 May 2018, No. 12955, reduced available space in cells can be compensated by sharing a cell between two people and accompanying the detention with recreational and sports activities outside the cell.

E. Life Sentences

The Constitutional Court delivered two rulings that contribute to reduce the rigidity of Article 4-*bis* of penitentiary law (law 354/1975, and successive amendments), the legislation that introduced some forms of so-called life sentences "without parole".

Judgment 149/2018 refered to persons convicted of kidnapping for purposes of terrorism or subversion and kidnapping for purposes of extortion who caused the death of the victim. In this case, Article 58-*quater*, law 354/1975, citing Article 4-*bis* of the same law, provided that these prisoners were not eligible for penitentiary benefits (assignment to outside work, premium permits, and alternative measures to detention) unless the convicted person effectively served at least 26 years of prison. According to the Court, these mechanisms are contrary to the objective of re-education and reinsertion into social of the prisoner, which the punishment strives to achieve in all phases of implementation. The rigid nature of this mechanism does not allow any room for manouver for the judge to adapt the implemation of the punishment to the convicted person, going against the principle by which the punishment must be applied progressively.

A similar reasoning followed by the Constitutional Court in the decision 174/2018 regarding Article 21-*bis* of the penitentiary law, which lays down, refering to Articles 21 and 4-*bis* of the same law 354/1975, that women condemned for drug crimes (among crimes considered "first-tier without parole" in relation to recognising benefits such as access to alternative measures to detention), cannot enjoy the benefits of caring for children under ten years old outside prison, unless they have effectively served at least a third of the sentence, unless they collaborate with the judicial authorities. The question of constitutionality concerns a person, condemned for a crime "without parole" and a sentence of four years and ten months, who would have had to serve almost two before being able to look after her three children outside the prison, all of whom were under 6 years old. In this case (see *Yearbook 2015*, p. 284), the Court also found a violation in the legislation of Article 31 on the protection of the rights of the child. Even if it were possible for the convicted women to colloborate with the judicial authorities (which is not always possible, especially when the investigations have already clarified the criminal situation or when the role of the convicted person in the crime was marginal), the consideration of the rights of the child (and the objective of re-inserting the mother into society) should not be systematically subject to the interests of the investigation.

F. The Condition of Prisoners in Special Detention Regime (Article 41-bis of the Prison System Act)

In various judgments, the Court of Cassation, Criminal Division, established that the visits for detainees currently in section 41-*bis* regimes (that is, a special surveillance regime set up, in particular, for detainees associated with criminal networks such as the mafia) with the local ombudsperson for the rights of detainees follow the same norms that apply to other inmates with their families. The special legislation that guarantee the confidentiality of the visit for the National Ombudsman for the rights of persons detained or deprived of their liberty – in other words, national prevention mechanisms against torture - are not applied to Guarantors established at a local level by regional laws or local administration. These visits are therefore subject to authorisation of the prison institute management, and with monitoring of the conversation and take place through a glass separator. They do not, however, count in the total number of visits that the prisoner can have (Court of Cassation, Criminal Division, sec. I, judgments 27 June 2018, No. 46169; 11 July 2018, No. 53006; 7 December 2018, No. 11585).

According to the Constitutional Court, the explict ban on cooking food in cells for prisoners under the special prison regime of Article 41-*bis* of the penitentiary law is considered unconstitutional, as it is a measure that presents no function other than punitive, and limits the prisoner from expressing their personal freedom by carrying out everyday tasks (judgment 186/2018).

> According to the Court of Cassation, the constant videosurveillance, in low definition, of the detainee within the special regime of Article 41-*bis* of the penitentiary law does not constitute inhuman or degrading treatment. The cell is not a living place of the prisoner, but public place and the need for privacy of the detainee must be balanced with the need to guarantee public order, which must be defined on a case by case basis. The limit is constituted by inhuman and degrading treatment, which must be assessed while taking account of the distressing character of the imposed sentence (Court of Cassation, Criminal Division, sec. I, judg. 16 April 2018, No. 44972).

G. Extradition, European Arrest Warrant

The implementation of the arrest warrant issued by a judicial authorities of the EU based on the Council Framework Decision 2002/584/JHA of 13 June 2002, as established in Italy by law 69/2005 and successive amendments, is inhibited by the fact that the person affected by the provision is firmly rooted in Italy, having already, for example, brought their family there and established a work activity (Court of Cassation, Criminal division, sec. vacation, judg. 28 August 2018, No. 39240); furthermore, it requires "double punishment" for the crime, by the requesting country and the country to which the request is sent, but the case correspondence may not be precise when the crimes concern matters of taxation (Court of Cassation, Criminal Division, sec. III, judg. 1 March 2018, No. 10251); the Italian Court must always establish that detention conditions in the requesting State protectthe individual from the risk of inhuman or drgrading treatment: see. Court of Cassation, Criminal Division, sec. VI, judgments 11 January 2018, No. 931 (concerning the case of Bulgaria) and 21 February 2018, No. 8916 (concerning the case of Belgium, in which according to ECtHR case studies and reports from the CPT, there are serious conditions of suffering due to the state of unrest of the local prison police; although the same section recognised shortly afterwards that, in the light of the positive Council of Europe assessments on the Belgian prison system and clainming of the aforementioned state of unrest, verifying the prison situation is not necessary: Court of Cassation, Criminal Division, sec. VI, judg. 28 February 2018, No. 9391). In the case of a request from Romania, the fact that the punishment would be carried out in parole, and therefore the majority of it spent outside the prison institution, but in conditions that are not clearly specified on the arrest warrant or knowable to the Italian Court, the refusal to implement the arrest warrant is justified (Court of Cassation, Criminal Division, sec. VI, judg. 5 June 2018, No. 26383).

H. *Aggravating Factors for Racial, Ethnic and Religious Discrimination*

The Constitutional Court (judg. 59/2018) ruled on the appearance of impartiality, raised by the Court of Bergamo, concerning a procedure of aggravated defamation by a Senator of the Republic who, during a meeting in 2013, insulted a female minister calling her an "orangutan" (*"orango"*). When requested to comment on the authorisation to procede, pursuant to Article 68 of the Constitution, the Senate excluded the absolute immunity for what the Senator had said regarding the accusation of defamation, but maintained that the aggravating circumstances of acting to racially discriminate could not be ascribed to the Senator in question (these aggravating circumstances were established with l.d. 122/1993, converted in law 205/1993). The Court complains about the encroachment of their prerogative by the political body which would have unduly restricted the criminal charge.

The Constitutional Court, after recalling the principles confirmed by the Court itself and the ECtHR on protecting freedom of expression of members of parliamentary bodies, both within parliament and outside the halls, concluded that there was a conflict between State bodies. The Senate should have limited itself to establishing whether the opinions expressed by the Senator were related to his parliamentary function. It is for the judial body to establish if the opinions expressed are protected by Article 21 of the Constitution on the freedom of expression, which are applicable to all citizens, or if they could be considered a crime. The Senate intervened on the legal classification of the expressions used by the Senator, holding that the offensive phrases used were triable in one respect (concerning the crime of aggravated defamation), and not triable for another (as an expression of racial discrimination). In this way, the Senate encroached on the competencies of the judicial authorities. Furthermore, it seems clear to the Court that there was no connection between the insulting remarks of the Senator and his parliamentary activities on irregular immigration, with the consequence that the exonerating provision for the protection of members of Parliament cannot be recognised. In conclusion, the Senate's deliberation recognising the "selective" immunity of the Senator has been annulled.

The aggravating factor of acting to racially discriminately, established by law 205/1993, is present when expressions are used to discriminate against the victim for religious or ethnic reasons and can focus on wording that recalls a prejudice on the inferiority of a certain race, or can focus on behaviour that, in specific contexts, appears to intentionally aimed to arouse ethnical hatred in others and is perceivable as such, creating a real risk of promoting discriminatory behaviours, both immediately or in the future (Court of Cassation, Criminal Division, sec. V, judgments 23 March 2018, No. 32028 – in this case, the perpertrators had beaten up some immigrants, while accompanying their actions with phrases such as "what did you come here to do…you should leave" (*"che venite a fare qua…dovete andare via"*) (14 February 2018, No. 14200).

It should be noted that the abrogation of the crime of insulting behaviour, established by lgs.d. 15 January 2016, No. 7, Article 1, implies that not only must the defendent be acquitted of the offence, even when the conduct was aggravated by the purpose of discrimination and racial hatred, but also that any decision concerning compensation for non-material damage to the victim must be revoked. The person who is the victim of the decriminalized conduct and referred to a civil offense will therefore have to start a civil procedure for compensation for damages (Court of Cassation, Criminal Division, sec. V, judg. 18 January 2019, No. 2461).

I. Measures of Personal Prevention

Further to the *de Tommaso* judgment of the ECtHR (see *Yearbook 2018*, p. 321), the Court of Cassation reiterated the princple that, for the application of prevention measures concerning individuals suspected of belonging to Mafia-type organisations, it is necessary to assesss the ongoing "dangerousness" of the individual. Regarding the relationship between the individual and the criminal organisation, according to the Court, the concept of "belonging" to, which is less intense than "participating in", takes the form of (sometimes isolated) actions that are functional to the aims of the group, excluding situations of proximity to the criminal group (Court of Cassation, joint sections, judg. 4 January 2018, No. 111). The *de Tommaso* judgment also criticised the vague and indeterminate nature used to characterise the offence against the accused, particularly the ban on participating in "public meetings". Some judgments of the Court of Cassation Criminal Division identified two different approaches to the issue. The first identified the possibility to interpret the reference as any meeting, even informal, that put the individual in contact with members of criminal organisations, including the meeting of the municipal council held to celebrate a distinguished citizen (even if this was then cancelled due to the absence of a quorum: see Court of Cassation, Criminal Division, sec. I, judg. 19 June 2018, No. 28261). The second approach required the "public meetings" to be categorised. In this way, the Court of Cassation, Criminal Division, sec. I, judg. 30 October 2018, No. 49731 judgment held that this did not constitute a violation of the special prevention regime, which included a ban on participating in "public meetings" and in electoral meetings. Similarly, Court of Cassation, Criminal Division, sec. I, judg. 10 July 2018, No. 31322, holding that it was legal for the accused to go to the stadium, the judges also ask that the joint divisions rule on this point.

Italy in the Case-law of the European Court of Human Rights

I. Ban on Torture, Inhuman and Degrading Treatment, Right to Liberty, Right to Life

With the judgment *V.C.* (No. 54227/14) of 1 February 2018, the European Court of Human Rights (ECtHR) ruled in merit of the situation of vulnerability of the applicant, who was a minor at the time of the facts, and had been left to wait for the authorities to adopt concrete measures to protect her.

> The applicant had been arrested during a party where there were drugs and alcohol. Following this incident, proceedings before the Youth Court were instituted, in which the girl was placed in a specialist care institution, with a view to rehabilitation treatment, having been evaluated as anti-social and drug-dependent. Between the first contact with the Court, on 23 April 2013, and 14 April 2014, the applicant was a victim of sexual exploitation and rape. The criminal proceedings concerning the sexual exploitation and rape of the applicant, which concluded in 2016 and 2015 respectively, are not subject to the ECtHR decision. The applicant alleged that, during this period, despite the fact that she had been the victim of a prostitution ring, the Italian authorities, particularly the Youth Court and the competent social services, had not taken all the necessary measures to protect her. According to the applicant, even though the risk of sexual assault, and therefore the certain and immediate risk to her life, had been foreseeable, the Italian authorities had not acted with the requisite diligence and had not taken account of the risks that she faced. It concluded that they did not take, in a timely manner, all reasonable measures to prevent the abuse.

The ECtHR concluded that the applicant falls into the category of "vulnerable individuals" (*Khlaifia and others v. Italy*, No. 16483/12 – see *Yearbook 2016*, p. 255) ("persons in vulnerable situations") who are entitled to State protection. The judge takes note that in the period in which she should have been protected, the minor was subjected to abuse as the victim of sexual exploitation and rape. The ECtHR further observes that the abuse to which the applicant was subjected, and which took the form of physical assaults and psychological duress, was sufficiently serious to attain the degree of severity necessary to bring it within the scope of Article 3 of the Convention, and interfering with her right to respect for her physical and moral integrity, it is also considered as a violation of her right to private life (Article 8 ECHR).

From the moment in which her parents had informed the authorities of the mental and physical condition of the minor and the consequential risks, the national authorities were aware of the vulnerable situation of the applicant and of the real and immediate risk that she faced. Despite the fact that the authorities immediately instituted a criminal investigation, no measures were put in place to protect the applicant, who was aged 15 at the time. Therefore, the ECtHR unanimously held that there had been a violation of Articles 3 and 8 of the ECHR, and condemned the State to pay the costs and expenses of the applicant and compensation for non-material damage.

> On 16 January, the ECtHR decided to strike out the *M.K.* case (No. 31031/16) of the list. The Italian authorities had already annuled the decree of explusion from Italy, with the consequent repatriation in Russia, which according to the applicant, would have exposed him to the danger of being subjected to treatment contrary to Article 3 ECHR. The applicant complained that, while the criminal investigation of the Russian authorities had been concluded with, excluding his responsibility in a bombing in 2008 near a mosque in Cechnia, the militants close to the Chechen president were still convinced of his guilt and had threatened him with death.

In the case of *Provenzano* (No. 55080/13), the ECtHR, with the judgment of 25 October 2018, considered the compatibility of the special prison regime foreseen by section 41-*bis* of the Prison Administration Act given his age and health conditions.

> The applicant, Bernardo Provenzano, who had been a fugitive on the run from the authorities for over forty years, was arrested on 11 April 2006 and after several sets of criminal proceedings, was sentenced to life sentences in solitary confinement pursuant to Article 41-*bis* for a series of crimes, including: membership of a mafia-type criminal organisation, mass murder *(strage)*, multiple homicide, aggravated attempted homicide, drug trafficking, kidnapping, criminal coercion, aggravated theft, and the illegal possession of firearms.
>
> During his incarceration period, the applicant was admitted a number of times to various hospitals. On 9 April 2014 he was admitted to the

correctional wing of San Paolo Hospital in Milan, where he was hospitalised until his death.

The applicant suffered from a number of chronic medical conditions (including Parkinson's disease, vascular encephalopathy, hepatopathy linked to HCV and arterial hypertension) which was also characterised by a decline in his physical and cognitive functioning. His lawyers lodged applications with different courts responsible for the execution of sentences, seeking the suspension of his prison sentence for medical reasons, especially the regime of solitary confinement regulated by Article 41-*bis*, for medical reasons under Articles 146 and 147 of the Criminal Code and the replacement of his detention with more lenient custodial methods. Each application was rejected by various Courts, though reiterating the deterioration decline of the health of the applicant. It underlined that all necessary treatment could be provided administered in the correctional facility, including frequent medical examinations and diagnostic tests, and if necessary, with admission in a civilian hospital. The Courts also considered that, given that the applicant was a "socially dangerous" person, the special prison regime should not be suspended. Notwithstanding the applicant's proven cognitive deficit, the Court could not exclude his – albeit fluctuating and diminished – ability to comprehend and communicate with other mafia contacts.

On this foundation of the principles developed by the ECtHR on a case to case basis, according to which a person must be detained in conditions which are compatible with respect for human dignity that the manner and method of the execution of the measure of deprivation of liberty do not subject him to distress or hardship of an intensity exceeding the unavoidable level of suffering inherent in detention, guaranteeing that the health and well-being of the detainee are adequately secured, the lawyers of Provenzano brought the case before the ECtHR.

Regarding the adequacy of treatment, the ECtHR reiterated that the health of the applicant was monitored by medical and nursing staff and his medical assistance was adequate, as demonstrated by his last admission into the civilian hospital, albeit in a correctional wing. On this point, the ECtHR found that there had been no violation of Article 3 of ECHR: the applicant's detention per se could not be considered incompatible with his health conditions and advanced age, or that, given the practical demands of imprisonment, his health and well-being were not adequately protected.

Concerning the continued application of the special prison regime, despite the applicant's age and illness, above all the ECtHR noted that, as it has already had ample opportunity to assess in previous cases, the imposition of the regime provided for in section 41-*bis* does not give rise to an issue under Article 3 ECHR, even when it has been imposed for lengthy periods of time (see cases *Enea, Argenti, Campisi, Paolello*; see also *Yearbook 2016*, p. 257). The ECtHR questioned whether the restrictions provided for in section 41-*bis*, in the light of the specific circomstances of the case, could be said to raise an issue under Article 3 ECHR, focusing on whether renewing or extending these restrictions could have been justified.

If, as recognised by the ECtHR, the nature of the special measures provided for in section 41-*bis* constitute a preventive and security measure – thus serving no punitive purpose - whose primary aim is to prevent the detainees (who, in this case, was the boss of one of the biggest criminal organisations) from maintaining contact with members of their criminal network, the State authorities must carry out periodic assessments of the continued danger of the detainee, to avoid the risk of abuse or arbitrariness. According to the ECtHR, this reassessment was correctly carried out in 2014 by the Rome Court; however, the Minister of Justice's renewal order in 2016 (a few months prior to Provenzano's death) was not carried out so correctly; the Court considers that the applicant's further cognitive deterioration should have been taken into account. The ECtHR therefore concluded the there is not suffient evidence demonstrating that the extended application of the section 41-*bis* in 2016 was justified, and therefore unanimously holds that there was a violation of Article 3 ECHR on account of the renewed application. The finding of a violation is sufficient to compensate for the non-pecuniary damage sustained.

II. Fair Trial, Right to Private Property

The *Cipolletta* case (application No. 38259/09, judgment of 11 January 2018), concerns the procedure of administrative liquidation of a cooperative housing company, with a judgment of 30 April 1985 by Macerata District Court. During this procedure, the applicant complained that his claims as a creditor had not been recognised, and consequently had asked the liquidator managing the administrative liquidation procedure to admit his list of claims subject to the verification of the insolent company's debts. The applicant complains about the unreasonable duration of the procedure, which began in 1985 and had not been resolved after 20 years. The Pinto remedy (law 89/2001) could not be accessed by the applicant since it was limited to the mere challenging of the insolvency declaration or opposition to the list of claims, thus excluding the administrative proceedings conducted by the liquidator, with no remedy to which Article 6 ECHR is applicable. The ECtHR therefore found that the creditor's application for admission to the list of claims constituted a genuine and serious dispute as to a civil right and therefore should be applied the guarantees within Article 6 ECHR.

To evaluate the reasonable duration of procedures, many criteria laid down by ECtHR case-law must be considered, including: the complexity of the case, the behaviour of the applicant and of the competent authorities, as well as what is at stake in the dispute for the applicants (*Cocchiarella v. Italy*, judgment of the Grand Chamber, 2006). In this specific case, the procedure began in 1985, when the applicant presented the liquidator with the list of claims, and the administrative proceedings for the assets of the debtor company were still ongoing in 2010. Therefore, while recognising the complexity of the procedure, the ECtHR decided that the disputed duration was excessive and did not meet the "reasonable time" requirement. The ECtHR therefore ruled, with six votes to one, that it was a violation of Article 6 ECHR. Regarding the applicant's lack of remedy available under the Pinto Act, the ECtHR found, with six votes to one, a further violation of Article 13 ECHR by Italy.

> In the *L.M.* case, which joined six other complaints (Nos. 30290/15; 30346/15; 30324/15; 30355/15; 30448/15; 14824/16; 50830/16) the applicants had contracted various viruses (HIV, Hepatitis B or Hepatitis C) following blood transfusions or surgical interventions that took place in national health service structures. The applicants had presented their complaint of the violation of Articles 2, 6, 8 and 13 ECHR and Article 1 Protocollo No. 1 before the Court, due to the introduction of new criteria that prevented them from reaching a friendly agreement at a national level of their cases, and for the excessive duration of the procedures to receive compensation. They also complained about the rejection of their claims for compensation. On 16 January 2018, the ECtHR struck the complaints from the list, since the applicants had accepted and, in some cases, already received compensation from the State, by way of just satisfaction.
>
> In the *Vito Rizzello* case, which combines eight complaints (Nos. 17799/10; 27923/10; 67551/10; 18230/11; 37764/11; 47181/11; 65762/13; 11409/14; 26949/14), the applicants alleged a violation of Article 6 ECHR on the grounds that the introduction of an interpretative norm with retroactive effect was contrary to the principle of a fair trial. The norm in question was introduced through the financial act of 2007 (law 296/2006) regarding the calculation of pensions, which would damage Italian citizens

who had already reached a certain pension level after working in Switzerland. The Italian Government recognised the existence of the violation of Article 6 in the cases reported, in light of ECtHR case-law (see *Yearbook 2013*, p. 320-321), and therefore decided to award each applicant a sum by way of compensation for material and non-material damages. For this reason, on 20 February 2018, the ECtHR decided to strike these complaints from the list pursuant to Article 37 ECHR.

On 16 January 20018, the *Concetta Cacciato and Michele Cacciato* (No. 60633/16) and *Alessandro Guiso and Vincenza Consiglio* (n. 50821/06) cases were declared unadmissable by the ECtHR in accordance with Article 35 ECHR, given the dispute of the alleged violation of Article 1 Protocol No. 1 by the Italian authorities through the imposition of tax on expropriation compensation to the applicants was unanimously declared unfounded.

With the judgment of 22 February 2018, the ECtHR ruled for the second time on the *Drassich* case (No. 65173/09).

The case concerns an Italian judge, sentenced for three years for corruption pursuant to Article 319 of the Criminal Code (forgery and abuse of office) by the Tribunal of Venice. This sentence was then raised to three years eight months on 12 June 2002 by the Venice Court of Appeal. In the Court of Cassation, the count of corruption was transformed into corruption in relation to judicial acts. The applicant presented a complaint before the ECtHR against this final decision, claiming a violation of Article 6 ECHR. According to the applicant, the Court of Cassation had not fully informed him on the nature and reason of the new drafting of the accusation, denying him the time necessary to prepare his defence and not allowing him the possibility to argue against the new accusation. If the material element of the two definitions of corruption is the same, i.e. carrying out actions contrary to the duties of a public official to obtain benefits, the subject elect is different: in the case of corruption in relation to judicial acts, specific intent is required. It was therefore plausible to claim that the measures chosen to defend himself would have been different than those used to challenge a previous accusation. The ECtHR, with the judgment of 11 December 2007, found a violation of Article 6 ECHR and, even if it is outside the scope of the ECtHR to indicate the way and methods in which a State must fulfil its obligation to comply with its decisions, in this case it identified the reopening of procedures in the Court of Cassation or the opening of a new procedure the best way to remedy the offence.

As established by the Committee of Ministers in Recommendation No. R (2000) 2, and in line with the practice of the Committee of Ministers in supervising the execution of the Court's judgments shows that in exceptional circumstances the re-examination of a case or a reopening of proceedings has proved the most efficient, if not the only, means of achieving *restitutio in integrum*, that is to say that where possible, ensuring that the injured party is put, as far as possible, in the same situation as he or she enjoyed prior to the violation of the ECHR.

On 25 May 2009, the Court of Cassation declared a new judgment, in which it once again condemned the applicant for corruption in relation to judicial acts. In this last case, the applicant also complained of a new violation of Article 6 ECHR. According to the applicant, the Court of Cassation again had not adequately informed him of the legal re-characterisation of the facts *in pejus*, nor had the Court informed him of their intention to handle the merits of the case directly rather than referring it to the Court of Appeal. In addition, the applicant complains about the denial of his request to participate personally in the trial by the Court of Cassation.

The ECtHR recalls that to rule on the fairness of the proceedings, the latter must be considered as a whole. Clearly the notification of the charge, as underlined by the ECtHR, has a fundamental meaning as it constitutes the act through which the person is officially informed not only of the facts but also of the legal classification of the charges against them. This constitutes a fundamental condition of the fairness of the proceedings. The Court acknowledges, however, that the provisions of Article 6(3) do not impose any requirement on the way in which the accused must be informed of the reason and nature of the charge against them.

From the moment in which the proceedings in discussion were reopened before the Court of Cassation to comply with the sentence of the ECtHR, according to the ECtHR, it is clear that the applicant knew of the legal re-characterisation of the facts as corruption in relation to judicial acts. Furthermore, according to the Court, in the five months after the partial revocation of the sentence and the reopening of the case, the accused was able to file two written pleadings before the Court of Cassation, and the defendant's lawyer orally discussed the case at the hearing on 25 May 2009. Under these conditions, the ECtHR does not see why the case should have been deferred before a trial judge. The re-examination concerned only legal reasons and not factual ones. Even the denied possibility to appear in person before the Court does not seem to violated the requirements of Article 6 ECHR. Keeping in mind the aforementioned reasons, the ECtHR unanimously considers that the rights of the applicant to be informed in detail of the nature and reason of the charges brought against and to have the time and facilities necessary to prepare his defense have not been violated.

The *Anna Maria Cristaldi* case (No. 29923/13) was unanimously declared inadmissible by the ECtHR on 22 May 2018 as manifestly unfounded. According to the Court, the fact that the applicant, a magistrate, did not receive the special judicial allowance (a part of the fees due to magistrates which is linked to the performing of judicial functions) during absence from work due to compulsory maternity leave, is not a form of indirect discrimination that affects only female magistrates. The allowance is given to all magistrates, men and women, in relation to the actual exercise of certain judicial functions. The fact that a female magistrate on maternity leave (who receives all other components of the wage during the compulsory period of absence from the service) cannot access this allowance does not constitute gender discrimination.

The ECtHR ruled on 5 July 2018 on the case of *Centro Demarzio S.R.L.* (No.24/11). The applicant is a company which manages a physical therapy and diagnostic radiology centre operating from 1991 in association with the national health service. Following the departure of one of the company's founding members, with resolution No. 383 of 8 April 1993, the health administration revoked the association. In 1996, the Apulia Regional Administrative Court annulled that decision, given that the departure of the partner who was originally responsible for the association with the national health service did not constitute a reason to revoke the association in se. Therefore, with Resolution No. 1143 of 28 June 1997, the health administration re-established the association with the applicant company coming to effect from 1 August 1997. On 23 November 1998, however, the applicant company asked for compensation for economic losses incurred due to the suspension of the association from 1993 to 1997. With the judgment of 22 February 2006, the Regional Administrative Court dismissed the complaint, holding that the illegitimate act was adopted after an "excusable error" by the administration. The company finally appealed to the ECtHR, arguing that the act by the Apulia Region, later aknowledged as illegitimate, constituted an interference with the right to respect for own's property, guaranteed by Article 1 Protocol No. 1 ECHR, from which there derived a substantial economic loss that is, however, not reparable given the decision of the Regional Administrative Court.

According to ECtHR caselaw, the concept of property does not only include existing property, but also credit on which an individual has a legimate expectation of seeing honoured. In this particular case, the ECtHR held that the State had interfered with the expectation of the company which is incompatible with the right to property, without any compensation; the excusable character of the health administration's error does not justify the interference in question. The Court unanimously orders Italy to pay 394,000€ for moral and material damages incurred by the applicant company.

In the *Therapic Center S.R.L.* case (No.39186/11), which united other nine complaints, the ECtHR with the judgment of 4 October 2018 ruled on the reasonable waiting period for the application of a cease and desist order of the Court.

> The applicants had obtained injunctions from the Court of Naples against a Local Health Authority for 2009 and 2010. However, the financial laws adopted in the successive years (laws 191/2009, 220/2010, 111/2011 and 189/ 2012) had introduced provisions (declared unconstitutional by judgment No. 186 of 12 July 2013 of the Constitutional Court) the effect of which was to prevent any legal action aimed at obtaining debt payments by the Local Health Authority. The Local Health Authority completely (complaint No. 39189/11, 39190/11 and 39194/11) or partially (complaint No. 39186/11, 39187/11, 39192/11, 39193/11, 39196/11, 39197/11, 39198/11) paid the debts contracted with the applicant companies after many years. With the recourse before the ECtHR, the companies therefore complain about the delay with which the Local Health Authority complied with the injunctions issued by the Court of Naples.

The ECtHR recalls having established that the principle of the right to recourse before a court would not effectively exist if the State legal system then allowed a final and binding judicial decision to remain inoperative. Regardless of the complexity of its implemetation procedures or administrative system, in view of the ECHR, the State must guarantee that the judgments are carried out within a reasonable time for the benefit of the right holder. The reasonable character of the implementation time must be assessed particularly taking into account the complexity of the necessary procedures, the conduct of the parties and competent authorities, as well as the amount and nature of the object of implementation. According to ECtHR caselaw, where executing a judicial act does not impose particular issues, given it is a simple transfer of money, a delay of one year and two months violates the applicant's right to court; whereas a waiting period of six months is not unreasonable. In this case, the ECtHR observes that the delays with which the Local Health Authority paid the applicant companies in cases No.39189/11, 39190/11 and 39194/11 are much longer than one year and two months; concerning other complaints, the Local Health

Authority still has not fully paid its debts more than seven years after the Court's injunctions were lodged. Furthermore, considering that the Government did not give any justification for the Local Health Authority inaction, according to the ECtHR, it is not necessary to try to establish whether proper balance between the general interest of the community and safeguarding individual rights has been maintained. Therefore, the ECtHR finds a violation of Article 6 ECHR and orders Italy to pay the expenses and material damage incurred by the applicants.

A similar issue came up in the *Casa di Cura Valle Fiorita S.R.L.* case (No.67944/13). The ECtHR, with a judgment of 13 December 2018, ruled on the failure to execute a final sentence on the eviction of an occupied building.

> The applicant is a limited liability company that owned a building which, from 1971 to 2011, was used as a clinic. From 2011, When the business terminated its activities, the building remained unused. From 6 December 2012, it was occupied by around one hundred people who entered the property by force. The same day as the occupation, the company filed a complaint with the public prosecutor's office, reporting a violation of their right to property and requesting the eviction of the people from the building. On 9 August 2013, the judge for the preliminary investigation of Rome arranged the preventative seizure of the property, assuming the illegal occupation of the building (Article 633 of the Criminal Code). From the investigations, it emerged that, upon entering, the occupants had immediately installed gates to stop others getting in. The situation had also caused serious damage to the building and constituted significant economic damage to the property. Despite the many initiative undertaken by the applicant company and the numerous requests to the public authorities, the eviction was never carried out.

ECtHR caselaw acknowledges the right to execute a judicial decision as one of aspects of the right of access to justice, an essential element of the rule of law. The implemetation phase of a judgment, regardless of what the judge ruled, must be considered an integral part of the "procedure" pursuant to Article 6 ECHR. The ECtHR therefore consider whether the measures adopted by the Italian authorities were appropriate and sufficient to ensure compliance with its positive obligations. In this case, the Court above all observes that the decision of the judge for preliminary investigations of Rome of 9 August 2013 concerned the protection of the right to property of the applicant, and that the seizure decision was urgent in order to preserve the integrity of the property. The ECtHR notes that not only was that decision not carried out, but there was no attempt at implementing it. The Government gave reasons as public and social order, although this does not justify the complete and prolonged inactivity of the Italian Authorities. The inactivity is also not justifiable for reasons of lack of resources or alternative accommodation for the occupants of the building. In this specific case, the national authorities deprived the provisions of Article 6 ECHR of any useful effect. The Court concludes therefore that there was a violation of Article 6 ECHR and of Article 1 Protocol No. 1.

III. Retroactive Laws with Effects on Ongoing Procedures concerning Property

The ECtHR ruled with the judgment of 5 July 2018 on the *Castello del Poggio S.S. and others* case (No. 30015/09, 34644/09, 10723/10). Since the 1980s, Italian agricultural companies, among which the applicants, have enjoyed a double benefit, represented by financial transfers and reductions in social security contributions for their employees. In July 1988, the National Social Security Institution (INPS) published a circular according to which the benefits and reductions were not accumulative but alternative. On different dates, the applicant companies filed actions against INPS, disputing the application of the circular. The applicants won the case at first instance, and INPS appealed the decision. In November 2003, while the actions brought by the appellants were still pending before Court of Appeal, the Italian legislator adopted law No. 326/2003, which expressly provided for the alternation between benefits and reductions, with the effect of determining the conclusion of the ongoing proceedings in favour of the State.

The ECtHR confirmed the position it has already delivered in a series of previous sentences in law and reason, including the *Azienda Agricola Silverfunghi S.a.s. and others v. Italy* case (Nos. 48357/07, 52677/07, 52687/07 and 52701/07, of 24 June 2014; see *Yearbook 2015*, p. 243). In this judgment, the ECtHR had held that the use of retroactive legislation that had the effect of determining ongoing procedures in favour of the State is incompatible with Article 6 ECHR. Such use of legislative power does in fact supplant the function of the judiciary and violates the right to a fair trial.

On this specific issue, Italian law, up to the 2003 legislative amendments, had consistently considered the two benefits to be cumulative based both on the literal meaning of the applicable ruled (considered unequivocal) and on the rationale of the two benefits, which had different functions and operated at different levels. The rationale of the "interpretative" legislation appears to be to remove any obligation to cumulatively provide the envisaged subsidies from the State. The ECtHR caselaw had already critised the practice of introducing interpretative laws with retroactive effect on economic issues on various occasions to guarantee more income for the Treasury (*Maggio and others v. Italy*; *Agrati and others v. Italy*; *Arras and others v. Italy*; *De Rosa v. Italy* – see also *Yearbook 2012*, p. 345-348; *Yearbook 2013*, p. 367-369; *Yearbook 2014*, p. 325-326). Given the lack of new arguments by the Italian Government, the ECtHR decided to follow its own case-law in this particular case, acknowledging a violation of Article 6 ECHR.

In the *Staibano and others* (No. 29907/07) and *Mottola* (No. 29932/07) cases, the ECtHR, with the judgment of 6 September 2018, ruled once again on the case of the so-called "coin-operated doctors". The ECtHR had already found the violation of Articles 6 and 1 of Protocol No. 1 of the ECHR in these cases with two judgments of 4 February 2014 (see *Yearbook 2015*, p. 317-322; *Yearbook 2016*, p. 215). From 1983 to 1997, the University of Naples general hospital hired a certain number of doctors with temporary contracts, before passing them over to permanent contracts. Starting from a certain date, on the basis of a law which reformed the distribution of responsibilities between ordinary courts and Regional Administrative Courts, some public civil servants, including the doctors hired at the University of Naples general hospital, found themselves deprived of the possibility of asserting their right to retirement benefits accrued during the period of permanent employment. Due to this, the Italian State prevented the effective execution of the judgments of the ECtHR. This latter sentenced Italy to pay compensation for moral and material damages of over 500,000 euros. In this regard, see also the judgment of the Constitutional Court 6/2018 – see this Part, Human Rights in Italian Case-law, I, A).

IV. Nulla poena sine lege: confiscation of land and buildings

In the *G.I.E.M. S.R.L. and others* cases (Nos. 1828/06, 34163/07, 19029/11), the ECtHR with the judgment of 28 June 2018, ruled on the confiscation of goods of abusive lotting in the absence of a criminal conviction and therefore potentially contrary to Article 7 of the ECHR.

At the end of its assessment of the case, the ECtHR first of all had to check whether confiscation, as regulated in Italian law, qualified as a "penalty" pursuant to Article 7 of the ECHR.

ECtHR caselaw identified a series of aspects that characterise a measure as a "penalty", according to the ECHR. It is therefore necessary to consider "whether it was imposed following conviction for a criminal offence, the nature and purpose of the measure in question, its characterisation under national law, the procedures involved in the making and implementation of the penalty and its severity". The fact that the confiscation was applied following a conviction qualified as a crime by domestic law is just one of several elements to be taken into consideration. In other words, the ECtHR, aims to prevent States from imposing substantially criminal measures without complying with the guarantees provided for by Article 7 ECHR, by means of not defining it as a "penalty".

If confiscation is ordered independently of a criminal conviction, the first aspect to assess this measure as a "penalty" is not fulfilled, although the other aforementioned criteria can be taken into account. Concerning this assessment within Italian law, "confiscation in matters of site development", in these cases, is governed by Article 44 of the Construction Code, which bears the heading "Criminal sanctions". With respect to the nature and purpose of the confiscation, the Grand Chamber confirms the conclusions of the Chamber in judgments *Sud Fondi S.r.l. and others* and *Varvara* cases (see *Yearbook 2014*, p. 325), according to which the confiscation for abusive lotting suffered by the applicants had a punitive nature and purpose against those responsible for the illegal transformation of the land. This measure is particularly harsh and intrusive, as it applies not only to the land that is built on, but also to all the other plots of land making up the site. As regards the procedures for the adoption and enforcement of a confiscation measure, the Court observes that it is ordered by the criminal courts. For all these reasons, the ECtHR concludes that the impugned confiscation measures can be regarded as "penalties" within the meaning of Article 7 ECHR. However, since in none of the cases examined were there any formal convictions that proved the existence of a crime, ECtHR ruled, with 15 votes to two (and in one case with 10 against 7), that the confiscation in matters of site development suffered by the applicants is incompatible with Article 7 ECHR.

The ECtHR also unanimously found that the measure violated Article 1 of Protocol No. 1 which requires for any interference of the right to peaceful enjoyment of the property to have a reasonable relationship of proportionality between the means employed and the aim sought to be realised. In these specific cases, the fact that less restrictive measures were not taken into consideration and the extent of the land confiscated, which also affected areas belonging to third parties, eliminated the correct relationship between the means employed and the aim sought to be realised. In the case of one applicant, for which the Court of Cassation had ordered an acquittal, while maintaining that criminal responsibility for the abusive buildings had been proven, the ECtHR, with 16 votes to one, also found that the violation by Italy of Article 6(2) ECHR, given that the judgment of Supreme Court had closed proceedings without referring them to a territorial judge had violated the principle of the presumption of innocence.

In the *Silvio Berlusconi* case (No. 58428/13) the applicant complained of a violation of Article 7 ECHR and 3 of Protocol No. 1 and 13 ECHR by the lgs.d. 235/2012 (Single Text for the provisions for the ineligibility and disqualification from standing for election or serving in elective roles following a final judgment for intentional crimes) breaching the principles of lawfulness, foreseeability, proportionality and non-retroactive application of criminal penalties. The decree in question was adopted as part of a National anti-corruption plan which had become essential, firstly in view of the conclusions of the evaluation conducted in 2008 and 2009 by the Group of States against Corruption (GRECO), and secondly because of the finding that most European States already had such a plan. Article 1 of the decree provides that anyone who has been sentenced in a final judgment to more than two years' imprisonment for an offence committed with malicious intent carrying a maximum sentence of at least four years' imprisonment is disqualified from standing for election or serving as a member of the Senate or the Chamber of Deputies. Pursuant to Article 3, where the ground for such disqualification arises or is established during the senator's or deputy's term of office, the house of Parliament to which he or she belongs must deliberate on the matter in accordance with Article 66 of the Constitution. The applicant, following the Senate election of 24 February 2013, was elected to the role of senator. On 1 August 2013, the Court of Cassation definitively confirmed Berlusconi's sentence him to four years' imprisonment of tax fraud in the context of the "Mediaset Trial". On 27 November 2013, the Senate invalidated the applicant's election. Berlusconi therefore decided to bring the complaint before the ECtHR.

On 8 March 2018, the Milan Sentence Supervision Court received the application for rehabilitation lodged by the applicant. On 27 July 2018, the applicant informed the ECtHR that he no longer intended to pursue his application, since as a result of his rehabilitation, the Court's decision on his application would serve no useful purpose given that his disqualification from standing for election had been lifted. The Grand Chamber received the application and struck the application out of its list of cases with a communication on 27 November 2018.

V. Private and Family Life

The *D'Acunto and Pignataro* case (No. 6360/13), on which the ECtHR ruled with a judgment on 12 July 2018, concerns the compatibility of measures adopted in Italy to foster the two children of one of the two applicants and the rights laid out by the ECHR.

> The fostering of two underage children of the first applicant at a family home was considered necessary given the unhealthiness of the family home and the mother's non-compliance with the remediation order for the condition of the premises. An evaluation had furthermore concluded that the first applicant, considered a "borderline" personality, was not able to care for the children. The fostering or custody of the grandmother (second applicant) was excluded due to the conflictual relationship between the latter and the first applicant. Visiting rights of the applicants had also been limited for the children, in order to preserve the well-being of the children.

The ECtHR acknowledges that in these kinds of cases, the Courts often address interests that are difficult to reconcile; it emphasises, however, that in the attempt to find a balance between these two aspects, the best interest of the child must always be a fundamental consideration. In this case, according to the ECtHR, the judicial authorities decided on foster care in a family home and family visiting restrictions on the basis of sufficient and adequate proof (including testimonials, expert reports and medical notes). The ECtHR further observes that although the diagnosis of a "borderline" personality does not require to be constantly reviewed (since it is impossible to evaluate its short term evolution), it is however the authorities' duty to request an update of the evaluation, to verify the ongoing existence of the aspects underlying the decision (see, for example, *Cincimino v. Italy*, Yearbook 2017, p. 247-8; *Improta v. Italy*, Yearbook 2018, p. 318). In this case, on deciding on the suspension of parental authority on 9 November 2012, the Court based its decision on the evaluation of 19 May 2010, furthermore partially disputed by an expert witness. According to the ECtHR, by not requesting a new evaluation, the Court was not able to take account of the evolution of the situation. The ECtHR therefore unanimously concluded that the Italian authorities had not respected the positive duties deriving from Article 8 ECHR. Considering the alleged violation of Article 3 ECHR, the Court holds that the applicants' arguments are insufficiently proven.

With judgment 27 September 2018, in the *Brazzi* case (No. 57278/11), the ECtHR ruled on the compatibility of the decision to search the home of the applicant with the rights recognised in the ECHR.

The applicant was born in Italy, and was habitually resident in Germany. Since 2009, he has been listed on the register of Italians resident abroad and owns a house in Italy. Suspecting him of tax evasion, on 13 July 2010, the Mantua public prosecutor's office authorised the tax police to enter Mr Brazzi's house in Italy in order to gather evidence, however he was abroad. He did, however, make himself available to collaborate via telephone and, provided documents concerning his earnings via the German authorities. On 13 July 2010, the Mantua public prosecutor's office opened an investigation and issued a warrant for a search of his house and vehicles. The search took place in the presence of the applicant's father on 6 August 2010. No document was seized as a result. On the request of the applicant, the preliminary investigations judge of Mantua archived the case with decree 7 October 2010. In the meantime, the applicant appealed to the Court of Cassation, complaining about the illegality of the search on 13 July 2010, but his appeal was declared inadmissible by the Supreme Court on the basis of current legislation which does not provide for appeal for such measures. The applicant therefore brought the case before the ECtHR for a violation of the respect for private life.

The ECtHR held that the violation of a right has to reach a minimum severity threshold to be deemed admissible; the applicant has to therefore have a significant prejudiciality at once. Severity must be assessed according to both the individual perception of the applicant and the objective value of a specific case. In this case, even if there was an economic prejudiciality, as the search did not conclude with the seizure of any property, the complaint is sufficiently relevant as it touches upon a matter of principle related to the respect of the applicant's property and home and to the existence of an effective jurisdictional control over a search measure in Italian law. Article 8(2) ECHR imposes that this measure be legally provided, based on one or more legitimate objectives among those established by the same regulation and deemed necessary in a democratic society. There is no doubt that the search was juridically legitimate (Article 247 and successive articles of the Criminal Procedures Code). However, the principle of the rule of law imposes that adequate guarantees be available against abuse and arbitrarity. In this specific case, the search took place in a preliminary phase of the criminal procedure. National legislation does not foresee an *ex ante factum* jurisdictional control on the legality and necessity of this investigative measure. According to ECtHR, conversely, guarantees should exist, such as the possibility to establish *ex post facto* control of the de jure and de facto need and legitimacy of the measure and, in case of abuse, the possibility to receive adequate compensation. In this case, however, there was no prior-assessment of the legitimacy and necessity of the search mandate, therefore the applicant could not request adequate compensation, as Article 257 of the Criminal Procedures Code provides for this only when the search is followed by the seizure of property. According to the ECtHR. the unavailability of ex ante or ex post factum jurisdictional control leads to insufficient procedural guarantees against abuse or arbitrarity by the authorities. Consequently, the ECtHR held unanimously that the search was conducted by the competent authorities in violation of Article 8 ECHR.

In the *S. V.* case (No. 55216/08), the ECtHR ruled, with the judgment of 11 October 2018, on the name changing of a trans person.

> The applicant was registered as male at birth, and as a consequence, pursuant to Article 35 of d.p.r. 3 November 2000, the name given to her corresponded to the sex in the civil-status register. During her gender transition process, in November 2000, the applicant applied to the Rome District Court on the basis of section 3 of law No. 164/1982, stating that she wished to complete the transition process by permanently changing her primary sexual characteristics, and sought authorisation to undergo gender reassignment surgery. Having obtained authorisation, in May 2001, while awaiting the surgery authorised by the District Court, the applicant applied to the prefect of Rome for a change of forename under Article 89 of Presidential Decree No. 396/2000 to a female one. The applicant argued that in view of her physical appearance, the fact that her identity papers indicated a male forename was a constant source of humiliation and embarrassment. The prefect refused the applicant's request on the grounds that, under Presidential Decree no. 396/2000, a person's forename had to correspond to his or her gender. In the prefect's view, in the absence of a final court ruling ordering the change to her legal gender status for the purposes of law No. 164/1982, the applicant's forename could not be changed. Only in 2003, after the gender reassignment surgery, the Savona municipal authorities altered the indication of the applicant's gender and consequent change to the forename. The complaint before the ECtHR concerned the inability of the applicant to change her forename for the two and a half years before the surgical intervention to change her sexual characteristics.

Although the ECtHR has ruled on various occasions on the legal recognition of the gender identity of transgender persons and on the conditions of access to gender reassignment surgery, this is the first case in which the ECtHR has ruled on the situation that many transgender persons find themselves in, concerning the inability to obtain a change of forename prior completion of the gender transition process by means of reassignment surgery. According to the ECtHR, this case undoubtedly falls into the context of the application of Article 8 ECHR, in line with its own case-law regarding the choice or change of surname or forename of individuals. The Court observes that, when it comes to laying down the conditions required in order for individuals to obtain a change of name, the Contracting States enjoy a wide margin of appreciation, justified in the public interest to ensure accurate population registration or to safeguard the means of personal identification. The ECtHR emphasised the particular importance of matters relating to a most intimate part of an individual's life, namely the right to gender identity, a sphere in which the Contracting States have a narrow margin of appreciation. The ECtHR, therefore, without taking the place of the competent national authorities in determining the most appropriate policy on this argument, addressed whether Italy struck a fair balance between the general interest and the individual interest of the applicant in having a forename that matches her gender identity. In this case, according to the ECtHR, the Italian authorities did not adequately evaluate the specific situation of the applicant, who had clearly announced her intention to undergo gender reassignment surgery, had been undergoing a gender transition process for a number of years and that her physical appearance and social identity had long been female. The rejection of the request to change her name was based on purely formal arguments. The ECtHR notes that the rigid nature of the judicial procedure for recognising gender identity of transgender persons as applicable at the relevant time was not only contrary to Recommendation CM/Rec(2010)5, which urges States to make possible the change of name and gender in official documents in a quick, transparent and accessible way, but also placed the applicant for an unreasonable length of time in a situation of vulnerability, humiliation and anxiety. The ECtHR unanimously concluded that there had been a violation of Article 8 ECHR by Italy, given that the public authoritiy did not fulfil its positive duties to guarantee the right to respect for private life of the applicant.

> In the *Francesco Luca Costa Sanseverino Di Bisignano* case (No. 58330/16), the applicant complained about a violation of Article 8 ECHR due to the lack of diligence by the competent authorities in implementing his right to visiting his children in the custody of another person, in conditions established by the national judge from 2009. The Italian Government acknowledged the violation of the right to respect of family life of the applicant and will pay a sum of money as compensation for damages suffered and expenses. Therefore, on 15 May 2018, the ECtHR decided to strike the case from the list.

Italy in the Case-law of the Court of Justice of the European Union

I. Limitation to the Possibility of Appeal Decisions regarding International Protection

In case C-422 (FR against the Minister of the Interior – Internal Territorial Commission for the Recognition of International Protection at the Prefecture - Territorial Government Office of Milan), the judge requests the intervention of the CJEU about the compatitbility of some Italian laws relating to international protection with EU law. Those in question provide that decisions rejecting the application for international protection must take place after an examination by the collegial territorial commission, and that these decisions may be challenged before the Courts; the Court decision that rules on these appeals, under l.d. 17 February 2017, No. 13 (urgent provisions for accelerating the procedures regarding international protection, as well as for combating illegal immigration), converted into law, with amendments, by law 13 April 2017, No. 46, cannot be challenged before the Court of Appeal. If the application for international protection is rejected, and confermed before the Court, the possible appeal by cassation does not suspend the executive effectiveness of the rejection. According to Article 373 of the Civil Procedures Code, the judge ruling on the decision can, at the request of one party and where the sentence may cause "grave and irreparable damage", arrange an order from which no appeal shall lie that the implementation is suspended or provided appropriate security. This was the procedure that a Nigerian asylum seeker followed, who had given his homosexuality as motivation for his asylum application, which in his country of origin exposed him to grave risk of persecution and inhuman treatment. The Court of Milan, which was requested to suspend the implementation of the decision of refusal and the consequent expulsion, brings up the question of compatibility of Italian law with EU law, specifically with Directive 2013/32 (procedural directive), together with

Article 47 of the CFREU. The CJEU resolves the preliminary question by recalling a previous ruling (C-180/17), also decided in 2018, in which it concluded that no provision of EU law establishes the Member States must grant the right of appeal to asylum seekers whose first-instance appeal against the decision to reject their application has been rejected, nor that the latter is automatically accompanied by a suspension of its effects. The principle of effectiveness of judicial remedy is limited to first-instant procedures and does not extend to appeals. Other legal remedies, precautionary or in the Supreme Court, do not necesssarily have to involve a suspension of the implementation effects of the application for international protection. It concludes that the Italian legislation introduced in 2017 is compatible with EU law.

II. Gender Discrimination among Theatre Workers

In the joined cases C-142/17 and C-143/17, concluded on 7 February 2018, the Italian judge asked if the legislation introduced with l.d. 64/2010, which set the retirement age for workers in the performing arts sector, in the category for dancers, was 45 years old for men and women. It also introduced a transitional option of two years in which they could continue to work towards the pension limits of the previous legislation set at 47 years for women and 52 years for men, where compatible with Directive 2006/54 on non-discrimination between men and women.

The disputes in the main proceeding and the question referred for preliminary hearing took place between the Opera Theatre of Rome and some female dancers who, having reached the age of 45 or 47, were fired, while the same did not happen to their male counterparts.

The CJEU considers the legislation that lowers the pensionable age of dancers within the meaning of the provisions of Directive 2006/54 which prohibits discrimination in relation to dismissals and in general the termination of work. The Italian legislation introduces a difference of treatment directly based on grounds of the sex of the worker.

La CJEU sees no objective reason justifying differential treatment and therefore considers the Italian legislation a form of direct discrimination based on sex, incompatible with EU law.

III. Administrative and Penal Sanctions: Ban on ne bis in idem

With three decisions adopted on 20 March 2018 by the Grand Chamber in cases C-524/15, C-537/16 and in the joint cases C-596/16 and C-597/16, the CJEU reiterated the position it gave in case C-617/10, Fransson, 26 February 2013 (see *Yearbook* 2017, p. 250-251), which criticised Italian law for imposing a "double" sanction – both criminal and administrative – for certain conduct. The aforementioned judgments concern these sanctions, criminal and administrative procedings for market manipulation and insider trading (in these cases the administrative sanctions are imposed by the *National Commission* for Companies and the *Stock* Exchange (CONSOB)), as well as for failure to pay VAT due.

According to the CJEU, Italian legislation which provides for an administrative penalty and a criminal penalty for the same acts, is compatible with EU law only if it is limited to what is necessary for those proceedings and penalties, pursuing additional but complementary aspects of the same offence, ensuring that the severity of all of the penalties imposed is limited to what is strictly necessary in relation to the seriousness of the offence concerned. This evaluation is left to the assessment of the referring court. The "double" sanctions, therefore, are not imcompatible with EU law, but requires the Italian court to carefully assess the actual disadvantage resulting from the application of these sanctions on a case by case basis.

Index

A

Abruzzo, Region of: 42, 69, 70, 144, 146
Afghanistan: 174, 283
Albania: 49, 105, 113, 170, 173, 175, 203, 210, 211, 229, 230, 243, 246–248, 260, 283, 284, 310, 321
Algeria: 170, 203, 204, 211, 212, 221, 248
Andorra: 231, 249
Angola: 210
Antigua and Barbuda: 169, 172, 177
Apulia, Region of: 43, 68–70, 72, 144, 147, 191, 360
Argentina: 208, 210, 248, 332, 333
Armed conflicts: 29, 61, 65, 85, 86, 131, 132, 148, 149, 206, 281, 306, 308, 310
Armenia: 170, 176, 182, 243
Asylum, refugees – see Migrants, foreigners
Australia: 141, 172, 174, 175, 185, 210
Austria: 18, 174, 175, 180, 181, 185, 211, 246, 260, 271
Azerbaijan: 174, 186, 231, 249

B

Bahamas: 210
Bahrain: 209, 284
Balkans: 284
Bangladesh: 188, 208, 307
Basilicata, Region of: 43, 68, 71, 73, 144, 145, 147
Belarus: 107, 169, 179, 180, 209, 248, 257
Belgium: 170, 214, 237, 244, 350
Belize: 169, 172, 174, 209
Benin: 309
Bioethics, biomedicine: 24, 77, 82, 87, 95–97, 99, 104, 107, 128, 138, 215, 216
Bolivia: 172, 189
Bolzano, Autonomous Province of: 71, 144, 145, 147, 158
Bosnia and Herzegovina: 209, 243–245, 247, 278, 284
Brazil: 168, 170, 184, 216, 248
Bulgaria: 18, 179, 180, 209, 211, 231, 237, 244, 283
Burundi: 179, 180, 281

C

Calabria, Region of: 43, 68, 69, 71, 73, 125, 131, 144, 147, 191
Cambodia: 80, 95, 97, 98, 102
Cameroon: 95, 102

Campania, Region of: 42, 68, 69, 71, 147, 243, 314
Canada: 169, 183, 185, 209, 216, 248, 296
Cape Verde: 208
Central African Republic: 186, 208, 284
Children and adolescents: 18, 26–28, 31, 32, 36, 42, 65, 67, 69, 71, 77, 79, 80, 84, 85, 87, 88, 90–92, 96, 97, 99, 104–110, 112–115, 117–119, 121–124, 147, 149, 151, 155–158, 160–162, 169, 170, 172, 179, 180, 190, 191, 196, 198, 212, 219, 220, 222, 249, 250, 252–255, 259, 260, 267, 271, 288–290, 293, 295, 297–300, 311, 312, 314, 328–338, 348, 368
  Adoptions, foster care: 28, 78, 90, 104, 106, 112, 157, 160, 253, 289, 293, 298–300, 330–336, 367, 368
  Best interest of the child: 117, 220, 252, 253, 255, 291, 301, 331, 334, 337, 338, 367
  Foreign children: see Migrants, foreigners
  Public protection of children: see Independent institutions for the protection of human rights
  Violence and exploitation against minors: 27, 33, 35, 37, 42, 65, 84, 87, 88, 91, 92, 105–107, 122, 124, 190, 191, 198, 212, 220, 222, 247–254, 259, 260, 271, 289, 329, 334–338
Chile: 167, 182, 202, 209, 210, 248
China: 95, 99, 107, 169, 171, 173, 187, 209
Civil society organisations: 19–21, 27, 29, 37, 38, 42, 47, 77, 85, 86, 110, 111, 125–129, 145, 146, 157–159, 165, 166, 178, 184, 192, 198, 199, 202, 216, 218, 230, 244, 245, 248, 249, 251, 253, 255, 259, 264, 265, 275, 306
Colombia: 107, 183, 185
Congo, Democratic Republic of: 188, 189
Congo, Republic of: 210
Constitutional Court (Italian): 32, 77, 87, 115, 116, 289, 293–300, 304, 313, 316–319, 323, 324, 329, 331, 336, 337–3350, 361, 364
Corruption: 20, 24, 25, 73, 83, 177, 182, 192, 194, 224, 256–258, 272, 290, 358, 359, 366
Costa Rica: 181, 184
Court of Justice of the EU: 32, 59, 62, 116, 264, 289, 291, 292, 304, 324, 343, 371–373
Croatia: 141, 231, 244, 246
Cuba: 172, 173, 181, 186–189, 209, 323
Cultural heritage: 158, 179
Culture of peace: 67, 150, 153, 155, 157–159, 163
Cyprus: 141, 179, 203, 210, 231, 284
Czech Republic: 18, 185, 209, 231, 246

D

Death penalty: 78, 168, 174
Democracy, rule of law: 88, 115, 116, 139, 148, 154, 168, 184,

201, 215, 223, 224, 245, 246, 248, 265, 271, 281, 282, 287, 315, 316, 363, 369
Denmark: 182, 214, 260
Disabilities – see Persons with disabilities
Diversity and intercultural dialogue: 37, 130, 132, 140, 214
Djibouti: 189, 286

E

Ecuador: 96, 188
Education, training, research: 17, 19, 21, 23, 26, 35, 37, 38, 40–42, 55, 64, 65, 67, 70, 72, 73, 78, 82, 87, 89, 90, 94, 96, 104–108, 112, 115, 116, 119, 120, 122, 124, 126–143, 145, 146, 150–152, 155–159, 161, 163, 165, 179, 180, 184, 193, 203, 212, 214, 215, 217, 218, 221, 239, 240, 242, 250, 252–254, 258, 260, 266, 271, 272, 275, 280, 282, 283, 289, 290, 297, 312–314, 324, 328, 338
Egypt: 99, 113, 168, 171, 174, 182, 221, 264, 284, 285
El Salvador: 209, 210, 324
Elderly people: 72, 87, 88, 227, 243, 328, 335
Elections: 17, 18, 25, 58, 69, 92, 118, 194, 225, 273–276, 303, 367
Emilia-Romagna, Region of: 42, 49, 68, 71, 106, 114, 144, 147, 150
Enforced disappearances, extraordinary rendition: 83, 93, 95, 110, 205, 207, 211

Environment, pollution, waste: 58–60, 62, 71, 82, 87, 88, 91, 108, 120, 127–129, 181, 193, 217, 261–263, 269, 290, 326
Eritrea: 95, 101, 102, 113, 189, 203
Estonia: 18, 243, 246, 249
European Court of Human Rights: 26, 32, 115, 116, 223, 225, 226, 230, 231, 256, 289, 292–294, 296, 302, 306, 315, 316, 324, 331, 333, 343, 345, 346, 350, 352–371
Expropriation: 358
Extradition: 61, 349

F

Female genital mutilation: 106, 168, 169, 184
Fiji: 210
Finland: 237, 246, 247, 249
Former Yugoslavia: 30
Former Yugoslav Republic of Macedonia/Republic of North Macedonia: 209, 210, 243, 248, 249
France: 231, 237, 244, 247, 252, 272, 299, 301
Freedom of expression, pluralism in the media: 18, 25, 59, 95, 126, 192, 193, 195, 197–201, 214, 241, 242, 269, 272, 275–278, 327, 350, 351
Defamation: 25, 194, 199–201, 276, 328, 350, 351
Friuli-Venezia Giulia, Region of: 42, 47, 69, 71, 114, 147, 149, 151

G

Gambia: 101, 113
Gender, gender discrimination: see Women, equal opportunities, gender issues
Georgia: 183, 231, 246, 248, 271
Germany: 181, 185, 208, 214, 231, 243, 249, 266, 368, 369
Greece: 182, 203, 204, 231, 237, 243, 245
Guatemala: 185, 209, 210
Guinea: 113, 203, 209
Guyana: 212

H

Haiti: 211
Hate speech: 19, 86, 90, 95, 117, 239
HIV/AIDS: 184, 357
Holy See: 203, 248
Homosexuality, transsexuality (LGBTI): 106, 291, 298–300, 370, 371, 373
Honduras: 210, 211
Horn of Africa: 285
Human dignity: 19, 47, 61, 65, 86, 100, 106, 120, 151, 161, 162, 215, 219, 243, 255, 295–301, 320, 327, 355
Human rights defenders: 19, 20, 127, 143, 144, 149, 151, 160, 164, 191, 193, 194, 198, 200, 264
Hungary: 18, 95, 96, 107, 209, 231, 246, 248, 249

I

Iceland: 18, 60, 249, 274, 283
Independent institutions for the protection of human rights: 20, 25, 31, 67, 70, 71, 77, 80, 81, 94, 95, 117, 121–125, 146–151, 155, 160, 161, 243, 244, 251, 267
 National Commission: 25, 93
 Ombudsperson for the Rights of Persons in Prison or Deprived of Liberty: 20, 70, 77, 116, 123, 125, 158, 161, 230, 350
 Ombudsperson for Children and Adolescents: 69, 77, 79, 116, 121–124, 151, 153, 158, 250, 268
 Ombudspersons: 25, 68, 69, 71, 95, 146–151, 155, 160, 161, 267
India: 284
International Criminal Court: 26, 94, 265, 281
International solidarity, development cooperation: 20, 32, 56, 67, 70, 96, 101, 102, 111, 128, 130, 132, 133, 136, 140, 143, 146, 151, 152, 155–161, 165, 187, 200, 201, 216, 281, 317
Iran: 175, 182
Iraq: 203, 210, 282
Ireland: 184, 225, 237, 246, 247, 267, 269
Israel: 188, 248, 283
Ivory Coast: 113, 203

J

Japan: 209, 211, 248

K

Kazakhstan: 248, 279
Kenya: 156, 186

Kosovo: 247, 248, 283, 284
Kyrgyzstan: 209, 248

L

Laos: 209, 210
Latvia: 210, 243, 246, 286
Lazio, Region of: 42, 68, 71, 105, 113, 125, 131, 144, 147, 191, 196, 315, 321, 322
Lebanon: 209, 285
Lesotho: 210
Liberia: 209
Libya: 45, 95, 100, 103, 104, 183, 199, 203, 256, 283–286, 306, 319
Liechtenstein: 210, 249
Liguria, Region of: 68, 144, 147, 324, 341
Lithuania: 209, 231, 247, 249
Lombardy, Region of: 68, 69, 72, 105, 113, 125, 145, 145, 147, 303, 321
Luxembourg: 210, 214, 248, 249

M

Madagascar: 212
Malaysia: 210
Maldives: 209
Mali: 183, 203, 208, 285
Malta: 203, 211, 244, 245, 246, 248
Marche, Region of: 68–72, 73, 144, 148
Marginalisation, social exclusion: see Poverty
Marshall Islands: 210
Mauritania: 96, 102, 209, 210
Mauritius, Republic of: 210

Mediterranean Basin and North Africa: 17, 23, 58, 131, 199, 202, 219, 223, 271, 273, 285
Mexico: 174, 182–185, 208–211, 248
Middle East: 284
Migrants, foreigners: 20, 24, 29, 32–37, 39, 40, 42–44, 56, 59, 61, 64, 71, 84, 86, 90, 92, 93–97, 99–101, 104–107, 111, 113, 115, 116, 123, 126, 127, 136, 151, 161, 162, 165, 166, 169, 171, 190, 192, 194–196, 198–200, 202, 203, 213, 220–223, 225, 230–235, 240, 242, 249, 251, 254, 255, 262, 264, 265, 267, 271, 272, 289, 290, 301, 306–311, 317, 320–323, 337, 351, 373, 374
  Asylum, refugees: 19, 20, 29, 30, 37, 41–43, 56, 59, 61, 84, 86, 92, 96, 97, 99–101, 104, 111, 123, 127, 136, 165, 166, 169, 171, 194, 195, 200, 202, 203, 220, 222, 223, 230, 232, 234, 242, 251, 253, 255, 262, 264, 290, 303–311, 320, 373, 374
  Centres for migrants: 30, 95, 99, 101, 113, 190, 222, 225, 230, 274
  Expulsion, refoulement: 29, 58, 121, 199, 227, 233, 236, 239, 256, 323, 338, 371
  Minors: 38, 61, 90, 106, 111–117, 121, 161, 162, 165, 203, 220, 221, 232, 234, 267, 271, 317, 337
  Residence: 35–37, 39, 42, 57, 60, 66, 199, 301, 310, 318, 321, 323, 324, 337

Minorities: 19, 67, 68, 71, 84, 87, 91, 92, 95, 98, 101, 126, 155, 181, 185, 192, 195, 196, 200, 221, 223, 244, 247, 248, 262, 265, 271, 273, 275, 276
Moldova, Republic of: 231, 246, 248
Molise, Region of: 42, 68, 70, 73, 144, 147
Monaco: 260, 272
Montenegro: 210, 247, 248
Morocco: 176, 248
Mozambique: 170, 171, 212
Myanmar: 175, 179, 180, 185

N

National plan of action on human rights: 23, 25, 26, 30, 31–46, 107, 110, 114, 116, 190, 196, 213, 251, 266
    Against human trafficking and serious exploitation: 26, 30, 31–46, 190, 213, 251, 250
    Business and human rights: 27, 110, 191
    Violence against women: 27
    Women, peace and security: 20, 27, 110
Ne bis in idem: 342, 343, 373
Nepal: 209, 210
Netherlands: 143, 209, 214, 225, 246, 247, 249
New Zealand: 182, 208, 210
Niger: 208, 210, 221, 285
Nigeria: 45, 49, 95, 101, 122, 125, 203, 249, 307, 371
Non-discrimination: 21, 26, 80, 82–84, 86–90, 95–98, 100, 101, 105, 106, 110, 113, 127, 155, 169, 170, 172, 181, 182, 184, 194–196, 198–200, 202, 204, 209, 210, 222, 240, 241, 244, 245, 265, 266, 289, 290, 307, 309, 310, 312, 317, 323, 344, 374
    Antiracism: 21, 26, 82, 84, 86–90, 95–98, 100, 101, 105, 110, 113, 169, 170, 172, 184, 192, 195, 196, 198–200, 202, 204, 211, 222, 244, 245, 265, 266, 311, 310
    Gender discrimination: 26, 83, 87, 90, 105, 106, 127, 157, 171, 196, 200, 211, 222, 245, 290, 312, 372
Non-pecuniary harm: 356
Non-retroactivity, retroactivity: 294, 315, 316, 330, 344, 360, 363, 364, 367
North Korea: 175, 179, 180
Norway: 60, 184, 209, 210, 214, 231, 246, 343

O

Oman: 211

P

Pakistan: 95, 102, 185, 187, 203, 284
Palestine, Occupied Palestinian territories: 173, 183, 187, 191, 211, 247, 281, 283
Panama: 210
"Peace human rights" norm: 67, 68, 143
Personal freedom and prison conditions: 20, 26, 80, 83, 86–88, 90, 91, 96, 97, 101,

117, 123–126, 151, 160–163, 171, 176, 182, 200, 230–233, 274, 295–297, 346–350, 354–356, 367
  Mistreatment: 83, 87, 90, 96, 171, 176, 182, 200, 230, 231, 232, 233, 345–347, 349, 350, 353, 373
  Overcrowding: 28, 89, 347
Persons with disabilities: 20, 27, 68–70, 77, 83, 86–90, 93, 95, 99, 106, 109, 111, 112, 114, 115, 127, 163, 170, 182, 198, 200, 204, 211, 261, 267, 268, 275, 291, 292, 312–315, 323, 337
Peru: 185, 188, 209, 211, 248
Philippines: 97, 188, 211, 281
Piedmont, Region of: 68, 73, 105, 125, 141, 144, 147, 264
Poland: 18, 181, 210, 231, 243, 246
Portugal: 181, 184, 203, 211, 219, 231, 238, 295
Poverty: 37, 40, 41, 71, 82, 88, 104, 111, 126, 172, 322, 324

Q
Qatar: 180, 209, 210, 284

R
Racism, xenophobia: see Non-discrimination, Antiracism
Reasonable length of proceedings: 26, 34, 124, 227, 228, 339–342, 357
Right to health: 26, 40, 53, 60, 70, 71, 82, 86, 89, 90, 92, 94–96, 101, 120, 125, 126, 191, 222, 234, 236, 240, 241, 252, 266, 297, 299, 300, 333, 355, 356
Right to accommodation: 82, 181, 191, 195, 200, 217, 236, 237, 253
Right to peace: 24
Right to private and family life: 95, 100, 230, 294, 299, 301, 308, 323, 325–329, 337, 366, 370
Right to strike: 119, 120
Roma, Sinti and Travellers: 19, 27, 30, 95, 101, 196, 197, 201, 223, 238, 239, 243
  Eviction: 98, 195, 201, 236, 238
  National Strategy for the inclusion of: 27, 30
Romania: 105, 230, 231, 243, 246–248, 350
Russian Federation: 107, 171, 175, 186, 209, 211, 230, 231, 244, 246, 247, 262, 354

S
Sahel: 285
Saint Vincent and the Grenadines: 212
Samoa: 210
San Marino: 203, 246, 249
Sardinia, Region of: 42, 69–72, 144, 147
Saudi Arabia: 95, 99, 101, 102, 175, 210
Senegal: 209
Serbia: 231, 243, 248, 249
Seychelles: 209–211
Sicily, Region of: 113, 144, 147, 241, 243, 250, 315, 316, 320, 329

Slavery, exploitation, smuggling, trafficking: 26, 30–50, 80, 84, 86, 92, 95, 106, 107, 124, 171, 177, 190–192, 197–200, 213, 220–222, 247–255, 261, 269–271, 277, 289, 290, 305, 306, 320, 331, 353, 354
Slovak Republic: 231, 243, 271
Slovenia: 67, 180, 181, 211, 246, 247, 249
Social security, pensions: 23, 82, 88, 90, 92, 94, 114, 229, 237, 241, 242, 316–318, 323, 339, 360, 363, 364, 374
Social services: 39, 49, 113, 134, 136, 139, 140, 153, 309, 324, 353
Somalia: 186, 189, 285
South Africa: 187, 208, 211, 248
South Korea: 185, 211, 248
South Sudan: 183
Spain: 185, 210, 211, 231, 244, 246, 249, 302
Sri Lanka: 210
Stateless persons: 30, 203, 240, 291, 322
Sudan: 190, 203, 209, 211, 266
Suriname: 210
Sweden: 182, 184, 209, 214, 244, 246, 247, 249
Switzerland: 20, 181, 183, 184, 245, 247, 249, 271, 317, 358
Syria: 18, 79, 175, 179, 180, 187, 188, 225

T

Tajikistan: 209, 210
Tanzania: 95, 99
Temporary measures (art. 39 of ECtHR's rules): 230
Terrorism: 55, 60, 64, 72, 174, 182, 251, 262, 271, 347
Thailand: 95, 98, 186
Togo: 182, 183, 185, 190, 191
Torture, inhuman treatments: 24, 32, 83, 86, 90, 91, 96, 97, 101, 102, 110, 111, 124, 169, 170, 182, 200, 201, 204–206, 210, 221, 222, 230–235, 291, 345, 351, 353
Trent, Autonomous Province of: 66, 70–72, 127, 129, 131, 139, 143–149, 151, 158
Trentino-Alto Adige, Region of: 42, 47, 67, 70, 72, 144, 150, 153
Tunisia: 58, 123, 190, 203, 248, 284, 286
Turkey: 95, 99, 203, 230, 231, 243, 245, 248, 249, 286
Turkmenistan: 208, 210
Tuscany, Region of: 42, 68, 70, 72, 144, 145, 147, 250, 315

U

Uganda: 281
Ukraine: 18, 175, 230, 231, 244, 245, 247–249, 271
Umbria, Region of: 42, 49, 68, 69, 71–73, 125, 144, 147
United Arab Emirates: 284
United Kingdom: 180, 181, 186, 225, 231, 244, 272
United States of America: 182, 247, 256
Universal Periodic Review (UPR): 21, 178, 190
University Human Rights Centre (University of Padova): 23, 128, 146, 151, 152, 161, 165, 166

Uruguay: 248
Uzbekistan: 248

V

Valle d'Aosta (Aosta Valley), Region of: 70, 72, 146–150
Veneto, Region of: 31, 43, 49, 66–73, 105, 143–145, 147, 150, 153–164, 248, 299, 300, 303, 315
Venezuela: 185, 187–191
Vietnam: 188, 209
Volunteering, Civil service: 63, 71, 72, 168

W

Women, equal opportunities, gender issues: 21, 26, 27, 31, 32, 56, 70, 83, 85–87, 89, 90, 96, 97, 105, 106, 109, 110, 123, 124, 127, 130, 135, 136, 145, 151, 156, 157, 163, 164, 169–171, 183, 190–192, 195–200, 203, 204, 209, 211, 213, 216, 221–223, 226, 240, 245, 251, 260–263, 271, 273, 290, 299, 300, 305, 311, 312, 330, 350, 360, 370, 371, 374
Violence against women, gender violence: 26, 31, 32, 56, 70, 83, 86, 90, 96, 97, 110, 123, 124, 151, 156, 170, 171, 183, 190–192, 195, 196, 198–200, 203, 204, 209, 211, 213, 222, 226, 240, 260–263, 271
Workers' rights: 24, 53, 55, 70, 82, 84, 86, 91, 127, 190, 191, 204, 211, 213, 235, 239, 241, 290, 302, 316

Y

Yemen: 95, 102, 185, 190

Table of Cases

Constitutional Court

Judg. 14 October 2005, No. 385: 332
Judg. 25 February 2014, No. 30: 344
Judg. 10 March 2015, No.70: 318
Judg. 26 May 2017, No. 123: 295
Judg. 25 October 2017, No. 250: 318
Judg. 18 January 2018, No. 5: 300
Judg. 18 January 2018, No. 6: 367
Judg. 30 January 2018, No. 12: 317
Judg. 9 February 2018, No. 22: 346
Judg. 9 February 2018, No. 24: 296
Judg. 2 March 2018, No. 43: 344
Judg. 23 March 2018, No. 59: 352
Judg. 19 April 2018, No. 77: 341
Judg. 26 April 2018, No. 88: 343
Judg. 26 April 2018, No. 89: 330
Judg. 27 April 2018, No. 93: 295
Judg. 11 May 2018, No. 96: 318
Judg. 23 May 2018, No. 105: 332
Judg. 24 May 2018, No. 106: 325
Judg. 13 June 2018, No. 120: 304
Judg. 26 June 2018, No. 135: 235
Judg. 11 July 2018, No. 149: 350
Judg. 13 July 2018, No. 158: 314
Ord. 19 July 2018, No. 163: 320
Judg. 20 July 2018, No. 166: 325
Judg. 20 July 2018, No. 167: 342
Judg. 23 July 2018, No. 174: 350
Judg. 12 October 2018, No. 186: 351
Judg. 19 October 2018, No. 190: 341
Ord. 16 November 2018, No. 207: 297
Judg. 22 November 2018, No. 212: 299
Judg. 5 December 2018, No. 222: 347
Judg. 14 December 2018, No. 236: 338

Court of Cassation, Civil Division

Judg. Sec. I, 19 January 2018, No. 1431: 333
Judg. Sec. Labour, 30 January 2018, No. 2286: 318
Judg. Sec. VI, 6 February 2018, No. 2875: 307
Judg. Sec. VI, 6 February 2018, No. 2861: 307
Judg. Sec. II, 16 February 2018, No. 3831: 293, 346
Judg. Sec. I, 20 February 2018, No. 4096: 349
Judg. Sec. I, 21 February 2018, No. 4197: 339

Judg. Sec. I, 23 February 2018, No. 4455: 309
Ord. Sec. I, 2 March 2018, No. 6919: 326
Judg. Sec. I, 6 March 2018, No. 5255: 348
Judg. Sec. I, 6 March 2018, No. 5256: 333
Judg. Sec. Labour, 19 March 2018, No. 6798: 313
Judg. Sec. I, 20 March 2018, No. 6963: 297
Ord. Joint Sec., 30 March 2018, No. 8044: 308
Judg. Joint Sec., 8 May 2018, No. 11018: 348
Judg. Sec. I, Judg. 11 May 2018, No. 11554: 334
Judg. Sec. 1, 24 May 2018, No. 12954: 335
Judg., Sec. I, 24 May 2018, No. 12955: 349
Judg. Sec. VI, 31 May 2018, No. 13858: 308
Judg. Sec. I, 31 May 2018, No. 14007: 302
Judg. Sec. I, 4 June 2018, No. 14238: 339
Judg. Sec. VI, 12 June 2018, No. 15238: 335
Judg. Sec. III, 26 June 2018, No. 16816: 330
Judg. Joint Sec., 27 June 2018, No. 16957: 300
Judg. Sec. I, 14 May 2018, No. 16969: 301
Judg. Sec. VI, 28 June 2018, No. 17072: 309
Judg. Sec. I, 2 July 2018, No. 17274: 347
Judg. Sec. I, 5 July 2018, No. 17717: 305
Judg. Sec. I, 9 July 2018, No. 18006: 328
Judg. Sec. I, 10 July 2018, No. 18148: 336
Judg. Sec. I, 16 July 2018, No. 18827: 333
Judg. Sec. VI, 17 July 2018, No. 19040: 306
Judg. Sec. I, 25 July 2018, No. 19780: 335
Judg. Sec. VI, 1 August 2018, No. 20375: 333
Judg. Sec. I, 29 August 2018, No. 21362: 327
Judg. Sec. lav., 10 September 2018, No. 21958: 337
Ord. Joint Sec., 13 September 2018, No. 22412: 308
Judg. Sec. I, 2 October 2018, No. 23957: 324
Judg. Sec. Labour., 2 October 2018, No. 23763: 325
Judg. Sec. II, 5 October 2018, No. 25686: 328
Judg. Sec. VI, 29 October 2018, No. 27336: 307
Judg. Sec. 1, 30 October 2018, No. 27700: 305
Judg. Sec. VI, 30 October 2018, No. 27504: 308
Judg. Sec. V, 30 October 2018, n 27564: 346
Ord. Sec. III, 5 November 2018, No. 28084: 327

Judg. Sec. I, 5 November 2018, No. 28119: 305
Judg. Sec. I, 7 November 2018, No. 28433: 307
Ord. Joint Sec., 27 November 2018, No. 30658: 308
Ord. Joint Sec., 28 November 2018, No. 30757: 308
Judg. Sec. I, 24 October 2018, No. 30826: 334
Judg. Sec. III, 6 December 2018, No. 31556: 347
Judg. Sec. II, 6 December 2018, n 31632: 346
Judg. Sec. II, 6 December 2018, n 31634: 346
Judg. Sec. II, 6 December 2018, n 31635: 346
Judg. Sec. I, 6 December 2018, No. 31676: 307
Ord. Joint Sec., 11 December 2018, No. 32044: 308
Judg. Sec. I, 13 December 2018, No. 32319: 306
Judg. Sec. I, 19 December 2018, 32862: 306
Judg. Sec. I, 14 December 2018, No. 32533: 329
Judg. Sec. I, 30 December 2018, No. 32319: 306
Judg. Sec. V, 7 June 2018, No. 53731: 349

Court of Cassation, Criminal Division

Judg. Sec. III, Judg. 9 January 2019, No. 345: 337
Judg. Sec. V, 18 January 2019, No. 2461: 354
Judg. Joint Sec., 4 January 2018, No. 111: 354
Judg. Sec. VI, 11 January 2018, No. 931: 352
Judg. Joint Sec., 26 January 2018, No. 3775: 348
Judg. Sec. VI, 25 January 2018, No. 12866: 336
Judg. Sec. VI, 1 February 2018, No. 10763: 337
Judg. Sec. V, 14 February 2018, No. 14200: 353
Judg. Sec. VI, 21 February 2018, No. 8916: 352
Judg. Sec. VI, 23 February 2018, No. 18833: 338
Judg. Sec. VI, 28 February 2018, No. 9391: 352
Judg. Sec. III, 1 March 2018, No. 10251: 352
Judg. Sec. V, 23 March 2018, No. 32028: 353
Judg. Sec. I, 16 April 2018, No. 44972: 351
Judg. Joint Sec., 31 May 2018, No. 51815: 331
Judg. Sec. VI, 5 June 2018, No. 26383: 352
Judg. Sec. VI, 7 June 2018, No. 39920: 337
Judg. Sec. I, 19 June 2018, No. 28261: 354
Judg. Sec. VI, 19 June 2018, No. 42918: 337
Judg. Sec. I, 27 June 2018, No. 46169: 351
Judg. Sec. I, 10 July 2018, No. 31322: 354

Judg. Sec. I, 11 July 2018, No. 53006: 351
Judg. Sec. III, 11 July 2018, No. 45736: 336
Judg. Sec. V, 12 July 2018, No. 42630: 330
Judg. Sec. vacation, 28 August 2018, No. 39240: 351
Judg. Sec. VI, 9 October 2018, No. 55737: 337
Judg. Sec. I, 30 October 2018, No. 49731: 354
Judg. Sec. III, 6 November 2018, No. 17810: 336
Judg. sec. VI, 5 December 2018, No. 6506: 337
Judg. Sec. I, 7 December 2018, No. 11585: 351
Judg. Sec. III, 17 December 2018, No. 56673: 337

Administrative Courts

TAR Lombardy – Brescia, Judg. Sec. I, 22 January 2018, No. 68: 321
Council of State, Judg. Sec. V, 7 February 2018, No. 809: 315
TAR Lazio – Rome, Judg. Sec. III, 28 February 2018, No. 2250: 316
TAR Lazio – Rome, Judg. Sec. I, 19 March 2018, No. 1736: 322
Council of State, Judg. Sec. III, 19 March 2018, No. 1736: 322
TAR Sicily – Palermo, Judg. Sec. III, 23 March 2018, No. 644: 316
TAR Tuscany – Florence, Judg. Sec. I, 26 March 2018, No. 439: 316
TAR Lazio – Rome, Judg. Sec. I, 12 April 2018, No. 4002: 322
Council of Administrative Justice for the Sicily Region, Judg. 3 May 2018, No. 258: 316
TAR Lazio – Rome, Judg. Sec. I, 16 May 2018, No. 5469: 322
TAR Lazio, Rome, Judg. Sec. III, 23 May 2018, No. 5740: 315
TAR Lazio – Rome, Sec. I, Judg. 24 May 2018, No. 5775: 322
Council of State, Judg. Sec. III, 28 May 2018, No. 3184: 321
Council of State, Judg. Sec. III, 29 May 2018, No. 3208: 303
Council of State, Judg. Sec. III, 5 June 2018, No. 3411: 324
TAR Lazio – Rome, Judg. Sec. I, 18 June 2018, No. 6824: 323
TAR Lazio – Rome, Judg. Sec. I, 28 June 2018, No. 7212: 322
TAR Lazio – Rome, Judg. Sec. I, 23 July 2018, No. 8318: 322
TAR Lazio – Rome, Judg. Sec. I, 26 July 2018, No. 8466: 323
TAR Sicily – Catania, Judg. Sec. IV 6 August 2018, No. 1671: 320
TAR Lazio – Rome, Judg. Sec. I, 28 August 2018, No. 9048: 323
TAR Lazio – Rome, Judg. Sec. I, 6 September 2018, No. 5262: 323
TAR Lazio – Rome, Judg. Sec. I, 1 October 2018, No. 9659: 323
TAR Lazio – Rome, Judg. Sec. I, 1 October 2018, 9678: 323
TAR Sicily – Palermo, Judg. Sec. III, 2 October 2018, No. 2030: 316

Table of Cases

TAR Sicily – Palermo, Judg. Sec. III, 2 October 2018, No. 2031: 316
TAR Lazio – Rome, Judg. Sec. I, 4 October 2018, No. 9735: 323
TAR Lazio – Rome, Judg. Sec. I, 4 October 2018, No. 9739: 323
Council of State, Judg. Sec. VI, 11 October 2018, No. 5851: 314
Council of State, Judg. Sec. IV, 12 October 2018, No. 5896: 311
TAR Lazio – Rome, Judg. Sec. I, 15 October 2018, No. 9993: 323
TAR Lazio, Rome, Judg. Sec. III, 19 October 2018, No. 10132: 315
TAR Veneto, Judg. Sec. I, 19 October 2018, No. 976: 316
Council of Administrative Justice for the Sicily Region, Judg. 30 October 2018, No. 614: 315
TAR Lazio – Rome, Judg. Sec. I, 19 November 2018, No. 11192: 323
TAR Lazio – Rome, Judg. Sec. I, 20 November 2018, No. 11249: 322
TAR Lazio – Rome, Judg. Sec. I, 20 November 2018, No. 11253: 322
TAR Lazio, Rome, Judg. Sec. II, 21 November 2018, No. 11321: 323
TAR Lazio – Rome, Judg. Sec. I, 5 December 2018, No. 11796: 322
TAR Lazio – Rome, Judg. Sec. I, 12 December 2018, No. 12063: 323

Ordinary Tribunals

Tribunal of Rome, Judg. Sec. XII, 11 January 2018, No. 613: 340
Tribunal of Modena, Judg. Sec. II, 12 January 2018: 314
Tribunal of Brescia, Judg. Sec. III, 17 February 2018, No. 508: 324
Tribunal of Bologna, ord., Sec. I, 7 March 2018: 309
Tribunal of Rome, ord., Sec. I, 11 May 2018: 302
Tribunal of Milan, ord., Sec. I, 6 June 2018: 309
Tribunal of Florence, ord., Sec. Labour, 26 June 2018: 311
Court of Appeal of Venice, ord., Sec. III, 28 June 2018: 302
Tribunal of Bologna, ord. 7 July 2018: 302
Tribunal of Venice, Judg. 27 July 2018, No. 4243: 307
Tribunal of Monza, ord., Sec. Labour, 1 August 2018: 319
Court of Appeal of Perugia, ord. 22 August 2018: 302
Tribunal of Modena, Judg. Sec. II, 6 November 2018, No. 1827: 323
Tribunal of Genoa, ord., Sec. IV, 8 November 2018: 302
Tribunal of Milan, ord., Sec. VIII, 15 November 2018: 302
Tribunal of Milan, ord., 13 December 2018: 310

European Court of Human Rights (in alphabetical order)

A and B v. Norway [GC], Nos. 24130/11 and 29758/11, 15 November 2016: 345

Adefdromil v. France, No. 32191/09, 2 October 2014: 304

Agrati and Others v. Italy (just satisfaction), Nos. 43549/08 and 2 others, 8 November 2012: 366

Arras and Others v. Italy, no. 17972/07, 14 February 2012: 366

Azienda Agricola Silverfunghi S.a.s. and Others v. Italy, Nos. 48357/07 and 3 others, 24 June 2014: 366

Berlusconi v. Italy [GC], No. 58428/13, 27 November 2018: 368

Brazzi v. Italy, No. 57278/11, 27 September 2018: 370

Cacciato v. Italy, No. 60633/16, 16 January 2018: 360

Casa of Cura Valle Fiorita S.R.L., No. 67944/13, 13 December 2018: 364

Castello del Poggio S.S. and Others, Nos. 30015/09, 34644/09, 10723/10, 5 July 2018: 365

Centro Demarzio srl v. Italy, No. 24/11, 5 July 2018: 362

Cincimino v. Italy, No. 68884/13, 28 April 2016: 370

Cipolletta v. Italy, No. 38259/09, 11 January 2018: 358

Cocchiarella v. Italy [GC], No. 64886/01, 29 March 2006: 359

Costa Sanseverino di Bisignano v. Italy, No. 58330/16, 15 May 2018: 373

Cristaldi v. Italy, No. 29923/13, 22 May 2018: 362

D'Acunto and Pignataro v. Italy, No. 6360/13, 12 July 2018: 369

De Rosa and Others v. Italy, Nos. 52888/08 and 13 others, 11 December 2012: 366

Drassich v. Italy (no. 2), no. 65173/09, 22 February 2018: 360

G.I.E.M. S.R.L. and Others v. Italy [GC], Nos. 1828/06, 34163/07, 19029/11, 28 June 2018: 367

Improta v. Italy, No. 66396/14, 4 May 2017: 370

Khlaifia and Others v. Italy [GC], No. 16483/12, 15 December 2016: 355

Guiso and others v. Italy, No. 50821/06, 8 February 2018: 360

L.M. an others v. Italy, Nos. 30290/15, and 6 others, 16 January 2018: 359

Maggio and Others v. Italy, Nos. 46286/09 and 4 others, 31 May 2011: 366

Matelly v. Francia, No. 10609/10, 2 October 2014: 304

Moreira Ferreira v. Portugal (no. 2) [GC], No. 19867/12, 11 July 2017: 295

Mottola and Others v. Italy (just satisfaction), No. 29932/07, 6 September 2018: 366

Pretty v. the United Kingdom, No. 2346/02, 29 July 2002: 298

Provenzano v. Italy, No. 55080/13, 25 October 2018: 356

Rizzello and Others v. Italy, Nos. 17799/10 and 8 others, 20 February 2018: 360

Staibano and Others v. Italy (just satisfaction), No. 29907/07, 6 September 2018: 366

Sud Fondi S.r.l. and Others v. Italy (just satisfaction), No. 75909/01, 10 May 2012: 368

S.V. v. Italy, No. 55216/08, 11 October 2018: 372

Therapic Center S.R.L. Nos. 39186/11 and 9 others, 4 October 2018: 363

Varvara v. Italy, No. 17475/09, 29 October 2013: 368

V.C. v. Italy, No.54227/14, 1 February 2018: 355

Zhou v. Italy, No. 33773/11, 21 January 2014: 294

Court of Justice of the European Union (in chronological order)

Judg. C-422/18, F.R., 30 November 2018: 306

Judg. C-180/17, X e Y, 26 September 2018: 376

Judg. Joint Cases C-142/17 and C-143/17, Maturi and others, 7 February 2018: 376

Judg. (Grand Chamber) Joint Cases C-596/16 and C-597/16, Di Puma, 20 March 2018: 376

Judg. (Grand Chamber) C-524/15, Menci, 20 March 2018: 376

Judg. (Grand Chamber) C-537/16, Garlsson R.E., 20 March 2018: 376

European Committee of Social Rights, decisions on collective complaints

Conseil Européen des Syndicats de Police (CESP) v. France, No. 101/2013, 4 July 2018: 304

Unione Italiana del Lav. U.I.L. Scuola – Sicily v. Italy, No. 113/2014, 24 January 2018: 229

Associazione Professionale e Sindacale (ANIEF) v. Italy, No.159/2018: 242

Confederazione Generale Sindacale (CGS) e Federazione dei Lavoratori Pubblici e Funzioni pubbliche (FLP) v. Italy, No. 161/2018: 242

Nursing Up v. Italy, No.169/2018: 242

Sindacato autonomo pensionati Or.S.A v. Italy, No. 167/2018: 243

Unione sindacale di base (USB) v. Italy, No. 170/2018: 243

Sindacato Autonomo Europeo Scuola ed Ecologia (SAESE) v. Italy, No.166/2018, 16 March 2019: 243

Research and Editorial Committee

Andrea Cofelice, MA in Institutions and Policies of Human Rights and Peace, University of Padova. PhD in Political Science – Comparative and European Politics, University of Siena.

Pietro de Perini, Lecturer of Human Rights in International Politics in the Master's Degree Programme in Human Rights and Multi-Level Governance at the University of Padova. MA in Institutions and Policies of Human Rights and Peace, University of Padova. PhD in International Politics, City, University of London.

Paola Degani, Aggregate Professor of Women's Human Rights in the Master's Degree Programme in Human Rights and Multi-level Governance at the University of Padova. She is National Expert in respect of Italy of the Group of Experts on Action against Violence against Women and Domestic Violence (Istanbul Convention) of the Council of Europe

Paolo De Stefani, Aggregate Professor of International Law of Human Rights in the Master's Degree Programme in Human Rights and Multi-level Governance at the University of Padova. He is National Director for Italy of the European Master in Human Rights and Democratisation (E.MA).

Ino Kehrer, PhD candidate in Human Rights, Society and Multi-Level Governance, University of Padova Human Rights Centre. LLM, University of Bologna.

Marco Mascia, Associate Professor of International Relations, UNESCO Chair "Human Rights, Democracy and Peace", Director of the Master's Degree Programme in Human Rights and Multi-Level Governance, University of Padova.

Peter Lang – Italian Yearbook of Human Rights Series

The legal and political significance of human rights has increased enormously at the international and European levels. Awareness has risen that the respect and the promotion of human rights must be at the centre of States and local communities' public policies and that human rights are at the basis of civil society initiatives and movements. There is a large machinery monitoring, at all the levels of governance, the way in which States implement the obligations assumed toward each person under their sovereignty.

The **Italian Yearbook of Human Rights Series** provides year by year, a dynamic and up-to date overview of the measures Italy has taken to adapt its legislation and policies to international human rights law and to comply with commitments voluntarily assumed by the Italian Government at the international level. The Series thus intends to contribute to the continuous monitoring activity on the situation of human rights in Italy undertaken at the local, national and international levels by relevant intergovernmental and civil society actors.

Each volume of this series surveys the activities carried out, during the year of reference, by the relevant national and local Italian actors, including governmental bodies, civil society organisations and universities. It also presents reports and recommendations that have been addressed to Italy by international monitoring bodies within the framework of the United Nations, the Council of Europe and the European Union. Finally, each Yearbook provides a selection of examples from international and national case-law which cast light on Italy's position vis-a-vis internationally recognised human rights.

The Yearbook is edited by the Human Rights Centre of the University of Padova, in cooperation with the UNESCO Chair in Human Rights, Democracy and Peace of the same University, and with the support of the Region of Veneto. The Centre, established in 1982, carries out research and education following a global and interdisciplinary approach. It hosts the Jean Monnet Centre of Excellence on intercultural dialogue, human rights and multi-level governance.

www.peterlang.com

www.ingramcontent.com/pod-product-compliance
Lightning Source LLC
LaVergne TN
LVHW010307070526
838199LV00065B/5465